The Art of
Scandal

Isabella Stewart Gardner, a pencil sketch by John Singer Sargent, 1888. *Isabella Stewart Gardner Museum, Boston*

The Art of Scandal

The Life and Times of Isabella Stewart Gardner

DOUGLASS SHAND-TUCCI

HarperPerennial

A Division of HarperCollins*Publishers*

A hardcover edition of this book was published in 1997 by HarperCollins Publishers.

First HarperPerennial edition published 1998.

Designed by Elina D. Nudelman

The Library of Congress has catalogued the hardcover edition as follows:

Shand-Tucci, Douglass.
    The art of scandal : the life of Isabella Stewart Gardner / by Douglass Shand-Tucci.
  –1st ed.
     p. cm.
    Includes bibliographical references and index.
    ISBN 0-06-018643-7
    1. Gardner, Isabella Stewart, 1840–1924.   2. Art–Collectors and collecting–United States–Biography.   3. Women art collectors–United States–Biography.
  I. Title.
709'.2–dc21   97-10676
   [B]

ISBN 0-06-092977-4 (pbk.)

98 99 00 01 02 ❖/RRD 10 9 8 7 6 5 4 3 2 1

For Richard Rothmund and Jamie Hardigg.
Their judgment saved the day, and me from complete disillusionment.

Contents

Illustrations

COLOR PLATES
(between pages 208 and 209)

Preface and Acknowledgments

. . . music heard so deeply that it is not heard at all,
but you are the music
while the music lasts.

–*T. S. Eliot,* The Four Quartets, *"The Dry Salvages,"* V

These words of Eliot resonate urgently for me at Fenway Court. Somewhere between first love and great love, this biography was conceived there as a kind of memorial to the former (under whose influence I first saw the Gardner Museum), even as its writing has been chiefly sustained over the last two years as a sign of commitment to the latter, a relationship so heartfelt and fructifying–and challenging!–it puts me in mind time and again of the life of the formidable figure who is the subject of this biography. I am fond of quoting Jackson Lears: "All scholarship is–or ought to be–a kind of intellectual biography." My scholarship, I see more and more clearly, hardly develops at all except as I am faithful to that standard as enforced by my muse.

Whether or not what is so often true of fiction in this regard can also be true of nonfiction is a nice question: I write history, not poetry, and more than psychological or experiential evidence needs to be found and weighed to create a work of historical scholarship; but because it is Lears's kind of scholarship I aspire to, I am much struck by something May Sarton once said. Asked (according to Margot Peters, in her biography of Sarton) if she was writing again, the then sixty-five-year-old poet replied: "Yes. Because I have a Muse again. . . . Poetry is a gift; you can't make it on will. . . . It doesn't matter if I go to bed with her or not." Sarton continued, asserting: "with me it's the Muse who causes poetry by focussing the world." *Focussing*. It seems just the right word to acknowledge how I came at last to write this book after a personal and professional perigrination of close to twenty years.

It was in 1976 that I made my first scholarly pass at Isabella Gardner, when I was but four years out of Harvard College, where, in the spirit of the Class of 1972 I learned more of tear gas than of history and on the whole am glad of it. But I am happy to have also found the best sort of education, after all, from coming to know men and women like that legendary scholar Kenneth Conant, famous still for his pioneering reconstruction of the great medieval abbey of Cluny, and an early mentor of mine.

I remember well how happy my mother, Geraldine Groves Tucci, was when in 1976 I told her of the forthcoming publication by the Gardner Museum of my first work on Isabella Gardner and of Conant's part in stimulating it. Both my mother and my mentor had their reasons for being glad for me. My mother, in both her professional and her personal life, had survived, with real courage, a great deal–though hardly without fault herself for some of it–including an anguished and much-publicized divorce from my father, which she contested pretty much on her own and in the face of my father's prominence and influence. She had over the years found no little peace and quiet for herself at the Gardner Museum. Having earned her A.B. from Simmons College next door, she knew Fenway Court well and was always keen for me to make this resource my own and close a book long enough, as she put it more than once, to learn to smell the flowers. Conant, on the other hand, from rather a different point of view–he became Isabella Gardner's godson as a graduate student in art history at Harvard when he became an Episcopalian, and he knew Gardner's secrets as only a much younger admirer could!–was trying, I can see now, to teach me an allied lesson: "Mrs. Gardner," he always said, "abided only true knights. She could spot a phony in a minute."

It was a long time before I cared to smell even Isabella Gardner's flowers, but when in midlife I was sought out (brought out, really) by my own muse and soul mate and learned that although one may live for awhile on brains and spirit, unless the heart also comes into play, the game soon becomes, so to speak, half-hearted, the key, as I now see it, to this biography was given me as just my mother and Conant would have wished. "To one only will I tell it, do I tell it all day long," Isabella Gardner's friend, Amy Lowell, wrote, adding boldly she was "certain of nothing but the heart's affections and the truth of imagination." These things Isabella Gardner learned in ways I've come to recognize, and how she learned them and how she always tried to stand up for them is the story of her life as I see it in every aspect, as muse, mentor, patron, and artist.

The exchange between soul mates is indeed a critical theme of this biography. But other relationships and other debts proceeding from them also make me marvel at the links in time and history so many such debts disclose. Josephine Pomeroy Hendrick, the great grandmother of Jamie Hardigg, one of the two dear friends and mentors without whose counsel this book would never have seen print (and to whom, in consequence, it is dedicated), knew Isabella Stewart Gardner. So did the mother of another friend, my colleague H. A. Crosby Forbes, who recalled his mother saying that the founder of Fenway Court was always kind to New Yorkers newly arrived in the Hub of the Universe–or is it just the Promised Land? Tweed Roosevelt, who came promptly to my aid on very short notice in a vital archival matter, is a great-grandson of the president of the United States who caused Mrs. Gardner more than a few ruminations recorded here, not all laudatory.

And then there is the St. Botolph Club, where Sargent's famous portrait of Isabella Gardner was first seen more than a century ago now. The club's Long Table provides, in fact, nourishment of many kinds: the perspective of that sage *Atlantic* editor, Robert Manning; the persistence of Bradford Washburn (who found Mount Gardner for me); the dry psychiatric eye of John Sturrock; the window John Axelrod opens for me on one art collector's mind–each and all have helped. Furthermore, each in very different ways, Martin Smith, Eldridge Pendleton, and Russell Page, brothers all of the Society of St. John the Evangelist (respectively, superior, historian, and sometime archivist), inherit in some strange institutional way an intuitive knowledge of and feeling for Isabella Gardner they themselves hardly recognize. So does Susan Sinclair, the Gardner Museum's superb archivist. To each of them and, more formally, to the trustees and director of the Isabella Stewart Gardner Museum and the Society of Saint John the Evangelist, I express my thanks for their preservation of Isabella Gardner's correspondence, from which I have quoted so liberally. I am especially happy that I have been able to give to Susan Sinclair for the museum's archives a number of letters written by Gardner herself, not many of which survive, all discovered during my research for this biography.

Susan is also due special thanks for not discouraging me in one of my more controversial contentions, that Gardner was in her own way very much a modernist. That Isabella Gardner was an artist of that caliber in the first place I am able to argue here all the better for the insights of the architect Thomas Fox, John Singer Sargent's friend and collaborator. For access to Fox's unpublished manuscripts I am particularly grateful to the Boston Atheneum and to Stephen Nonack, the reference librarian of that wonderful institution, where so much of this book was written. I am equally thankful for access to the correspondence of John L. Gardner Sr. to the president and fellows of Harvard College and to Harvard's inde-fatigable archivist, Harley Holden, who made that possible.

For hardly less important help I wish to record as well my indebted-ness to Timothy O'Donnell and Robert Douglas Hunter for much good talk on art, and on the subject of religion, Betty Hughes Morris and Robert Evans, while the composer Rodney Lister did me a similar service with respect to the music of Charles Loeffler. For good counsel generally I thank Stuart Myers, Robin Bledsoe, Anita Lincoln, and Llewellyn Howland III. My agent, Upton Brady, has been patient, diligent, and sup-portive throughout. And without the skillful word processing of Diane Myers nothing would have been possible. Even more is this true of Cass Canfield, Jr., who has contributed more than a few ideas in aid of my work here and proved always an alert and persuasive critic. He is that great rarity, a good editor.

For the rest of it I will only add that for this historian, as, I believe, for the founder of Fenway Court, it is true to say the music does last! And love is only love when its origin is remembered and it is understood to be unconditional; when, in fact, it is finally given away.

Part One

————•◦•————

Madonna

The society [Henry] James knew was a performance . . . in which the performers wore masks and costumes. . . . the audience was expected to imagine the actual bodies beneath the costumes and the secret acts of love and violence that occurred offstage. The performance was a dance of the powerful, who loved, abused, and sometimes freed their beloved victims, and of the victims themselves who, all too rarely, succeeded in achieving freedom and power.

–Sheldon M. Novick

1

Reverie

COMEDY AND TRAGEDY: Isabella Gardner and John Sargent, the fourteenth of September, 1922. It was a wintry business, though it was still autumn–his last portrait of her. What was it Oscar Wilde had said? "The soul is born old, but grows young. That is the comedy of life. The body is born young and grows old. That is life's tragedy."[1]

This last portrait was a very different portrait than Sargent's first, painted nearly thirty-five years previously. Then she had been a vigorous woman of forty-seven, in high middle age: with its striking disclosure of her strength of character–that steady, appraising gaze–and hardly less so of her bohemian nature–Sargent had looped great ropes of pearls around her waist!–that portrait had in many ways in 1888 heralded her growing repute as a cultural maverick. By 1922 there was no doubt about it. Nor that she had become a formidable leader in her field; muse, mentor, patron, collector, connoisseur, and designer. And a scandal too–for so many people everywhere whom she had alternately vexed or fascinated. In 1886 it had been she, through Henry James, who had searched out Sargent. Thirty-six years later it was Sargent who sought her out.

She was eighty-two now, paralyzed so that she could no longer walk; for this last portrait they had had to prop her up like a dummy on a sofa, braced by pillows. Yet after her death, her friend Corina Smith, studying Sargent's brilliant farewell of his friend and patron,[2] saw in Isabella Gardner's eyes the most improbable thing–*elation*. The body is born young but grows old. The soul is born old, but grows young. Tragedy and comedy. It was Mary Berenson who had written Gardner: "Nothing, has ever been wasted on you?"[3] Yes, elation. As soon as she could (she had to wait for the return of her secretary; all her letters had to be dictated now), Isabella Gardner confided happily to Bernard Berenson that her last portrait, no less than had the first, was keeping "everyone's tongue busy wagging," adding in her ironic way: "even I think it is exquisite."[4] Dying wouldn't be wasted on her either. How many people die exquisitely? But there would always be Sargent's portrait to prove it.

She was burning her letters now too.[5] There were many fireplaces in her apartment high above perhaps the most unusual art museum in the world—the only institution anywhere, after all, both envisaged and designed by and then named after a woman[6]—where the woman herself was seeing to her legacy as surely as in another way was Sargent; keeping this, destroying that, she was editing her life as passionately and as determinedly as once she had formed the first and for years the greatest of all the private art collections of the New World, the glories of which still surrounded her. "Dearest Isabella," Bernard Berenson wrote, "we are all playing a losing game; you play it better than anyone else in the world."[7] Was that why she triumphed in the end? Did that explain the elation? She had been called the most optimistic of women; her museum, the pride of her life, the most joyful of creations. Yet she had had to hold on to that optimism, that joy, pretty tightly in her life. The fastest of runners as a girl, as an adult Isabella Gardner's carriages were also always driven, her friend and amanuensis Morris Carter recalled, "at top speed." It was her great contemporary, Theodore Roosevelt, who wrote: "Black care rarely sits behind a rider whose pace is fast enough."[8]

◆

Venice—there, certainly, were the finest memories of her youth. "Rising like water-columns from the sea; Of joy the sojourn, and of wealth the mart"[9]: so Byron hymned that legendary Italian city in its elegiac nineteenth-century twilight. And so in his way did Wagner, who, as it happens, died there: the drama of his funeral flotilla making its way up that age-old stage set, the Grand Canal, evokes in my mind's ear the long passionate rapture of longing and finding, or, it may be, betrayal, that one hears in *Tristan*; themes that resonate in all our lives. The opera itself was well known to Isabella Gardner; she loved Wagner's music. And in her old age she probably had learned that *Tristan* was the work the composer began writing in the very year that at the age of seventeen, in 1857, Isabella first saw Venice. All the story of her life suggests she lost her heart there. She once queried a friend, "Does your heart ache with mine for Venice?"[10]

She was Isabella Stewart then, Belle to family and friends, born April 14, 1840, not quite but almost the brash young "American girl" Henry James would shortly explicate so well; in Italy with her parents, David and Adelia Stewart of New York.[11] Educated at the sort of front-parlor school then so popular among the well-to-do of Manhattan, but also, briefly, at a Roman Catholic convent school (though the Stewarts were earnestly low church Episcopalians, parishioners of New York's fashionable Grace Church), Isabella had been brought up under a genteel though somewhat restricted regime—her mother had the reputation of being strict enough—in the sort of overstuffed mid-Victorian town house whose decor in her maturity Isabella doubtless preferred to forget.

Her father, a second-generation Scots immigrant, had been a self-made man, an importer turned mine owner, descended (his daughter might have boasted and probably did, for the Stewarts were "new money" and a lively, competitive as well as rather a romantic spirit had showed itself early in Isabella) from an ancient branch of Scotland's and, later, England's royal house of the same name. Isabella's mother, Adelia Smith, as she was when David Stewart married her, had been, however, of decidedly more humble background. Though the Smiths were of seventeenth-century New England stock, with at least this much of romance to offer Isabella—that one of her mother's uncles had been a scout for George Washington—Isabella's maternal grandfather, Selah Smith, had owned a prosperous Brooklyn tavern! In later years the founder of Fenway Court was reticent about this, but devastating enough. She talked little about her childhood and her family, Morris Carter declared: "she admired her father, was loyal to her mother, and loved her brother, David." Period.

It was Isabella's paternal grandmother, Isabella Todd Stewart, who as Sully painted her was certainly a striking old grandee, evidently imperious but stimulating, after whom young Isabella had been named and on whose Long Island estate she spent many happy summers as a girl, for whom she reserved her deepest affection. Alas, when Grandmother Stewart died in 1848, her young namesake was only eight. It was another loss, the death in 1854 of Isabella's sister, Adelia, and a natural enough tendency thereafter to focus on their only surviving daughter, that probably accounts for the Stewarts' European tour three years later with Isabella, a curious, high-spirited girl her parents no doubt felt would profit from such a trip. First they had lived in Paris, where they enrolled their daughter in a school about which nothing is known, not even its name, except that Mrs. Stewart insisted it be Protestant, a memory Isabella Gardner in later years must have smiled at given the ardent Anglo-Catholicism she had been so quick to take up after her marriage. They moved on thereafter to Italy for another long but largely undocumented sojourn, staying chiefly in Rome. There, David Stewart, called urgently back to New York on business during the financial panic of 1858, left Isabella and her mother in the care of the American minister to the Papal States. Mrs. Stewart, so eager to avoid "popery" in Paris, was thus left to await her husband's pleasure (nervously one may be sure) in the very shadow of the pope's court, all the more nervously because—rather astonishingly in her late forties—Isabella's mother was apparently again pregnant. (A son, James, was born on their return to America.)

Isabella's memories of her time in Italy also reflected what the willful look and shapely profile of her portrait-photographs in this period suggest: her increasing sense of self as well as her evidently blooming physical charms. Though plain of face and all her life sensitive about it, Isabella at eighteen had developed a noticeably "beautiful figure and lovely complexion [and] exceptionally quick [personality]," as evident in their Italian classes in Rome to her then classmate, Ida Agassiz, as they surely were as well to the man who was their teacher, with whom Agassiz noticed "Miss Stewart amused herself by mildly flirting."[12] Indeed, in future years, Isabella Gardner never pretended to have been a diligent student. Asked once in her prime if she had studied hard in school, a friend recalled her tart reply that "if it was against the rules she probably did."[13]

It had not escaped her classmates either that Belle Stewart was actually quite as quick at her lessons as on her feet. And as it turned out Italy had been an inspired finale for the Stewarts' long odyssey; it became the golden thread that ran through Isabella's life. From her famously grand passion for a certain novelist to her art collecting, Italy struck deep into Isabella. How deep Ida Agassiz Higginson, as Isabella's ultimately lifelong friend became, documented decades later when she recalled that such was the effect of Milan's Poldi-Pezzoli Museum, a fine house and splendid art collection left to the citizenry by a local notable, that Isabella told Ida when they were girls in Italy that if she ever had any money of her own she would like to "have a house . . . like the one in Milan filled with beautiful pictures and objects of art, for people to come and enjoy."[14]

How simply put, that dream—to have a house filled with beauty for people to come and see. That money of her own was, to be sure, rather demanding of fortune, but no more so perhaps than Virginia Woolf's later and more celebrated room of her own. In Isabella's case too it was all rather unlikely (she had in 1858 a brother, after all, and another sibling on the way). Yet what had been a dream in Milan would become a vision in Venice, and, in America, decades later, she had only to look up from her lapful of letters before the fire and across the courtyard of her remarkable museum to see what she had achieved: a significant episode in the history of art and a cultural revelation to the New World. She herself, both dreamer and maker, had already been counted more than once as among the most remarkable women of her time.

Venice for Byron had been "as a fairy city of the heart," and he averred that he had "loved her from [his] boyhood."[15] So, from her own youth, had Isabella Stewart Gardner, as she became after the Stewarts return to America when in 1860 she married John Lowell Gardner, Jr., of Boston, and apparently lost her heart again.

◆

Sixty years later, consigning to the flames what she had thought better of in her life, not only letters were burned but the Stewart family Bible—an astonishing act so at odds with her devoutness in her old age that the Bible's family associations, perhaps even its likely genealogical data, seems the only possible explanation.[16] Certainly hers was a life of more than one secret, not all of which she could be sure were disappearing into her fire. Nor could Isabella Gardner be sure either of her more-or-less chosen and all but authorized biographer: admitted Morris Carter after Gardner's death in 1925, when he was at work on her biography: "I felt constantly that Mrs. Gardner's friends were afraid of me—there was so much that might be said that ought not to be published."[17] Was some of it in the Stewart family Bible?

Exactly when or where Belle Stewart and Jack Gardner first met is really not known, nor what Jack's mother, the haughty scion of a great Salem family, made of the granddaughter of a Brooklyn tavern owner. It was Jack's father and Belle's father, so the authorized version had it, who so liked each other when they met in Paris, where their daughters were both enrolled in the same school, that they encouraged the visit to Julia Gardner back home in Boston of Belle Stewart in 1859 that yielded her romance with Jack Gardner and their subsequent engagement. But there had always been a variant version of events that after Isabella Gardner's death Carter felt bound to rebut: there were those in Boston, he huffed in his 1925 biography, who "repeated the tale that Belle Stewart jumped out of a boarding school window and eloped with Jack Gardner."[18] It is a tale newly credible today for it is now known that the one fact omitted from the authorized version–omitted surely for a reason–is that young Jack too had planned to be in Europe at the same time as young Belle, a fact newly documented by recourse to Harvard's archives, where a letter survives from his father withdrawing Jack from college for that purpose.[19]

Followed up, new evidence has also now surfaced documenting the fact that Jack Gardner did indeed accompany his parents to Europe during the period Belle Stewart was a student there.[20] Furthermore, according to the journal of General Nicholas Longworth Anderson, there was even more to tell: "Jack Gardner is . . . said to be," Anderson noted on March 29, 1858, "the most popular young American in Paris."[21] If Belle Stewart eloped with anyone, those who knew Isabella Stewart Gardner at all in later years knew it would have to have been with such a man! And if the oral tradition that has come down to us about Jack Gardner would seem to challenge such a characterization of him, that is only a better reason to look more closely at a man who was in fact so much overshadowed by his wife in later years that we know very little of him in any period.

Such an inspection, moreover, taking due note both of the compliments lavished on him in his maturity as "prince of hosts," club man and yachtsman and such, and also of the more dismissive remarks (of A. J. Phillpott, for instance, that Jack was "easy-going and not over-energetic")[22] suggests that while all this is, perhaps, dull enough sounding of middle age, in his youth "Jack the Lad" may, so to speak, have led the dance, which is by no means incompatible with his college record! Indeed, that record is a catalog of reprimands (the exact nature of which it is hard to determine) and accords also with the only other glimpse we have of Jack Gardner at Harvard. It is also from Anderson's journal: "According to the wager, this evening we spread out a fine supper of oysters, ale, and brandy punch in Jack Gardner's room. My room is in too close proximity to people who might inform the college faculty of our proceedings to have a real 'blowout,' and Jack kindly offered his room," wrote Anderson. "Seven individuals ate twelve dozen stewed oysters and drank six quarts of ale, besides much punch. From the riotous singing which they made I should think that the spree was a decided hit. . . ."[23]

A year later in Paris Jack Gardner's habits were not likely amid the temptations of the French capital to have become more sober. Nor, back home again in Boston, did he return to Harvard to complete his educa-tion. Whether or not he and Belle met in Paris, or fell in love there, or eloped (or whether or not James Stewart, who died at age twenty-three, "half-witted" according to Morris Carter,[24] was their child and not the elder Stewarts'!) Jack Gardner certainly preferred leaving school in order to get married, surely against the advice of his father, himself a Harvard graduate. Nor was Isabella Stewart likely to have opposed these events. Jack Gardner, after all, was quite a catch: in the words of a contemporary, "Boston's most eligible bachelor." Over six feet tall and with arresting if rather ravaged youthful good looks as well as penetrating eyes, he was self-assured and socially graceful, widely popular, and a thoroughgoing gentleman; the sort of man, Carter recalled, who would always "think of the other fellow."[25] Nor was there any doubt, all witnesses agree, that he had fallen headlong in love with Isabella.

No such report ever surfaced about Belle's feelings for Jack. And that her decision to marry Jack Gardner was a soberer one than his to marry her is the implication as well of the few surviving early letters Carter had access to after Isabella Gardner's death, in one of which she refers not so much to her own but rather to her "mother's bright visions of the future"[26] (the Gardners being for the Stewarts, of course, decidedly a step up the social ladder), suggesting that Isabella had struck out for freedom more than for love when in New York's Grace Church in April of 1860 she and Jack were married. The wedding trip thereafter was to Washington. Isabella Stewart Gardner was making a good investment in a good man and a devoted husband. But she was going, not to Venice, but to Boston.

◆

From the vantage point of her old age she must have wondered more than once if it had been worth it. State Street, Beacon Hill, Back Bay and

Cambridge, all solemnly united, with assorted colonies distributed from the North Shore to Maine: who was it who said Boston has always been more a state of mind than a place? A close-knit, gifted, stubborn, Yankee elite, self-sufficient and only grudgingly beginning to draw in to itself in cultural and intellectual alliance, through means marital and otherwise, a more cosmopolitan cast of characters, Boston's ruling class as it approached the late nineteenth century did not doubt then (any more than does its more diverse elite today), that it was leading Puritan Governor John Winthrop's visionary city on a hill, America's first and brightest beacon, always testing, measuring, valuing, illuminating. There was no more judgmental place anywhere. On the other hand, it would as things turned out offer Isabella Gardner considerable scope.

To be sure, the country's intellectual capital, as Boston was then becoming as Harvard and then MIT and one institution after another began to form what would become a striking constellation of learning, was forced more and more in Isabella Gardner's lifetime to acknowledge that New York was emerging as America's business and also its cultural capital, even as both Boston and New York increasingly deferred to Washington as the nation's third (governmental) capital. But already, so to speak, it was the traffic back and forth, the intercourse, that told the tale and pointed to the future. In Gardner's time, Boston would lose not just writers like William D. Howells to New York, but painters like Childe Hassam and Maurice Prendergast: the Puritan capital even lost Henry Adams to Washington, to say nothing of Louis Sullivan to Chicago. But New York's tribute to Boston in this period was also substantial: consider just two men, each preeminent in America in their fields, who moved from New York, preferring to work in Boston: the architect H. H. Richardson and Frederick Law Olmsted, the landscape designer. By the time of her death, many would have put Isabella Stewart Gardner in their league. But when first she came to the hilly red-brick and brownstone city on the Charles she had been only on Jack Gardner's arm and with no repute of her own at all, nor much likelihood of any. She was, furthermore, seen on all sides very much as an intruder. If her memories of Venice in her youth were the most joyful of her life, those of her first years as a bride in Boston could not but have been the most painful.

She had become, of course, Mrs. John L. Gardner, Jr., in the style of the day; no small thing. Being a New Yorker she had not been able to count, however, on the familial support on which most young brides depended to make their way in Cold Roast Boston, where she had also faced a good deal of envy and resentment because so many Boston women had had their own eye on Jack Gardner. Jack and Belle meanwhile moved in with the senior Gardners, then to an apartment hotel, while their new town house, a present from Belle's parents, was being built on Beacon Street in the Back Bay, then being developed as the city's most fashionable quarter of elegant tree-lined streets centering on the two-hundred-foot-wide Commonwealth Avenue. With its towering churches and gracious parks, adorned with sculpture, the Back Bay was truly an example of the city as a work of art not lost on the impressionable bride from New York.

Civic art, however, was not at the forefront of the Boston mind in this era: slavery was. And whatever Isabella's view, it was certainly the case that the Gardners' most important business interests were closely linked to a settled economy in the American South; "lords of the loom" as the Gardners were, they had been in those days deeply anxious about anything likely to cause instability. Though they doubtless did not favor slavery in and of itself, they appeared willing to tolerate the evil in aid of peace, and–it must be said–profit. Jack Gardner's sister, Julia, Isabella's old classmate from Paris, had also married into a Southern family.[27] Jack Gardner himself was no more likely to have voted for Lincoln than he would have been a hundred years earlier to have dumped British tea into Boston Harbor. Resented in the first place as an intruder, inevitably suspect to those with abolitionist sympathies, Isabella Gardner had, too, another problem. For while it is true that the Abolitionists (like the Sons of Liberty a century earlier) were not favored by Boston's ruling class, Boston society *was* staunchly pro-Union. Yet when Lincoln appealed for volunteers to preserve the Union, Jack Gardner declined; throughout the Civil War he evaded the call, presumably buying a substitute to fight for him.[28]

How vigorously these issues were joined on Beacon Street in Isabella Gardner's twenties she must vividly have remembered all her life. Above all there had been the story of the all-black Massachusetts 54th Regiment, marching up Beacon Street to death and glory–only to be met at Boston's preeminent club of the era, the Somerset, by lowered shades! Walter Muir Whitehill disproved the story but not the truth that bred it when in his study of the matter he concluded that nearly a quarter of the Somerset's membership resigned when Lincoln's assassination brought to a head the bitterness felt by those who walked out to found what the remaining Somerseters called the Sambo Club! Actually, the new club was called, naturally enough, the Union (as it still is). According to Whitehill, "feeling ran very high indeed . . . it was for a few years *after the war* so acute that members of the respective clubs did not greet one another in the streets."[29] Yet in just that period Jack Gardner joined, not the Union, but the Somerset![30]

Had either Jack or Belle Gardner read, I wonder, "The Lamp of Psyche," a short story by Edith Wharton that focuses on Boston's view of just such actions as those of Jack Gardner, who though in later life much liked, was also thought as we've seen to have been "easy-going," not Boston's highest praise? So was newly married Delia Corbett's husband in Wharton's tale; he was called "cosmopolitan" and "pleasure-loving." Brought somewhat nervously home to Boston to visit the highly "moral" and incurably serious "do-gooder" aunt who raised Delia, the husband, though liked well enough by the aunt, when he admits he evaded war service, is neither ashamed nor much embarrassed, which is to make the correct historical point that no shame attached generally to Jack Gardner's actions. But neither would any praise have either! And the aunt's judgment, though unspoken, was unmistakable. So much so that Delia, like the mythical Psyche who when she shines a light on her great love is disillusioned, sees that her husband, impressive enough elsewhere, "cannot survive being viewed in Boston light." And though she resists judging him, in the very need to resist she discovers the power of a moral issue that won't go away.

Evidence this was true of Belle Gardner too might be found in the more liberal than conservative (as we would say today) and decidedly inclusive views of her maturity, when, for example, she declared herself an admirer of the militant abolitionist, Wendell Phillips. Certainly, too, Belle had been as quick as the wife in Wharton's story to lay claim to just such a highly "moral" aunt as friend and mentor in Boston, that other transplanted New Yorker, Julia Ward Howe—she of *The Battle Hymn of the Republic*, whose lifelong and affectionate friendship with Isabella Gardner must be accounted telling of the younger woman's views of such matters.[31]

On the other hand, among the men at least, Jack Gardner seems to have survived "Boston light" very well! General Anderson, his Harvard classmate and a much decorated war hero, remained a close friend after the war. Similarly, there was Jack Gardner's lifelong friendship with Henry Lee Higginson, which brings to mind Henry Adams' relationship to Higginson and Adams' brother, Charles, whose service with Higginson in the Massachusetts Cavalry made Henry Adams (as one might have thought Jack Gardner!) feel like a "civilian shirker"[32], in Edward Chalfont's words, if not an outright coward. Yet Higginson, who all his life proudly bore a saber wound on his cheek as a mark of his war service, and donated "Soldier's Field" to Harvard in memory of fallen comrades, continued Jack Gardner's close friend, calling him not only "charming–such a gentleman, with his courteous, cordial manners," but also "high-minded [and] . . . full of careful thought as to his duties and his conduct, wise, honorable to the highest point"–hardly words a war hero uses to describe a shirker.

What may be missing here by way of explanation is that whatever Isabella Gardner's political views, if she had not protested Jack's draft evasion of military service, had she perhaps been the cause of it? That would explain his friends' otherwise curious acceptance of his actions. Sixty years later this was perhaps the sort of issue Isabella Gardner in her old age might well have felt was best forgotten. How relevant could it be so many decades later? Certainly Carter recalled that in later years when anyone brought up the Civil War, Isabella Gardner was only too apt to give the impression she was too young to remember it.[33]

◆

Had the founder of Fenway Court been able to read perhaps the best of her obituaries, written in 1925 by her old friend, John Jay Chapman, she might perhaps have been convinced that those early, unhappy years as a bride in the Boston of the Civil War period were, in fact, vital to recall if sense were to be made of her life. For the fact is that though Isabella Gardner was high-spirited enough to have provoked at least the rumor of scandal before she was twenty, by twenty-two, as a young bride, she seemed to many so delicate and nervous her husband could hardly have been faulted if he decided not to leave her for war service. Isabella Gardner, wrote Chapman in a memorable phrase, had appeared at first in Boston to be akin to "a fairy in a machine shop," so at odds did she seem "as a bride . . . [in] the bosom of one of Boston's old Brahminical families."[34] He was talking about the Gardners. Being from New York was one thing, negotiating the political shoals of Boston during the Civil War was another; living with the Gardners was apparently something else again.

Cold Roast Boston as lifestyle has always had much to be said for it. Talk can be cheap, emotions misleading, sacrifice more controlling than kindly. Undoubtedly there are some emotions so deeply held and keenly felt that to say nothing about them is sometimes to say everything superbly. But a perennial refusal to face up to an issue with forthright discussion, at worst cowardly, at best immature, is inevitably disastrous; frustrations mount and emerge often in bizarre ways; the explosion, when it comes, really a kind of panic, is invariably deeply harmful and

Isabella and John Gardner in the early years of their marriage, ca. 1861. *Isabella Stewart Gardner Museum, Boston*

very long in the healing. It is not for nothing, in Nathan Hale's words, that "American psychotherapy . . . develop[ed] primarily in Boston,"[35] and that in the 1900s Freud and Jung would find when they visited New England that Boston was on the leading edge of this field.

Whether or not it was so simply remedied a matter as Belle and Jack Gardner having to spend part of their marriage in his parents' house (their move to an apartment hotel is telling) before their own was ready–it took nearly two years before it was–their marriage had not seemed to begin well. Indeed, like many a spouse before her, Isabella Gardner's in-laws seem to have led her to cast her own family in a better light; at least that is the impression in her last years she must have given Carter, who she was doubtless coaching in the morning, so to speak, as eagerly as she was burning letters in the evening! And Carter duly reported in his biography that early on Belle was "glad to escape frequently to New York and to stay with her parents until her eager husband came to fetch her," a pretty clear portrait of an unhappy and disappointed woman who had long since lost patience, one imagines, with husband, family, *and* New England's capital city.

Significantly, such report as survives of Isabella Gardner when she was in Boston during those first two years of her marriage implies she was "much of an invalid." So much so that when she and Jack "would drive to Danvers to see their Peabody relatives . . . she was sometimes so weak that she had to be carried into the house."[36] And there, surely, is the key to understanding for us in the post-Freudian age: As Jean Strouse has pointed out in her path-breaking biography of Henry James' equally complicated sister, Alice, a contemporary of Gardner who was herself the invalid all her life that Isabella Gardner is said to have begun her marriage as, "nervous women who took to their beds with fainting spells . . . were, in fact, opting out of the roles society had prescribed for them. . . . Though the terms neurasthenia and hysteria were inexact, . . . [the doctors who named them] pioneered in recognizing that . . . their patients were neither malingerers nor madwomen but people who were in intense pain."[37]

The cause of that pain is always a complex issue; but as Peter Gay points out, neurasthenia, as first defined in the 1880s by the neurologist Dr. George Beard, was at once observed to be sexually related.[38] To appeal to an example from the same social milieu and overall time frame, it is possible that Belle Gardner was, like Edith Wharton, somewhat at a loss as a sexual partner. Perhaps Paris had been only romantic! Wharton, though from a more sophisticated New York family and a generation later, was entirely "unprepared for almost everything that marriage . . . would require of her" according to her biographer, who adds that when Wharton "at last recognized her sexual needs, she felt betrayed not only by her mother['s lack of guidance] but also by the cultural system that kept

young women in a state of false modesty and innocence."[39] Including, perhaps Gardner too. It seems a safe bet that so sternly evangelical a mother
as Isabella Gardner's was just such another as Wharton's.

Of none of this did Isabella Gardner leave any evidence at all, but it is
possible that lifelong sexual frustrations were rooted in this era. On the
other hand in her husband and lover Isabella Gardner had certainly been
more fortunate than Wharton, and perhaps it was Jack Gardner's
patience and kindliness that had made the difference. Certainly that is
implied by his devotion to a wife who would clearly have puzzled if not
exasperated most husbands. Whatever was wrong, it was well over
three years into their marriage, but finally achieved, after all–and, significantly, after nearly a year in their new home at 152 Beacon Street–that
Belle and Jack Gardner celebrated the birth on June 18, 1863, of a son,
John Lowell Gardner III.

It was, however, an ordeal for the new mother, and Peter Gay has well
explained why when he points out that in the nineteenth century "the
processes of pregnancy and giving birth were attended by severe pain
and often by excruciating sufferings, and the ever-present threat of death
to child and mother alike. It is true that from 1847 on, chloroform
became available to ease the pangs of labor. . . . But while women's terror
of pain, anticipated and actual, diminished in the second half of the nineteenth century, the far more ominous specter of death continued to haunt
them."[40] This was true even in Boston, then as now a medical center,
whose best doctors it was entirely Isabella Gardner's to command. It was
Dr. Walter Channing of Harvard Medical School, who first used anesthesia in obstetrics (in 1847), and Isabella Gardner's own doctor, Dr.
Henry Bigelow, was the son and namesake of the "apostle of anesthesia"
as his father was called (he was the author of the first scientific paper on
the subject).[41] But doctors were often reluctant to use anesthesia because
of the possibly adverse consequences; Queen Victoria had used chloroform in 1853; in 1856 the Empress Eugénie of France had declined it.[42]

Of Isabella Gardner's decision we know nothing. Only that visiting
family members, according to Carter, recalled no elation on Isabella's
part, reporting that they found her "lying in bed, very straight and very
quiet, waiting stoically for the return of health and strength." And even a
year and a half later she would complain in one of very few letters from
this period still extant that though "quite well again" she had to admit her
"strength and flesh haven't come back yet." Meanwhile, though, young

Gardner and her son, John L. Gardner III ("Jackie"), ca. 1864. *Isabella Stewart Gardner Museum, Boston*

Jackie, as they nicknamed him, yielded his parents many joys: "backward with his walking," Gardner reported to her mother-in-law, Jackie was, however, "quite advanced in talking and says any quantity of words quite distinctly."[43] For her part all the evidence—including a touching portrait of mother and son—suggests Belle was the kind of attentive, even doting, parent who would have listened closely.

Alas, John Lowell Gardner III would have little enough to say. Peter Gay again: "quite as many nineteenth-century children died between the ages of one and five as died in their first year. And even five was no threshold of safety. Physicians stood largely helpless before childhood diseases."[44] Jackie Gardner survived at least one siege of high fever and vomiting, in the fall of 1864, probably measles and whooping cough, and even achieved the coming of four double teeth. But the Gardners' little boy had not proved able to withstand the bad cold of March 1865 that turned soon enough into pneumonia, and on the fifteenth of that month, John Lowell Gardner III died.

So much suffering, so intensely felt; so much grieving; more than the death of parents or friends' betrayal or lover's rejection, the loss of a child, by all accounts, is of all calamities the most devastating. Neither husband nor wife, stressed as severely, perhaps, as can be, hardly is able from their depleted resources to support the other spouse's great need. Recklessly, perhaps, the Gardners seem to have determined to have another child almost at once, even though Carter reported that Jackie's birth had been "such a terrible ordeal for Isabella Gardner that the doctor told her she could never have another child."[45] According to a no longer extant letter of Mrs. John Amory Lowell cited by the author Louise Hall Tharp (but not made available subsequently to the Gardner Museum or any other archive), Isabella Gardner, whether enthusiastically or not, became pregnant again four or five months after her infant child's death, at the same time as did her sister-in-law Harriet—who put a very immediate human face on all the doctor's warnings by having her son—but at the cost of her life. Exhausted by that trauma, and doubtless unnerved generally, Isabella Gardner suffered a miscarriage according to Lowell's letter and herself came quite close to death.[46] How anguished Jack Gardner must have been as well. In all likelihood it was probably his entirely understandable wish to continue the family line which had led him and his wife on a course that had so greatly imperiled her life. The year 1865, only Isabella Gardner's twenty-fifth year, and Jack Gardner's twenty-eighth, must have been the most searing of their young lives, and a decline back into invalidism and depression was both natural and predictable.

The conventional analysis, however, that Isabella Gardner had been plunged into depression by the loss of her son never quite accounts for why (or so at least she gave Carter to understand) she had already been mired in a similar depression *before* the birth of the child, any more than the conventional explanation for that earliest period of depression—that she was childless—explains why that was true in the first place. Of Isabella Gardner's depressions in general more will be said here soon. Of this specific period in her life it is important, however, to avoid the conventional assumptions of Carter's authorized version. That the child himself made all things briefly bright and beautiful (Isabella Gardner kept all her life a miniature of her son inscribed with his name and dates and with a lock of his hair encased in the back in a closed case)[47] is really beside the point, which is that Jack Gardner surely badly wanted a son and heir and that both he and Isabella had loved little Jackie very much, but that *none of this means that Isabella Gardner herself wanted children*. The fact may well be that it was increasingly borne in upon her that the roles of wife and mother did not come naturally to her, for all that she would be made to feel again and again in her life that they *should*, and that in the aftermath of her trauma she had been *relieved* not to be able to have more children. Of none of this either is there any surviving documentation. But in her long life it was to be other roles than wife and mother to which she seemed to take more naturally, in the end so much so they made her famous.

It was not, of course, a thing that could ever have been said. Isabella Gardner's relief, however, perhaps explains why her Commonplace Book in this period seems so much more cheerful than her public life; what little there was of it according to Carter, given her decline back into invalidism. Perhaps it also explains why she seems to have been so miraculously revived in 1867 by a long journey she and Jack took to Scandinavia and Russia, followed by rather a frivolous finale in Vienna and Paris. Of this trip she would have, surely, all her life, the fondest possible memories. They had both returned home in high spirits. Perhaps in the end Jack Gardner was relieved too; Belle (like his brother's wife) might easily have died in childbirth. And perhaps their joint survival of all this proved the one thing needful to cement their relationship, which all these anxieties must have strained considerably. What other explanation can there be for the improbable tale of Isabella Gardner having had to be carried on board the steamer in Boston, so weak was she, whereas by her return home she had transformed herself into "one of the most conspicuous members of Boston society. Effervescent, exuberant, reckless. . . ."[48] It was as if Belle Stewart had been reborn.

2

The Capacity of Enjoyment

LOOKING BACK FROM the perspective of an invalid in the 1920s to her youth in the 1860s and 1870s, Isabella Gardner, seeing how the world revived in her old age from the cataclysm of the First World War, must have been reminded of how in an earlier time America had rebounded from the Civil War—and how she too, at more or less the same time, had got to her feet again, so to speak, after the trauma of the death of her son. As an old woman she would live to see very little of the "roaring twenties," and that little from an invalid's chair; but had she not had her fun in the 1860s and 1870s? And this too, Mary Berenson reminded her in her old age, was no trivial blessing: Isabella Gardner had indeed been given, Berenson wrote her in 1923, "the capacity of enjoyment, by no means the least of the gifts of the gods."[1]

Yet for all that Berenson was right, Gardner did not really like society in the way, say, the late Duchess of Windsor did. The better comparison of our day might be Jacqueline Kennedy Onassis, who as she grew older was seen to be a more and more serious person. Certainly Isabella Gardner was never the gilded age grand dame perfect hostess of some-body's legend who devised elegant dinners renowned for good food and drink, trained a perfect staff, scintillated all evening and exuded tact and charm from every pore, bringing out everyone's best, and so on. It was *Jack* Gardner who set the table, as it were, at the Gardners' house, and he might as well have been the classic bachelor host for all his wife did in that respect. Carter (always a better observer than historian) saw at firsthand that it was actually "Mr. Gardner [who] managed the household and engaged the servants,"[2] and that it was *his* social skills, not his wife's, which made their entertainments a success. The Gardners' par-

The entrance hall of the Gardners' Back Bay town house at 152 Beacon Street. *Isabella Stewart Gardner Museum, Boston*

ties, Carter recalled, were overall distinctly uneven in quality because "although the men were ready to accept Mrs. Gardner's invitations, some of the cleverest women were still unfriendly." The supper, on the other hand, always under "Mr. Gardner's personal supervision [was the] one element of [their] parties [that] was always a triumph." Mr. Gardner was, in fact, "the perfect host, and [the reason] the Gardner dinners were the best in Boston,"[3] wrote Carter, who recounted amazedly how different husband and wife were in this respect: Jack Gardner, for example, prized their visits to the house of a couple noted for serving "the best burgundy in the world, for which [Isabella Gardner] cared nothing whatever."[4] Maude Howe Elliott concurred, calling Jack Gardner "the prince of hosts," while his wife, recalled another friend, Corina Smith, was as far as food and drink were concerned "indifferent to both."[5]

Nor had Isabella Gardner ever mastered the art of presiding at table with anything like grace and wit. She was far too outspoken for that! Smith also recalled that while Jack Gardner was the soul of tact, Isabella spoke always with "a startling frankness,"[6] so intrusive her husband nicknamed her "Busy Ella."[7] Nor had she ever any repute for wit.[8] Rather, she was that very different thing—quick-witted. In fact, Isabella Gardner was, in the old phrase, distinctly a handful, by no means everyone's cup of tea, and attractive really only to those who could forgive her the lack of so many of the "feminine" social skills of those days because of what was perhaps her most attractive characteristic: her eager (indeed, irresistible) spirit, most especially, in Carter's words, "her readiness for any kind of lark."[9]

When, for instance, she and Jack had once missed the train from town that was to take them to a country coaching party, who else would have suggested they hire a special engine. Their friends, downcast at their country rendezvous by the failure of the Gardners to make it, must have been startled by the sudden appearance of a belching locomotive, from which soon appeared Isabella Gardner, in her latest Worth gown, followed by her "hugely pleased" husband.[10]

It was the stuff of which newspaper society columns are made, even in New York (especially in New York) and this too was to be always held against her by the Back Bay. Indeed, long after Isabella Gardner's death no less than Time magazine (in 1936) retold this particular tale with characteristic embellishments: Gardner had driven the engine herself, reported Time. Moreover, she had done so at eighty miles per hour![11] A half century earlier it had been that infamous New York society rag of the 1890s Town Topics, which had often laid the groundwork for such tales, regaling readers then about how "Mrs. Jack, as she is familiarly called, is easily the brightest, breeziest woman in Boston, . . . the idol of the men and the envy of the women. She throws out her lariat and drags after her chariot the brightest men in town. . . . Let the wives of giddy and wayward husbands scold and stamp their feet . . . the spell of Mrs. Jack's enthrallment cannot be broken."[12]

Nonsense? Of course. Yet Isabella Stewart Gardner, who had always been both an athletic and an adventurous, flirtatious woman, loved to dance as much as to run. And now that we can read the thank-you notes she received many a morning after, Town Topics seems to have been not too wide of the mark sometimes! If "Mrs. Jack" had her foes, she had her friends too. From one admirer, for example, came this favor: "No wonder so many gentlemen admire you," he wrote. "The trouble is you excite all these emotions in other people's bosoms. . . . As it is, there seems to be no alternative but to sit on top of Oak Hill and think of the way your dress fits. . . ."[13] Not too many years later, furthermore, she was receiving similar notes from that admirer's son! One such announced that "as a gloom-dispeller, corpse-reviver, and general chirker-up, you are as unrivaled in the fragrance of your flowers as in the sunshine of your presence. . . . I wish you would stop in again when you have a minute to spare, and exhilarate me some more. I did not have to take any champagne the last day you came."[14]

It sounds trivial, of course, but that is perhaps because, like so much about Isabella Gardner, the tale is told from the male perspective. More insightful were the views of several of Gardner's female contemporaries who were what we'd call today professional women. Maude Howe Elliott, for instance, Julia Ward Howe's daughter, herself a beauty as well as a writer and intellectual, proffered rather a more thoughtful analysis of Isabella Gardner. While not failing to notice that Gardner was increasingly "conspicuous for her equipages, her entertainments and her toilettes" and that she was "one of [the Paris designer] Worth's most valued clients,"[15] Howe found even in purely society matters better reasons than those to admire Gardner. It was, for example, in the postbellum era the custom for ladies to carry at a ball bouquets sent to them by partners who had engaged to dance with them, and–Isabella Gardner being a superb dancer–Howe recalled Gardner was "always among the most favored" with flowers: "I have a vision of her now . . . resplendent in a Worth dress of white uncut velvet, her arms filled with flowers," Howe remembered, and then added: "It was an open secret that, while outside the houses of many of our belles one could see on Friday mornings, before the city carts made their rounds, the faded bouquets of the week thrown carelessly into the ash barrels, the flowers Mrs. Gardner had worn or carried were never thus desiccated. It was said that she herself committed the faded blossoms to the clean flames . . . a small instance indicative of [her] good taste. . . ."[16]

And not the only one. Carter too had a tale about bouquets: it seems that in this rather Jane Austen world of Boston dances of Gardner's early years, she and another woman were so streaks ahead in this matter from anyone else that various young men laid wagers on who would arrive at the next ball the most heavily laden with floral tribute. With a nice appreciation of Gardner's style, Carter recalled that whereas "the other lady arrived carrying more bouquets than ever," a few minutes later "Mrs. Gardner, who would never have made the mistake of arriving first, did the only effective, amusing and also dignified thing–she entered the ballroom without a single flower."[17] A small matter, but a sure touch, heralding the nature of Gardner's eventual career hardly less than did her spectacular wardrobe.

As Howe indicated, Isabella Gardner began to collect artistic gowns from Paris–and splendid jewels too–long before she collected anything else. But there was a difference; witness the testimony of another "professional" woman of the era, a lifelong observer of Gardner, who though admiring of her in many respects was critical enough to keep her distance, the composer Clara Rogers. In later years, writing of Boston in the 1870s and 1880s, Rogers recalled a growing

> relaxation from the rigorously modest cut of the regulation evening dress, and a more generous display of the person. . . . this change followed in the wake of a certain lady from New York who had come to live in Boston, and who was plentifully supplied with Paris gowns,–creations of Worth–very attractive from a purely artistic standpoint, but very shocking as viewed by some of the good Bostonians of Puritan ancestry. . . . righteous indignation–meetings were held in quiet corners at luncheons.

> Meanwhile the lady in question [Gardner is never named, even though Rogers was writing in 1932] gave dinner parties in her attractive house, to which many of her detractors accepted invitations. . . . And so it came about that little by little these same detractors found arguments sufficient to themselves for modifying their general attitude. . . . A different standpoint began to assert itself slowly but surely until the old characteristics were well-nigh effaced by a new order of things.[18]

Here was a larger thing, and the position Gardner took up was more obviously significant. So, too, was the response of the Back Bay, which liked the newly effervescent Isabella of the late 1860s and early 1870s even less than the nervous newcomer and intruder of the early 1860s. As another of Gardner's contemporaries, Margaret Chanler, recalled, more and more Isabella Gardner "stood out in vivid contrast to the people among whom she lived, and seemed to belong to another age and clime, where passions burned brighter. . . . Some of the more conservative groups," Chanler added, "looked askance at [Gardner]; Grace Minot was not allowed to go to her parties, nor were several others of the Sewing Circle I belonged to."[19] Indeed, Isabella Gardner herself was never invited to join that centerpiece of female society in Boston in those days, a sewing circle (and truth to tell it's hard to imagine her in one). Yet it is very likely for most of her life she was the hottest topic of discussion in all of them. There it was, perhaps, that was born that distinctive liter-ary genre, the Gardner Tall Tale.

◆

One thing in her old age Isabella Gardner did not burn, nor even cull through to any appreciable extent, was her great treasure trove of news clippings, which survives to this day. An inveterate reader of the daily press (it was as she grew older a more and more useful way to keep up with what was going on), Gardner right up to her death regularly clipped a wide range of stories that interested her, usually about sports, music, or art, and not excluding, as she became better known, stories about herself, though it is likely her widespread circle of friends and acquaintances rained many of those clippings amusedly down upon her.

Like New Testament parables and ancient sagas and folktales, these stories about Gardner fall easily into recognizable categories and types, each with its own inner meaning or core truth about Isabella Gardner. They are, moreover, key to a sophisticated understanding of her life. Clara Rogers saw this when she wrote in the 1930s of Gardner: "the eager attention of the public is neither excited nor held by merit alone. The sensational element must intervene. Even *conduct* must be original to be interesting."[20] Carter also saw it, and saw the good in it so many miss even today: "In the magazines that circulate scandal," he wrote, "there were frequent paragraphs about [Mrs. Gardner]. A public curiosity was thus developed, which was vulgar enough at the time, but from that thorn grapes were ultimately gathered."[21]

One group of tall tales proceeded from the enormous interest that attached to Isabella Gardner's modes of transport, which were indeed conspicuous, and on the element of dash and speed I've suggested disclose hardly less about her than similar stories do about Theodore Roosevelt! "Boston's jaw dropped, Boston's eyes bulged," declared Carter, "when it was heard that besides a butler the Gardners kept two footmen, and when it saw Mrs. Gardner drive out with [not the usual one but] two men on the [carriage's] box." Dashing along, she does not seem often to have ceded anyone the right of way either–even on a sidewalk! Perhaps Carter's masterpiece of a Gardner tall tale–which was always, he perceptively observed, about "one of those little vagaries [of Gardner] which exasperated the victims and entertained the rest of the community"–is the one about how Isabella Gardner coped with curbside snowbanks:

> Something had annoyed her; to recover her composure, some selfindulgence which should prove her above the law was needed; ... the coachman, driving a booby-sleigh, stopped in front of [a friend's] door [upon whom she was calling], but between Mrs. Gardner and the sidewalk was a mountain of snow. "It's impossible for me to get out here," she said irritably, "drive up on the sidewalk." When her order had been carried out, and the sleigh had made a barricade completely blocking the passage of the hundreds of pedestrians who were taking the air after the storm, Mrs. Gardner descended in a perfectly happy frame of mind.[22]

Another variant of a Gardner tall tale was what could be called the animal type, and this achieved extraordinary dimensions, reflecting not only Isabella Gardner's great love for animals but how she found animal exuberance an absolutely necessary counterpoint to Victorian convention and artificiality. Dogs and horses Isabella Gardner cared for extravagantly all her life, but in this area as in so many others her tastes were wide-ranging and exotic. Thus she was a frequent visitor to a small zoo on downtown Boylston Street opposite Boston Common, where she was given to taking unusual liberties with the lion cubs without much regard, let it be said, to any protest of the cubs' mother, who on at least one occasion seems to have been restrained with some difficulty.

One time, nothing daunted, Gardner reportedly actually secured permission (permission? it was a publicity bonanza for zoo and newspapers alike) to bring home for a bit two of the best-looking cubs–doubtless to the consternation of more than one shopper on Boylston Street as her carriage passed. Back home at Beacon Street she reportedly frolicked about with them and some Back Bay children invited over for the fun. Reported one correspondent: "the sensation created in the Gardner residence was a sublime one." Gardner typically returned the cubs to the zoo that night with a red bow beautifully tied around the one she liked best, which was, of course, promptly nicknamed "Mrs. Jack" after Isabella Gardner by the zoo's operators, who by this time must have been gleefully feeding the newspapers news of any and all escapades, not least that

> on Monday last [so reported one paper] Mrs. Gardner extended her special attention to a fine young lion called Rex. He is nearly three years old, about the size of a large mastiff and with every promise of being a magnificent specimen of his kind. He is a newcomer, and Mrs. Gardner had been putting in a claim for his notice and good will for several days.... knowing him to be thoroughly tamed ... Manager Bostwick [allowed Mrs. Gardner to] saunter about old Bates Hall with an immense yellow-eyed lion by her side, her hand resting on his neck and he swinging along as contentedly as though he had been under Mrs. Jack's care every day of his life. Surprise reigned among the spectators present.[23]

A contemporary newspaper sketch of Isabella Gardner at a Boston zoo. *Isabella Stewart Gardner Museum, Boston*

That fine understatement betokens one of the staider newspapers, but, inevitably, a Gardner tall tale was begat, the telling of which over the years has not dulled the event by any means. Within five years of the first relatively sober report, probably in the *Transcript*, the *Herald* or the *Globe*, another paper, the more sensational *Post* in all likelihood, had considerably recast the tale and in a much bolder palette, Gardner by now bedecked with jewels, guarded by gentlemen who quailed in terror while she bravely led a full-fledged lion on so merry a peregrination as to have caused a near riot. Year by year, moreover, it only gets better. By Walter Terry's biography of Ruth St. Denis in 1969, for example, Gardner was described as known to walk along Boston streets with "a wild animal on a leash."[24] In the most recent report, in 1982, according to Jane Smith, Elsie De Wolfe's biographer, Gardner actually "rode through the streets" on–not a lion, but an elephant![25]

Yet Isabella Gardner's leonine frolics, in a wider contemporary perspective, were not as eccentric as they have too often been made to seem, and really signaled the fact–then as now–that she needs to be more and more seen as a true original and on a larger stage–and judged accordingly. How many people today, for instance, recall that the celebrated Victorian actress Sarah Bernhardt also had a lion? She actually tried for a time to keep it as a pet in a cage in her house! To be sure, Bernhardt's Paris was more blasé about such things than Gardner's Boston, but as between the two cities–moreover, as between the two women–there was more to be said than might be supposed.

Bernhardt, who though she thought New York "a place of American boastfulness, philistinism and greed," much liked the "more elevated values" and "tradition of learning and ... love of beauty" she found in Boston, which Bernhardt visited for a long engagement in 1880, was reportedly "captivated by what she called the 'Bostonian race,'" particularly by the females, and it has been said that "the cultivated ladies of Boston rushed to her every performance." It did not hurt, of course, that they all spoke French, or that Boston's critics raved about Bernhardt's acting (one called it "perfection that defied analysis"), or that the Divine Sarah's "suite at the Hotel Vendôme [was] filled with works of art ... sent by welcoming Brahmins."[26] Among them, Gardner surely saw to it, were numbered a few treasures from her own house a few blocks away. Less likely than many to be put off by the fact that Bernhardt was Jewish, and probably more intrigued than shocked that she was as much courtesan as actress and known to be sexually active with both men and women, Gardner, whether or not she helped enrich the star's hotel suite, forged a warm relationship with the legendary Sarah, as their surviving correspondence attests, and not by any means an unequal one either. Not for nothing, as Isabella Gardner's increasingly picturesque persona of the 1870s, 1880s, and 1890s unfolded, was she later called "Boston's precinema star,"[27] and several of her friends and Bernhardt's were quick to compare the two women.

Usually they had in mind the flamboyance and style of each woman, their similar personalities and, above all, their willfulness. But to my mind they may have been most alike, Gardner and Bernhardt, in the unusual but characteristic way each dealt with depression. Neither woman, though each was neurasthenic, ever cast herself in the role of victim; both, for instance, took great strength from the stimulation of travel. Bernhardt, to cite another example, who led an incredibly strenuous life, was much given to such neurasthenic symptoms as copious weeping, fainting spells, vomiting blood, and what she called in her memoirs "agonizing bouts of exhaustion," bouts her biographers, however, thought correlated so intimately with her being denied acting roles she coveted that they wondered "if perhaps she used illness (self-induced, if necessary) as a pretext in order to have her own way."[28]

There comes at once to mind Isabella Gardner's sudden recovery in 1867 during her and Jack Gardner's European trip, intended to rouse her from depression after their son's death and her subsequent miscarriage and the relief, as I have argued, she may have felt over being unable to have more children. Not the perennial and deepening passivity of invalidism of the Alice James variety, but a more active, willful neurasthenia of the Sarah Bernhardt sort suggests itself. Writing of such a dramatic recovery in Bernhardt's life, her biographers suggest of Bernhardt what I suggest of Gardner: that she "had either exaggerated her condition or . . . success is a wonderful cure for neurasthenia!"[29]

Does it not accord perfectly with Isabella Gardner's golden rule for deflecting criticism, according to Carter: "if criticism ever influenced her—which is doubtful—she never let it appear to, but preferred to excite more criticism."[30]

Whether to her husband and his family then, and to Carter later, Isabella Gardner had exaggerated her invalidism, it was certainly true that though she would always be a highly nervous woman, success would increasingly be a wonderful cure! What William James wrote of his potentially brilliant sister, Alice—that always there was "a unique and tragic impression of personal power venting itself on no opportunity"[31]— could so easily have been true of Isabella Gardner—even at her most rambunctious. But the tale as it unfolded, would play out, of course, very differently.

3

———•◦•———

On Pilgrimage

As SHE RECOVERED more and more her native buoyancy, Isabella Gardner also began at some point to do all that, so to speak, with her left hand, as she would continue to do all her life; while with her right hand she began, unbeknownst to most, to steer for more distant stars and for more serious goals–literary, intellectual, artistic, and religious. It was the start of what would turn out to be quite a long personal journey, even an odyssey, a *Künstlerroman* as the Germans call it, an "artist's novel" of the sort more and more characteristic of the late nineteenth and early twentieth centuries–Proust's *À la recherche du temps perdu* is one such; another would be Joyce's *Portrait of the Artist as a Young Man*–whereby the protagonist through many experiences and crises comes eventually to the mature recognition of his or her true identity and vocation.[1] To this more earnest endeavor, furthermore, Isabella Gardner brought the same "capacity of enjoyment" as she did to matching wits with the Back Bay.

The earliest important experience of this journey for Gardner was not (as might seem to us likely now) artistic, but religious; and though it was only when eventually she fused religion to art and intellect that she would famously find her ultimate calling and identity (in a finale still cel-ebrated a century later), religion remained Isabella Gardner's most long-standing lifelong interest, enduring as it did until the very end of her life in 1924, and having first arisen as far back as the early 1870s when there appeared at the Church of the Advent in Boston a charismatic young priest by the name of Charles Chapman Grafton.[2]

A Bostonian of old family and liberal abolitionist sympathies, educated at Harvard, Grafton would go on to be a bishop of the Episcopal Church and the leader of its high church or Anglo-Catholic wing. Of his early period in the ministry Advent historian B. Hughes Morris has written:

Father Charles Grafton, a founder of the Cowley Fathers and Isabella Gardner's earliest confessor and spiritual director. *Society of St. John the Evangelist Archives*

The Cowley Fathers, as the Society of St. John the Evangelist was popularly called, had really begun at the behest of Charles Chapman Grafton, who went to England in 1865, hoping to take part in a revival of [monastic life]. He and [another] sought the help of Dr. Pusey [who with John Keble and John Henry Newman are universally acknowledged as the Fathers of the Oxford Movement], who suggested they see his great friend, the Reverend Richard Meux Benson. They did so, and soon asked Benson to act as their superior in a monastic order. . . . [founded in] December 1865 . . . in Oxford.[3]

The result was the first Anglican order of monks, still thriving today, and in America headquartered since 1870 in Boston, where it became quickly known not only for a special ministry to intellectuals and academics but, in Morris' words, for "the exotic flavor of their appearance [monkish habits had never been regularly seen before in the Puritan capital], their direct, extemporaneous manner of preaching, and the zeal of their social outreach."[4] In this last especially the Cowleys were early allied with an Anglican order of nuns, the Society of St. Margaret, which came to Boston in the same decade to staff Children's Hospital.[5] Both orders were also much interested in church art and liturgy and one of Grafton's first tasks was the erection of a magnificent new Ruskinian Gothic Church of the Advent between 1878 and 1883, by which time Isabella Gardner's devotion was evident in the first of many princely gifts to Cowley and the Advent, the church's high altar.[6]

Isabella Gardner doubtless found in Grafton, who was still corresponding with her three decades later, wise pastoral counsel and probably close friendship; he is, in fact, described in a contemporary letter as her spiritual director.[7] But it went much further than that. In the first place, the Cowley Fathers' work with the immigrant poor and especially with blacks (Grafton, after all, had been a disciple of Wendell Phillips, who as we've noted here Isabella Gardner greatly admired) would importantly shape Gardner's own interest in what would come to be called the social gospel. At the same time Gardner's intensely emotional nature and developing aesthetic sensibility, allied unusually to a high critical taste, drew her even more ardently to the artistic dimension of Cowley's ministry, so evident in the Advent's famously beautiful liturgy, designed by Grafton.

The extent and nature of her response may well be illustrated by one instance (in the reign of Grafton's immediate successor, Father Frisby) recounted by Morris: Having "discovered in her reading a rite for Maundy Thursday in which the altar is scrubbed with vinegar, salt, and water during the ceremonial stripping of the church for the austerities of Good Friday," Gardner, always persuasive, won the rector's agreement, according to Morris' parish history, "to revive the rite, and she and two ladies of the Altar Guild, dressed in figure-fitting blue habits Mrs. Gardner herself designed, [one assumes Gardner chose women whose figures were as good as hers!] and wearing Madonna-blue veils and Franciscan sandals, solemnly washed the altar and the steps with palm branches."[8] Notice that Isabella Gardner was now not only ordering artistic clothes, she herself was designing them, as well as, one may be sure, the choreography of the rite.

Alas, for an alert and lively imagination. To have a flair for such things was for some as unforgivable in religion as in anything else, it seems. And this rather too picturesque (even by the standards of those days) liturgical drama begat of all Gardner tall tales by far the most bizarre, which in its most outrageous forms suggests that it was not the altar steps, but the front steps of the church itself Gardner washed—*barefoot*, no less, in one version, shod in another (but in that version she is *crawling* up the steps!), and in yet another version, whether shod or not, lugging a great pail of water—all as a penance (what a Calvinist Bostonian projection!) for any number of sexual transgressions.[9] It's so good a story in any form it has

A page of Isabella Gardner's sketches and notes from the travel diary she kept during her trip of 1875 to Egypt and the Holy Land. *Isabella Stewart Gardner Museum, Boston*

been told and retold even by Gardner's admirers; told, be it noted, as if they had *seen* it, rather than only been *told* it. Never mind. I doubt Isabella Gardner ever gave any of it a second thought. It had more to do with true religion, perhaps, that in 1874–75 she and Jack were on another pilgrimage, this time an actual voyage–to the Holy Land and to Egypt.

◆

This journey too as it turned out was to be a long and memorable one, especially significant in that Isabella Gardner kept a very complete travel diary that includes her earliest attempt to set down her inner thoughts in a continuous, sustained way,[10] and at a time when she was greatly stimulated, as she often was throughout her life, by foreign travel.

How varied and characteristic were her impressions. Her response to Cairo? "Oh, the grace and beauty of the men. . . . What graceful languor and what perfect postures, as they lean against . . . a wall." At another time she disengaged, also characteristically: "I felt that I was disappointed when I stood close to Cheops . . . but when I got away from carriages and many of the people, and could lie in the sand near the Sphinx, with the silent desert beyond and on every side, and the pyramids a little away from me–then solemnity and mystery took possession and my heart went out to the Sphinx." Equally she was moved by native music, noticing while cruising up the Nile, "the crew, with their turbans and many-colored robes, squatt[ing] in a circle about their lurid, flickering fire, cook[ing] their coffee and chant[ing] their low, weird songs," and at the museum at Boolak she had what seemed to her "a revelation. . . . I was surprised by [Ancient Egypt's] high state of art. Some of the statues seem to me unequaled."

Indeed, the whole journey was a revelation, as her travel diary attests:

[At Karnak by moonlight] I have never had such an experience and I felt as if I never wanted to see anything again in this world; that I might shut my eyes to keep that vision clear. It was not beautiful, but most grand, mysterious, solemn. I *felt* it, even more than saw it. . . .

What nights we have! The [Nile] runs liquid gold . . . and then the sun sets and the world has hardly time to become amethysts and then silver before it is black night. And the moonlit nights! How different from ours! Nothing sharp, clear and defined, but a beautiful day turned pale. It was so beautiful, inexpressibly lovely tonight on deck and everything was so still when the muezzins call to prayer was wailed through the air that the tears would come.

[At Abu Simbel we] all climbed through the sand [and] . . . then with candles we examined the interior with its hall supported by eight Osiride pillars. . . . And then to make it perfect the moon rose directly opposite the temple, in at the very door, so that all the lights were put out, and the great hall was the strangest thing I have ever seen, with its shadows and ghostly light.

> [Then, at sunrise] I was the first to be there and almost buried
> myself in the golden sand as I lay watching the light streak in the sky
> getting deeper and deeper, and by and by a yellow light began to
> creep down the rock and over the benign calm of the great Rameses.

Isabella Gardner was also alert to more practical and contemporary
aspects of her travel. The housing, for example, of a donkey boy she visited ("one room which had only a window looking on a court to lighten
it, and even that was barred") depressed her. So (though in a more philo-
sophical way) did her experience, while determinedly sitting on the deck
on their small yacht going up the Nile during a gale, of "a poor woman
who came to the river to fill her water jar. It was a terrible struggle [in
such a storm], but it was to be that or thirst." On the other hand, at an
American mission school she was elated by the fact that "in this country
of woman's intellectual depravity it was good to see young girls who
could read and write."

Self-disclosure of that sort permeates this travel diary. Above all, there
is her *eye*, her discernment, whether of the contraposto of a well-formed
man leaning against a wall or of the color hues of Egyptian light. What
an imagination she had: "a lovely evening. . . . went up as usual [to the
deck] after dinner and found the steersman at his prayers, his forehead
touching the deck and little Alee at the helm. As I lay upon the couch
with the fragrance of the frankincense stealing over me, the wake of the
moon was a fit path by which my thoughts went straight to Cleopatra–
and I forgot it was Christmas Eve!" She was that sort of traveler! Indeed,
she and Jack made their entrance into Jerusalem as it turned out quite in
the Gardner style so reputed back home: a great storm–"everything in
darkness," wrote Isabella, "thunder roaring and the lightning flashing on
the walls and towers." Though she was often ill–she ate *everything*, never
seeming to learn her lesson–her mind was on other things. "It is hard to
realize," she mused at one point, "that we are living in Jerusalem; it is a
fact that seems to *grow into one*, and to be living here is like nothing else
in the world." Here it was the Jewish women who were beautiful, she
thought, not the men.

They traversed the Mount of Olives (it was, she wrote, "the road by
which David fled when Absalom rebelled"); traveled through the wilder-
ness of Judea ("the scene of the [parable of] the Good Samaritan"); bathed
in the Dead Sea, collected wildflowers (duly pasted into her journal),
drank at the River Jordan, evaded some Muslim fanatics at Hebron, sur-

vived being robbed, spent a night in Jericho, and in Bethany saw the house of Mary and Martha and Lazarus' tomb. Journeying back into time as much as into the Holy Land (for theirs was not the average tourist tour—Jack and Isabella traveled in their own caravan, of eight horses, five mules, and two donkeys, led by their dragoman and assorted retainers), they rode horseback, living in the open ("tents pitched in a beautiful place, hanging over the valley") and, seemingly lost to time and care, had one of the great experiences of their lives together, by now, surely, the sort of friends whose regard, when it can survive that level of intimacy, is forever secure.

For a glorious pendant there was classical Athens ("took rolls of bread in my pocket and ate them with the coffee between the pillars of Jupiter Olympus") and then Constantinople: "Most beautiful. . . . very like New York. . . . Saint Sophia a little disappointing . . . Dome really wonderful." Determined to do everything, Isabella Gardner, confronted doubtless by her cautious and determinedly unromantic husband, pressed an otherwise anonymous Mr. Hurel into service, so as to go out in a caique (which Gardner was quite capable of rowing herself, as she often did in Maine) on the Bosphorus by moonlight. And then there was a long, languid return to the West up the Danube to Vienna and Salzburg and Munich and Nuremberg—evidence as religion more and more kept company with music of another growing interest in Gardner's life. Interestingly, though increasingly drawn to high church Anglican religion and always a lover of the art and literature of Italy, the music Gardner responded to was neither religious nor Italian, but German and French and rather more secular than not.

That response was ardent enough that after their return to Boston, Isabella Gardner sometime in the mid- to late 1870s conceived the first of what would be several building projects in her life, the purchase and remodeling (with the help of architect John Sturgis, who at the same time was designing the new church for the Advent) of the town house next door to the Gardners. It was an undertaking that certainly enhanced their state! By the project's completion in 1881 the Gardners' newly doubled town house, already one of the grandest on Boston's legendary Beacon Street (*Artistic Houses of Boston* raved about the Gardners' "noble flight of stairs" and such), rejoiced as well in a splendid new music room carved out of the newly acquired neighboring town house.[11] In this music room the interest in art and music so evident in Gardner's dedication to the liturgical arts of the Church of the Advent would be considerably intensified and focused as she began to feel her way toward her role of patron of the arts. At the same time, in 1878, she took another decision for art, as it were, one that would shape her life decisively–to enroll in a course of lectures given by a notable Harvard professor in the field of the Italian studies.

◆

"Plain in appearance but with a dashing air, [she] had early made up her mind to be 'bright and ugly'; and always the center of an admiring group, [seeking] out the cleverest Harvard boys to talk [with]"[12]: an apt enough description of Isabella Gardner, it was, however, written to describe Margaret Fuller, the Boston woman who in the early nineteenth century in many ways was Gardner's precursor. And not only in Fuller's enthrallment with all things Italian, from art and literature to the great love affair of her life; as Christina Zwarg has asserted, "the swamp of gossip and petty response to Fuller," the inevitable response of most men *and* most women in a patriarchal society to female accomplishment, led to a parade of "stories that cover[ed] and in a literal sense disguise[d] almost everything there was to know about [Fuller]."[13] So too with Isabella Gardner. And if Gardner in her time, at the dawn of our own media age, was able in my view deliberately to use such a "swamp of gossip and petty response" for her own purposes (the art of scandal!), it was because both Boston society and the New England intelligentsia had already discovered common ground a generation before Gardner, ground on which Fuller had already won something of a foothold for women, a foothold the feminist leader Julia Ward Howe, whose friendship with Gardner has already been touched on here, held with some distinction and was able in turn to welcome Isabella Gardner to explore.

Still, in setting her sights on the superior intellectual opportunities of Harvard University Gardner was considerably pushing out the boat, so to speak; for the whole question of women's education at Harvard was then highly controversial. The very year Gardner decided to enroll in the lecture series was the year a women's college at Harvard was first really seriously mooted, and it was in the fall of the year following that the "Private Collegiate Institution for Women," the embryonic Radcliffe College (the "Harvard Annex" as it was soon nicknamed), opened its doors for the first time. Its leading spirit, not surprisingly, was a friend of Gardner's,

Elizabeth Cary Agassiz, who would become Radcliffe's first president, herself an esteemed colleague of her famous husband, the zoologist-geologist Louis Agassiz. Perhaps it was the Agassiz connection (it was the Agassizes' daughter, Ida, who had been Isabella's classmate in Rome and thereafter a lifelong friend) that turned Gardner's thoughts toward what the Harvard faculty had to offer not only to women generally but to Gardner personally. Certainly Isabella Gardner, so alert to female education in Egypt, was equally so at home: her support of the cause of women's education at Harvard is documented by the fact that twice at least Elizabeth Agassiz wrote to Gardner on the subject, once to thank her for "your sympathy as well as your generosity to the Annex," another time acknowledging Gardner's "affectionate line of loving congratulations" on the project's success.[14]

In seeking access to Harvard's resources Gardner was very much at the leading edge of her time not only with respect to women's education generally but in her choice of field as well, for when the teacher whom she had chosen to sit at the feet of, so to speak, Charles Eliot Norton, was appointed a professor only four years previously, in 1874, Harvard became the first university in America with a professorial chair in art history. Moreover, behind Norton stood John Ruskin, Norton's intimate friend, who claimed Norton as his "first real tutor,"[15] and in a cause both preached in and out of season: what Maureen Cunningham has called "an entirely new view of the life of the past,"[16] a view in which not classical, but medieval Italy, its art, literature, and architecture (celebrated in Ruskin's book, *The Stones of Venice*) become central to nineteenth-century thought. Especially in thirteenth-century Florence and in the work of Dante and Giotto, Norton saw, furthermore, the American future as well as the Italian past, for as Cunningham notes, both Ruskin and Norton saw in medieval Italy

> an example of integrity and civic pride and beauty, all of which Norton found missing in America. To the knowledge of these glories Norton led those in whom he discerned the stirrings and sensibilities he felt.
>
> Mrs. Gardner was one of these initiates. . . . There is no doubt he influenced her greatly, in effect pointing out a new course in life. . . . Later Mrs. Gardner would branch out, finding Norton's view restrictive. But for the while she was his pupil.[17]

And an ardent one, for Norton possessed gifts Gardner valued: "a magnetic sympathy with generous ideals, whether in life or in art,"[18] as well as an "exquisitely light social touch." It was as if a light had gone on in Isabella Gardner's head.

It was not, actually, quite so straightforward as that; it never was with Isabella Gardner. There had been three years earlier, in 1875, yet another family tragedy; Jack's brother Joseph,

Charles Eliot Norton. *Courtesy of the Harvard University Archives*

the widower of the sister-in-law whose death in childbirth had had so much of an effect on Isabella's miscarriage, despite having three boys to rear and being their only parent, "blew his brains out" in Henry Adams' vivid phrase[19], and it had devolved upon Jack and Isabella to raise children after all–three of them, Joseph's orphans. By 1878, the eldest, Joe, was seventeen, and ready for Harvard; William Amory, a precocious fifteen, was not far behind, and Augustus, coming on fast enough, was already thirteen. Isabella Gardner, herself nearly forty in 1878, by enrolling in Norton's lectures, was keeping up with her young men–a habit she would persevere in to very good point all her life.

Of Gardner's parenting, opinion seems to have been divided. "It was a mixture of devotion and rigor," John Jay Chapman remembered, and the result was "highly organized, clever, sensitive, conscientious children, apt at all things intellectual, and they become noted both as boys and men for integrity–every kind of integrity," he continued, "–mental, moral, social–and for the extraordinary devotion to their aunt."[20] Geoffrey Lowell Cabot, on the other hand, though he thought Isabella Gardner "an able woman," thought her influence on these boys problematic. Pointing to what might well have seemed a moral vacuum to a future leader of Boston's Watch and Ward Society (which would become in

Jack Gardner's three nephews, the children of his brother, Joseph (*left to right*): William Amory Gardner, Joseph Peabody Gardner, Jr., Augustus Peabody Gardner. *Isabella Stewart Gardner Museum, Boston*

the early twentieth century the city's most notorious censor of plays and books), Cabot, already a considerable prude, had this "fault to find with her, she evidently considers that the two things best worth having in life are intellectual ability and courteous manners," suggesting to him that, for the eldest boy, "she is a dangerous leader for Joe."[21] Still, if Gardner would, arguably, turn out to be a better mentor to other young men than a parent to her nephews, her devotion to "her boys" was evident. Witness the fact that, judging William Amory needed to wait a year before entering Harvard, and that a delay would do Joe no harm, Gardner decreed in 1879 that she and Jack would lead all three of them on another pilgrimage, as much educational as religious, focusing on the cathedral churches of England and France. "Those brilliant boys,"[22] Henry James called them, were always for Isabella Gardner (who was often called selfish) as much a matter of *her* education as theirs.

It was during this ecclesiastical peregrination in the summer of 1879, midway between cathedrals English and French—eighteen of them!—that James emerged as a definite presence in the life of Isabella Gardner, along with Henry Adams and his wife, Clover. Leon Edel, one of James' biographers, writes of one occasion in Paris when the Gardners and the Adamses and Henry James dined

> at a *cafe chantant* in the open air and then went to the *Cirque*, after which they ate ices at a wayside cafe. The experience could not have been lost on Henry [James]: an imperious-aggressive "Queen" [Isabella, of course already with this repute] juxtaposed with a "Voltaire in petticoats" [Clover Adams] in a setting such as Manet painted. "I remember those agreeable days last summer in London and Paris," Henry wrote Isabella later, "those talks and walks and drives and dinners."[23]

This was, of course, heady intellectual company; but for those who saw through the Gardner tall tales of lions and such to the less widely suspected Isabella Gardner who was Charles Eliot Norton's ardent student it was no surprise Gardner sought such company so avidly.

4

The Awakener

"THE MOMENT MY eyes fell on him I was content."[1] The words of Edith Wharton, and not of her husband, they also, I believe, represent the feelings of Isabella Gardner for Frank Crawford, who was not her husband either.

The eyes ever leading the psyche, an awakener will usually be fair to look upon. Awakener, however, does not necessarily mean lover, at least not in our modern sense of that word; what is meant is more akin to soul mate, lover or not. In Wharton's case, for example, it was neither her husband (who in the end sickened and betrayed her) nor the lover Wharton was so strongly drawn to physically (whose character was such as to eventually empty even good sex of any worthwhile meaning) but a third man (with whom she was never physically intimate, so far as we know), whom Wharton called "the great love of all my life"[2]–a soul mate with whom she preferred in her biographer's words, "the promise of a long friendship to fleeting hours of romance."[3] But Wharton was lucky. Walter Berry was not afraid of such a demanding relationship. It suited his values; if he was not entirely a true knight, he was still (the best sort of) intellectual snob, who would esteem the meaning of a book dedication, for example, more highly than a sexual liaison. What is the old Italian proverb? Love is for the person who knows how to make it. Alas, it would seem neither Isabella Gardner nor her soul mate did know, though to be fair the world did not make it easy for them. In a long life neither ever met anyone else who would mean to the other so much and become so heartfelt a friend; yet the only legacy of what might be called the first act of their drama in 1882–83 was the scandal that finally gave the Back Bay what it had for so long felt cheated of by Isabella Gardner.

There were actually two bachelors who were noticeable callers on Gardner in the winter of 1881–82. The first was Gardner's fellow traveler of Paris days, Henry James. Just recently in the public eye for his first major success, *Daisy Miller*, James, already a formidable intellect in early middle age, had kept up with Gardner after Paris, though his letters display the mock-ironic tone that so often reflected his conflictedness about someone. In his first missive to Isabella Gardner, for example, he bows with a flourish: "so indelible is the image you imprint on the consciousness," only to at once insist on a certain distance, remarking how their times together in the French capital had possessed "a tenderness which the past, directly it recedes a little, always awakes in my sympathetic soul"; and concludes by seizing the high ground: "Look out for my next big book," he purred. "It will immortalize me. After that, some day, I will immortalize you."[4] In fact, though James never dedicated a book to Gardner and, indeed, took care to try to obscure her appearances in his work, he did immortalize her in the end. But it was a very gradual unfolding, the experience of Gardner for James. That "such letters [as James wrote Gardner; in the end over 100] could have been written only by someone who, at bottom, really liked the self-inflated, willful, and driven Mrs. Gardner,"[5] ought not to obscure the fact that it would be many years before James took Gardner's measure. And with good reason: she would develop enormously. Gardner, on the other hand, seems at once to have seen the promise of the other bachelor conspicuous among her callers that winter of 1882, Francis Marion Crawford.[6]

The son of the well-known nineteenth-century American sculptor, Thomas Crawford, he of the figure of *Freedom* that surmounts the dome of the U.S. Capitol, and of Louisa Ward, Julia Ward Howe's sister, though Frank (as he was always called) was of American parentage, he was born in Tuscany in 1854. His father, who like so many American artists then, preferred to work in Italy, died of cancer there at only forty-seven, when Frank was a boy, and except for brief and not very successful educational episodes in Britain and America (including a three-year stint at St. Paul's School in Concord, New Hampshire), Frank was raised in Rome. Very carefully; there was little money.

Francis Marion Crawford. *Isabella Stewart Gardner Museum, Boston*

Crawford was not only gifted intellectually, he was also socially graceful, adventuresome, idealistic, and, not least, beautiful physically; Maude
Howe Elliott described him as "one of the handsomest men I have ever
seen–tall, splendidly built, with a noble head, classic features, and hands
and feet of sculpturesque beauty. His eyes were blue, dancing, full of
light, real Irish eyes." Elliott also noticed that Crawford was distinctly
narcissist, though she recalled that "his vanity was of the simplest and
most disarming variety. . . . He would pose before a mirror quite openly,
rejoicing in his strength and beauty like any vigorous young animal."[7] On
the other hand, his mother, not surprisingly, found ample occasion to
protest Frank's "extraordinary selfishness" and his conspicuous "self
love,"[8] while his biographer added that along with all his virtues
Crawford evidenced "obstinacy, moodiness and proud spirit,"[9] adding

that neither "in his personal affairs or his literary work did Crawford willingly accept criticism."[10] Still, these were things that one might expect to be righted by maturity. Crawford was only twenty-seven in 1881 when he journeyed to the United States, very much the young man in search of fame and fortune, to live with his celebrated aunt Julia Ward Howe, Gardner's close friend, on Beacon Street, a block or so from the Gardner town house.

Close by, Henry James was enmeshed in a task as typical of early middle age as was Crawford's of youth, sorting out family affairs after the death of his mother–"the central figure of all his years, and so she would remain"[11]–lying low and feeling fragile in rooms James had taken in a modest brick house in the shadow of the Charles Street Meeting House at the foot of Beacon Hill, a block north of Beacon Street. There, after a walk across Boston Common and a mid-morning breakfast at the Parker House, he would most days spend the rest of his time at his writing desk. His daily round with his muse completed, when "in the gathering winter twilight" James didn't walk across the river to Cambridge for dinner with his father and sister,[12] he was known to turn instead toward Beacon Street and Isabella Gardner's town house, hardly a ten-minute walk away.

Crawford was much slower to put in an appearance at "Mrs. Jack's." He had begun his quest for success, as would most men of his hormonally driven age group, not with friendship in mind, however potentially romantic, but marriage, a good marriage; and given Gardner's domestic state and that she was also fourteen years older, not with her! Rather, the object of Crawford's affections at first was the entirely age-appropriate Mary Perkins, the lovely and wealthy unmarried daughter of Boston's legendary China Trade merchant prince, Thomas Handasyd Perkins. But Crawford was innocent, as Maude Howe Elliott later recalled, of "the American girls' habit of leading a man on, several men simultaneously."[13] Highly honorable (the sort of man who if he sent a person a valentine would regard it as a commitment and mean what he said on it!), he hardly realized he was being misled. Mary Perkins, we now know, was accepting his attentions insincerely. Crawford, of course, persevered.

The middle-aged James, meanwhile, found more reason to call upon Isabella Gardner. In Paris their relationship had it would seem been almost wholly frivolous; though it is interesting that the day James finished the book he was working on there, *Hawthorne*, it was Gardner with whom he went out to celebrate. Now, in Boston, James' chosen task was a dramatization of the book that had so recently made him famous, *Daisy Miller*, a choice he must have made carefully at a time when he was natu-rally recollective. ("All those weeks after Mother's death," he wrote, "had an exquisite stillness and solemnity.")[14] And this time Gardner would play a bigger part than celebrant: if James did not exactly seek her advice, he nonetheless paid her the enormous compliment of in some sense seeking her understanding. He rejoiced, in one of his biographers' words, in "the joy of his creation, and when his play was written he carried his script to Mrs. Gardner and read it to her, during the long evenings. She was a sympathetic listener." Thus, writes Leon Edel, "Henry had long ago imag-ined Benvolio reading his plays to the irresistible countess–[James] had, so to speak, his private performance at the Court of Isabella."[15] Behold, our first glimpse of Isabella Gardner (with perhaps the greatest novelist of the age) playing the part for which she would become famous, as muse and mentor; for James surely shared with her the difficulty he was having placing the play (in fact, it failed) at a time when he was very vulnerable, generally, and concerned to follow up promptly his first literary success. But if this was the sort of situation in which Gardner was apt to come into her own, on James' side it was a situation in which he could not long be comfortable, especially with a woman. Consider his relationship with Gardner in the light of his response to both her and Edith Wharton.

Very striking indeed is the way James over the years spoke on the one hand of Isabella Gardner–that she was "not a woman, she is a locomo-tive–with a Pullman car attached"[16]–and on the other of Wharton, who again seemed to him not so much a woman as, in this case, an eagle, sub-jecting James to "general eagle-pounces and eagle-flights of her deranging and devastating, raving, burning and destroying energy."[17] Locomotive and eagle, both female, terrified James equally, as happened so often when he spied "the masculine conclusion . . . crowning the feminine observation."[18] In James' view, Wharton's biographer writes, Wharton and Gardner were each distinctly a "bird of prey."[19] Indeed, when James compares Wharton to George Sand and George Eliot, Leon Edel rightly concludes that James was cataloging Gardner as well as Wharton as one of the "'queenly' women" James was so leery of.[20] Moreover, Edel comes close to the heart of the thing when he notes that though it was "Gardner's assertiveness [that] had attracted [James] to her," he always preferred Wharton because she did not "assert her queenliness in the eccentric ways of Mrs. Jack."[21] Eccentric? Of course. Wharton was old money; the Stewarts new money, a little bolder. James' sharpest comment about Gardner's mentoring, however, was that "she tries too hard," as he complained to a friend, "and listens too sympathetically."[22] It is, after all, the response of a man perhaps not entirely at ease with himself, especially about women. It was, too, the response of a man who was confessedly the great observer (no small part of his being the great novelist); James would always be more comfortable observing than being observed; always he wanted to know but resisted being known.

If Gardner's "countess" was not quite right for James, neither was

Henry James in early middle age, when he first became a part of Isabella Gardner's circle. *By permission of the Houghton Library, Harvard University*

James' "Benvolio" for Gardner, for whom, too, James' brilliance and distinction would be somewhat offset by the fact that he not only withheld himself, emotionally, from Gardner, rejecting her as either muse or mentor, but in early middle age he was also beginning to let himself go physically. Balding rapidly, James was (like Jack Gardner!) becoming stout. By contrast, Crawford's appearance was as dashing as his mind was brilliant. And most important of all, if James was alike to Gardner in being a realist, Crawford was more alike to her in being also an idealist and a romantic. And whereas James retreated in some alarm from Gardner's sympathy, Crawford undoubtedly signaled to her that, whether or not he found her sexually attractive, he felt (in the wake of the final collapse of his romance with Mary Perkins) drawn strongly to Gardner emotionally. So much so that Crawford's biographer, John Pilkington, wrote that "of all those who helped to mend Crawford's broken heart none assisted more satisfactorily than Mrs. Gardner."[23] Crawford's infatuation with Mary Perkins (it was not to prove an enduring love) was not, to be sure, as worthy a trial to mentor a friend through as the catastrophe of a mother's death, but it is significant that Crawford, "probably attracted to Mrs. Gardner because she seemed the American equivalent of the women he had known in Roman society ... mature, intelligent, glamorous, cosmopolitan," found according to his life's chronicler that Gardner "listened sympathetically, ... and greatly encouraged him."[24] Exactly what James had found off-putting in Isabella Gardner was what most attracted Frank Crawford.

Did it matter to Crawford that Gardner was also by repute a woman of strong personality, possessive and dominating and even manipulative? One might as well ask if Crawford's "obstinacy [and] moodiness" gave Gardner pause! If Crawford's own biographer pronounced him "proud, defensively aggressive and ... stubborn,"[25] pointing to the often fatal flaws of the self-absorbed, the fact was that both were well matched in that as in other respects. Because, for instance, of his unusual life experience—having lost his father in his boyhood, for example, and growing up in a foreign country with mostly older people—Crawford was culturally complex beyond his years and psychologically interesting in a way few young people are, yet also doubtless lonely, perhaps, because such complexities naturally were appreciated more by an older person like Gardner than by his peers. Crawford also shared with Gardner exacting interests and standards and values, cultural, social, and religious, which neither wished to compromise. Gardner especially, much battered by life, was no doubt also rejuvenated by the way Crawford renewed in her ideals she perhaps had sensed she was beginning to lose track of. Though very different from each other, Gardner and Crawford were distinctly worthy of each other.

Crawford, moreover, was not just fair to look upon. He was a man of considerable intellect. Not for nothing had he already, though still in his twenties, taken first-class honors in Mathematics, Divinity, Latin, and Greek at Cambridge, subsequently pursued scientific interests at Heidelberg, even studying Sanskrit at Harvard.[26] He traveled widely, including India. He actually wrote his diary in Urdu (doubtless to keep it up!). He had also acquired strong religious beliefs, converting to Catholicism in his early twenties. Even insofar as the physical side was concerned, he did not just pose! At Heidelberg he fenced; he loved both hiking and sailing; and at Cambridge he boxed, quite as well, actually, as Isabella Gardner danced![27] And both Crawford and Gardner not only loved Italy, both spoke and read Italian. In fact, they first came seriously

Gardner's and Crawford's copies of Dante's *La Divina Commedia*, interleaved and bound together by Tiffany in 1893 according to Crawford's designs. *Isabella Stewart Gardner Museum, Boston*

together to read Dante—fatal choice!—and in the Gardner Collection today, amid such editions of that poet's work as a superb one of 1482 with engravings after drawings by Botticelli (an edition of such surpassing historic importance that Charles Eliot Norton called it a "treasure"), perhaps the most moving is the book made up from Gardner's and Crawford's own everyday copies of *The Divine Comedy*, interleaved and bound together by Tiffany, which also made the binding of silver tendrils and enameled flowers inlaid in dark green leather Crawford designed for this volume.[28]

It is all that is left of Crawford's strong, tenor voice and mellifluous Italian, answering Gardner's own deep contralto, stirring up many a youthful dream, doubtless, for Gardner especially. She had not, for all her growing interest in Italian studies, seen Italy since her earliest youth, and Crawford, as one contemporary put it, knew Italy "as a man might know the rooms of his own house."[29] Gardner was not slow, I suspect, to respond to Crawford's vitality; nor was Crawford slow to react to her devotion. He soon chose Gardner not only as his mentor but–far more important–as his muse, perhaps the most intimate of all soul mate relationships. Every artist, every author, has one, though everyone doesn't admit it; mine once wrote to me of how he had got through a difficult time in his life by being buoyed up by "the strength that you found in yourself [to write] through the agency of loving me,"[30] an elegant description from the muse's point of view of the importance on each side of such a relationship. From the author's vantage, Crawford was equally forthright soon enough, writing to Gardner of his first book, *Mr. Isaacs*, published by Macmillan in 1882: "I think of it as someone else's work, as indeed it is, love, for without you I should never have written it."[31]

Love? The word is Crawford's, though the arrow, surely, was Dante's–so much more Bostonian than Cupid's! Dante was, in fact, a sort of household god in nineteenth-century Boston, and had presided over more than one Back Bay romance. When, for example, John Jay Chapman and Minna Timmins "climbed to the top floor of the Athenaeum" it was to read Dante to each other in that "broad, chastely lighted room [which gave them] the illusion of being lost." There "Chapman was scarcely conscious of having fallen in love"; he was only aware "of his great pleasure in hearing Minna Timmins read aloud and listening to his own voice answering hers."[32] So, perhaps, with Crawford. Yes, love; or so, at least, Crawford's sonnet to Gardner of May 1882, a copy of which survives in his own hand, suggests: "My lady late within my chamber tarried/In sweet dark vesture, all her fair hair flowing/In ripples o'er her shoulders; and she carried/Her beauty with such royal air, so sowing/ Her path with jewels from love's treasure quarried/That I was awed, and low before her bowing/Felt all my body by sweet love-stings harried/And all my soul with silent pleadings glowing./Such love doth surely purify and hallow/The earthbound spirit from all common dross/Such blossom, bursting forth in life's green fallow/Blooms heavenly red, as roses among moss–/The heart's sweet soil is not so scant or shallow/But it may feed a rose–or hold a cross."

Prophetic words, those last, for both of them, especially if they made physical love to each other, as this sonnet suggests. Certainly they made several unchaperoned visits to New York,[33] and during the summer of 1882 Crawford spent with Isabella Gardner at the Gardners' summer estate in Beverly, Jack Gardner would probably have often returned home only on weekends. It was there perhaps Crawford contrived this valentine for Isabella Gardner: "Come and let me whisper you/Half the things Madame can do./She can read terrific Dante/In a manner calm and canty./She can sit in Music Hall,/Heavenward raised at Music's call,/She can turn again to earth/At the plea of modest Worth./She can ride and she can row,/She can dig and she can hoe,/She can dance and she can–what?/Not say flirt? she'd like it not?/Nay! then I can't tell to you/Half the things Madame can do!"[34] Or would not do! Once Isabella Gardner had lost her heart to Crawford, a *marriage blanc*, to be sure, would thereafter have been the only proper course for the Gardners. But Isabella Gardner was an ardent Anglo-Catholic; she also much valued for a host of reasons not only her husband and their marriage but their adopted orphan nephews too. She was, moreover, known always as a proud woman, one who never broke her word. That she violated her marriage vows, or that Crawford, a devout co-religionist, joined her in what both would have considered a serious moral lapse according to their lights, is surely problematic.

That they were deeply, passionately intimate, however, is clear. But a hundred years ago even passionate, sexually charged romantic love did not require for emotional bonding the kind of physical sexual validation insisted upon in our own sex-obsessed age where it is almost to the point that the primary relationship in a person's life *has* to be a sexual partner. Even today such a view is impoverishing. In my own life the most intimate experience I have ever had of another human being was not sexual intimacy, privilege though that was, but the lending to me to read of a college diary! Soul mates *talk*–physical sex in such a relationship can seem almost incestuously wrong. Crawford and Gardner may or may not have been physical lovers. Certainly they were soul mates.

A related aspect of their relationship difficult to understand today is that while on the verge of the twenty-first century we remain tantalized by the attractiveness (even the erotic dimensions) of money and power (as opposed to just physical beauty), Isabella Gardner–who likely agreed with Gerard Manley Hopkins' view that beauty is of three kinds–of body, mind and character–celebrated equally the powerful (even possibly erotic) attraction of creative genius, an attraction which no longer seems to draw us quite so powerfully today. Not, certainly, solely, but often chiefly, Gardner was drawn to people for their mind, for their *work*, in this too reacting against the values that underlay the then widely held contemporary distinction between men and the creation of original works of art and women and the creation of–children! Isabella Gardner, as will emerge shortly, was hardly capable of liking a piece of music or a novel, say, because she liked the composer or author romantically or socially. Instead, she was much more likely to value the composer or the novelist or whomever *because* she admired that person's work! She always sought the best, which meant the best work, and beauty of character and intellect mattered to her sometimes even more than physical beauty. Isabella Stewart Gardner always was moved, and sparked, by genius.

In this connection Walter De la Mare has written of a deeply felt love that "the moment arrives when a self hitherto kept in reserve and unrealized looks out of the eyes. . . . It is above all an instant of self-revelation," and what is revealed is a quality of love chiefly discernible in the fact that "whatever it may sacrifice of life's other interests and incentives, [it] is all-creative," even as "envy and hatred are no less poisonously . . . destructive."[35] The love of soul mates, after all, as Plato declared, aims too at fusion, as love always does, but union with a beloved can take many forms, and the one that is most obviously documented in Crawford's and Gardner's case, is a creative collaboration between author and interlocutor so vital to the author's work that Crawford as we've seen all but declared Gardner the co-author of his first book. Certainly, in the case of that book and of several others, Gardner, whom Crawford trusted with his work (the greatest trust), critiqued his manuscript and suggested plot lines, sharpening characterization, serving both as muse and mentor, resource and sounding board. Each such situation is different. What exactly Isabella Gardner coveted I cannot say, nor that she found it fully with Crawford. But before too many more years passed she certainly would achieve part of it with Bernard Berenson! The thing is always there for the making–if one knows how to make it.

That Berenson's name, like Henry James', can arise here without further explanation, however, whereas Crawford's, largely forgotten today,
could not, points to another difficulty that troubles our attempt to focus
on the artistically creative rather than the passionately lustful in explor-
ing Gardner's relationship with Crawford: Crawford's genius has waned
as James' has waxed; they are hardly plausibly any longer equals in our
eyes a century and more later. Even Crawford's biographer admits that
today "in the critical argument with Henry James, Crawford appears to
have lost,"[36] the "psychology of Sigmund Freud" being Pilkington's explanation, in which I concur. Alas, it was Crawford's fate to become one of
the last masters of a genre–the romantic action novel–that could hardly
survive Freud's influence, even as it fell to James, on the other hand, to
"catch the wave," so to speak, and become a foundational author for the
post-Freudian twentieth century. In his own time, however, Crawford's
success was such that James himself, never mind Gardner, once admitted,
according to Gore Vidal (who appears to be leading something of a
Crawford revival today), that Crawford was "a prodigy of talent–and of
wealth. It is humiliating." The "humiliating," Vidal believes, was "pure
James irony," but the "prodigy," Vidal concludes with equal fervor, was
James at his most sincere. Of course, Vidal admits Crawford does not
take rank as an artist with James or Proust, but retorts at once–"how
many do?"[37] Even that most fastidious of critics, Van Wyck Brooks,
agreed that "a few of Crawford's novels were almost as good as the
best."[38]

Which few? The last? The earliest? If only about the core facts of
Crawford's and Gardner's intimacies we knew more! Carter's lament
that there was of Isabella Gardner "so much that might be said that ought
not to be published"[39] (his biography says nothing of the Crawford affair)
is particularly tantalizing in this respect. Some of Yeats' early work is
now thought to have been largely the work of Lady Gregory. Bernard
Berenson's wife, Mary, played a major role in her husband's achievement.
I suspect too that some of Crawford's early work may largely have been
the work of Gardner. But what is to be said? Suddenly we are back with
Isabella Gardner in her old age before her fireplace. Crawford also
burned *her* letters. It is all probably beyond knowing now.

Crawford's uncle, Sam Ward, writing to Julia Ward Howe of his
nephew's *affaire du coeur* with Gardner did focus on what is to me the
key point–that Gardner seemed to stimulate Crawford to literary

achievement–but how or why were less important to Ward, of course; parent-like, he worried if the stimulus was healthy. That was Gardner, of course. And Crawford? He was busy laying down a special smoke screen for his mother's benefit: assuring her that if rumors came to her ears of him and a certain married woman she was not to worry, despite the Back Bay.[40] *Town Topics*, of course, was also heard from–on a theme of how "the doors of Boston's really best society [were] slammed in [Crawford's] face . . . more than once" because of his "affairs with married women."[41]

Was Crawford, in fact, the pursuer? We don't know that either! Margaret Chanler recalled of the "much-talked-of flirtation" that it was Crawford who "escaped."[42] Chanler was Crawford's sister and thus perhaps not the best witness, but Gardner's own closest confidante through it all was another Crawford relative, Maude Howe, which only underlines how involved the Howes were on both sides of the affair and in the middle too; quite half the cast, in fact, of what really was as much Italian opera as psychological drama–as fit for Verdi as for James–even perhaps for a Freudian case study.

For me Rainer Maria Rilke's perspective rings truest: "love consists in this," he wrote, "that two solitudes protect and touch and greet each other."[43] Christopher Isherwood writes of an axis on which two "utterly different" people turn. Of all of which there survives a very tangible memento indeed: a photograph of clasped hands wearing matching bracelets taken on Boston's North Shore, dated August of 1882 in Gardner's own hand and inscribed in Crawford's: "*Due son le mani unite d'all'amore–Un spirto delle unisce, ed un sole core*"/:"Two are the hands united in love–One spirit–united and a single heart."[44] In loss, too, after all: both had experienced in some sense very much the same loss– Crawford as a child of a parent, Gardner as a mother of her child. In 1883 when their affair was at its height, Crawford was still in his twenties, while Gardner's long gone but one may be sure well-remembered son, Jack Junior, would just have turned twenty had he lived. Not all women marry their fathers, nor all men their mothers, nor do all children remind parents of *their* parents, but that dimension ought not to be discounted here. Though, of course, this was yet another problem for Gardner and Crawford in haute bourgeois Back Bay.

The secure and well-established Mrs. John Lowell Gardner–so long as she was reasonably discreet and did not become a sort of Bostonian Anna Karenina–had no need at all, and scant disposition, to be concerned with conventional "appearances," even if it were not increasingly her vocation to challenge them. But Crawford, a young man of good background and education and some gifts but neither family money nor as yet recognized genius, had to be worried as he made his way in the world, about his repute, and among his peers as well as his betters. Bourgeois worries these were, to be sure, disclosing a certain lack of security and strength of character. But Crawford was *not* John Lowell Gardner III! And he was very young. And while he could easily have been the first, he would certainly not have been the last young artist or writer talked of in Boston "because he was conveniently 'kept' by a social butterfly," as one chronicler wrote of Gardner's relationship in later years with no less than John Singer Sargent himself.[45] Besides, intergenerational relationships, whether soul mate, lover or whatever, ranging from the casting couch liaison of despised renown to an honorable romantic friendship, are as tough on the "trophy wife" or the "house boy" as on the "older" partner. True, because it is the older who is looked to for emotional stability, he or she is allowed (inhumanly!) *no* mistakes; yet there's no denying the destabilizing effect of any mistake, once made, chiefly on the younger. Gardner herself, though only forty-three, had by no means herself achieved complete maturity. It was a very delicate equilibrium for Isabella Gardner and Frank Crawford that was in 1883 somehow upset, possibly by Jack Gardner, but more likely it seems to me by a demand either of Gardner of Crawford or of him of her that the other did not feel able to accede to. Whoever precipitated the crisis, it was Crawford who panicked, betraying his most devoted friend and mentor and abruptly and cruelly ending their two-year-long relationship. He turned his back on Gardner utterly, walked out on her, and, with whatever unilateral declaration (apparently allowing of not even the courtesy of a response) dropped her cold.

How and why could such a betrayal (in some fundamental sense it had to have been mutual) ever happen? Can one profess loving admiration in February only to demand a divorce in March? Clearly the break was desperate and only desperate actions could have caused it. We know Crawford was selfish, indeed, narcissist, stubborn and moody, and doubtless the likes of Mary Perkins had made him a cynic too. What Gardner had immediately to offer must have seemed to him problematic. As he could not hope to marry her he may well have lost sight of his long-range self-interest and in his selfish way have felt badly treated and repressed the ethical qualms he must have felt (perhaps using her strong personality as an excuse), concluding he had exhausted the benefits of the relationship and that it was time to cut his losses and run. This is to speak, of course, of Crawford as victim, a sorry enough tale but one he may have invested in heavily.

If the demand was sexual and his of her, we have already touched on the reasons Gardner might have resisted breaking her vows and risking her marriage and "family." If the demand was hers of him, his view, if theirs was as I have suggested a soul mate relationship, may well have been the visceral "incest" response. More likely, it was a third, more complex situation: that Crawford projected onto Gardner a sexual demand of him that, though she could hardly help telegraphing it, she never really made (or even consciously felt, except very generally, knowing it was impossible), a demand that despite Crawford's actual physical reluctance (because of her age and closeness to him) he nonetheless needed to impute to her, not just for his ego's sake, but because of his youthful inexperience of the varieties of love. To confuse romantic love, however passionate, with sexual fulfillment is a mistake more characteristic, after all, of twenty- than of forty-something, and, perhaps, more of men than women, for there are men who are capable of feeling personal connection with another person (for which, sometimes, read: personal power) only through sex. Instead of a spiritual life, for example, such a man might speak instead of that mirage of Hollywood, his "romantic center." Moreover, he would be open to a soul mate relationship, if ever, only between lovers! And would always mistrust it. Indeed, it may even be that for such a man a nonphysical intimate relationship would not be possible; the only soul mate for such a man *is* bedmate. Of course, like the person who has but one language, the result is impoverishing. Nonphysical intimate relationships can be key. But that knowledge comes only in middle age, when, significantly, it was Frank Crawford who sought Isabella Gardner out again. Meanwhile, of act one of their friendship there is little more to report than their breakup.

All Crawford's own biographer can proffer is the bald statement that Crawford's "sudden departure has been linked to his friendship for Mrs. Gardner. . . . he left [the] country unexpectedly for reasons that Crawford [and his family] did not wish to reveal. . . . the best explanation seems to be that Crawford suddenly found that his friendship with Mrs. Gardner was on the verge of deepening beyond the bounds of what he considered proper." Continued Pilkington: "He hastily departed, and after reaching London, he held himself in readiness to 'be on the march' instantly if Maude Howe cabled that an additional move was necessary."[46] Howe, who moved into Isabella Gardner's house to pull her through, apparently had reason to fear Gardner might actually pursue Crawford across the Atlantic. Or, perhaps, that too was only Crawford's ego. But Howe surely had her hands full and Isabella Gardner a brutal loss to endure, the worse for the fact that she was herself by no means without responsibility for what had happened. She was, even before people guessed she was a genius, already a very taxing friend; intense, demanding; altogether, as it were, the graduate course; and Crawford must have decided it was the least trouble to flunk it, however high the price for such violence. Pythagoras, says Marsilio Ficino, teaches that of this highest mode of friendship Gardner and Crawford forged: "nothing in life is more rarely found, nothing more dearly possessed. No loss is more chilling or more dangerous than that of a friend."[47] So both learned. Though Henry James never entirely approved, Isabella Gardner and Frank Crawford were both very Jamesian characters after all.

◆

That celebrated novelist was also leaving town that fateful spring of Gardner's and Crawford's breakup in 1883. Though James was back in Boston for the first half of the year, this time to settle affairs in the wake of his father's death, he must have known it was for him "the end of an era . . . : the death of both parents, the sale of the house in Cambridge . . . which had been his home as a young man. . . . During the intervening years," Charles Anderson continues, "searching for his ideal observation post as a novelist, the young Henry James had tried in succession Italy, Boston, New York and Paris, each for a year or more. Since 1876 he had been living in London. . . . In 1883 he knew it would be his residence for the rest of his life."[48]

James was for all this the more alert to the old Puritan city he was taking his leave of, and which meant more to him than he yet guessed. We know this not only from the two short stories he wrote on Beacon Hill that winter of 1883–"The Point of View" and "A New England Winter"–but from that "masterpiece of James' middle period," in R. D. Godder's words, in which he summed up as he saw it "the history of New England . . . [as] the only serious cultural tradition which America might be argued to have had,"[49] *The Bostonians*, the first idea for which James recorded in his notebook in Boston in April of 1883, a time when Isabella Gardner and Crawford were also much on his mind and his sympathies, apparently, decidedly with Gardner: "Crawford appears to act in his novels as well as write them," James complained, sounding (improbably) jealous. Yet the terms in which James bid farewell to Boston and America are significant: "I am surrounded by the social desolation of Boston," he protested to William Dean Howells, only "one feature" of which, James wrote, interested him: "Mrs. Jack Gardner's flirtation with Frank Crawford, the American novelist of the future.... Have you read *Mr. Isaacs?*," James queried, "and do you see a future in it?"[50] It would be interesting to know if James asked the same question of Gardner when he took his leave of her.

The Gardners were also leaving–for Japan. But Back Bay Boston was not to be left entirely without diversion; it is a good bet that soon enough, from Beacon Street to Japan to Italy (whence Crawford had retreated), everyone was, in a sense, back in touch, which is to say reading Crawford's latest book, *To Leeward*, published in December of 1883 by Houghton Mifflin in Boston. Another work by Crawford, *A Roman Singer*, had begun appearing the previous July in the *Atlantic*, but it was *To Leeward* which the Back Bay must have devoured avidly: "a fictional account ... of what *might* have happened in the 'tragic situation' [Crawford] had recently avoided in America," according to Crawford's biographer, *To Leeward* was "a warning both to himself and to Mrs. Gardner of the unhappiness that was latent in transgressions of the social code."

I will invoke again the words of Jackson Lear: "All scholarship is–or ought to be–a kind of intellectual biography."[51] Crawford was seeking to understand the truth of his own experience. And if it was primarily *his* point of view, Gardner's is easily enough found too–in the colloquy, for example, Lornora Carantoni (the Gardner character) has with herself on the subject of how wrong she had been to leave her husband, to do, that is, what Crawford implies Gardner wanted to do:

> There was no more self-deception then, no more possibility of believing that she had done well in leaving all for Julius; she could no longer say that for so much love's sake it was right and noble to spurn away the world,–for the world came to mean her husband,

her father, and her mother, and she saw and knew too clearly what
each and all of them must suffer. Their pale faces came to her in her
dreams, and their sad voices spoke to her the reproach of all
reproaches that can be uttered against such a woman. Her husband
she had never loved; but in spite of all her reasoning she knew that
he had loved her. . . . [And when Julius tries to quiet her by asking]
"How can true love, like ours, not be right?" [he answers his own
question:] "God has put it into the world dear, and into our hearts."[52]

Offensive as such preaching may seem to most ears today, there is in it
nonetheless much of the truth of both Gardner and Crawford. Both
were devout adherents of the Catholic moral law. And even though
Gardner would not probably have put it the way Crawford did, her own
religious beliefs were strong enough that in a letter of sympathy to a
friend she once wrote words I suspect bore for her the weight of her
breakup with Crawford as well: "Thank God for it all. . . . The lover is
always yours, as you are always his."[53] To the pages of her Commonplace
Book she also confided her conviction that "indifferent souls never part.
Only passionate souls part–and always come together again because they
can do no better."[54]

◆

Even a lifetime later it was fragments of Crawford's letters that surely
made the most poignant bonfire in the aged Isabella Gardner's fireplace,
though some few fragments–having been quoted here we know why–
even Gardner could not bring herself to destroy. It is possible there was
some lingering bitterness; certainly the increasing incidence of divorce in
America did not escape her (conflicted?) attention in later years.[55] But
whether or not she ever intuited that there would be advantages to her
not being tied to Crawford (though she was the older of the two, it was
she who would grow; Crawford much less so), Isabella Gardner surely
saw, if not when they broke up, nor yet when they reconciled some years
later, then surely by her old age, how good she and Crawford were for
each other. Crawford's national (even transatlantic) success was early
evidence of how much Isabella Gardner too had to offer, disclosed perhaps ambiguously with Henry James' early work but much more definitely with Crawford's. Berenson was right. Nothing had been wasted
on her. Sargent did well to see elation! And Crawford's letters should

indeed have burned the brightest. Not as wife or mother or Back Bay matron then, would Isabella Stewart Gardner's life unfold, but–famously–as muse, mentor, and patron. In her early forties, as youth fled away with the departing Crawford, whatever he had done with her heart, she had still her brains and her spirit. Isabella Gardner had found her role.

Part Two

———— ∙ ————

Muse

The [Isabella Gardner] I knew was not the figure of romance, who lived and died as a Maecenas–Strawberry Hill–Sarah Bernhardt personage, but a simple, inquiring woman, very much moved by the endeavors of workers and thinkers, but dreading the step that might put her at their side to share their effects of discovery.

–Matthew Prichard

5

Jamesian Perspectives

Madonna, muse, seductress—three ways, Anne Higonnet suggests, American art tended to portray women in the nineteenth century. They are of course either idealized projections of male desire or demonic projections of men's sexual fears.[1] But along with "mentor," which I've added to muse as necessary to compass Gardner's role (and as leavening somewhat the sexism), these are also in a deeper sense enduring classic archetypes. And Isabella Stewart Gardner, widely perceived at varying times to have been all three, found herself in each archetype. As she matured, moreover, and one role seemingly eclipsed the other, each in fact tended to layer up, so to speak, one upon the other as she became more and more her own person. Always complex, as her life experience deepened Henry James would liken her to "a figure in a wondrous cinquecento tapestry."[2] And as she headed through early middle age in her forties during the decade of the 1880s toward the 1890s and the high middle age of her fifties, she set a pace that would be more recognizable today than then, when women who weren't married by twenty-five were spinsters, and then old by fifty, however long they lived.

As so much she cared for departed so abruptly with Crawford, in mid–1883, Jack Gardner rallied to his wife's side loyally. As Crawford had loomed more and more in the projected expedition to the Orient—which at one point was mooted as a Howe family affair, with Isabella Gardner joining Julia, Maude, and (of course) Frank, the venerable Julia reluctantly serving as chaperone–it had become less and less likely that Jack Gardner would make the trip. (All things considered, it is an interesting question whether he would have been faithfully there on his wife's return–if she did return!) Now, however, he took up the idea: *he* would take Belle to the Orient himself; indeed, virtually around the world. Content always, in Carter's words, "to provide the setting and background for [his wife's] fascinating personality"[3]–remarkable enough in a husband in that patriarchal era–Jack Gardner also could take the bridge when necessary, and especially if he had had anything to do with Crawford's abrupt withdrawal, it was all the more fitting he did so now.

They sailed in May of 1883. Japan, China, Cambodia, Java, Burma, India; followed by a long, leisurely return through the Mediterranean, Italy, France, and England–it was a year to busy the whole person and especially to captivate the restless mind, as her travel diary and correspondence with Maude Howe disclose. Though Gardner, an aesthete, was never one to compromise her critical standards ("if the Japanese were only handsomer," she wrote, "they would be perfect. Such charming manners, so gentle"),[4] the invigorating effect travel always had on her was already evident in Japan in June: "I am wild with excitement," she blurted out in one letter, and whatever her inmost thoughts, this heady feeling hardly flagged throughout their voyage. "I ate my first peacock!" she announced at one point from Phnom Penh triumphantly! Equally she could absorb rather a more subtle experience, an audience with the emperor at Java, where, fascinatingly, she describes very well hardly anything happening at all: "a very large and handsome palace.... dim lights, rain pouring in the outer courts.... women dwarfs in attendance. A large orchestra in the shadow, that played most strange music ... The whole thing under one's breath, and as if something were going to happen. Twice eight or nine soldiers came in in procession, once with tea; once with wine, liqueurs, etc. No conversation except between the Resident and the Emperor.... In perhaps three quarters of an hour we left."

The highlight of the trip was their last-minute expedition to Angkor Vat, the great temple complex of the Khmer Empire (pilgrims attempting its ritual circumambulation face a twelve-mile walk) built about the first century B.C.E. Rising out of the Cambodian jungle on five great terraces to a final height of over 200 feet, it is so astounding a sight that even in the mid–twentieth century Rose Macaulay could describe the experience of going there as "being caught into some delirious dream."⁵ When the Gardners saw it the great temple and the nearby capital of Angkor Thom had only quite recently been rediscovered, having for over 500 years, since the fall of the Khmer empire, been abandoned and all but engulfed by the jungle of banyan and fig trees, which in the end had overgrown everything. Isabella Gardner's travel diary fairly pulsated:

> in about two hours the boats could go no further. . . . Then we started again in carts, I lying on my back, through a wonderful forest, in two hours arrived at Angkor. . . . The great temple opposite. Such a scene. Tropical forest all about us. . . . Directly on our left the four great stone gryphons. . . . Early to bed. Moon rose. . . . Up at five, coffee, and off on elephants. . . . About three quarters of an hour to Angkor Thom's gateway, great moats and wall. Then a tramp through the jungle to see the wonderful ruins. The forty-eight great towers, high, and with each side carved with huge Buddha heads.

The spiritual dimension of all this and the openness to the indigenous culture and religion of the region Gardner's travel diary discloses reflects, I suspect, her experience of the Cowley Fathers, and particularly the teachings of Richard Meux Benson, the English cleric, who with Simon Wilberforce O'Neill and Charles Grafton founded this monastic order which has functioned over the years in many cultures. (Indeed, at this time O'Neill was serving in India).⁶ Gardner was also, as we have seen, a good friend in this period of William Sturgis Bigelow, who spent much time with her and Jack in the Orient. Ultimately an important American authority on Japanese art, Sturgis had been inspired to this avocation by Sylvester Morse, whose lecture on Japanese architecture in Gardner's own music room in 1882 had fired her to make this trip.⁷ Thus not for the first time forces religious and artistic, eastern and western, combined to stimulate Gardner. She responded wholeheartedly, as when on a drive back from an afternoon expedition through the palm forest by moonlight she caught sight of "a beautiful little Siamese temple. So I got out of the gharry and walked through the trees to it. And there, all alone, was a yellow-robed priest chanting his evensong to his gilded Buddha. I crept up softly—no light but the moon and the service lamps and the burning incense, and I stood behind the priest, who never heard or noticed me. It was exquisite—but *very* sad."

It was not, I suspect, a difficult feeling to engender in Gardner at this time. Her mood, of course, was bound to be problematic. It is known that she had constantly with her on the trip *The Imitation of Christ*, a book Maude Howe had given her which Gardner described as "precious" to her, and that she was specially alert to her inner life is suggested by her description of their visit to Malacca. It was, she mused

> an uncanny sort of place, as if under a spell. The sea was pink and yellow and green. . . . A fringe of palms hung over the water and the houses had red roofs shining and bright. In the center was a green hill with a ruined church on it. . . . [We] climbed up the hill to the ruined church—Saint Francis Xavier's—and I wished I had had a taper, and I wished that it were all those years ago when the whole populace wound up the hill with tears and lights, as [the saint's] body was brought back to rest for a while in his own church and tower that he had loved so well. Mount Orphir (the Golden) was dreamy and misty in the distance. . . . It was all so still and quiet. . . . I don't know where the enchanted princess was—but the prince surely had not come. And when we got back to our ship a mist had come down from Mount Ophir. . . . everything disappeared. . . . —so perhaps it was a vision after all.

At the Anglican cathedral in Hong Kong she actually broke down; the liturgy, she wrote Maude Howe, "chanted by the beautifully-voiced choristers in this strange land made me cry." The psychological pain she was working through was never more clear, nor the deep undertow of depression the loss of Crawford had caused, than when she heard from Maude that by the time of their return to Boston that fall Maude herself—her closest link to Crawford—would likely be away on a trip of her own. Now it was Gardner's turn to panic:

> Oh! oh! oh! I could cry and sob and break my heart. . . . that you think of coming abroad for *three* months this summer? So when shall I ever see you again?.. . . I can scarcely bear to think what my coming home will be without you. . . . You see I am a SELFISH BRUTE, but I am too wretched to be unnatural just now. . . . Do, the very moment you get this, sit down and write to me every detail about yourself. . . . Oh, if I could only be unselfish I should say what I

know, that you ought to have a change and a very good time (with Lords and Dukes at your feet)—and I *do* hope your book will bring in returns of money untold and fame. . . . and, dear one, I feel it will. But we must meet somehow. Your little four-leafed clover is fastened in my portfolio and is my constant companion. You ask for a flower. Those of this country [are] not for pressing. I have a dear little cornflower . . . I put it . . . in that precious book you gave me, "The Imitation of Christ," and I think I would rather leave it there. But flowers will come, and to you always.

Gallant, determined, stubborn: supported by a constant loyalty and devotion on Jack Gardner's part that must have made her wonder more than once whether the price she paid was too high or, on the other hand, whether she was a fool not to count him her greatest blessing, Isabella Gardner was trying to rally her resources. And, as always, healing for her was found at the intersection of art and religion: on the return trip, she turned, as if instinctively, toward Italy; never mind how much it brought Crawford to mind. Can it have been only chance that now she determined to renew her experience of Venice? She dedicated no less than five weeks to a serious study of painting, something that had until now taken second place to music and literature in her life. She devoted herself to Titian and to Tiepolo; studying Bonifazio and Tintoretto; diligently pasting photographs of them all into her album like any student. That one day originals of all of them would hang on the walls of a museum bearing her name she probably did not yet surmise. But through the storms of her great love seemingly lost is heard here the persistent theme of first love now renewed. Strange and heartening it was, the way Gardner's and Crawford's love was just as nurturing and creative in its blackest passages as in its brightest. Though she was with Jack Gardner, the eyes through which she rediscovered Venice must, of course, have been Crawford's. How could it be otherwise?

It was, to be sure, a battle. Despair can never have been far off, and when Gardner reached London and confided in Henry James he saw it too, writing to one of his own confidants:

"Mrs. Jack Gardner has just passed through London, at the close of her universal tour and on me *her* hand too was laid: but very discreetly. She is worn and tired by her travels, but full of strange reminiscences, and in despair at going back to Boston, where she has neither friends, nor lovers, nor entertainment, nor resources of any kind left. She was exceedingly *nice*, while here, and I pity her."[8]

Poor James. Though right to sympathize with her, he was still struggling to understand her. Gardner wanted nothing of pity–Isabella Gardner would be no one's "victim"! And because she continued to care deeply for Crawford (enough ten years later to forgive him and resume their relationship) Gardner may even have saved herself from that worst possible response to friends' betrayal or lovers' rejection–self-righteousness! Instead, though James hardly seemed to have much confidence in her carrying it off, Gardner would embark upon a course reflective of James' own counsel (one she would succeed better at in the long haul than Crawford), for to Gardner herself James had taken a different line earnestly begging her: "Fix your thoughts on your future then–and forget your past–if you can."[9] She couldn't (who can, or should?). But she did fix her thoughts on the future, in aid of which (well in advance of inheriting her own fortune[10]) on her very next trip abroad, in 1886, Gardner asked a special favor of James. What she had begun to focus on, because his work was both brilliant, and, lately, scandalous (a fascinating psyche, hers: recall her rule about when criticized giving critical people *more* to criticize), what she very soon had, indeed, set her heart on, was meeting James' friend, John Singer Sargent.[11]

◆

No other painter at that time would have interested her more. Yet another American expatriate, born and raised in Italy, after studies in Paris, where his work began to attract attention in the annual salons, Sargent, only thirty in 1886, had already caused such a sensation with his highly sensual and daring portrait of *Madame X* that he had subsequently quit Paris for the calmer air of London. From his studio there in South Kensington Sargent wrote to Gardner at once: James, he announced, had told him of her arrival and "authorized" him to call on her. He confessed, however, that his invariable afternoon sittings were "dreadfully in the way"; all this by way of apology. "I hope that if I do not make my appearance as soon as I should wish you will not mistrust the above statement," he concluded, remarking that James had told him he and Gardner would be at the academy that Wednesday and that "afterward he might bring you to my studio if you felt inclined." The purpose of Sargent's letter became clear: "it would be doing me a great pleasure."[12]

As eager, apparently, to meet Gardner, as she him, neither appears to have been disappointed. Their rendezvous was a success and it certainly seemed a commission was in the air.

But the Gardners were only passing through London at that time and under severe time restraints before sailing. In the event it was James McNeill Whistler, not Sargent, whose turn it was in 1886 to immortalize Gardner. But she returned home perhaps just a little bit less despairing than she had seemed to James during her previous visit in 1884, not only because of the charming portrait Whistler[13] had done of her but because her idea had now surely become a definite project; at some point in her near future she intended that there would be a portrait of her by Sargent even bolder than that of *Madame X*, and even more scandalous! Nor had she long to wait. In November of the following year, in order to paint a great number of American grandees, Sargent came to America, including in his plans a considerable stay in Boston.

His was, in fact, an old New England family (Charles Sprague Sargent, the then director of Harvard's Arnold Arboretum, was a cousin), and though guarded in his private life, Sargent in his public life was a man of the sort of broad culture and sophistication, well regarded both in London and in Paris, that went over very well in Boston society. His genius aside, Sargent thus had both regional and cosmopolitan credentials of a high order; he was at once accepted as an equal by Boston's most patrician families. Probably he painted as many New Yorkers as Bostonians, but all his murals were done for Boston, necessitating extended stays at the elegant old Hotel Vendôme on Commonwealth Avenue, or, after 1918, at the splendid new Copley Plaza in Copley Square, visitations that registered the more importantly for Sargent's decades of membership in the city's elite art clubs, the St. Botolph and the Tavern. In fact, Sargent would become more closely identified with Boston than any other American city.[14]

The New England capital played, furthermore, a key part in the making of Sargent's career, for his visit to Boston in late 1887–early 1888, his first, came at a critical time in his life. Following an admiring essay on his work by Henry James in the October 1887 *Harper's*, Sargent painted a number of portraits, including Isabella Gardner's, in anticipation of his first one-man exhibition anywhere at Boston's St. Botolph Club the following February. Furthermore, several of these Boston portraits had a part in earning Sargent's medal of honor the following year in Paris. And the Gardner portrait was, perhaps, the most striking of these American pictures that quite rejuvenated Sargent's career, somewhat in eclipse since the scandal of *Madame X*. However, the Gardner portrait itself never made it to Paris. In fact, it was never exhibited publicly again in Jack Gardner's lifetime, so much of a fracas did it arouse.

As difficult to paint as any subject Sargent ever attempted ("portraitists," one of the painter's biographers has asserted of Gardner, "like biographers, have had a hard time with her,") the sittings were said to be long and frustrating. Actually, it was only that, as Carter tried to explain, "Mrs. Gardner was having such a good time she sought to prolong the pleasure [of the sittings]").[15] Sargent, meanwhile, produced a masterwork. *Woman—an Enigma*, as he called the completed portrait, like all the portraits of Gardner through the years,[16] evoked a wide range of reactions.

The most ambitious came eight years after its completion from the

John Singer
Sargent.
Private Collection

pen of the French author and critic Paul Bourget in his *Outre-mer, Impressions of America*. Captivated by the way Sargent had caught Gardner's "head, intellectual and daring, with a countenance as of one who has understood everything," and equally struck by Sargent's treatment of her "firm hands, the thumb almost too long, which might guide four horses with the precision of an English coachman," Bourget ascended to considerable raptures, whether about Gardner's rubies, which he thought "(almost after the manner of Huysmans) like drops of blood" or about the way the picture seemed to him truly an "American idol," symbolic of "a whole social order" after the manner of a Renaissance portrait. Defining the spirit of American idealism as ". . . a faith in the human Will, absolute, unique, systematic and indomitable,"[17] Bourget, in Trevor J. Fairbrother's words, "proclaimed that Sargent deified Mrs. Gardner 'as a supreme glory of the national spirit.'. . . 'a human orchid'; . . . the ultimate expression of the subjects frenzied capitalist habitat. . . . an idol whose jewels and whims were the raison d'être of all of America's imponderable labor force, from the endless wheatfield to the Wall Street battleground."

It was certainly an immense vision![18] Others, more immediately, saw something no less imaginative but perhaps more personal, though for that reason even more suspect in so patriarchal an era. The nature of these other reactions were nicely conflated by Carter: "One critic wrote, 'She is not a beautiful woman, but she has arms that are perfection–beggaring description'; another said the picture challenged speculation regarding the audacity of both sitter and artist. . . . No old master had left a more puzzling personality on canvas. . . . the painter would, of course, be severely censured by people who could understand propriety better than they could art. . . ." And so forth. No wonder Jack Gardner was so incensed. Isabella, on the other hand, told Carter that she thought hers "the finest portrait Sargent ever did," and Carter affirmed that she "often tried to make [Sargent] commit himself to the same opinion."[19] (What Carter *didn't* like to mention about Jack Gardner's irritation was that it was widely believed to have been sparked by much more salacious comments put about in Boston men's clubs, quite the sharpest of which to survive in the oral tradition is that in displaying so much of Isabella Gardner's bosom Sargent had "painted her all the way down to Crawford's Notch."[20] The wit of which play on the name of a then well-known New England "artistic" resort was naturally lost on Jack Gardner, and I suspect that remark particularly explains why Sargent's striking portrait was never seen either at the Paris Salon or at the Venice Biennale, for both of which Sargent proposed it, according to Trevor J. Fairbrother.)

That historian's analysis of *Woman—an Enigma* seems to me definitive: "it is likely that the self-contained isolation of the standing figure paid homage to [Gardner's] commanding individuality.... Mrs. Gardner exercised considerable authority in literary, musical, scholarly and artistic circles, in her own right and as a patroness; but she was more bohemian than blue-stocking, [she] understood the uses of her willful and aggressive nature in shaping affairs. Sargent responded with an audacious portrayal of a cultural maverick."[21]

Indeed, here was no grand dame of the gilded age, as so many still like to imagine (and trivialize) Isabella Gardner. Rather sooner than most, Sargent, it would seem, saw (as James had not) how formidable a figure she would become. Alone, perhaps, among Sargent's pictures of women (no bravura here, no dash or color, nor any hard socialite gloss), the Gardner portrait is an evocation of power, and comparable to such male evocations of power as Sargent's masterful portrait of Gardner's dear friend (and fellow traveler up through ascending cultural heights) Henry Lee Higginson, the founder of the Boston Symphony Orchestra. Like Higginson's portrait, Gardner's is somberly brownish in tonality, at once unexpectedly informal and human and yet utterly magisterial, and in Gardner's case, iconic. Indeed, Sargent had painted, as it were, the frontispiece of James' *Portrait of a Lady,* and it is thus perhaps not surprising that when he saw a reproduction of the picture James famously got it in two words, though they were mysterious enough; Sargent's depiction of Gardner, he wrote, put him in mind of a "Byzantine Madonna."[22]

But James may not have guessed how timely as well as penetrating his insight was: the Gardner portrait which prompted his evocation of the archetype of the Madonna coincided, in fact, with the purchase of Isabella Gardner's first old master, a Madonna and Child from the studio of Francisco de Zurbarán. Purchased in Spain, to which the Gardners had sailed just after the fracas over Sargent's depiction of her—such a trip was by now their usual surcease from conflict and scandal—the Zurbarán was a souvenir, more or less, of the medieval pageantry of Holy Week in Seville, which had moved Isabella Gardner particularly; it was, Carter recalled, "never to her merely a work of art—it was a religious picture, her altar-piece." Her private altarpiece, let it be added. On her way home from Spain, Gardner purchased what could be called her public altar-piece, another Madonna and Child, a marble relief attributed to Rossellino; and while the Zurbarán (like the "Byzantine Madonna"!) never hung in the public rooms at the Gardner town house, the marble relief Gardner placed in her entrance hall, hanging before it an antique sanctuary lamp in which a votive candle always burned.[23] What must the Back Bay have made of that Marian devotion? Muse and mentor might be more natural roles for her, but as she developed these new roles the archetype of the Madonna would remain fundamental to Isabella Gardner; though as both Sargent's portrait and James' response to it demonstrate, Gardner would be a very modern Madonna indeed!

◆

The imagination of Henry James was moved time and again by Isabella Gardner, for all that she had proven a better mentor to Crawford than to him. But James was always oblique with respect to Gardner. For instance, in his "A New England Winter" of 1884, though his evocation of 152 Beacon Street ("there is a special charm there") nicely documents James' view of the Gardner town house, the Gardner character, Pauline Mesh, an "outsider" in Boston, is from Baltimore rather than New York, allowing her to be all the more plausibly a descendant of cavaliers, an obvious allusion to us today to Isabella Gardner's devotion to Charles I and the Stuart cause.[24]

Often, too, Gardner's appearances in James' fiction tended to reflect an experience of her by James rooted very much in the idea of Americans abroad, where Gardner herself spent more and more of her time in the 1880s and 1890s, particularly in Venice.

Indeed, since she had renewed her acquaintance with the queen of the Adriatic at the end of her post-Crawford world tour, Isabella Gardner never willingly forsook Venice again for long. She and Jack Gardner returned again and again through the 1880s and 1890s, taking up residence on the Grand Canal for long periods every other year for the better part of two decades, staying usually for several months: "mornings in still, productive analysis of the clustered shadows of the Basilica, . . . afternoons anywhere, in church or campo, on canal or lagoon, . . . evenings in starlight gossip at Florian's feeling the sea-breeze throb languidly between the two great pillars of the Piazzetta and over the low,

Isabella Gardner and Gaillard Lapsley in Venice, ca. 1894. *Isabella Stewart Gardner Museum, Boston*

black domes of the church,"[25] theirs was a Venetian idyll. The words were James', but he may well have had in mind his time there as Gardner's house guest at the Palazzo Barbaro, a considerable portion of which then as now was owned by the Curtis family of Boston, cousins alike to both the Gardners and the Sargents, from whom (complete with its superb staff of servants) the Gardners fell into the lovely habit of fre-quently renting an ample suite of rooms, including state apartments of great splendor.[26]

Of "the Barbaro's dark, pervasive opulence," at once rich and somber, Stanley Olson has written that "the atmosphere was compellingly sympa-thetic to the arts and the location was narcotic,"[27] while F. Hopkinson Smith went so far as to call the palazzo's splendid rococo *salone* "by far the most beautiful in Europe."[28] Certainly Gardner made free of all these splendors with her usual flair, entertaining royally, giving musicales to exhibit the talents of artists she was interested in, evenings to which Jack Gardner added his usual elegant supper parties, and even on one occasion, when James was staying, placing the author's bed in the palazzo's famous library! . . . According to one of his biographers, James "reveled in the grandeur . . . and in this game of modern life carried on within the frame of the past. He had always enjoyed it, and as for dreams of power and glory, he had but to walk across marble floors and great spaces to feel almost as if he were a doge himself—conferring in this instance favors on a great Lady from Boston,"[29] a lady with whom, moreover, James had distinctly Venetian moments. An expedition to Asolo, for example, seemed to Gardner "so romantic, so Italian,"[30] while James thought their ride there "in the fragrant Italian evening . . . one of the most poetical impressions of my life."[31] Nonphysical intimate relationships were never a problem for Henry James.

Was Fred Kaplan correct, however, that in the final analysis James "feared the sensual relaxation, the emotional complications, . . . the fantasies and fantastic images provoked by the flicker of the canal on [the] gilded roof of the Palazzo Barbaro"?[32] Probably. If Rachel Brownstein is right to pronounce James himself "the ultimate Jamesian character (having taught us to search for the sexual secret that illuminates character),"[33] as between the celibate, oedipal James of Edel, his first biographer, the deeply closeted homosexual of Kaplan, and, now, the more straightforward if discreet figure of Sheldon Novick,[34] James' latest biographer, we are, in turn, still right to be wary about James, if only because of his manifest intent to obscure himself hardly less by writing so much than Isabella Gardner did by writing so little.

Fortunately, there were others not so bedeviled by such Jamesian frets; among them the artist son of the house, Ralph Curtis. Thirty-something, tall, blond, as intelligent and charming as he was handsome, in his late youth Curtis was strongly drawn to Gardner, probably not erotically because he was so much younger (his sexual orientation is also unclear) but both emotionally and intellectually; certainly he was enough a man of the world to be able to enjoy ambiguity of a sophisticated kind, and he found Gardner sufficiently interesting to muster the necessary gallantries: a distinctly romantic friendship ensued, the intimacies of which were not really much affected even by Curtis' later marriage. One can sense him playing often to her strengths ("your musical, mellow voice [is] so suited," he wrote her once, "to confidences by moonlight in

Venezia"),[35] and it was Curtis who bucked her up no end in her fifties by suggesting tactfully to her that fifty-something was actually preferable to forty-something: "forty is the old age of youth," he insisted, quoting, he said, Victor Hugo; "fifty is the youth of old age."[36] Whether or not it was Hugo, it was vintage Curtis: gallant but not implausible.

Needless to say they went everywhere together. And, when apart, wrote constantly back and forth (Curtis to Gardner in 1894, typically: "Lady de Grey, I am afraid often breaks the Devil's 9 commandments of vice–and her spinal column would be even more elliptical had she all the loves she poses for").[37]

Isabella Gardner for her part fascinated Venetians as surely as she did James or Curtis: recalled one admirer, Count Hans Coudenhove from Vienna, writing to her years later: "I remember you conquered the Cardinal [Patriarch Agostini of Venice] in an inkling (twinkling?")."[38] Nor did royalty disdain her musicales in the Barbaro's gorgeous *salone*, for Gardner took care to be duly presented at the Italian royal court in Rome in 1895. Indeed, T. Jefferson Coolidge wrote of Gardner in his memoirs as holding her own "little court at the Palazzo Barbaro,"[39] so consistently idyllic that even Jack Gardner was once moved to put pen to paper to describe one of their more romantic evenings in a letter to a friend back in Boston: "After dinner we . . . were enjoying the moonlight from the second story when Guillermo and his music boat arrived and gave us a delightful serenade. We all five then got into [our] gondola and floated along . . . the music [boat] accompanying us and the moon sinking into the lagoon. . . . It was nearly one o'clock when we got home and of course I growled about keeping the servants working all day and all night. Still it was a success. I wish you could have been there."[40]

One thing is clear: James, ever the observer, whatever he made of it, missed none of this. And he deliberately explicated her in the succeeding phases of her life, as we will observe later on here more than once.[41] A small instance, but remarkably evocative of the world of Isabella Gardner in Venice, occurs in *The Wings of the Dove*, where James not only calls to mind the Palazzo Barbaro, "with its *piano nobile* and the shuttered light playing across the floor"–the superb photograph of the Barbaro by Alvin Langdon Coburn commissioned by James for the book's frontispiece removes any doubt of this–but also Gardner herself, whose characteristic pearls (the Gardners marked every European visit by buying another string, amassing nine in all) are also tellingly evoked in this novel: that "long priceless chain, wound twice around the neck, hung, heavy and pure, down the front of the wearer's breast–so far down that Milly's trick, evidently unconscious, of holding and vaguely fingering and entwining part of it, conduced presumably to convenience."[42]

It is an exquisite word picture, as intimate in its way as Sargent's treatment of the same pearls famously roped about Gardner's waist in his portrait, though perhaps even more marvelous was James' depiction in *The Golden Bowl* of Gardner's waistline! For Robert Coles is surely correct that this was very much in James' mind when, wishing to convey a notion of "the litheness, glitter and sensuality of the ... thin-waisted Charlotte Stant," he wrote of "the extraordinary fineness of her flexible waist, [so like] the stem of an expanded flower, which gave her the likeness also to some long loose silk purse, well filled with gold-pieces, but having been passed empty through a fingering that held it together." Isabella Gardner also pervades *The Golden Bowl* in terms of overall design, as we will see later, but more significant were Gardner's appearances in James' notebooks, those fascinating diary-like and very personal source books. And it is these which suggest how seriously, overall, Gardner's influence came to be: "Ah, to squeeze a little, a little, of what I felt, out of that,"[43] James mused of time spent with her.

The first hint of what was to come, of what it would be about Isabella Gardner that would grow in James' mind, has been brilliantly explicated by Stephen Donadio, who writes that there is an

> evident parallel between Nietzsche's sense of the relation between extraordinary individuals and the society which serves to produce them and James' view of the matter with respect to his own American heroines. For in James' view, American society is ultimately vindicated of the many charges lodged against it (which include pushiness, coarseness, and lack of culture)–it is, in Nietzsche's formulation, "justified"–only by its ability to produce human specimens of such inexhaustible vitality and exquisite sensitivity as those who figure as the central focus of so much of his own fiction, characters whose energy ... serves as a sharp judgment on the relative moral indifference or exhaustion ... characterizing the European relation to experience.
>
> A striking passage in Paul Bourget's *Outre-mer* ... speaks unexpectedly but distinctly to this point [when] Bourget ... describ[es] a

portrait which he claims is "that of a woman whom I do not know"; but there is little doubt that the portrait in question is one of Isabella Stewart Gardner executed by John Singer Sargent.[44]

John Singer Sargent, as his portrait discloses, was perhaps quicker than James to understand Isabella Gardner.[45] But Sargent's feelings for her were nonetheless widely misunderstood by others, and have continued to be despite his biographer's disclaimers.[46] Witness this beautiful reminiscence of a lovely Sunday morning in the late 1880s when a schoolboy, protected from nosy masters behind rolled-up wrestling mats in the gymnasium of Groton School, was reading Ben Hur:

> suddenly the gymnasium door was thrown wildly open and a woman's voice thrilled me with a little scream of mockery and triumph. Cautiously I peeked from my concealment and caught sight of a woman with a figure of a girl, her modish muslin skirt fluttering behind her as she danced through the open doorway and flew across the floor, tossing over her shoulder some taunting paean of escape. But bare escape it seemed, for not a dozen feet behind her came her cavalier, white-flanneled, black-bearded, panting with laughter and the pace. The pursuer was much younger than the pursued but that did not affect the ardor of the chase. The lady raced to the stairway leading to the running track above. Up she rushed, he after her. She reached the track and dashed round it, the ribbons of her belt standing straight out behind her. Her pursuer was visibly gaining. The gap narrowed. Nearer, nearer he drew, both hands outstretched to reach her waist. . . . "She's winning," I thought. "No, she's losing." and then at the apex of my excitement, "He has her!" But at that crucial moment there came over me the sickening sense that this show was not meant for spectators, that I was eavesdropping and, worse, that I would be caught at it. There was not one instant to lose. The window was open. Out I slipped and slithered to safety.
>
> For me that race was forever lost and forever won. . . . What I did know was the Atalanta of that Sunday morning was Mrs. Jack Gardner and Milanion Mr. John S. Sargent. It was that same year he painted the famous portrait of her with her pearls roped about her waist, her beautiful arms glowing against a background that might have been the heart of a lotus.[47]

Ellery Sedgwick certainly got his dates wrong. Sargent was in Boston that year only during the winter,[48] when neither white ducks nor an open window will do; but sixty years later such a mistake is only too likely. Yet for Sedgwick to have misremembered the identities of two such famous people (one of whom, Gardner, he came to know as an adult) would have been for the distinguished *Atlantic* editor not at all likely. But if this is not another Gardner tall tale, it is a charming reminiscence of Gardner's lightly flirtatious style; what it is *not* is evidence of a passion-ate love affair of the type she had with Crawford, though it does beauti-fully document the perception that waxed through the years that there was such an affair (which one may be sure troubled neither Gardner nor Sargent), a perception that flowered gracefully enough in Eleanor Palfrey's charming novel about Gardner and Sargent, *The Lady and the Painter*. Less charming but equally fictional is another author's view: Charles Mount in his biography of Sargent imagines Gardner's "quick but shallow mind" taunting a Sargent "seething with a hatred he could but ill conceal" and unable to "look at [Gardner] without some little wave of revulsion."[49] I wonder how many portraits in the history of art have inspired such wide-ranging and divergent imaginings?

Sargent's actual relationship with Gardner, like that with James, can only emerge here gradually, but it certainly began in a frank enough exploitation on both sides that as their interests coincided and their acquaintance grew ripened into true friendship and really a mutual patronage. Consider, for example, the case of the Spanish dancer, Carmencita, the sort of exotic figure Sargent loved to paint. Carmencita did indeed inspire such a work, which, as it was done quite on his own, the painter needed to sell. Knowing how much Gardner admired his ear-lier but long since sold painting of another Spanish dancer, *El Jaleo*, and thinking Carmencita herself would excite interest in his new picture, Sargent talked Gardner into giving a party with him in New York, where the dancer was then appearing, a party at which Carmencita would dance and someone (Gardner?) would be moved to buy the painting.

Alas, the dancer showed up with both her hair and her makeup not to Sargent's taste and his attempts to bring her appearance more into line with his painting so irritated Carmencita that, told to play up to the great lady, she made instead a rude gesture and threw a rose in Gardner's face. Retrieved quickly by a friend who saved the night by having the pres-ence of mind to put it in his buttonhole as if he thought it intended for him,[50] a good time forthwith ensued. Gardner, who understood Sargent's purposes and would have found no fault in them, understood her own better and did not buy the picture. It was *El Jaleo* she wanted, not Carmencita. In the end though, as we will see, whereas we do not know who won the race at Groton, we do know (though it seemed an impossible coup then for Gardner to get it) that *El Jaleo* ended up in Gardner's possession.[51] We know too that as Gardner's and Sargent's interests more and more coincided, and especially when in later years they were much thrown together, they became quite close friends. Sargent was himself drawn to paint Isabella Gardner twice more, the last time as a precious gift to a dear friend, while Gardner for her part not only would devotedly collect his work but commission some of the best of it (including a superb Rocky Mountain watercolor). Moreover, it was she who secured for the painter a job he dearly coveted and would undoubtedly have called in his maturity the greatest commission of his life, one which he had quite given up on at the time—the murals of what is today the Sargent Gallery of the Boston Public Library.[52]

In Sargent's case, no more than in James's, however, was there any romance. Both men were more likely to have been covertly studying the likes of Crawford, not Gardner. Indeed, the year before James had introduced the painter to Gardner, James had proved so ardent in his own pursuit of Sargent that Stanley Olson has described the author as "mesmerized" by the painter. "James's entertainment [of Sargent] was the closest thing to courtship" that could be imagined, the painter's biographer reports, though adding that in the event "their relationship was strangely, though not clearly, chaste."[53] A wonderful phrase, that, echoing as it does the ambiguities—at once gloriously innocent but sorely repressed—of the lives led in the pre-Freudian era by men like James and Sargent, both of whom were gay.

6

⚬

Figure in the Carpet

ACCORDING TO THE musician George Proctor, a "great big real love affair [that would] knock everything and me into the bargain to pieces *for my own sake and art's,*" was urged on him once by Isabella Gardner.[1] Perhaps her most vivid counsel ever as muse and mentor, into which central venue of Isabella Gardner's life first James and then Crawford and now Sargent have conducted us, that advice reflects the fact that just as it has been argued of Alfred, Lord Tennyson's friendship with Arthur Hallam that although their relationship lasted a mere four years, those "four years probably [were] the equal in psychic importance to the other seventy-nine of Tennyson's life,"[2] so with act one of Gardner's and Crawford's affair, which lasted barely two years. Gardner's awakener lacked, to be sure, the imagination and staying power to quite rise to the occasion, but in the long run Crawford had truly gifted Gardner, who just because of her pluck and her quest for emotional and intellectual outlets of her own, had stood in great need of such an awakener. Crawford had sparked as vital forces in her as she in him, yielding a whole new self-identity for Isabella Gardner as mentor, muse, and patron of the arts.

Margaret Fuller again comes to mind, she whose "exuberant nature made her a foreigner in cautious New England,"[3] according to Emerson. Her beloved, the Marchese Giovanni Ossoli, Fuller's junior by about a decade as Crawford was Gardner's by a decade and a half, and as much as Crawford, intensely Italian and artistic and Catholic, had too a greater influence on the older partner than had the older on the younger. As Fuller's biographer points out, young Ossoli transformed Fuller from an arrogant and selfish, rather narcissist person to one much more sensitive to the human exchange and more generous and understanding of others, and, finally, of herself. All this, furthermore, at the crucial point of mid-life, a point as it turned out in Gardner's life in which the trauma of Crawford's departure and marriage proved only to be the beginning of a decade of still more family tragedy.

The Gardners suffered a dizzying series of losses in the 1880s: Jack Gardner's mother died in 1883; his father in 1884; Isabella Gardner's mother in 1886 and five years later her father; in nine years all four parents had died and Isabella Stewart Gardner herself had become the last of her father's line, and she childless. Of course, even the worst news has always its good news: Green Hill, the Gardner country house in Brookline, inherited from John L. Gardner, Sr., was a joy; and Isabella Gardner's own inheritance on her father's death was, of course, the foundation of her independence. But the accumulating losses were formidable even before the ghastly climax of 1886, when the Gardners suffered a family catastrophe that certainly may be ranked with the death of their son and Isabella Gardner's rupture with Crawford–the death of the eldest of their three adopted orphan nephews, Joe Junior. Like his father, moreover, Joe Junior committed suicide. And to understand this tragedy, is, I believe, to begin to understand why in the wake of the Crawford affair Henry James and John Sargent were only the first and foremost of an ever-widening homosexual circle of Isabella Gardner's friends.

For this homosexual repute Gardner has suffered grievously for many years at the hands of the sort who, just as they liked to call Margaret Thatcher "the only man in the room" in the 1980s, or Eleanor Roosevelt a "nigger lover" in the 1930s and 1940s, cannot but see Isabella Gardner in her day as what is boorishly called a "fag hag." To be sure, Jack Gardner probably *was* less threatened by, and Isabella Gardner less vulnerable to, gay men, and if the Gardners did not equally love each other, they had learned to appreciate each other; he for the distinction and ultimately the luster she lent to his name; she for the liberty and support (the rarest of combinations) which he appears to have nearly always proffered. But the homosexual aura of Gardner's circle derived primarily from the far more fundamental trauma of Joe Junior's suicide.

Two explanations have surfaced in the historical record to explain this tragedy. The first, put forward in Joe Junior's Harvard Class Notes, attributes the suicide of this young man, who after college had gone on to take a further degree at Harvard's Bussey Institute and enter the field of veterinary medicine, to the fact that "being subject from early childhood to fits of depression," he returned from a summer in Europe in 1886 "only to feel that his fate was growing on him," and killed himself that October "under the dreadful impression that he ought not to live because he had been so destructive to insect life"![4] The less said of this bizarre idea the better. The second explanation makes much more sense of the overall pattern disclosed by the Gardner nephews we are beginning to explore here. Like the story of Isabella Gardner's miscarriage, the second expla-nation is, however, dependent on documentation seen only by one per-son, Alan Simpson, and not independently verifiable. Simpson, however, having had no more imaginable reason than had Tharp about Gardner's miscarriage to falsify his sources about Joe Junior's suicide, I incline to Simpson's explanation for the same reason I accept the earlier miscar-riage story, because it is most consistent with the other known facts.

Simpson points out, in his *Artful Partners,* that of Charles Eliot Norton's four protégés at Harvard in the mid-1880s–Bernard Berenson, George Santayana, Charles Loeser and Logan Pearsall Smith–all Joe Junior's friends–the last three were widely known as homosexual when they appeared at the Gardners', where open house was always kept for the friends of Joe, who Simpson asserts

had been causing the Gardners some concern. He had bought himself a remote homestead at Hamilton to the north of Boston. . . . [Logan Pearsall Smith] said that Joe Gardner had bought the Hamilton home-stead as a refuge from the censorious eyes of Boston, and his aunt's constant urgings to find a "suitable girl and settle down."

Logan and his sister Mary had been frequent visitors, but it was Mary who had been the chaperone, for the object of Joe's attentions was Logan himself and it was Logan who had broken Joe Gardner's heart.

Jack Gardner half suspected the truth and quickly included Joe on his annual [sic] European tour. The traditional solution for a broken heart did not work. On October 16, 1886, Joe Gardner committed suicide.[5]

Logan Smith was not by repute the Christian gentleman Joe Junior was. Robert Gathorne-Hardy recalled that to Smith the golden rule had no meaning at all, and that the "sorrows and perplexities of the heart were not allowable in his life [and that even in later life he always said he hadn't] the slightest feeling of guilt,"[6] however cruel his actions and however much harm they caused. The role Simpson casts Smith in, in other words, is on the basis of independent documentation, highly plausible. Far from Smith's guilt-free feelings, of course, were Isabella Gardner's. Like any parent, she must have been moved to much thought by the nightmare of, in effect, losing a *second* son, and be only too likely to have blamed herself for a lack of sufficient sympathy and understanding. As a failure of parenting that with Joe Junior must have been devastating. Gardner, who had failed so conspicuously in several aspects over the years in the established roles of wife and mother, had now failed all over again.

Yet here again, Gardner, even so greatly stressed, waxed rather than waned, and while she certainly no more got over Joe's suicide than Jackie's death or Crawford's desertion of her, nonetheless she made even this catastrophe constructive, both for herself and for the many gay men she seems from now on to have felt especially drawn to and even to identify with in the wake of Joe's suicide. Increasingly she found that although she was likely to always be rejected by Back Bay society, among Boston's Bohemia she found a ready acceptance that became more and more enabling, as much for her as for Bohemia.

The culture of secrecy so pervasive in the Victorian era on the subject of homosexuality (though it was often, so to speak, the figure in the carpet), requires of us today both a highly critical and a highly imaginative response in order to understand it. In aid of compassing, first, Jack Gardner's likely experience, and, then, Isabella's, the testimony will prove useful here of Henry Adams, as we've seen a friend of the Gardners, who also in 1886 suffered his own loss in the suicide of his wife, Clover, another of those dark Victorian tragedies, the truth of which (like the reasons for the Adamses' childless marriage) it appears may never be known.

As librarian or "Alligator" of Harvard's Hasty Pudding Club in 1857, the year of Jack Gardner's withdrawal from Harvard, young Adams essayed in the club's minutes a highly homoerotic and priapic hymn (a "giant oak" is found—aren't they all?—in the middle of "love's garden") as

seen through the eyes of a young woman (for we are still in 1857 in the
world of Shakespeare's sonnets, where the thing to note is not the gender of the balladeer, but the significance of the subject sung to!) whose
performance of oral sex on said giant oak is lovingly described.
Attributed jokingly but knowingly to Lord Byron (widely known for his
homosexual liaisons), the poem is introduced by Adams with a discourse
on Greek professor Cornelius Felton's recent travels, the highlight of
which is a discussion this time about the joys of anal sex, and who best is
made for it, Harvard chambermaids or Greek boys.[7] Both poem and introduction, though quickly passed over by Adams' biographer as "smutty
doggerel"[8] (fair enough as literary criticism, but not in respect to the subject matter), document the nature of the male upper-class discourse on
homosexuality in mid–nineteenth-century Boston, more than anything
else a matter of collegiate sexual fantasies.

Adams is also, interestingly, a good witness to gay male discourse of
the time of rather a different sort that would also have compassed upper-
class women because of his and Isabella Gardner's close mutual friendship with Theodore Dwight. Historically a kind of "don't ask, don't tell"
character in both their lives, those who have written about Gardner have
scanted Dwight, while Adams' chroniclers, though they can't ignore
Dwight, also can't agree on what to call him: "caretaker," "seneschal,"
"secretary of sorts," "research assistant," "family archivist," "friend," "companion"[9]–in ascending order each has been advanced as a characterization of a relationship which began when Adams made friends with
Dwight, the State Department's archivist, while doing research, and continued with Adams' attracting Dwight away to become the Adams
archivist at the family home outside Boston. Initially apparently an
entirely professional relationship, it clearly also became a social one and
eventually quite intimate, it would seem: Certainly, when they traveled
together to Cuba in 1888 Adams confided to John Hay that "Dwight and
I had a captivating dinner at the Restaurant de Paris last evening, and
became quite glorified over a bottle of Burgundy."[10] It was not the sort of
thing Henry Adams did with everybody.

Adams himself described his friendship with Dwight (which was a
stormy one, though lifelong) curiously. "Dwight worries me a good deal,"
Adams wrote a friend in 1890. "His depression is as bad as last summer. . . ."[11] A year later Adams was more explicit: "Poor Dwight is a
worse moral dyspeptic than I am; which is saying much. He is greatly to

be pitied, too; and I do not want to make him–or myself–worse by attempts to make either of us better. Willy Phillips is a third lunatic."[12] It was the second of the three, Adams announced after his wife's suicide, who seemed most needed: "for the present," wrote Adams to a friend, "Theodore Dwight is coming to live with me"[13]–a declaration Gardner surely understood. Theodore Dwight's framed photograph stood alone for years on her writing desk and he signed Gardner's guest book more than fifty times. A gifted person, with just the sort of range of interests Gardner liked in a man–rare books to baseball–Dwight, with Adams' full support and perhaps with Gardner's too (we have seen that she brought her influence to bear at the library in Sargent's behalf) ascended in 1892 to one of the nation's preeminent archival positions, as head of the Boston Public Library.

Of Dwight's homosexuality, Roger Austin has written:

> Dwight's private library was well stocked with pictures of naked young men [including] some Neapolitan photographs he had pur-chased from Pluschow, the notorious purveyor of erotica. . . .
>
> While touring Europe with Mrs. Gardner during the summer of 1892, Dwight purchased some additional material. . . . Dwight was also taking pictures of naked young men in Boston–and, if possible, going to bed with them. Sometimes his models were Irish, but more often they were Italians who had been procured for him by his bar-ber. After he began earning five thousand dollars a year from the library [as director], he usually had one of these models living with him as his "valet."[14]

A less public side of Dwight, and necessarily so then, to be sure, it is nonetheless clear that, whatever Adams knew, Gardner knew just about everything. She and Dwight were very close; so much so that at John LaFarge's urging Dwight once smuggled in a watercolor for Gardner along with his erotica.[15] They may even have had, Theodore Dwight and Isabella Gardner, similar tastes–what was homoerotic for Dwight, of course, being heteroerotic for Gardner: in her scrapbooks are several photographs of nude males of the sort Barbara Hardy calls "high pornog-raphy" after the manner of the Rokeby Venus in London's National Gallery, the one smashed by the suffragists.[16] Certainly, Gardner was Dwight's mentor and confidante; their extant correspondence leaves no doubt of her knowing involvement in his life. Admitting in one letter that what he writes to Gardner (only Dwight's side of the correspondence survives) "is of a nature quite too confidential to have been written with propriety,"[17] in another he frankly confesses himself smitten by the two young men who attended to Gardner's gondolas in Venice: "I never cease," he insists, "thinking and talking of Angelo and Tito."[18] Dwight, apparently quite bisexual, was also at one point passionately interested, seemingly, in virtually all the LaFarges, writing to Gardner after lunching with them: "the aesthetic John appeared. (Under breath–entre nous–I like Bancel very much–very much–the other–well, there is an infinite ques-tion involved). (Again–sotto voce–I like Mabel in the same way.")[19] Dwight's was a prodigious libido.

Yet he was by no means free of angst. Homosexual acts in this era were not yet seen as evidence of disease, but were widely judged to be sinful and even criminal. Dwight confided to Gardner: "You would be amused could you know how in my secret thoughts of late I have been chiefly engaged in trying to penetrate my own disguise to find the real Dwight, for it is really ridiculous that I should all unconsciously have played a part so well as to deceive so many intelligent and respectable people. I dare not think of the time when they will discover their mistake."[20]

Meanwhile Dwight led a grand and stylish Bohemian life both in the Back Bay and in Cambridge, where his circle extended to another mutual friend of his and Gardner, George Santayana. Both he and the Harvard philosopher were fellow members of Boston's bohemian Tavern Club[21] (as was also Jack Gardner), where in 1894 Santayana introduced Bertrand Russell's older brother, the second Earl Russell, one of Santayana's great loves, and with whom the philosopher's biographer reports Santayana was then having "an intensely physical affair."[22] Dwight lived nearby the Tavern, on Beacon Hill, in bachelor rooms at 10 Charles Street, where he shared a servant, one Jacques Medus, late of the French Army in Morocco, who valeted them both, with Russell Sullivan, a well-known author, playwright, and clubman (also a Taverner) who was also close to Isabella Gardner, and often, in fact, kept Gardner up to date on comings and goings in Boston's Bohemia when she was abroad. Dwight, he wrote her once, frankly enough, was "having his photographs [of young men] framed, one by one. I go up[stairs] for tea, and find him sighing before them, with clasped hands, wrapped in bro-cades."[23] In another he reported that Sturgis Bigelow was about to carry "me off to dine with him tonight, with the resident literati and tutti fruitti. . . ."[24] So close was Sullivan to Gardner he even ventured play-by-play, so to speak, on his and Dwight's spats: "our breach has been repaired," he notified her once, "and we have kissed and made up."[25]

A dinner party at the Gardners' Back Bay town house prior to a Myopia Hunt Club ball. Jack Gardner is standing; Isabella (*seated, second from right*) is pouring. *Isabella Stewart Gardner Museum, Boston*

They foregathered with the Gardners regularly. After dinner one night, both the Gardners and Dwight and Sullivan, entertaining the French novelist Paul Bourget and his wife, "adjourned to 10 Charles Street . . . Dwight opened his rooms [on the floor above], and we moved about between the two [floors], smoking, talking, and laughing. Then Bourget and I were left for a while alone. We talked of books. . . . They stayed late. . . . One more pleasant association for this small *salon!*"[26] Sullivan was also particularly close to another figure in Gardner's circle, the painter Dennis Bunker, who came to Boston in 1885–86 to teach at the Cowles Art School. And Bunker brings us full circle, so to speak, and back to Sargent, whom he met, very likely through Gardner, in 1887.

The two were at once deeply attracted to each other, and became intimate friends, of which Bunker's depiction in Sargent's *Frieze of the Prophets* at the Boston Public Library is perhaps the most public souvenir; though Gardner, always the friend of lovers, put their photographs side by side for all to see (still today) in her array of friends' portraits.[27] Another rather more problematic memorial, a not brilliant Sargent portrait of Bunker neither could recall quite the occasion of but neither denied was "their" work, was said to be the result of rather a wild night at the Tavern. More productive artistically was their summer together painting in the following year. Well might Sargent's biographer write of Bunker that he "was a romantic figure, short, very handsome, lively, colorful, funny, while at the same time shadowed by unhappiness. . . . He and John were ideally suited as companions. . . . Thirty years later John confessed that 'he could remember no one whom he had held in greater affection.'"[28]

Gardner also cared deeply for Bunker, mentoring him devotedly. A "moody" man, according to Carter, Bunker "suffered from violent headaches and fits of depression; at such times he would lock himself in his room, go without food and admit no one. Mrs. Gardner alone could persuade him to face the world again."[29] One wonders how she did it. Sullivan, told once that "Bunker means to give us up," opened the door alit on all this when he advised Gardner: "Don't let him. And put a little more of the arlecchino [Harlequin] into him, if you can. It's the only role to play–except that of Colombina [the flirt]–and those who play it best (whether it hurts or not) get on best. . . . Give him a grip from me, and tell him to stay with us. But don't read him my moral philosophy, or he will swear strange oaths."[30] Bunker, to be sure, was not Crawford!

The most significant clue, however, to what was going on is Carter's remark that Isabella Gardner "remained tolerant of any moral or perhaps immoral code."[31] That, surely, was the legacy (it may even have been the occasion) of Joe Junior's tragedy; certainly Isabella Gardner was not left without explanation when others proved less tolerant, especially in the wake of Oscar Wilde's sensational trial in 1895. Dwight was soon caught up in a scandal (the exact nature of which is predictably vague) and forced out of Boston, marrying and moving to Italy (both Adams and Gardner kept in touch); Sullivan also married, leaving Gardner's circle abruptly; Bunker, too, married, though in his case probably most unwisely. "You are marrying a man . . . whose highest ambition is to conceal his identity,"[32] he wrote his wife-to-be. It is not surprising Bunker's earliest biographer, R. Ives Gammell, did not doubt that Bunker's death in his first year of marriage was by his own hand.[33]

The painter Dennis Bunker costumed here as "The Gay Troubador" for the 1889 Artists' Ball. *Isabella Stewart Gardner Museum, Boston*

Dennis Bunker went to the 1889 Art Students' Association Ball as the Gay Troubadour; in the nineties *Town Topics* referred to another of Gardner's circle, the musician Tymoteusz Adamowski, as "the gay young bachelor, smiled on by all women, but conquered by none." So too Henry James, in "The Sense of the Past," calls his protagonist both "gay" and "queer," "favored adjectives of the fin-de-siecle and after, which in the fullness of time," Karl Miller writes, "were to become in succession the names which the English-speaking homosexual community has used to identify itself. James' use presages this."[34] Indeed, Gardner's circle was so often described as gay the origin of the word ultimately to become the favored neologism for homosexual in the twentieth century could hardly be more obvious. Nor was it understood then any more than now as necessarily ironic: sensitized (her consciousness raised we would say today) by Joe Junior's tragedy, and as time went on by Dwight's and Bunker's and others, Gardner nonetheless had a wide enough experience of homosexuality by the 1890s to know as much of happy lives as unhappy ones. Indeed, she had to look no further than another of her nephews, for improbable as it may seem Joe Junior was not the only one!

William Amory Gardner, for all the commonality of sexual orientation and circle of friends with Joe Junior (again, Ned Warren is in evidence; he lived across the hall from Joe at Harvard and also traveled to Greece with Amory), though his life was hardly without its conflicts, was to turn out as happily as Joe's did not.[35] At Harvard, WAG as he was called, became both a passionate classicist and an ardent high church Episcopalian (two other signals of homosexuality in this era) becoming one of the leading classical scholars of his class, which presumably offset his rather effete mannerisms when he was invited at a relatively early age to be one of the three founders of Groton School, to which he dedicated his life, becoming a much honored and beloved figure there.

In fact, the magnificent chapel he gave Groton in memory of Joe Junior—given by one gay man in memory of another and designed by a third (Henry Vaughn)—is not only an important marker of the Gardners' contributions to New England Anglicanism and in turn of New England's contribution to the American Gothic Revival, but is also a landmark of the emerging self-identifying gay subculture of the period. It was a subculture that would make a significant contribution to the intellectual and cultural history of a New England that was not, as some have thought, in this period, declining, but, rather, transforming itself into a new and more diverse society. (Consider just the contribution of Ned Warren to Boston's Museum of Fine Arts—one of America's greatest collections of classical sculpture—never mind WAG's to Groton.) True not only in terms of race, ethnicity, and gender but also of sexual orientation, that new diversity was increasingly by no means beside the point to the life of Isabella Gardner, who was very much in the forefront of it. Consider for instance, Joe Junior's foursome of friends at Harvard, so cheerfully received on highest Beacon Street by Mrs. John L. Gardner: Berenson and Loeser were Jewish, Smith a Quaker, and Santayana half Spanish and Roman Catholic and all but Berenson were gay.

A similar diversity, in Eurocentric terms, was evident in the musical circle that in the wake of her new music room began to emerge around Gardner in the 1880s, the central figures of which were Clayton Johns,[36] a Harvard-trained musician Gardner thought so highly of that on at least one occasion she stood at the door of a public hall handing out programs to a concert of his, knowing full well her presence would pull in a large audience (the art of scandal again!); Tymoteusz Adamowski, the much lionized first violinist of the Boston symphony; Charles Martin Loeffler,[37] his co-first violinist and a virtuoso of his instrument as well as in later years a distinguished composer (to whom—talk about being muse and mentor!—Gardner lent once the poems of Verlaine, some of which Loeffler set to music); and William Gericke,[38] the symphony's conductor. All kept frequent company with Gardner in what Johns referred to as those "halcyon days . . . when Russell Sullivan and I called Mrs. Gardner 'The Queen,' while Gerricke was her 'Kapellmeister.'"[39]

Needless to say neither Adamowski, who was of Polish descent, nor Loeffler, who was Alsatian, were very fond of Germany. But Gericke was unmistakably German! And, years later, when his successor as con-ductor of the Boston Symphony, Karl Muck, also German, was hounded into prison by anti-German hysteria during the First World War, Gardner was one of the few who withstood the wartime media's hysteria and stood up for him, even visiting him in jail.[40]

Similarly, though Gardner much favored German and French music over Italian, she was a patron of two Italian musicians.[41] The most impor-tant was the composer and pianist Ferruccio Busoni,[42] of whom more soon, whom Gardner was close enough to that when Busoni asked her, after his not very successful American tour of 1894 (including an appear-ance in Gardner's music room) for the loan of a thousand dollars—a huge sum then—Gardner sent him the money at once.[43] Busoni, who dedicated several of his piano pieces to Gardner, went on to become a significant figure in the history of music in the twentieth century. The other Italian composer Gardner helped, Pier Adolfo Tirandelli,[44] would today be accounted a quite minor figure; then he was director of the Venetian Symphony. He is of interest, however, as illustrating yet another mode of Gardner's mentoring and patronage; for his opera, Atenaïde, did not fail because of any lack of interest on Gardner's part! She attended the rehearsals as well as the Venice opening, encouraging composer, soloists, and casts, and actually reviewed the opera for the Times of London with the connivance of that journal's correspondent, when a political crisis kept him in Rome—for which she received a gold sovereign she used to say was the only money she ever earned. When all else failed, further-more, she helped Tirandelli, who was a better performer apparently than composer, to find his musical (and financial) niche with the Cincinnati Symphony. Loeffler, on the other hand, who would become a significant composer (and who dedicated his Divertimento in A Minor for Violin and Orchestra to Gardner), she was able to help in quite a different way: Loeffler's decision to pursue his composing, according to his biographer, was directly related to the decision to publish his music by Gustav Schirmer, as it happens a close friend of Gardner, who it is virtually cer-tain advanced Loeffler's cause.[45]

Not only classical music interested Gardner. Although she could be scathing on occasion of mass musical taste, popular music was also made in Isabella Gardner's circle. Adamowski, in fact, was the then conductor

of the Boston Pops and Clayton Johns was a composer of romantic bal-
lads. Was there "a summer hotel in this broad land," someone wondered
once, "that has not echoed to [Johns' song]: 'I cannot help loving thee'?"[46]
Indeed, not only composers like Busoni and Loeffler dedicated work to
Gardner; John's *Scythe Song* was also written for her.[47] (For that matter,
so were a flower–a dahlia[48]–and even a mountain dedicated to her:
Mount Gardner in the state of Washington, the highest peak in the
Isabella Range, so named by a classmate of Joe Junior, who climbed it in
her honor.)[49]

Notice too the varied ways Isabella Gardner pushed and inspired and
cajoled the diverse band she mentored. Even with critics she was a force
to be reckoned with. A distinguished Boston music critic, Philip Hale, "at

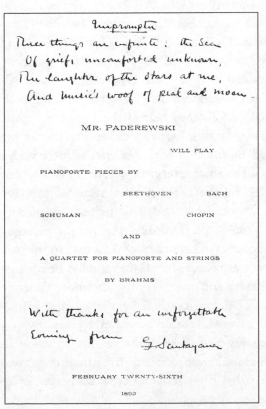

A program for the concert by the legendary
Paderewski in the Gardners' music room, on which
George Santayana has written verse and thanks, top
and bottom. *Isabella Stewart Gardner Museum, Boston*

first unconvinced of [pianist Charles Copeland's] artistry, allowed Mrs. Jack Gardner to bring them together," according to a music historian, "and thereafter listened to Copeland with understanding."[50] Usherette, pub- lishers' agent, impresario, initiator of ideas to set this or that poem, finan- cial backer, mediator with critics, job-broker, and even reviewer were just some of the jobs Gardner was not too proud to do in her capacity as muse, mentor, and patron. Although her name more properly arises later in this narrative, the legendary Australian opera star, Nellie Melba,[51] is worth mentioning as another such at this point to dispel any idea Gardner's mentoring was in any way restricted to men, gay or not, or only to European artists.

Here again, of course, Isabella Gardner's music room, and her patron- age, generally, though a sincere expression of her love of music and of her desire to help musicians, had a social as well as an artistic dimension. Even her "lion-hunting," however, as more than one critic called it, took unusual form and yielded its share of good deeds. Clayton Johns recalled, for example, when the wildly idolized concert pianist, Ignace Paderewski, visited Boston, "Mrs. Gardner . . . individual in everything she did, engaged Paderewski to play a recital for herself alone at her house. . . . I sat and listened behind the tapestries," Johns wrote, and "after the music was over, I was invited to join the supper party, which was composed of Mr. and Mrs. Gardner, Paderewski, and myself."[52] Furthermore, when the conservatory students (for whom Gardner had paid Paderewski to give a free concert) returned the favor and invited Paderewski to a concert by their best performers of only his composi- tions, and a protégé of Gardner's, the pianist George Proctor, was praised by Paderewski, Gardner more than rose to the occasion: Proctor there and then was promised by Gardner what he took good advantage of for years: tuition and expenses to study under Paderewski's old mas- ter in Vienna, Théodore Leschetizky, the greatest piano pedagogue of the era.[53] And although Proctor, nor in later years any of his students at the conservatory, never achieved the heights of fame Gardner coveted for them all (and for herself, of course), the investment was a sound one. Proctor proved that pearl above price, a man who let appearances be damned and continued Gardner's faithful friend and cavalier even into her old age.

Nearly all the qualities Isabella Gardner sought in a man seemingly were Proctor's. Blond, good-looking in a rather boyish and yet sophisticated way; eager, gallant, frank, athletic, distinctly a good sort, Proctor lacked only genius. When he confessed to her that to "row heavy boats" was perhaps not the best thing for a pianist's fingers, it was the sort of range in a man Gardner always liked. Both loved the outdoors: and when he reported to her in a letter one summer he was "as brown as a berry and strong as a bull; all the forenoon I hoe in the fields.... In the afternoon I go swimming (I love the water by the way) and then [go] off for a [bicycle] ride,"[54] he was sharing with Gardner pursuits she craved as much as art or music.

Isabella Gardner and George Proctor (*far right*) with others of her house guests at Green Hill, the Gardners' country house in Brookline, Massachusetts, in 1902. *Isabella Stewart Gardner Museum, Boston*

Although in later years it is not clear Proctor was as frank with his wife, he made a point of sharing his homosexuality with Isabella Gardner as well, and in an era when it was by no means accepted that sexual orientation is entirely precognitive, which is to say discovered, not chosen, it says much for the character and quality of Gardner's counsel. Indeed, when Proctor's marriage lasted barely a year it cannot have surprised Gardner, to whom Proctor had "come out," as we would say today in a moving correspondence with his patron:

In answering your letter this afternoon [he wrote in an addendum to an earlier letter headed "Night! P.M."] I missed one point (to my great surprise) which really is of importance.

I am something of a lawyer when I correspond with some people and look out to answer everything that needs an answer.

It is only that I am much obliged for your good wishes in regard to the "great big love affair. . . ."

I have just tipped my ink bottle over and everything is swimming, but I must let things swim until I have asked you if it is your private desire that the person to whom I–in a moment of folly–might say "je t'aime" will be a sort of second Sandow? Now I will clear things up![55]

Sandow, it will be recalled, was the terrifically well-built Victorian strong man so much admired in those days–not least by Gardner.

Gardner's musical circle was too cosmopolitan and diverse in ways other than sexual orientation, to be called only gay, reflecting the new world of late-nineteenth New England, but Proctor as a gay man was in that respect more characteristic than not, as were also I believe the three men who with Proctor stood at the center of Gardner's set musically, Johns, Adamowski, and Loeffler, though it must be said that while the most authoritative studies both of Sargent and of James document their sexual orientation conclusively in my judgment, neither Johns nor Adamowski nor even Loeffler has had the benefit of such sophisticated, in-depth scholarship. Admittedly a novelist's or a painter's work is more likely to be revealing of sexuality than a musician's–even a composer's (witness the continuing controversy over the sexual orientation of Schubert and of Tchaikovsky)–but like both Sargent and James, each of these three musicians in Gardner's circle were artists who were either "confirmed bachelors" or involved in long, anguished courtships or prob-lematic marriages, and men also notably reclusive about their "private lives," which, moreover, when scrutinized, typically disclose same-sex "significant others"–all signs scholars have repeatedly documented as characteristic of homosexuality in the nineteenth century.

It is possible, of course, to quarrel with such evidence. Loeffler's biog-rapher, disdaining what she calls "speculation," does not identify the composer as gay, insisting, as she puts it, that Loeffler's life disclosed no "Bohemian habits. . . . There was no question of his moral uprightness"–a judgment which, apparently seriously pronounced in 1993, is itself telling, it being a sure sign of a negative (which is to say, in this case, a homophobic) attitude to be so judgmental and to insist as well on a standard of evidence more stringent than the norm. After all, in eras when it was either or both a sin and an illness and, too, a crime, it is even less possible to "prove" homosexuality than it ever is to prove *any* sexuality, including heterosexuality!

What would be the evidence? Marriage? Children? Oscar Wilde rejoiced in both. Physical sex? Not in the Victorian era! Besides, homosexuality, no more than heterosexuality, is only a matter of physical sex. As Robert Martin has noted in *The Homosexual Tradition in American Poetry*, we are too apt today in our sex-obsessed age to "assume that everyone is heterosexual until there is proof, not of homosexual feelings, but of homosexual acts."[56] Nor is the word bisexual helpful. Everyone is bisexual to some degree. Perhaps Julius Caesar was, in the old phrase, every woman's husband and every man's wife, but how many of us are to be found at just the exact midpoint of the Kinsey scale that famously measures sexual orientation? Most of us fall to one side or the other, whether by a little or a lot, and there can be very little doubt which sexual orientation was pervasive in Isabella Gardner's circle. Or of her wholehearted role as facilitator! Loeffler, for example, was drawn specially as it turned out to Sargent, whom he met the night of November 11, 1887, when Loeffler performed brilliantly Édouard Lalo's *Symphonie Espagnole* as soloist with the Boston

Portrait of the composer Charles Loeffler by John Singer Sargent, 1903. *Isabella Stewart Gardner Museum, Boston*

Symphony. Sargent, in the audience, went backstage, where, of course, a man of his stature would always be welcome, to congratulate Loeffler after the concert, arranging, Loeffler later recalled, for "our meeting at a friend's house."[57] The mutual friend, of course, was Gardner, to whom years later Sargent gave as a birthday present the portrait he painted of Loeffler.

It was much better than the one Sargent had painted of Bunker, who had meanwhile also caught Loeffler's eye. Forthwith Loeffler and Bunker spent rather a fructifying summer together: "the two artists worked together in Medfield throughout the summer of 1889, and the serial nature of Bunker's paintings," Erica E. Hirshler has pointed out, "seems reflected in Loeffler's quartet for strings, its fourth movement, a rondo pastorale, expressing the Edenic rhythms of country life that Loeffler and Bunker shared."[58] Indeed, what better evidence could there be of how diverse and wide ranging and enabling Gardner's influence was on some of the most distinguished American art of her day than a surviving photograph of Loeffler's study which shows a reproduction of Sargent's portrait of Isabella Stewart Gardner.[59]

◆

From another nephew, Isabella Gardner gained a yet more varied view of these diversities, for there were not only the two of her own three–Joe Junior and WAG–who were bachelors, but the son of Jack Gardner's sister Julia, Archibald Cary Coolidge.[60] And if the effeminate WAG was a classic example of the aesthete or effete gay archetype, Archie Coolidge, not at all effeminate–indeed, he was a varsity wrestler at Harvard–could equally be seen as an example of the athletic gay archetype, a type "whose bisexual inclinations seemed [in the words of one scholar studying sexuality at nineteenth-century Yale] innocent to [him] and apparently to others, because his bearing and behavior, including his emotional attachments to others of his sex, did not affront current codes of conduct."[61] Indeed, it would never have occurred to Archie Coolidge to be anything other than manly in his bearing, and at any Gardner family gathering he and WAG must have stood out as utter opposites.

Their similarities they conveyed with equal force, WAG at Groton and Archie at Harvard, where each "bachelor don" was both wealthy enough and artistic enough to give full-fledged architectural expression to his collegiate lifestyle. WAG at Groton built a home for himself; Archie at Harvard built a private dormitory, Randolph Hall, with an apartment for himself. But each was, in fact, much more than that. To each building each nephew appended what at Groton WAG called a "Pleasure Dome" and what at Harvard Archie called a gym (priceless distinction; one can all but hear irreverent undergraduates lampooning the "fairy" don and the "jock" don–two classic types, after all)–each facility different and yet the same even as was true of WAG and Archie: WAG's included a small theater, Archie's squash courts; but both centered around a student-faculty swimming pool that in each case certainly focused homoerotic passions in the most anciently Greek way each nephew admired.[62]

WAG's aesthete mode at Groton, of course, is more easily discerned as homosexual by many than Archie's athletic mode at Harvard, but that sort of stereotyping is post-Wildean. Scholars have long since documented the way "the great commercial artist J. C. Leyendecker [he of the turn-of-the-century *Saturday Evening Post* covers and Arrow collar advertisements] popularized the image of the athletic homosexual,"[63] for instance, and as Archie, however much he was a jock, was Isabella Gardner's nephew, it will not surprise that his view of the matter (of which Gardner certainly approved), resulted in a series of murals at Randolph Hall of aesthete athletes, powerful but languid, self-absorbed and thoughtful, and all strikingly homoerotic. The muralist was Leyendecker's presager, Edward Penfield. What James Gifford calls "the Athlete-Aesthete dialectic," is very evident in Penfield's stylish "marriage of sinew and sensitivity."[64]

Isabella Gardner avoided the usual stereotyping from which so much of what we now call homophobia arises not only as a result of the variety of gay modes she was confronted with in her own family, but also, I think, because her own core romantic values about the man of her own ideals were so strong they pervaded all her relationships with men, gay or not. It is perhaps not surprising then that the narrative of her life as it unfolds here will disclose a well-known man, heterosexual but effeminate, and thus forever parrying homosexual advances and, on the other hand, gay friends who were not artists or musicians but scientists and economists, most immediately, in fact, the figure of a gallant officer and famous explorer, to whom Gardner also offered herself as muse and mentor as completely as to any artist.

Isabella Gardner loved Arthur J. Monteney Jephson.[65] Nothing is clearer. Whereas Proctor, seventeen in 1890 to Gardner's fifty, was clearly a crush that would have to wait, Jephson in 1890 was thirty-two; handsome, intelligent, athletic, beautifully formed, adventuresome, if a bit of a rolling stone and tending to be scatterbrained and impulsive, Jephson offered just the exchange of late youth and high middle age Gardner needed at fifty. He had been an officer in Stanley's expedition of 1888–89 to relieve Emin Pasha, the Egyptian governor of the Sudan, and the book he had written about it had made him, if only briefly, world famous. Indeed, Gardner carried him off to Groton School to give a talk to the boys that no one found boring.

So much in Isabella Gardner's life happened in the orbit of her Beacon Street neighbor, Julia Ward Howe, where all visiting celebrities in Boston eventually were feted. It was at a luncheon party at the Howes' that Gardner had met Oscar Wilde in 1882. In town to lecture in connection with the Boston premiere of that parody of Pre-Raphaelite aesthetes like himself, *Patience*, Wilde was then living only a few blocks

away from the Gardners' at the Hotel Vendôme on Commonwealth Avenue, his headquarters during the northeast leg of his lecture tour. Howe's having "entertained this pornographic poet" caused such a furor she had recourse to the letters page of *The Boston Evening Transcript* to deny anyone's "right to decide who should be received socially." Isabella Gardner, one of the small party Howe invited to meet Wilde, must have been delighted that for

Arthur J. Monteney Jephson, the explorer. *Isabella Stewart Gardner Museum, Boston* once her own mentor had stolen Gardner's lead in livening up the Puritan capital.[66] But Jephson, more than Wilde, was Gardner's type. And when at another meal at the Howes', a dinner party for Jephson during his and Stanley's American tour of 1891, Gardner was first seen in Boston to accept Jephson's attentions, it was the beginning of a long and close relationship. Jephson would thereafter be her devoted cavalier.

Stringing together bits and pieces from correspondence and such, Jephson's relationship with Gardner seems somewhat to carry forward a pattern which has already emerged here. Midst much talk of history and music and the arts and politics and not a little gossip, barely veiled references to his sexuality are evident. For example, he writes quite freely to Gardner of an acquaintance introducing him to "what one may call the 'under-side' of New York [city]" and how they had enjoyed an "afternoon in a Turkish bath," many of which were gay gathering points in this era and that at the baths he had been "introduced to some of his [acquaintances'] friends," an experience, Jephson assures Gardner, that was "one of the most unique introductions I have ever seen, the picture in my book [about Africa, presumably of someone naked] was nothing on it."[67] Later when the same man, who becomes a friend, marries, he asks Jephson, so the latter writes Gardner, not only to the wedding but to "travel with them on their honeymoon." Confides Jephson to Gardner: "how simple and naive, is it not?"[68]

Then there is the intimate and confidential "coming-out" experience, not by letter this time, as with Dwight and with Proctor, but in person, one assumes, during an idyllic time at the late summer retreat the Gardners owned in Maine, Roque Island: "that enchanted island," Jephson writes Isabella Gardner later, "where we were out of doors the whole day long and you read Walt Whitman to me, and his 'Song of Joy' till the shadow that was over me lifted a little and I seemed to feel quieter and better."[69]

The tale unfolds through the predictable scandal and a covering marriage, though this time we are spared a suicide. Perhaps this is due to the ministrations of a mutual friend of Gardner's and Jephson's living in Florence, to whom Gardner confesses what a "dear friend" Jephson is ("tell Jephson his photograph is before me as I write,")[70] and who in turn reports back to Gardner in Boston the predictable nature of his difficulties: "Poor dear Jephson. The scandal about him was to the effect that he had come to Florence to have improper relationships with men."[71]

Advised of Jephson's marriage plans (it was the universal cover then), Gardner's response was brief and telling: "don't advise Jephson to marry. He wouldn't be happy."[72] She knew well enough that the real gulf was not between heterosexual men and homosexual men, but between the effete homosexuality of Proust's world and the more robust homosexuality of Walt Whitman's.

It may seem at first glance an unlikely distinction for Gardner to have made, but the fact that her personal library[73] remains intact documents the breadth and even some of the specifics of her knowledge of such things. In addition to books of known pertinence to the Boston gay subculture of the 1880s-1890s—Charles Flandrau's *Harvard Episodes*, for example, and Henry James' *The Bostonians*—and to classics by foundational authors of modern homosexual discourse such as Baron Corvo, Verlaine, Swinburne, Huysmans, and John Addington Symonds (in whose work the word "homosexual" first appeared in English in 1891) and, of course, Whitman's poetry—Gardner also owned two books whose personal associations make them doubly significant: Lord Alfred Douglas' *Poems*, a gift (*after* the Wilde trial) to Gardner from her dear friend, of whom more soon, Matthew Prichard, who knew Douglas well,[74] and to whom it had been a gift from the original owner, to whom Douglas himself had inscribed it, and another book which particularly documents her familiarity with exactly the distinction we are developing here of the aesthete and the athlete: Edward Carpernter's *Iloaus, An anthology of Friendship*—another gift to Gardner by Prichard.[75]

An Anglican priest (curate, indeed, to a founder of Christian Socialism, Frederick D. Maurice), Carpenter, a Socialist gay thinker and friend to both William Morris and George Bernard Shaw, was the founder of the Milthorpe community in England. It was intended to express his belief that "homosexuality could become a positive, spiritual and social force, breaking down the barriers of class and convention,"– akin to the policy we've seen the bohemian Gardner was herself pursuing –"and binding men together in comradeship . . . that current of affection which he had recognized with a leap of joy when he first read the poems of Walt Whitman." Well known in advanced circles in Boston, Carpenter and the book by him Prichard gave Gardner are distinctly a red flag: *Iolaus*' "homosexual content was scarcely veiled," Warren Johansson has written; indeed the book was nicknamed among bookmen "The Bugger's Bible."[76]

Isabella Gardner was, of course, too sophisticated to be trapped in any mode.[77] At least one report does exist of Gardner in company with "a couple of very young and very fashionable and very nice young gentle-men. . . . their canes [hanging] trembling from their '"limp hands'"[78]–a code not hard to crack–and, after all, one of her escorts might have been WAG! On the other hand neither of the limp gentlemen certainly was Dwight or Proctor or Jephson, or Archie Coolidge, with whom she was as likely to be seen at a baseball game or out rowing, for one reason, surely, she was so sensitive to the two contrasting gay archetypes of ath-lete and aesthete was that the one passion she had that almost out-weighed her love of art, and, indeed, played into it in fascinating ways–was her passion for sports.

A swift runner as a schoolgirl,[79] as an adult she remained a good swim-mer, rower, and horsewoman[80] and also seems to have studied and become proficient in jujitsu.[81] Had it been possible then I'm sure she would undoubtedly (why do I think of Joan Payson, the Mets owner of the 1960s) have bought a major league baseball club; nor is there any doubt which one it would have been, so devoted was she to the Boston Red Sox. In the event she was content to buy a horse, "Halton," which she raced quite successfully.[82]

Carter, whom she dragged one year to one game after another of the World Series, also remembered Gardner attending every Harvard hockey game in which George P. Gardner, Jr., another nephew, ever played–and often the practices too, though they were frequently held outdoors at Soldiers Field in below-zero temperatures.[83] To be sure fam-ily pride entered into this–George was also a hurdler and a tennis player and she missed few of those events either–but what is especially notice-able is that aside from baseball it really was the most violent male sports that Gardner liked best, whether boxing, hockey, or football. She was enough of a friend of Harvard's ruthless and controversial football coach, Percy Haughton, to have shared a Christmas meal with him, and she once wrote a friend this telling anecdote: "Yesterday at the Somerset, I was lunching. At another table was a man I knew eating with another I *didn't* know. This latter turned out to be *Dibblee* the Captain of [the Harvard] Football [Team]. Up got the man I knew, came to me and said 'Mrs. Gardner would you mind knowing Dibblee; he has asked to be pre-sented!' *Mind?* It was the proudest day of my life!"[84]

Significantly, Jack Gardner, though a member of the Myopia Hunt Club on Boston's North Shore, was only a nominal sportsman; owning a tenth share of the 1885 America's Cup defender, *Puritan*, is as athletic as the increasingly stout Jack was known to be. Proctor and Jephson, however, were both distinctly athletic, as was Crawford, of course, whose summer idylls with Gardner on the North Shore found him and Gardner rowing

A contemporary newspaper sketch of the boxing match Isabella Gardner staged for herself and a few friends. *Isabella Stewart Gardner Museum, Boston*

several miles in Beverly Bay every morning and then traversing as many miles on horseback every afternoon.

Crawford's best sport at Cambridge, moreover, was boxing, one of Isabella Gardner's favorites.[85] Indeed, she once went so far as to organize surely the most unusual boxing match in the sport's history, recalled amazedly in later years by the promoter she talked into it. Under the heading "MRS. GARDNER'S PRIVATE BOUT," the event was described thusly.

> The fight was held about two in the afternoon [in an artist's] studio. . . . The place was full of paintings and pieces of statuary. . . . Mrs. Gardner wanted the whole show and she got it all right—yes, it

was Mrs. Jack Gardner who put up the money.

Well, it was one strange fight. I was used to all sorts of crowds, but I never saw a fight crowd like that before. When all those sedate-looking, quietly-dressed women came into the studio, I confess I had my misgivings. Did they know what they were in for, or did they have an idea that a prize fight was like a game of Ping-Pong? Would they scream and faint when some one got a sock in the jaw, and a little blood spattered around? I didn't know ... but I had an idea that come what might, Mrs. Gardner would stick by the ship, because she had a reputation as a dead game sport.

I didn't need to worry any.... they were impartial in their applause, cheering either fighter when he socked a good one home. Mrs. Jack seemed to have a liking for Harrington—he was a good-looking fellow and won the bout—but after the fight she took pains to compliment [the loser] Doherty on his stand. The fight lasted 17 rounds.[86]

Talk about transgressing male terrain! More will be said later of Isabella Gardner's love of sports. But Gardner, like Joyce Carol Oates, who has written so perceptively on boxing, probably would have understood John Updike's comparison of Ted Williams to Achilles. (About a martial arts exhibition she once sponsored Gardner wrote a friend: "the jujitsu men ... are wonderful and beautiful too.")[87] She might even have seen in the bat and glove of baseball (as others have) the lance and chalice of the Grail quest.

There is no doubt at all that Isabella Gardner knew an aesthete from an athlete, or that her ideal was a man who was both. She did not always buy Madonnas either! One of the masterworks of her assemblage of paintings, which in the late 1880s and early 1890s she was just beginning to collect, and to which we will turn in Part Three, is Piero della Francesca's fifteenth-century fresco of *Hercules*, a highly masculine classical image for heterosexuals—and for homosexuals too—as John Boswell of Yale points out when he writes: "Plato thought homosexuals naturally the most manly and an equation of homosexuality with effeminacy in men would hardly have occurred to people [like the ancient Greeks] whose history, art, popular literature and religious myths were all filled with the homosexual exploits of such archtypically masculine figures as Zeus, Hercules, Achilles, et al."[88]

Forceful and graceful, the figure of Isabella Gardner's *Hercules* is noble, intelligent, and beautiful. On her wall, in history, Gardner had, perhaps, found her man. In real life her quest was to prove more difficult, even mysterious. In this as in so much else Gardner showed herself, on the eve of the Freudian era, a woman of, even ahead of, her times.

7

Diversities

To be a Jew in Boston in the nineteenth century was a different but by no means a less vexing problem than to be homosexual. Nor was Boston peculiar in this respect even among the most cosmopolitan of capitals: in Paris it was the era of which Peter Brooks could write of "the crucial Proustian figures of the homosexual and the Jew–two social outsiders," he called them, "who were disguised doubles for the artist."[1] It is a profound measure of the intensity and sophistication of Isabella Gardner's growing sensitivity to such issues that the whole story of her life in a sense was a coming to terms with the meaning of Brooks' observation for herself, who was neither a Jew nor a homosexual, but might just as well have been in the Back Bay. Meanwhile, if Boston's emerging gay and lesbian subculture was a dominant influence in her circle, it was the immigrant Jewish subculture which yielded the most brilliant of her protégés and ultimately played the key role in the most enduring of her achievements. Everyone, of course, knows it, but *none* of Gardner's earlier biographers have cared to say it:[2] Bernard Berenson was that much despised figure in Victorian Boston, a Jew.[3]

That he was not also gay must have surprised more than one interlocutor, though perhaps not Gardner herself, because Berenson, the one heterosexual among Charles Eliot Norton's protégés (as one affair after another documents) was also the most effete, an irony Gardner would surely have been quick to appreciate.[4] A young dandy notable for his luxurious pre-Raphaelite curls, Berenson, who was of diminutive stature with "a certain delicacy and sedateness in his walk," in the words of his principal biographer, Ernest Samuels, must have seemed to most Bostonians, let alone Harvard men, like a "strayed faun from Arcady."[5]

In fact, young Bernhard Valvrojenski, as he originally was, came from the village of Butrimonys, near Vilna, in Lithuania. The son of Albert and Judith Mickleshanski Valvronjenski, who had fled with their children from the pogroms of 1874–75 to America, where they settled in Boston, Bernhard grew up facing a less physically threatening but hardly less persistently bigoted culture, where too often Jews as much as any other group were disdainful of "Litvaks" like Bernhard, which doubtless explains the new family name of Berenson his parents were quick to adopt in an effort to shed a disadvantage in a new society pregnant with possibilities for them: for the Berensons, though desperately poor slum dwellers in Boston's North End, dependent on the slim income of Bernhard's father, a peddler, had reason to hope. It is true that the elder Berenson did not succeed, going from hand basket to peddler's pack to pushcart and, alas, no further; but he was well read if not well educated (indeed, often welcomed on his peddler's round into quite genteel houses) and as is so often the case the parents' values no less than their genes were advantages that in the event outweighed poverty and propelled Bernhard forward with the help of Boston's legendary public institutions, Boston Latin School and the Boston Public Library.

Quick to master English and eager to cultivate his mind, in the reading rooms of that library by day and in his little attic room by night, young Berenson persevered and earned his way into Boston Latin in 1881 and, two years later, Boston University. Ambitious, intellectual, a compulsive dreamer, romantic, supremely (even arrogantly) confident, his aim to be some sort of writer-scholar, Berenson, perhaps through his coaching of wealthy Harvard undergraduates who brought him to the attention of Charles Eliot Norton, somehow found the money to enable him to transfer in 1884 to Harvard College, where he sat at the feet of Norton and such other luminaries as philosopher William James ("Come," James would invite his class, "let us gossip about the universe") in what has come to be seen as Harvard's golden age. Intellectually stimulated, Berenson also experienced some kind of religious conversion at Harvard and was baptized by Phillips Brooks, a charismatic spiritual influence on Berenson's class. He achieved as well some small literary repute of his own, writing for the *Harvard Monthly*. Finally, as almost a finale, Berenson had been presented to Isabella Gardner, most likely after one of his lectures, by Norton himself, who may have had an arrangement with the Gardners about funding worthy students upon his recommendation.[6]

The young man's precocious intellect probably was what attracted Gardner to Berenson, who in turn liked athletic and intellectual women. He must also have been tremendously excited by Gardner's lifestyle: the magnificent music room, the many paintings, the majestic staircase, the footmen, and the full-dress dinners[7]–all of it must have constituted for Berenson a most astonishing contrast to his cramped, run-down garret in the North End slum only a half-hour's walk but worlds away from the Back Bay. At the Gardners' or in some nearby patrician abode, the young man must first have learned which fork to use and which wineglass to reach for, all the while singing, so to speak, for his dinner, brilliantly enough it seems to have been asked back again and again.

Bernard Berenson. *Courtesy of the Harvard University Archives*

It needs to be said that others, equally poor and seemingly as full of promise, struck out with Gardner, who was not so quick as many have thought to take up every latest thing, the more exotic the better. Another Boston slum child, for example, of despised race and great gifts and obvious need, Kahlil Gibran (he of *The Prophet*) never got to first base with Gardner, for whatever reason, despite efforts to call him to her attention.[8] On one occasion she pointedly remained quite disinterested in him though Gibran was sketching a guest of hers at the time. On the other hand, that Gardner intended to give a distinct lead in her increasing inclusivity and openness is quite clear if the relevant evidence is considered. Deliberate in receiving gays and Jews and Quakers into her Beacon Street town house, she was no less so in receiving Irish Catholics in an era when the Back Bay was a bastion of Yankee bigotry against the Irish.[9]

As always there was a personal side to Isabella Gardner's interest in things Irish: in this case Mollie Osgood, who though she was forty years younger was close enough to Gardner to be called her "girl friend." The sister of Gretchen Osgood Warren, of whom with her daughter Rachel, Sargent would paint one of his more dashing portraits under Isabella Gardner's auspices, Mollie Osgood married Robert Erskine Childers, an English writer who took up the cause of Irish independence so ardently he would later join the Irish Republican Army, only to be captured and shot. His wife identified so closely with the Irish cause that a mutual friend once wrote Gardner that Mollie Osgood Childers was "supposed to be behind the very worst excesses and follies of the Sinn Feiners," but that Isabella Gardner was not put off by this is clearly indicated by her sympathetic correspondence with Gretchen Osgood after Childers' death and by the fact that Gardner carefully clipped all the relevant newspaper stories.[10]

Furthermore, not only did Irish-Catholic cultural and literary figures like the poet Louise Imogene Guiney frequent the Gardners' circle; never one to do things in a small way, Isabella Gardner also received, indeed, courted, William Cardinal O'Connell. No stranger over the years to Gardner's set, her house must have been among very few in the Brahmin orbit to which the Roman Catholic Archbishop of Boston was invited regularly and enthusiastically, just as Gardner must have been among very few in Back Bay Boston who was active in the support of the religious institutions of Irish Catholic Boston, lending her name as sponsor, for example, to a charity benefit at Horticultural Hall for the Carney

Hospital. She was also a generous contributor as well to the Knights of Columbus,[11] and–most astonishingly–Gardner would become later an ardent supporter of James Michael Curley, Boston's legendary and highly controversial mayor, who made no secret of how well he and Gardner got along, nor of the fact that Gardner gave him generous campaign contributions. He did not exaggerate:[12] Gardner wrote once to her niece, Olga Monks: "I had a bad day yesterday but Curley's triumph makes me better today. . . . I try always to stick up for a friend in need and Curley is not a prig."[13] These were words as insightful of Gardner as true of Curley. Very few if any ethnic, religious, or sexual prejudices were safe from her.

Isabella Gardner's views on such matters may, in fact, explain rather a bizarre imbroglio later in her life.[14] One of the three nephews she and Jack brought up, Augustus Gardner, became eventually a Republican congressman from Massachusetts. When "Gussie," once announced his intention to relinquish the seat in order to run for governor, only to think better of it after being soundly beaten in that year's primary fight, a good friend of Gardner's, A. Piatt Andrew, who had meanwhile been encouraged by Isabella Gardner to run for Gussie's congressional seat, refused to give way, and Gardner backed, not her nephew, but her dear friend Andrew, reportedly infuriating all her Gardner in-laws.[15]

Although too loyal to have proposed Andrew if Gussie Gardner had not backed out, that Isabella Gardner when the chance presented itself did back the more progressive Andrew is very interesting. Indeed, it may be that perhaps more than just her friendship with Andrew was involved, for Congressman Gardner had led the fight in the House of Representatives that his father-in-law, Henry Cabot Lodge, had led in the Senate, to override the president's veto of a highly controversial literacy bill widely regarded by progressive forces as directed against further Jewish and Italian immigration to the United States[16] and, although Isabella Gardner's opinion of this specific legislation is not known, a startlingly cool letter to her in the Gardner archives from Senator Lodge strongly suggests she was not one of his supporters.[17] (Nor would it have been the first time she parted political company from her nephew, who would be quite strongly in favor of the Spanish American War, which Gardner despised as "a war of a bully."[18]) Most important of all, Gussie Gardner's and Henry Cabot Lodge's chief opponent in the immigration bill fight was then Congressman James Michael Curley.

Gardner's wide-ranging and openminded apprecation of diversity was not, for example, only Western; she had so keen and militant an appreciation of Asian sensibilities, for example, that Carter recalled she would not receive a distinguished Japanese visitor because he wore Western dress![19] Usually, it was some artistic aspect, of course, of a downtrodden but brilliant culture that attracted her. Thus while her sympathy with Ireland would find its strongest center, as we'll see, in the literary revival led by Yeats,[20] it was her love for the Church of Our Lady of Good Voyage in Gloucester that involved her in the Portuguese community there in its restoration.[21]

Many of these actions of hers were well enough known, but they have always been seen in rather an episodic way, as a series of rather flighty whims, reflecting, it is often said, her quirky egotism; it is only when one links her various affinities with and activities in aid of gays, Jews, and Irish and Portuguese Catholics that a pattern begins to emerge that gives new meaning, beyond socialite "scandalizing" to Morris Carter's careful observation that "the proprieties and conventions of a society where Puritan tradition still lingers had always been somewhat ostentatiously flouted by Mrs. Gardner."[22] After all, everything we know about how Isabella Gardner approached a work of art suggests that in her approach to life generally, no less than her friend Martin Loeffler, whom his biographer calls "a life-long opponent of political oppression," Gardner was moved by the underlying cause she thought artistically expressed—as was Loeffler, for instance, when he wrote his celebrated Irish songs, dedicated to the Irish tenor, John McCormack. Of course the Yeats texts he set appealed to Loeffler artistically, but as his effort to set one song in Gaelic suggests, so did the cause of Irish nationalism.[23]

When exactly Isabella Gardner began to be seen as an explicitly liberating force, nothing less, in the life of her era in Boston, and in ever-widening circles much beyond the old Puritan capital, as her repute became a national one, it is hard to say. But there are indications (her close association with Loeffler, or, indeed, Curley's attitude to her) that Gardner progressively registered more broadly and publicly in some way hard to pin down, but perhaps connected with her media image, and this despite the fact she took no high-profile role in such things as settlement house work among the poor. On one of the few occasions when she visited such an institution, in Boston's North End slum, she was greeted with the sort of rapturous, cheering reception usually reserved for politicians.[24] There is, furthermore, distinctly the oddest of the Gardner tall tales, where Marie Antoinette, as it were, is all but rescued from a mob by the city's leading ethnic sports figure of the era, and, appropriately enough, a boxer.

Carter tells the tale in his biography. Gardner was returning alone in her carriage from an evening engagement, passing through a very poor part of town, heavily Irish South Boston, when she was engulfed by a yelling mob in the middle of a very ugly street car strike. Not only were her carriage and her liveried attendants more conspicuous than was wise in such a situation, but, as she remembered she was wearing some of her grandest jewels, including

> her two large solitaires [very large diamonds] named the "Rajah" and "The Light of India," which [with her usual imagination] she had set on springs so that they waved above her forehead like antennae.... [In the midst of the mob] the thought crossed her mind that if the blazing diamonds irritated some angry eye, the result might be unpleasant; but, before any definite fear had taken shape, a heavy hand was laid on the carriage door, and a vigorous voice said, "Don't be afraid, Mrs. Jack, I'll see you through all right." When they had emerged from the mob, Mrs. Gardner leaned forward and said, "May I ask to whom I am indebted for this courtesy?"–"John L. Sullivan."[25]

Whether or not exactly this incident occurred, that the heavyweight champion of the world and the pride of Irish Boston was advertised so widely as so well disposed to the queen of Boston's Back Bay, as Isabella Gardner was sometimes called, seems significant. Moreover, it is clear that some at least of her contemporaries, even amid the tall tales and the media excess, saw Gardner as certainly more liberal (as we'd say today) than her husband, and as deliberately attempting to break down barriers on many levels and argue for a more inclusive society. This is evident both in private observations (such as Henry Adams' to Elizabeth Cameron to whom he wrote: "Jack [Gardner] is too good a Bostonian to care for Cuban heroes, though his wife would know better."),[26] and equally in public discourse as disclosed in any survey of the more serious of the Boston newspapers of the period at the height and at the end of Gardner's life when likely long prepared appraisals were naturally published as most timely.

This vector in Gardner's life appeared most strikingly, of course, in her bohemian attitude to every aspect of the Back Bay Brahmin code. Although Gardner's New York background was often cited by way of explanation for her "hardihood," as one correspondent put it, in being able to successfully oppose "Brahmin repressions," John Jay Chapman, on the other hand, no provincial, while he did not deny the trauma of her rejection by Boston in her early years in the city, argued that Gardner never acted primarily out of a sense of alienation from her adopted city. He insisted that she understood that "you must not expect the outpourings of spontaneous feeling–guitars in the moonlight–from the native Bostonian," and that the "tinge of theology in life and manners which has survived through three centuries of growth and change indicates a great native strength [that] is in its own way touching and beautiful." Argued Chapman, "Mrs. Gardner felt this and the rigidities of the New England temperament never annoyed her. I have never heard her say cross or critical things about Boston."[27] For Chapman there were much deeper reasons why Gardner not only repeatedly challenged the status quo and, indeed, seemed to wax rather than wane when criticized: "her native buoyancy and good humor seemed to make her float on the waves of moral controversy if they rose," he wrote, with enormous insight; "for her soul's interest lay in other directions."[28]

And some of the most vital of those directions, whether in art or in people, were plain enough to another correspondent whose article Carter clipped for the Gardner scrapbook. Almost certainly from a Boston newspaper, probably the *Post* or the *Globe*, the more serious of the middle-class Boston media of the time, its tenor obviously reflects a long consideration of Gardner, whose circle was said to have "approached more closely the salon of Mme. de Stael than [that of] any other woman of the nineteenth century." Gardner, the report asserted, "*broke down social barriers* [emphasis added] and evidenced her belief in society as a vehicle for the cultivation of art, music and intellectuality, [thereby intending to] create a social renaissance." And, finally: "the set which represented the old Puritan aristocracy of Boston and the set which represented the new Bohemianism met in her house on common ground."[29]

Here is a key point: Gardner was *not* by any means the most Bohemian Boston figure of her era, and not even the most Bohemian in Boston society. Carter, amplifying on the newspaper story above, identified the old Puritan aristocracy–that venerable tribe of the Cabots and the Lowells and such–with the Brimmers (headed by Martin Brimmer), and the new Bohemian set with the Apthorps (headed by the *Transcript*'s music critic, William Apthorp),[30] of whom some knowledge has survived in the reminiscences of Clayton Johns, who recalled "little dinners of six or eight people, usually having some highlight guest like Paderewski, Melba, Sarah Bernhardt–after dinner special friends were invited. . . . Mrs. Gardner and [Boston Symphony conductor] Gericke were always there. Besides, there were members of the younger set. . . . Late in the evening," Johns fondly recalled, "beer and cigars lent a Bohemian air. . . . Mrs. Apthorp appeared, carrying a large pitcher of beer in one hand, beer mugs hanging from each finger of her other hand"[31]–not something likely to happen at the Gardners. Isabella Gardner did smoke, and she did drink beer occasionally, but beer mugs hanging from each finger was not her style. If she was in no sense the conventional grande dame, Isabella Gardner was equally never the complete Bohemian either. She set herself the more difficult task of nurturing the more cosmopolitan common ground where the puritan and the bohemian might happily ferment together.

It was Santayana who spotted that Gardner was, in fact, one of "two leading ladies in the Boston of my time" and it is significant he did not think, like the popular press, that the other was Sarah Choate Sears (of whom more later), whose husband was much advertised as the richest man in Boston, but Sarah Whitman, the distinguished artist (primarily in stained glass). Of Gardner, Santayana wrote, "her vocation was to show Boston what was missing. . . . [and] she had an indefatigable energy and persever-ance that in spite of all murmurs and hesitations, carried the day." Whitman, on the other hand, he found "more in the spirit of Boston, more conscien-tious and troubled. . . . there were echoes in her of Transcendentalism," he felt: "she didn't [like Gardner] make a point of entertaining itinerant artists or other celebrities; but devoted herself to instilling the higher spirit of the arts and crafts into the minds of working girls." It was an inspired compari-son. So was his conclusion: "our good works, alas," he wrote of Whitman, "are often vainer than our vanities."[32]

Even Martin Brimmer himself, who Carter holds up as the represen-tative Brahmin figure, was no stereotypical Puritan (he founded Boston's Museum of Fine Arts). Chapman, perceptive as we just saw in his views of Gardner, cast also a clear enough eye on Brimmer. Puritan

Brimmer might be, but Chapman thought him "the best of old Boston; for he was not quite inside the Puritan tradition and was a little sweeter by nature and less sure he was right than the true Bostonian is. . . . there was a knightly glance in his eye . . . [he] lived always, in a little Camelot of his own," Chapman recalled. "He was not quixotic, but he was independent. There were portcullises and moats and flowered gardens around him. . . . there was nothing sanctimonious about his mind, and that is what really distinguished him from the adjacent Boston nobility." Bitingly, Chapman concluded there was in Mr. Brimmer "nothing of that austere look which comes from holding on to property and standing pat. And besides this he was warm; not, perhaps, quite as warm as the Tropics, but very much warmer than the average Beacon Street mantelpieces were."[33]

Although it was indeed "outsiders"–all along the continuum from immigrant to bohemian–who truly accepted and enabled Isabella Gardner even as the Back Bay rejected and tried to enfeeble her–the complexities of Brahmins like Sarah Whitman or Martin Brimmer–or of figures like Julia Ward Howe or Henry Lee Higginson–are critical to an understanding of Gardner's role. For all the war games she conducted with the Back Bay, she was by no means the one light in that dark room. Boston abounded in individualists worthy of meeting on common ground if only someone would clear away such a place. That too was Isabella Gardner's role.

◆

Sometimes, indeed, these others took the lead, as when Thomas Sargent Perry, so progressive as to have been among the first of Harvard's faculty to agree to lecture at the embryonic Radcliffe in the 1880s, became the moving spirit in a small group who when Berenson failed to win an expected travel fellowship raised a stipend to enable him to go to Europe on his own. Naturally though, the Gardners' contribution to the fund was by far the largest, despite the fact that Isabella Gardner was taking the risk of alienating Norton, her dear friend and chief mentor, who had judged Berenson unworthy.

An ill-advised risk it soon appeared, for if Berenson's letters to Gardner from Europe do show Gardner's, "way of inspiring men to confide in her," in Rolin N. van Hadley's words, drawing out of Berenson "a remarkable candor,"[34] they show much less on Berenson's part: though he sent her books he had read—by such sophisticated authors as Paul Bourget and Leopold von Sacher-Masoch—and though he reported on his trips to this gallery or that museum and his views of one composer and another, over time there seemed very little *development*, and when at the end of his year abroad in April of 1889 he wrote Gardner that he had secured financial support from elsewhere to stay abroad, she took umbrage, a point of view Berenson always seemed to understand. Certainly he admitted years later that time he "had nothing to show that could change the opinion you formed of me when you put a stop to our correspondence."[35] As always, Gardner had had her expectations; demanding, provoking, enabling, to some; to others her Socratic methods doubtless seemed controlling, too intense, even threatening. She was, certainly, a strenuous mentor. In a very real sense, for all the differences, Gardner's break with Berenson was not unlike the break with Crawford. Nor was their reunion half a decade later. Only when Berenson matured sufficiently for his ambitions to draw usefully abreast of Gardner's demands—one definition of mentoring—would Berenson seek to renew their relationship and Gardner agree forthwith.

Meanwhile, though Gardner's own mentor, Norton, continued her patron during the late 1880s, inviting her to join his prestigious Dante Society, to which honor Gardner responded by cheerfully funding Norton's project of publishing a Dante concordance, the divergence between the two over Berenson did not disappear. It was fundamental, for if it was Norton, as many suspected, who denied Berenson the fellowship, it was not because the young man seemed purposeless, Gardner's fret with him, but because—then as now these were frequently code words amounting to anti-Semitism—he found the young man brash and pushy.

Berenson's biographer, Ernest Samuels, seems hardly to disagree, writing of Berenson in this early period that his life had become, "a long calculation for a talented parvenu," a cruelly accurate observation. Furthermore, Berenson had "somehow to make the uncomfortably adhesive title of 'Polish Jew' a title of interesting distinction," and this despite the fact that "in assimilating the high culture of his greatly admired Boston, he assimilated as well the current anti-Semitism." Samuels concludes that for Berenson, "life would be a prolonged accommodation to the prejudices of the great world and its upper crust," going even so far as to assert that though Berenson "convinced himself that he had successfully escaped from his blighting heritage,"[36] Berenson would, "never

quite lose the traces of Jewish self-hatred which at the turn of the century his sharp-eyed friend, Henry Adams, was quick to spot in his emancipated Jewish friends." The path to personal identity would prove, in
Samuels' words, "strewn with unexpected hazards and ambiguous guide-
posts."[37]

Isabella Gardner, the "intruder," the granddaughter of the man who
owned a New York tavern, become Mrs. John Lowell Gardner, knew all
of those hazards and all of the signposts. It was a mentoring situation
made for her, though her affinity with Berenson in this respect, both of
them being outsiders, has hardly been given the attention it deserves,
perhaps because to do so one must face up to the fact, well known, but
never spoken of, that Berenson was Jewish. And not the least problem
with this approach is that it leaves the impression that Gardner herself
rather avoided the fact, which is to say was anti-Semitic. Yet such a characterization of Isabella Gardner greatly distorts the truth.

Of course, anti-Semitism in Boston a hundred years ago was far less
covert than it is now; at Harvard, for example, in the striking words of
John McCormick, it was "automatic, medieval and Shakespearean . . . a
social attitude as conventional as table linen."[38] But Isabella Gardner's
attitudes were quite otherwise, more complex and more interesting. So
were Berenson's. Was it really, I wonder, anti-Semitism that Berenson
had assimilated which prompted him to condemn the ill-mannered behavior of disadvantaged Jews, or to find disgusting the philistine values of
grasping Jewish businessmen? Was the "blighting heritage," in Samuels'
words, that Gardner was helping Berenson escape from, a matter of
being Jewish, or being poor, or perhaps sharp or vulgar? Surely, these are
separable from Jewishness; to think otherwise is what is anti-Semitic!
Granted, the fact that "Jew" is the word both Gardner and Berenson
used often as a synonym for less than creditable qualities says worlds for
what we would call today the "institutional" racism of Christian culture
generally, in which both Gardner and Berenson were caught up. But one
does not have to be a "believing," religious Jew to be quite openly and
frankly Jewish. Moreover, Phillips Brooks was a charismatic converter of
young men of all faiths in Berenson's era at Harvard. And, after all,
Berenson's religious journey resolved itself soon enough in an agnosti-
cism that would please Christians as little as it would religious Jews.
Furthermore, I would contend that Gardner and Berenson, if they were
anti-Semitic, must also be pronounced anti-Italian!

Outrageous on its face (was she not, finally, to become the most brilliant and imaginative interpreter of Italian art and architecture to
America of her era? Was he not ultimately to be the greatest connoisseur of Italian Renaissance art in the world?), the assertion can easily be
proved nonetheless by the same evidence as can the supposed anti-
Semitism: one need only compare Gardner's and Berenson's use of the
word "Jew" to their use of the word "Italian" in their correspondence,
bearing in mind that theirs was common usage *before the Holocaust.*
Whereas Virginia Woolf would confess before the Nazis "how much
[she] hated marrying a Jew," even though she loved Leonard Woolf
deeply, and then add in consequence, "We are Jews";[39] *after* the
Holocaust only in a private diary could such things be said as Harold
Nicolson's remark that, "although I loathe anti-Semitism I do dislike
Jews."[40] Not unnaturally we are wary of anything like such a distinction
today, having seen what a little supposedly harmless anti-Semitism can
lead to. *But neither Gardner's nor Berenson's generation had seen this.* And
one must not expect second sight of them! What both meant by "Jew" is
the same as what both meant by "Italian." "Do you fancy they realize
how their behavior appears to an Anglo-Saxon?" writes Gardner to
Berenson on one occasion.[41] On another: "some day I shall tell [a mutual
friend] my opinion of an Italian's opinion of honor."[42] She hardly makes
any distinction. Nor does Berenson, who later in the same year writes to
her: "for an Italian he has behaved splendidly."[43]

Given how devoted Gardner and Berenson were to *everything* Italian
(not just art; the latter lived there always; the former whenever she
could), and that this was in both their cases not a matter of heritage or of
convenience but of their free choice of, as it were, their "country of the
mind," with which they both so much identified, it would be ludicrous to
suggest personal prejudice on the part of either against Italy. There is
again, to be sure, an offensive "institutional" racism here—Christian in the
case of "Jews," it is Anglo-Saxon in the case of "Italians"–that reflects on
their participation in their overall culture from our point of view discred-
itably. But the values Gardner and Berenson are referencing personally
have much less to do with race than with *class.* It is all the more clearly
evident because in the case of both Gardner and Berenson they are, to
some extent, assumed values; when Gardner and Berenson call someone
a "Jew" or an "Italian" they mean pretty much what Samuels means when
he calls Berenson a "parvenu," a word he could also have used before her

marriage just as easily of Gardner herself, who (in Santayana's words) though instinctively "aristocratic" in the largest sense of being secure enough to disdain appearances and surround herself with whoever was "distinguished or agreeable," was, in the narrower sense, "*not* of good family,"[44] especially in Boston, where distant royal ancestry hardly canceled out a grandfather who owned a tavern. Who recalls that Van Wyck Brooks called Isabella Gardner "vulgar enough"[45] or that in *The Puritans* Arlo Bates declared: "Mrs. Wilson [the Gardner character] is like a banjo, more exciting than refined."[46]

Consider too that the bigotry Berenson (according to his biographer) felt most keenly was from Boston's firmly entrenched upper-middle-class *German* Jews. And while it can be argued that Jews can certainly be anti-Semitic in the sense of being self-loathing, if, as I am suggesting here, the issue was one of *class*, not race, it is the very perception of Berenson as self-loathing that seems to me is racist: *self*-loathing is the role any cultivated Jew *had* to be cast in by any anti-Semite, for whom the issue with any Jew was always, fundamentally, by definition, not class, but race. Do I mean Charles Eliot Norton? That being only a suspicion (it has never been documented why he did not favor Berenson's candidacy for the fellowship), let us fix on that other friend of the Gardners and of Berenson, Henry Adams; widely known for his anti-Semitism, his attitude was instructively different than Gardner's and will set hers off very well.

As Samuels points out, Berenson's "enormous financial as well as literary success was enough to give Adams painful pause during this period when he and his brother Charles were inventorying the failures of their patrician generation" of Adamses.[47] (So, indeed, must have Gardner's achievements later in her life, for as Isabella Gardner and Clover Adams would surely have agreed, Henry had as many problems with women as with Jews.)[48] Yet, if when confronted with Berenson, Adams bridled instinctively, Berenson himself was quite candid in his analysis: Adams and he, wrote Berenson, "had much in common but he could not forget he was an Adams and was always *more embarrassed than I* [emphasis added] that I happened to be a Jew."[49] It was something Berenson, in fact, did not find off-putting: Adams, he thought, was "like a glass of fine sherry" and Berenson was "determined to relish the whole bottle," wrote Samuels.[50] And that a deep affinity rather than inner insecurities is thus glimpsed is supported by the fact that Berenson's attraction for Adams was not unrequited: "in spite of himself," Samuels writes, "Adams was slowly drawn to this enormously 'cerebral' fellow Puritan. . . . The affinity ran deep, and the tie endured almost to the end of Adams' life."[51] So much so that Adams not only admitted that in a world of "dismal flatness" only Berenson "bites hard enough to sting," but once confessed in connection with some medieval music he was studying, that "there are just two people who really understand and feel these songs; one is Mrs. Jack Gardner, the other is Berenson, and I call them by 'publique d'elite.'"[52]

Well he might, for if Adams and Berenson had as much in common as Gardner and Berenson, it was Gardner who was able to have the easier and closer friendship with Berenson precisely because though she had her share of class prejudices, she was effectively without racial bias: she no more stereotyped Jews as inevitably vulgar or philistine any more than she stereotyped gays as invariably effeminate. Gardner was very much the exception, Adams very much the norm. And, of course, because Berenson surely so despaired himself of behavior that played into bigoted expecta tions, he was the more devastated when someone like Norton apparently saw the stereotype Berenson so despised exemplified *in Berenson himself.* And perhaps rightly! That Berenson *was* brash and pushy is not impossi ble, perhaps even not unlikely. (As someone has written, "Shylock and Anti-Semitism are *both* hateful.")[53] After all, no race or ethnic group has any monopoly on this vice or that virtue. (When Sargent painted his great patron, the Jewish art dealer Asher Wertheimer, he caught, as a matter of fact, the sitter's shrewdness; for anti-Semites, as Trevor J. Fairbrother sees, it confirmed their racial stereotype. It does not follow Sargent agreed.)[54] Minority status, moreover, quite aside from poverty, has its own consequences anywhere: Cardinal O'Connell was not the only Irish Catholic New Englander, for example, who discovered he felt better about himself in Dublin and positively triumphant in Rome–and conse quently less need in both places, as it were, to shout.

Back in Boston, because in the nineteenth century issues of race and class were often conflated, and because New Englanders of Puritan stock thought of themselves as distinctly "a race apart" and at *all* class levels–from New Yorkers–the disdain of many a Back Bay matron for Isabella Gardner was exactly analogous to that of Boston's German Jews for Berenson. That Gardner and Berenson understood this at some level, moreover, is suggested by the fact that in each case that disdain was a spur to achievement.

Consider Martin Smith's words. The purpose of expressing forthrightly our feelings, Smith insists, is, "not to convey information." (That Berenson was Jewish, for example, or Gardner of ambiguous social background or Santayana homosexual, was widely known.) Rather the purpose of being honest about feelings is "to bring them out of the safe realm of the unspoken and deal with them in the open–to stop trying to please the oppressor, as it were." Similarly, our interlocutor does "not seek information, but to bring the truth out of our hearts." It is only when "a loved one dies without warning," Smith explains, to cite a universal instance, or, to cite an example more exact to this discussion, when gay people learn that they are "welcome at [their] parents' home, even with their companions, only on the condition that complete silence is maintained on the subject of homosexuality" that we begin to realize that "what goes unsaid has enormous power. An iceberg moves not because the wind blows upon its surface, but because its vast bulk hidden beneath the water is moved by the currents of the depths,"[55] depths historians can clarify after all by study: to whatever extent a historical figure can be shown to have *cooperated* with the time-honored defense mechanism of the majority culture to invariably cast suspect individuals as trying (wanting? needing?) *to* please, to *pass*–whether a Jew as a gentile, a homosexual as heterosexual, or even a black as white (even a New Yorker as a Bostonian!)–to that extent self-loathing is indicated. Did Berenson cooperate? Did Gardner expect him to? Did *she* cooperate? With Adams, in retrospect, Berenson seems frank enough. But at the time, in the late 1880s and early 1890s, with Gardner? Therein lies the truth of the matter.

Yet it may generally be said that as a student at Harvard it does not seem that Berenson sought to avoid the subject of his Jewishness: he focused on it, indeed, and on exactly its most controversial aspect, when in his senior year at Harvard he submitted to the *Harvard Monthly* a story (published after his graduation) entitled, "The Death and Burial of Israel Koppel," which is about an apostate Jew who forsakes his Jewish character and in consequence draws down divine wrath.[56] It may have even been one of the undergraduate articles of that year he is known to have sent Gardner, and even if it was not, it is fascinating to note the first sentence of his first letter to Gardner when she became his patron, from Europe: "My dear Mrs. Gardner," he writes, "I wonder whether you have already received a book that I mailed to you. . . . I wish you to read the introductory essay, especially, written by a person born not many miles from my natal home."[57] That was the village of Butrimonys, of course, where

Bernard was not Bernard Berenson but Bernard Valvrojenski, about which Berenson, according to Samuels, always recommended anyone interested in his childhood to read one or more of four books he especially cherished, each of which emphasized variously the "humble round of life in a Polish village," the varied makings of "Jewish family [life] ... centered on the village synagogue," the long "ten-hour days" of boys in Hebrew school, and "the poverty and oppression ... of the ghetto."[58] All emphasized Jewishness. And it was one of these, H. A. Sienkiewicz's *Bartek*, Berenson not only suggested Gardner read but made it all but impossible for her not to read by his making her a gift of it. It was, he wrote her, so "true of myself in so many different ways that it seemed to me a confession written by myself."[59] A confession he insisted she read!

Is this frankness surprising? Certainly Gardner as muse and mentor seems to have had a liberating effect especially on Bunker (who only she could coax out of his depressions) and on Dwight and Proctor (whose moving "coming-out" correspondence has already been quoted) and on Jephson. So, too, it would seem with Berenson! Perhaps that is what Samuels means when he admits without explanation that "Berenson felt *curiously reassured* [emphasis added] of his identity in [Gardner's] presence."[60] With Gardner, Berenson was content to be himself; wherever else he may have felt the need to "pass," Gardner never signaled any desire for him to try and in fact would have disdained any such behavior.

Smith's analysis of the effect on the individual speaker or hearer, contemporary or posterity–of "trying to pass" and thus to cooperate with the culture of self-loathing and secrecy, explains as well how the historical record can have so warped our understanding of Isabella Gardner a century later that her instinct for social freedom–what we'd call today an inclusive society–comes now as so much of a surprise generally. Particularly, does it explain why all memory has been seemingly obliterated not just of Berenson's part in Boston's overall history (and, equally, in the city's Jewish history), but of Isabella Gardner's involvement in Boston's black history.[61]

◆

It is a sad commentary on many things that in the earliest biography of Gardner the only mention of her role in black history falls under the category of what is called her enjoyment of "red-blooded vulgarity"; by which was meant a show called "The Red Moon," put on by "octoroons" named Cole and Johnson who Gardner is said to have admired "not only for their sincerity but the way they put their feet down."[62]

In fact, the black American composer and singer, John R. Johnson, Robert Cole's partner, was most unlikely to have been in any way "vulgar"; he held a degree from the New England Conservatory of Music, his music appeared in Broadway shows of the period, and he enjoyed an international reputation, responsible as he was with Cole in the early 1900s in helping to "establish a new direction for Negro musical theatre," in Eileen Southern's words, "by discarding the minstrel show format and writing in operetta style." Johnson's famous song, "Lift Every Voice and Sing," is still widely felt to be a sort of African-American national anthem. Indeed, Edward Perry went so far as to write, in Nancy Cunard's *Negro*, that "perhaps no Negro musician has done as much for the musical advancement of his people as J. Rosamond Johnson."[63] Another fact, that the tenor Roland Hayes (the first black to appear as soloist with a major symphony orchestra, Boston's) sang also for Gardner in her music room, is not even mentioned in that or any other biographical sketch of Isabella Gardner.[64] Yet the fact was she was very interested in African-American music, whether it be the new Negro theater of Cole and Johnson or the spirituals interpreted (along with, one may be sure, German lieder) by Hayes.

To see the context for this interest, and how deep-seated and long-standing it was—and how comparable to her sympathies with Ireland and Japan, two small indigenous island cultures by then much endangered—it is only necessary to read a letter like Gardner's of 1884 from India about "a native, a beautiful, tall, lithe, Hindu strolling by . . . singing to himself or his god such a weird, soft strain";[65] not very different was her interest thirty years later in the African-American folk songs sung by Gerald Murphy to her, when that collector of folk songs (among many other artistic avocations) was brought to Gardner by Sargent and Loeffler for a private recital they knew would be welcome.

It was while Murphy, later so identified with Fitzgerald and Hemingway and Paris in the 1920s, was a student at Harvard that he had "discovered in the Boston Public Library the text of many songs sung by Southern Negroes before the Civil War (songs at that time unpublished anywhere, such as . . . 'Sometimes I Feel Like a Motherless Child')."[66] Later, in Paris, he and his wife would sing them for Erik Satie; in Boston they sang their repertoire for Gardner, in two-part harmony, and responded to her interest by sending her by way of thanks H. E. Krehbiel's pioneering *Afro-American Folksongs*.[67] This seminal book was by a white musicologist, who in the wake of W. E. B. Du Bois' *Souls of Black Folk* (in which Du Bois argued that the Jewish Psalter was the only analogue to these black spirituals), was the first serious musical analysis of this newly emerging black American folk music, which appropriately enough found its way in this period even into the Western classical tradition through Dvorak's "Symphony from the New World."[68]

That Gardner's attention to all this was more than casual is also suggested by her acquaintance with the Australian composer and pianist (whom she may have met through Busoni, one of his teachers, or Loeffler, a friend) Percy Grainger, a free spirit if ever there was one, who while he was a pioneer in the study of new sonorities also was a lifelong student and collector of folksong, whether of Iceland or Zanzibar, work commemorated today in the Grainger Museum, founded as an ethnomusicological research center at the University of Melbourne. The nature of Gardner's and Grainger's relationship is not clear but a surviving letter from him to her is significant: "I am sending you four of the Negro choruses by Negro composers you were interested in at our last delightful meeting," he wrote, "and I have marked with a blue cross the pages or bits I thought might interest you."[69] Clearly, he expected her to study the music!

Krehbiel, Grainger, Loeffler, and Isabella Gardner and their common interest in African-American music are part of a too-long-obscured pattern in Boston's cultural history, already evident here in Gardner's patronage of Cole and Johnson. Significantly, moreover, Loeffler, the musician most closely identified with Gardner, would later be, for all his "classical" credentials, conspicuous among American composers for his interest in jazz.[70]

Interestingly Isabella Gardner seems to have registered more generally on Boston's black community just as the John L. Sullivan encounter and the North End slum visit indicate she registered similarly on the Irish and Italian immigrant communities. Witness a news report of 1894 that a particular black leader, Lillian Lewis, was called "The Mrs. Jack Gardner of Her People" because Lewis was able to mediate between "two distinct, fashionable rival sets," possessing, it was said, "the independence and dominance that enabled her to set rather than to follow protocol—traits so characteristic of Isabella Stewart Gardner."[71]

Gardner's deepest involvement in Boston's African-American commu-nity was at the intersection of art and religion, so precious to her, though here again her interests centered on yet another suspect group (as sus-pect to the bigoted with their stereotypes as "cultivated" Jews, "athletic" gays, "refined" Irish Catholics)—black Episcopalians—yet another aspect of the result of Gardner's ongoing commitment to the Cowley Fathers,

St. Augustine's Church, designed by Clipston Sturgis, built by the Cowley Fathers for Boston's black community, and completed through Gardner's generosity. *Society of St. John the Evangelist Archives*

who ministered actively to Beacon Hill's black community. Led by Fathers Arthur Hall and Charles Field and their then novice Charles Brent, of whom more later, in association with the Sisters of St. Margaret, the Cowleys spearheaded in the 1880s and 1890s an active ministry to African-Americans dedicated to St. Augustine, that greatest of the African saints. On Beacon Hill they built in 1892 on Phillips Street St. Augustine's Church; nearby in 1895 they founded St. Augustine's Trade School, the outreach of which was widely influential in improving slum conditions; and in suburban Foxborough in 1900 they started St. Augustine's Farm for Colored Children.[72]

The Beacon Hill Church, a two-towered Italianate structure designed by R. Clipston Sturgis, the distinguished architect (in the wake of his uncle, John Hubbard Sturgis) of the Church of the Advent itself, was the centerpiece then of St. Augustine Ministries, as it is called today, and it was Isabella Stewart Gardner's generosity that made possible the completion of this large church[73] where, in 1894, the first African-American was ordained to the priesthood in the Episcopal Church in Boston,[74] a fact (when I observed its significance with respect to Isabella Gardner) that at once reminded me of when I first read in Trevor J. Fairbrother's seminal study of Sargent about his portrait of Thomas E. McKeller: for "this most intimate work of Sargent,"[75] in Fairbrother's words, a portrait in oils that must rank among the most strikingly beautiful works of that master, who seemingly painted every crowned head and merchant prince and social leader of the era, is not only manifestly homosexual in feeling, but depicts a bellman of a Boston hotel who was African-American. It is not the image we have of John Singer Sargent any more than St. Augustine's is our image of Isabella Gardner.

There is, furthermore, an interesting footnote to all this: Gardner's contribution to Boston's black history, so long overlooked, has sustained itself in a wonderfully underground way in that while old St. Augustine's Church had to be torn down to build the subway to Harvard Square, and St. Augustine's was merged with another black church in Boston's South End, Gardner's old high altar was transferred to St. Martin's, where an altarpiece for another altar was painted by a Boston artist whose work has long declared both his African-American roots and Anglo-Catholic beliefs, both nurtured by the Cowleys, Allan Rohan Crite, some of whose earliest memories (and sketches) date from a childhood visit to see Gardner's art collection early in this century, where he recalls Boston's by then leading patron of the arts inviting his mother to tea.[76]

Some of Gardner's friends foresaw what she was up to, including Congressman Piatt Andrew, who wrote to her once that, following her advice, he had gone to see, "Cole and Johnson in the 'Red Moon'–and come back so flurried with the merits of the show that I have been sending all of male Washington [to see it]. The theater is one to which female Washington could not go without being utterly emancipated." Having clearly understood Gardner's purposes, Andrew concluded his letter to her simply enough: "so the bread you cast upon the waters is helping Cole and Johnson to keep alive."[77]

That Isabella Stewart Gardner, legendary patron of the arts that she would become, not only numbered St. Augustine's but Cole and Johnson as well as Sargent or Loeffler among those she sustained, will doubtless surprise many. Indeed, there is also an unverified but persistent tradition that the Black Madonna at St. John's, Bowdoin Street, which may date from the fifteenth century, was given to the Cowley Fathers by Isabella Stewart Gardner.[78] As it turned out, Gardner's mentor, Julia Ward Howe, was not the only reformer to live on Beacon Street.

8

The White Rose

IN 1888 ISABELLA Stewart Gardner made one of her now lesser known appearances in American literature, in a book by the then quite popular novelist Arlo Bates. Entitled *The Puritans*, the title really says it all and Gardner, of course, was not cast as one of them. Nothing curious there. But Bates should have known better than to have the "scarcely fictionalized Mrs. Jack Gardner go from a posh Mardi Gras ball," in B. Hughes Morris' words, "to a Midnight Mass at a thinly disguised Church of the Advent on the Eve of Lent."[1] Gardner (though evidently not Bates) would have known better: Anglo-Catholics have never had midnight masses the night before Ash Wednesday, and by the late 1880s Gardner was ardently invested in that religious tradition–the beginning, so to speak, of another pilgrimage, one that bridges many apparently disparate strains in her life, and discloses particularly well her type of feminism.

Perhaps the most characteristic and exotic aspect in the spectrum of her religious interests was the Order of the White Rose,[2] a Jacobite-Anglican society (its name derived from the badge of the royal house of Stuart, with which Gardner identified all her life, naturally enough) whose purposes, at least in America, were more cultural and religious than political, though a more Hamiltonian than Jeffersonian cast to the proceedings is sometimes detectable. Its Boston members (though the society was well established in Britain, no other American branches are known to have existed) promoted the cult in the Episcopal Church of

Charles I, martyred under Cromwell and later canonized. Members undertook antiquarian studies for example and formed notable Jacobite collections (Gardner herself bought a magnificent Book of Hours thought to have belonged to Mary, Queen of Scots), and the group had a small but significant influence in its day while arousing no little ridicule and controversy. Van Wyck Brooks, for instance, protested heatedly that two of the most striking features of Harvard and Boston life in the 1890s, as he put it, was "the cult of Dante, which Mrs. Gardner also embraced [and the] semi-serious cult . . . [of the] Order of the White Rose," the second of which, he insisted, was yet another attempt of an increasingly diverse culture "to expunge all remnants of the Puritan past."[3] A large task indeed! But it could not be denied that this Jacobite group was made up of rather militant high church Episcopalians fueled by an ardent anti-Puritanism that was more and more politically charged in the changing Boston of the fin-de-siècle and played into Gardner's broader religious interests quite well.

It may seem at first glance that Anglo-Catholicism would be very much at odds with the broad-minded and increasingly inclusive philosophy I have contended here was characteristic of Isabella Gardner, but it must be remembered that the gays, Jews, Irish, Italians, and blacks Gardner was identified with all shared with her some important aspect of her world view, usually artistic or religious; neither racist nor sexist nor homophobic, Gardner nonetheless had strong beliefs and opinions and many could be characterized as, in the best sense of that now much abused word, traditionalist. Anglo-Catholicism, furthermore, was in the 1880s and 1890s much more progressive than it later became in the twentieth century. And what John Reed has called the "counter cultural themes in the Anglo-Catholic program [that] help[ed] to account not only for its opposition but *for its support* [emphasis added]"[4] ranged from such major developments as the emergence in the Episcopal Church of independent, female-led, orders of sisters as an alternative to marriage, to such perhaps minor but telling attacks on the patriarchal Victorian family as private confession by a woman to a man (only men could then be priests) not usually her husband. The distinction between Roman and Anglican Catholicism is key. Among Anglo-Catholic intellectuals "the dominant theology from the 1880's until the 1930's was a *liberal* Catholicism [emphasis added],"[5] David Hilliard has written, generally taking a more progressive view of such things as biblical criticism, Darwinism and feminism and more favorably disposed towards the newly emerging construction of homosexuality.

Here is to close a critical circle indeed in Isabella Gardner's life, explaining finally why Gardner, far from being drawn by her religion to public penances for sins heterosexual or homosexual, by her *or* her friends, was instead led by Anglican teaching–and more intimately by the guidance of the Cowley Fathers–to see her own family experience of gay men as not only encouraging her broad-minded views but also as stimulating her to be supportive; all this within the context of what Hilliard concludes is a definite historical "correlation between Anglo-Catholicism and homosexuality." It was a correlation at the heart of which was "an affinity of outlook between a sexual minority and a minority religious movement [that in Victorian times encouraged gays to] express their difference in an oblique and symbolic way [that was] a socially more acceptable type of rebellion."[6] In other words, seen in this context, Gardner's circle can be seen for what it was, historically: an example of the first stage of discreet gay rebellion in the emergence of the modern construction of homosexuality, a stage historians now see as a precursor to the later stage of gay anger and militancy that eventually yielded our own era of what is sometimes called gay liberation. If Gardner led the way in Boston, which because of the city's importance as an intellectual center had a wider national effect, it was not just her family history that led her: that coincided with and was shaped and disciplined by her "conservative" Anglo-Catholic religious tradition, to which, of course, precisely because of her family history, she had earnest recourse for guidance.

Consider the three leaders of the Order of the White Rose in Boston. Fred Holland Day,[7] a pioneer of American art photography of a highly homoerotic kind and a herald both of the aesthete and decadent movements (he was Oscar Wilde's American publisher), was at the extreme left of the gay continuum in Boston. Socially awkward and effeminate, a loose cannon if ever there was one, Day was never close to Gardner. On the other hand, the distinguished Irish Catholic poet Louise Imogene Guiney, so splendid a character she has been called "the first modern nun,"[8] so much does the women's movement and ecumenicism owe to her, was very much Gardner's friend: daughter of a *Republican* Irish Catholic Civil War general (there again is Gardner's "liberal" ethnic inclusivity coupled with her "conservative" political beliefs), Guiney was progressive and outspoken, but traditional in belief. The "liaison officer" between Gardner and the Beacon Street intelligentsia generally and Boston's younger, largely gay Beacon Hill bohemia, Guiney, a lesbian, was as different from Day as WAG was from Archie Coolidge.

The third and chief leader of the White Rose was a young architect and art critic in the 1880s of the prestigious *Boston Evening Transcript*, Ralph Adams Cram,[9] who became in later years the greatest American church architect of the twentieth century, and always shared not only Jacobite sympathies and architectural affinities, but a whole world view, with the Boston Anglo-Catholic scene. So much so Peter Gomes of Harvard has written: "It is in the ecclesiastical Gothic of Ralph Adams Cram, examples of which are often called 'sensuous,' that the Anglo-Catholic aesthetic sensibility and homosexual devotee blend in something of a Trinitarian evocation of beauty both furtive and at the same time flamboyant: beautiful buildings, beautiful music, beautiful men."[10] Always, these have been of Anglo-Catholicism the outward and visible signs, though of what inward and spiritual grace not everyone is prepared to say!

Cram first surfaced in Gardner's circle in 1890 when he was commissioned to design an elaborate stone credence as a companion piece to the towering stone screen of traceried saints erected over the high altar of the Church of the Advent at that time by Isabella Gardner from the design of Sir Ernest George[11] and Harold Peto,[12] the second of whom was introduced to Gardner by Henry James in just the terms we are enmeshed in here: "I have just given a letter to you to the beautiful Harold Peto, . . . a good friend of mine. He is a young architect, held in considerable esteem professionally here and much liked personally, though—but you will discover the 'though'—it won't mystify you."[13]

The "though" does not seem hard to fathom: Peto, who never married, was a Harrow man, a friend of Sargent's as well as James', thirty-six years old in 1890 and, unusually, was as interested in landscape design as in building. He was warmly welcomed by Gardner and her set and his trip to America had a decisive effect on him. And Isabella Gardner influenced Peto's architectural work as she would influence Cram's. Indeed, for Peto she was a kind of transatlantic muse, engaging with the young Britisher at what turned out to be a turning point in his career as he prepared to part company with Ernest George and launch out on his own. Much impressed by American Italianate design, Peto was greatly stimulated by Gardner herself; her introduction to Peto of her close friend, the artist she saw so much of in Venice, Ralph Curtis, offered Peto the opportunity he needed: for Peto would design for Curtis the first of a notable series of houses and gardens in the south of France, while Gardner's own aesthetic clearly influenced Peto in the interiors he designed for Illford Manor, his own house. Whether or not Peto ever propped up a reproduction of Sargent's portrait of Gardner against his drafting board, one thinks again of the desk in the study at Medfield, which did boast such a picture, and where Loeffler and Bunker did such good work. Thus in architecture and horticulture, in Peto's work as in Cram's, and in the music and painting of Loeffler and Bunker, in the environs of Boston or London or wherever, Gardner's influence was felt. After Peto's return to Britain Henry James reported back to Gardner that whenever her name came up "the placid mirror of [Peto's] countenance seems literally to crack with enthusiasm."[14]

In introducing Peto to Isabella Gardner, James was somewhat returning the favor, for Gardner, one suspects, introduced a few finds of her own to James! One that is definitely known of is Gaillard Lapsley,[15] an intelligent and handsome young man with the necessary grace and strength and security of self and sophistication to respond to an older person's devotion; he became one of the great loves of James' later years. Gardner had first met Lapsley when he was a student in Santayana's circle at Harvard; recall, too, that it was Gardner, as we've seen, who in all likelihood introduced Bunker to Sargent, and Sargent to Loeffler—and so on. Isabella Gardner was as much interested in matchmaking in people as in art and architecture. And she had more than one triumph to boast of in both respects, including a role (probably as donor) in yet another Cowley high altar reredos at St. John's, Bowdoin Street, Cram's own parish church, where this time his commission was not just for a credence table but the entire altar screen.

The artist for this work was Martin Mower,[16] one of Gardner's most cherished protégés, so much so she once sponsored a sale for profit of his works in her music room. A Harvard graduate who stayed on after taking his degree as an instructor in fine arts, as a painter Mower was best known for architectural art still to be found from Fifth Avenue salons to Palm Beach villas. Like Peto, Mower was a bachelor, and, as Louis Kirstein recalled, picturesque enough: "square-cut head, crowned *en brosse* by pepper and salt, and [with a] bristling trim mustache . . . Shetland-wool jacket, a burgundy scarf secured by a big garnet, suede shoes buckled in squared silver clad him in High-bohemian attire"; but, to the contrary of the image we are apt to form of Isabella Gardner's protégés, he was distinctly a severe and demanding artist-teacher–"by a brief, aphoristic phrasing," Kirstein, once his student, remembered, Mower "bent a careless attack; curt, prickly responses, distilled from a lifetime of looking, would every so often ignite and accelerate my innocent brain. How dared Martin Mower, a leftover . . . challenge . . . Manet? Much of this persiflage was Socratic goading." Nor was the hand and spirit of Isabella Gardner far away, as Kirstein's description of Mower's studio makes plain:

> He dwelt in a delectable house, up an unmarked alley off Brattle Street [near Harvard Square]. His large, sky-lit studio was tiled in dull red. . . . The proportions of the room were strict as in a Vermeer. . . . Light was controlled by linen shutters. Two sturdy oak easels . . . claimed that it was canny to play more than one game at a time. Dogged, doltish industry was exiled, his milieu spoke delight. . . . finished or unfinished canvases were stacked slant against his walls . . . of which Mrs. Gardner owned several. . . . [and] the room was perfumed by potted orange trees, bougainvillea, blue plumbago, and drooping nasturtium.[17]

The nasturtium was also from Gardner–from her legendary greenhouses–and its perfume and Gardner's stacked canvases against the studio wall presided over by an artist so peppery is an image that deserves to stand with that of Peto's London studio or Cram's in Boston or Loeffler's and Bunker's country living room as compassing the diversity of Gardner's influence.

Yet multiplying the many evidences of the influence Gardner had on individual artists by no means explains her success as muse and mentor, so likely to be overshadowed by her later work as collector and designer. It was in the nature of things that her mentoring role is hard to assess. In suggesting, for instance, that the work of Berenson and the other Boston aesthetes of the 1880s–1890s was more important in the long haul than even Oscar Wilde's ("the intentions as well as the dimensions of their work were more massive") Martin Green queried:

> was it that [the Boston aesthetes] were more intelligent as individuals? I doubt if Berenson at least was; it was, rather, that he belonged to a more intelligent community [than did Wilde] and had a better

idea of his historical role: he could guide himself by Henry James and Henry Adams, Mrs. Wharton and Mrs. Gardner . . . . I Tatti was another Fenway Court. . . . it was left to Harvard as a serious cultural monument . . . Wilde had no guides of comparable weight.

One does not have to share Green's view of the relative importance of Wilde's work and that of Berenson and the Boston aesthetes generally to see the merit in Green's insight that "the most characteristic-relationship [these Boston aesthetes] shared (because, wrote Green boldly, "all had a feminine streak in their natures"!) was with [Charles Eliot] Norton's former students, Mrs. Gardner and Mrs. Wharton."[18] That in turn points not only to Gardner's role in Boston's emerging gay subculture of the time, but to her role in the equally fundamental sea change represented by the city's increasing ethnic diversity and the emerging women's movement. And in Isabella Gardner's own life this last points us, first and foremost, back toward religion.

◆

Isabella Gardner was sufficiently a figure in religious circles in Boston that her role in the life of that city's Episcopalians was central to the quite popular novel by Arlo Bates already referred to here, *The Puritans*. Her own religion—under her own name—was also counted sufficiently newsworthy as to have been itself the subject of a newspaper profile by the mid-1890s which focused particularly on her devotion to the Church of the Advent: "The fine reredos [she has given is one] proof of affection, but of not half so much real interest to the parishioners generally as the sight of her handsome brougham standing at the door, with its prancing horses, staid coachman and dapper little footman, or of the well known figure seated Sunday after Sunday [in church]. In Lent," the report ended, "several times a week she dons a raiment of sackcloth, or its modern substitute, serge, and goes to clean the brasses in the chancel."[19]

In fact, as head of the altar guild, usually a prosaic enough task, Gardner brought to the tasks of arranging hangings and flowers a fecund imagination that presaged a certain later achievement, and hardly stopped there, if one recalls the stylish habits she designed as well as the Maundy washing ceremony she choreographed, which amounted to something like women's liturgical theater, after all, and was hardly less elaborate than the all-male performances (as they then were, before the ordination of women) during services! Today, of course, we react with skepticism to such ostentatious seeming public piety. Yet to be those things in religion was so consistent with the rest of Gardner's lifestyle as to argue convincingly for her sincerity. Indeed, there seemed no bounds at all to her forwardness: not even with the pope, by whom when she was in Rome in 1894 she was received in private audience. Though deeply impressed, she reputedly did not hesitate to talk back even to Leo XIII, famously anti-Anglican, when he asked her if she was Catholic: "*Anglican* Catholic," she retorted,[20] with the same passion Carter reported she showed during Holy Week in Seville in 1888:

> at all the ceremonies and pageants of the Easter season, Mrs. Gardner had been conscious of more than the superficial show; much as she enjoyed that, she was herself so sincere that, if it had been only a show staged to attract travelers, she would have hated it. Even an elaborate procession can be conducted with a spirit of simplicity, expressing the pleasure and the inherited faith of the participants; only so could it interest her. Her own emotions were so deep and possessed her so completely that she quickly detected the shallowness of mere organization and saw only its defects. The realism of the Spanish images was an expression of simple honesty of belief, and with her whole heart, Mrs. Gardner believed.[21]

That greatest, perhaps, of the Spanish saints, Ignatius of Loyola, the Jesuit founder, probably figured closely in Gardner's spiritual life. Chivalric and spirited, even merry, "characterized by great-heartedness, generosity, 'nobless,' even during his youth," and as a religious figure still "longing for nobility and distinction" in his maturity, Ignatius was in important respects very much like Gardner's ideal man![22] And her reactions in Seville in 1888 were similar to those when she visited the tomb of St. Francis Xavier on her Asian tour of 1883.[23] Given Gardner's intensity of passion and the Cowley Fathers' strong affinity for Ignatian spirituality—and, indeed, with the traditional Jesuit division of the spiritual life between two distinct roads: "one for ordinary folk, . . . the other for extraordinary folk who might be led to God by extraordinary ways about which the less said the better"[24]—it can be conjectured that Gardner's prayer life was as spirited and intense, even as flamboyant as the rest of her life.

In fact, Gardner surely would have responded keenly to two aspects particularly of the Ignatian meditation schemes: first, as put by W. H. Longridge, the Cowley Father who first translated them into English, the way "the outline of the course of the Exercises is [derived from] the Epistle to the Hebrews [with its strongly athletic image of] run[ning] with patience the race that is set before us"; second, the way the exercises seek to activate the *vista imaginativa*—the forming through the imagination of visual and therefore artistic images in the mind in order to better identify with Christ.[25] That Gardner's faith was receptive to such visual imagery is surely clear from one of her most vivid religious experiences, in 1897, when at another outdoor procession, this time in Venice, she was relieved of a pain so acute she had not been able to stand up straight until, as the Madonna of San Stefano passed before her, she was healed as the result of her maid's prayer.[26]

A more prosaic way to discern spiritual authenticity is to look for consistency in religion between public profile and private practice. Her repute in this respect was actually rather good. Even Arlo Bates, in *The Puritans*, a very anti–Anglo-Catholic novel, urges that though politic and cynical (she is cast as a notorious "mother confessor" to Cowley novices and her pride in the Advent's liturgy is likened to that of "a manager whose tenor succeeds in opera") she was sincere in her religion. It is a view not contradicted, now we can peruse them, by what remains of her private papers. From these it is clear that she tried to be strict in private discipline, fasting and meditating before Mass, for instance, and that she had an oratory for private prayer off her bedroom, all but unknown to others.[27] And we know too the contents of her private library, which includes many religious works, books by George Herbert, F. D. Maurice, Thomas à Kempis (a book of special importance to her she is known at least once to have made a present of to a close friend), St. Francis de Sales and William James (this last the most underlined of them all!)—and, found after her death in the prie-dieu in her private chapel, *A Treasury of the Psalter* and the *New Testament*, in which were several letters from various of the Cowley Fathers she was closest to.

In the 1880s and early 1890s the closest would have been her likely confessor, Arthur Crawshay Hall. An Englishman, possessed of a "tall and striking figure [with a] deep and powerful voice,"[28] Hall was both handsome and brilliant. A graduate of Christ Church, Oxford, he had come to Boston with the Cowley Fathers in 1874 and eventually led the

Boston community of the society. Notable for his ministry to young men, Hall was a popular preacher at Harvard, Williams, and Princeton and also at New England's leading prep schools like Groton and St. Paul's, where he never hesitated to establish the most informal relationships, even doffing his cassock to join the boys in their sports.[29] On the other hand, he had little patience with the sanctimonious sort monks often attract. When, for instance, "an officious lady had provided for him a [kneeling] hassock which he loathed," a colleague remembered Hall "kicked it several feet across the room." He was just the man for Isabella Gardner![30]

A number of Hall's letters to her survive in her papers and his direct, no-nonsense requests for money for financial aid of all sorts, and Gardner's openhanded response, as well as her concerns for his health and consequent invitations to rest up at her country estate, all argue for a close mutual understanding and sympathy—as, above all, does the fact—utterly overlooked and ignored until now—that this Oxford graduate's most widely read book of readings was dedicated to Isabella Gardner[31]—a dedication as key to understanding Gardner's role in Boston as the many better-known dedications of literary and musical works to her of which so much is always made. One of Hall's letters to her may be taken as characteristic in touching on more than just money in Gardner's involvement:

> Father Osborne has told me today of a case to which your alms would exactly apply. A little girl named *Bella Manning*, child of a struggling mother in the North End (with a drinking father who spends a good deal of time on the island) was run over by a coaster & is in the Masstts Hospital (*Ward 30*, will you see her?)
>
> During the 6 weeks or so that she is there the mother loses her wages .75 a week, wh. will be really a great loss. Wd you like to give the money to the child to hand (as her wages still) to the mother, or send it by us![32]

Note the clear understanding that Gardner was likely to visit these people herself. Like Grainger's expectation she would study the black music he sent her, Hall's expectation underlies the fact that Gardner did not just write checks and then dress up for the opera, as it were.

An interesting counterpoint to her straightforward charity is evident in her confiding of her philosophy of life once to a friend, Count

Coudenhove, as he remembered well enough to remind her of many years later: "one evening (you had a black dress on) in the fresco ceilinged salon of your palazzo, you denied the existence of merit, sacrifice. You said: 'If a man does a thing, he does it because he likes it, otherwise he would not do it. There is nothing meritorious in doing a thing which one likes to do.'"[33] What a different light this casts on her charities! And how refreshing. Declared at the height of her prime, in her fifties in the 1880s, and not gainsaid by her in her eighties, how does one explain such a belief by a woman whose place in history, even now when her gifts as a designer are coming to be more acknowledged, will probably always rest primarily on her roles of patron and donor, muse and mentor! For an Anglo-Catholic to seem to colonize Nietzsche (whose correspondence with Wagner, by the way, a close friend once gave her) is rather startling. But Gardner was by then too old a hand for that. More likely, friend to and close reader of William James that she was, and to Santayana too, whose *The Sense of Beauty* of 1896 "anticipated Freudian theory"[34] in John McCormick's words, Gardner was being herself proto-Freudian, as well as reflecting her fecund Ignatian imagination.

No secrets of the confessional are at hand to help us here. But Hall's effect on his lifelong best friend, Charles Brent, a Cowley novice who went on to be an Episcopal bishop and an international ecumenical leader, may be instructive. Because he was a spiritual figure whose inner life by the standards of those days could more properly be publicly scrutinized, his biographer ventured an appraisal that seems applicable to Gardner, for all its masculine imagery. (Gardner, after all, was as keen on sports as Brent, an outstanding athlete.) "The constituents of Brent's being were discordant...." wrote his biographer. "Limitless spiritual aspiration and a painfully acute conscience fought with physical appetites, pride [and] ... a strong man's desire to have his own way and a hot temper." Brent knew, apparently, periods of "abysmal depression" as well as "heights of ecstasy," and he was able to hold himself firm only by "captivating increasingly his imagination and emotions ... It was because Hall ... fired him to espouse this idea [and] taught him the necessary discipline ... that Brent felt under such profound obligation to him."[35]

Gardner's personality was very like Brent's, and so too may have been her debt to Hall, who would certainly have expected of Gardner what really is the supreme validation of her religious sincerity, a virtue we know of very dependably, moreover, by way of that old cynic Santayana:

Gardner, he wrote, "though she defied prudery, practiced the virtue most difficult for a brilliant woman in a hostile society: she spoke ill of nobody."[36] It is a virtue many saints have hardly achieved! Feuds imputed to Gardner usually, in fact, turn out to have been mainly prosecuted by others: Mary Cassatt did call Isabella Gardner a "poseur" to Louisine Havemeyer and Berenson did aver that the Havemeyers had "no real taste," while the Potter Palmers, "Monets by the yard cover[ing] the walls," lived in a house that looked like "an incredibly extravagant brothel."[37] But on all these subjects Gardner herself said nothing, and it would seem Santayana was correct that despite her volatile, outspoken personality, she really did join "kindness to liberty." If kindness be equated with Christianity–to do to others as you would have them do to you–and liberty with Bohemianism, there is another example, not only of Gardner's consistency across the board, but of her brilliant reach. And so to the most flamboyant example of her feminism.

◆

Ellery Sedgwick, the *Atlantic* editor already heard from before here as a boy in a gym at Groton, who in adulthood became a friend of Gardner's, ventured in his memoirs an even greater leap, reminiscent of the one cited at this chapter's opening by Bates in *The Puritans*, but more daring because not just from frolic to religiosity in aid of remorse but in Sedgwick's case from sports to art and religion by way of explanation for, of all things! the high altar screen Gardner gave the Church of the Advent. Wrote Sedgwick of Isabella Gardner:

> I have spoken of her inheritance direct from the Renaissance. The Lord, I verily believe, had not shaped another like her these four hundred years. She was profoundly, sometimes ecstatically, religious and she was without a worldly scruple. Her favorite saying: "Don't spoil a good story by telling the truth," had in it more than whimsical significance. What she wanted, that she would have.... She loved physical pre-eminence, the grace and symmetry of young athletes. One day when she did me the honor to dine at my table long after she was seventy, she told me the history of the day before. She had risen at six, caught a football train for New Haven at eight, watched the thrilling game, applauded the victors, returned in a crowded coach of rollicking, hurrahing boys, and then had refreshed herself

by going out to supper. There was no sacrifice she would not make to Beauty. She would pinch herself to the extremity of economy. She would go without her carriage; she would live . . . almost on a diet of herbs, but the magical canvas, the inspired bust, the glass of Chartres, the ruby that men must have died for, and the three great ropes of pearls which hung to her waist, these things she enjoyed, she adored, and out of the fullness of her joy would thank God for them, and in His Holy Name make offering to His Church of the intricate loveliness of a marble reredos.[38]

The high altar reredos Isabella Gardner gave the Church of the Advent.
Private Collection

Considering this towering altar screen today, two stories of Flemish Gothic as overpowering, almost, as Sedgwick's rather breathless prose poem in explanation of its splendor, it must be said that if it is not the most famous work of art commissioned by Gardner (the first Sargent portrait of her is that), the Advent reredos uniquely offers the viewer today the chance to stretch his or her mind so as to try and compass Gardner's own imaginative reach, only in the first place from sports to religion, perhaps seeing, as I think Gardner did, in the vivid and stately medieval pageantry of a choral High Mass swirling before and beneath her Advent reredos a Gothic religious spectacle that was something of a parallel to the more raucous classical pageantry and color of a football game in the colonnaded, coliseum-like Harvard Stadium she also often attended. Both reredos and stadium were visual backdrops which even in our era of the giant video screen retain their force and conviction.

Most telling of all is that looked at with knowing eyes, it is possible to see in the Advent altar screen, if not, strictly, a rebus, then certainly a kind of map, so little coded it hardly seems a riddle, of what was in the mind of Isabella Gardner when she and Peto conceived it. It is all there: her wealth, her pride, her downright egotism, her artistic and questing nature, her materialism, her spirituality, her love of history, her search always for the ideal (especially in a man!), her cares and causes, religious and secular, her open-mindedness and, above all, her vivid romantic feminism.

The altar screen is in three stages. In the first stage design and meaning center on a sculpted relief of the crucified Christ midpoint in a long frieze just above and behind the altar, but the small figures that immediately flank Christ, the Madonna and St. John the Evangelist, expand this foundational meaning, as do the larger flanking figures that dominate the frieze at each end, figures that suggest the truth of Sedgwick's explanation of the background of this reredos being both a sincerely religious offering but of a quite worldly and personal kind: both figures are namesakes of Gardner: one St. Isabella of France, daughter of St. Louis, the other St. Elizabeth or Erzsebet of Hungary, Isabella, of course, being a variant of the English Elizabeth. Both figures are the earliest evidence of that fascination with the Isabellas of history (particularly the royal Isabellas!) for which Isabella Gardner became notorious at a later point among the art dealers of two continents. The figure of St. John, meanwhile, clearly representing the Cowley Fathers, whose patron saint he is, as well as Anglican monasticism generally (the revival of which in the late nineteenth century Isabella Gardner participated in as a Cowley associate and donor), and also the figure of St. George in the second stage of the reredos, representing Anglicanism generally, may be said to root all the reredos's themes historically.

Four of these themes stand out in this second stage: service to the poor finds its focus in the figure of St. Francis of Assisi; Cowley's mission to blacks particularly in Boston in the statue of St. Augustine; while St. George, paradigm of knightly courtesy and courage, surely stands too for ideal Christian manhood, while St. John, who is called the Beloved Disciple because of his special relationship with Christ (depicted traditionally by his leaning against Christ's bosom) surely represents the theme of particular friendship, a theme prominent in Arthur Hall's writings, where he taught in his "Gospel of Friendship" that the bonds of such friendship were comparable to and in some respects superior to the marriage vow between husband and wife, surely a reflection of that Oxford Hellenism of the period, as it has been called, which a century ago laid significant groundwork for a more positive social identity for homosexuality and eventually a greater openness to same-sex unions.[39]

In this second stage of the reredos a much less discreet gay subtext is also evident in the naked and bound figure of St. Sebastian, not because he is thought to have been homosexual, but because (and presumably this explains the homoerotic resonance of his naked depictions here and elsewhere) Sebastian became something of a cult figure in the late nineteenth century for gay men at a time when an increasingly self-identifying homosexual community was beginning to emerge. Perceived widely or not, the historical association is there. Similarly, though more problematically, the association is also there in the figure of St. Theresa of Avila, who according to Lawrence D. Mass, was also becoming in this era an icon for lesbian writers, as we now know from Corinne Blakmer's remarkable essay "The Ecstasies of St. Theresa."[40] Above all, however, Theresa is a key figure in the over-arching theme that dominates all else here—women in the life of the Church.

Consider the scheme of meaning and its symbolism. In the first stage of the screen, the lower altar frieze portion of 1882, as we have seen, women dominate through the fact that three of the four saints depicted are women. Similarly, in the second stage, women also dominate; in this case there are actually more male (four) than female saints (two) but it is the two women who are given pride of place and precedence in the center of each rank, flanked to each side and behind by the male figures. Both women, moreover, are distinctly women like Gardner: St. Barbara rather notoriously so, having always been the "patron saint of certain dangerous crafts and professions such as those of fireworks makers, artillerymen," and St. Theresa, one of only two women in all Christian history given the title of doctor (or theologian) of the Church, a woman who combined both the contemplative and active ministries, founded dozens of convents and her own branch of the Carmelite Order that by Gardner's time had spread all over the world. Significantly, in *The Second Sex*, Simone de Beauvoir ranks Theresa with St. Catherine and three legendary queens–Elizabeth of England, Catherine de Médicis, and Isabella of Spain, all of whom, she writes, rose "to heights that few men have ever reached."[41] Note also that Isabella Gardner is the namesake of two of these queens.

The third stage of the reredos centers on its two topmost figures, crowning the entire altar screen: the Madonna and the Angel of the Annunciation, brilliantly poised atop the two towers to either side of empty space and profound darkness (just dimly visible through the stone tiers of tracery), each to each other enacting not only the great moment when the gospel of Jesus Christ begins but the one moment in Christian history unarguably controlled by a woman, St. Mary, who seems here less the dutiful and passive icon of patriarchy and more (like Gardner herself!) a leader who in the face of God's challenge, as Hans Urs von Balthazar has said, shows "not passivity; [but] radical, active confidence," despite her puzzlement. Here St. Mary is truly the God Bearer, the Queen of Heaven, whose exaltation in modern Catholic teaching Jung called "the greatest religious event since the Reformation," seeing in it the "deification of the feminine of Heaven."[42]

Of course, there is a necessary context to be borne in mind here. As Gardner's involvement with gays, with Irish Catholics, with Jews, and with African-Americans has unfolded here, something has already been said of her involvement with women's issues. Mentored as Gardner was–though the fact has until now hardly been emphasized–by Julia Ward Howe, the American feminist leader, founder of both New England and national suffrage associations, anything else would be surprising. Whether it was Gardner's aid in the founding of Radcliffe by her friend, Elizabeth Cary Agassiz, the support Gardner gave to women involved in literary and cultural work like the novelist Sarah Orne Jewett, the artist Sarah Whitman, or the singer Nellie Melba, or Gardner's mentoring of such future female leaders as Maude Howe Elliott, who in 1916 would share the first Pulitzer Prize in biography given to a woman, or of Elsie De Wolfe, who pioneered the field of interior decoration in America, Gardner played an important role in advancing the cause of women. (It may be said in passing that Elsie De Wolfe, like Bernhardt and Guiney and Jewett and also Amy Lowell, of whom more later, were all lesbian; Gardner's greater identification with gay men than women, a reflection, doubtless, of her ardent heterosexuality, ought not to be understood as implying any aversion on her part to lesbians.) Isabella Gardner was also a member of the New England Women's Club, whose catalog of causes–dress reform, election of women to local school committees, admission of women to higher learning (MIT particularly), and the establishment of college preparatory schools (such as Boston's Girls Latin School, perhaps the club's most enduring achievement)–reads like a roll of honor of causes led and won by women at the end of the nineteenth century. Sufficient to the 1890s was the way the reredos she gave the Church of the Advent declared boldly Gardner's interest in the signal contribution of women to church history.

In *The Anatomy of Prejudices*, Elizabeth Young-Bruehl has recently isolated "the four prejudices that have dominated American life and reflection in the past half-century–anti-Semitism, racism, sexism and homophobia."[43] Significantly, Isabella Gardner, according to her own lights to be sure, took a hand in striking down each, celebrating Jews, blacks, women, and gays, in ways her posterity can to a remarkable extent still enjoy a century later, not least in the Church of the Advent's high altar screen. Can it be accident or coincidence that, leaving aside Christ and the angel figures and considering only the human figures, the Advent's high altar reredos celebrates three saints historically identified as gay and lesbian cult figures, an African saint identified through Cowley with their ministry to Boston African-Americans, and more female saints than male? One of them, moreover, as Jaroslov Pelican points out in *Mary Through the Centuries,* is not only the great Christian saint but a Jew.

Bedecked as it usually is with myriad flickering candles and blossoming plants, successors to those Isabella Gardner arranged once herself, the Advent's altar screen may still be thought a hundred and more Easters later an enduring inspiration to artistic worship–and a glorious feminist riposte to Boston's Puritan patriarchy.

9

A Paradoxical Character

A RTISTS–INCLUDING, OF course, musicians and architects and writers–were the people to whose interests Isabella Gardner was devoted above all, and in no small measure because it was in their company that she was always happiest. Whether it was the world-famous Sargent or the hardly known young Proctor, it was in the exchange with artists that there is most to learn of Gardner, not just as muse and mentor, but of her overall personality, which we have been layering up here, so to speak, heading toward her prime, the proper time, I think, to take a complete reading.

A Gardner tall tale: Another one! This time from the "posing" category, which, because of the sexual implications, offers some rich material. Here again fairly outrageous behavior on Gardner's part got the ball rolling, for although the conventional sissy in front of a mirror "sculpting" himself would not have interested Gardner much, a beautifully built young athlete like Sandow the strong man, Proctor's hero, aroused her in just the way as did her portrait of *Hercules*. So it does not surprise that when she went to see Sandow she was not content until as she told Carter proudly, she actually "felt" his muscles as he posed for her.[1] In the tall tale, however, it was Gardner who did the posing; if, that is, one can believe the well-known Harvard-trained scholar, S. Foster Damon, who embedded his tale in a most carefully crafted paragraph:

Was there actually a White Rose League dedicated to the Jacobite cause? Did its members constantly remark that the best of the Stuarts had come to America, the proof lying in the person of Mrs. Jack Gardner? Did a certain lady have a room lined with black velvet, in which she posed nude before a select company of gentlemen? Did she repent something else by washing the steps of the Advent one Good Friday? Was a Boston publisher [Damon is referring to Fred Holland Day] photographed as the crucified Christ? And did his friends once appear in the South Station robed as Apostles? Did another gentleman actually burn off the hand that had slapped a friend's face? Those who should know swear that at least some of these things are true.[2]

As a matter of fact, virtually *all* of these things are now documented these many years later *except* for those relating to Gardner, and so long as Jack Gardner or her nephews never heard about it, I for one am quite prepared to believe that by the 1880s if an artist Isabella Gardner respected had proposed such a thing she might very well have agreed to it. But it is hard to see how she really could have kept such a thing from her husband. Never mind. That she would at the very least have *wanted* to agree is more important. Though actually that is only the short answer.

The long answer, and the better one, is a kind of hinge between the importance of artistic media in Gardner's life and the way she herself became a media object. And it was a variant of Gardner's own well-known dictum: "Don't spoil a good story by telling the truth."[3] Gardner was an aesthete, but keeping up appearances in the bourgeois sense never interested her. She never took to the media age in the way, for example, Theodore Roosevelt did. Gardner shunned reporters and photographers. But she intuitively knew how to use the media, as Clara Rogers saw.[4] I don't know if Gardner knew the Confucian rule that a gentleman should never do anything in private he would be ashamed to do in public, but Gardner surely knew of the Marquess of Queensbury's observation that "to pose as a thing is as bad as to be it."[5] For Gardner it was as *good* as to be it! "If people *like* to believe such things," she was reliably reported as saying, "please don't contradict them."[6]

If this is all very modern sounding, an unidentified newspaper clipping of the last century in the Gardner archives explains why: "no woman in

Boston," it reads, "has been so much discussed, both privately and publicly, as Mrs. John L. Gardner; indeed, here is a case of a woman's reputation having been made entirely by the [news]papers."⁷ A hundred years ago, in that before anything else, Gardner was on the leading edge of the twentieth century, and not least in her invariable attitude of never protesting, never explaining. If like the late Mrs. Onassis, Gardner effectively never gave an interview, like the late Princess of Wales she never missed an opportunity to court notoriety either! Indeed, Gardner's own response to the tale of her posing in the nude was surely clear from her placement of her own (fully clothed) portrait by Whistler right next to an anonymous nude by the same artist, in which case the "fact" of Gardner's own much admired figure, and the pride she took in it, certainly becomes the key factor, not whether Whistler's nude was Isabella Gardner. In deliberately juxtaposing the two Whistlers, Gardner transferred the matter to the viewer's *imagination*, in which contest, of course, she did not doubt because of her repute she would win. And so she has; I am reminded of the Oxford don's response to an American student skeptical of the tale of George Washington and the cherry tree: did he think, queried the don, that after two hundred years posterity would be telling a similar story about Richard Nixon?⁸ That we *are* telling tales like this about Isabella Gardner a century later testifies not only to her media skill but to the fact that in her prime, in the 1890s and 1900s–in her fifties and sixties–Gardner's increasingly more bohemian, free-spirited (artistic, if you will) values reflected the fact she was by then really coming into a much fuller kind of self-understanding–not shedding the roles of muse, mentor, and patron, but making use of those roles increasingly as a creator in her own right–as, indeed, *a creative artist* herself.

That fulfillment was long in coming to Isabella Gardner. Not until her late middle age, on the edge of sixty, did it flower finally and conclusively. And in this connection the artist she identified most closely with was Joseph Lindon Smith,⁹ later notable for his remarkable paintings of ancient Egyptian architecture and art as seen first after excavation by the staff of Boston's Museum of Fine Arts, of which Smith eventually became honorary curator of Egyptian art.

They met in circumstances picturesque even for Gardner, who first spied the artist in the Square of Sts. John and Paul in Venice, as the painter was perched astride the marble pedestal of the equestrian statue of Bartolomeo Colleoni. Smith recounts the story too well not to quote him:

I had taken advantage of a ladder, placed against the statue and not yet removed after some repairs to the head. No one had protested as I mounted it and I returned to climb it again with a roll of canvas and paints. Three days later I had completed the picture [of the figure's head] without being ejected by officials. I was about to roll up my canvas when a cultivated woman's voice called up to me, asking what I was doing. "Painting [a] portrait . . ." I answered.

"Come down and steady the ladder for me!" she said.

Her manner was that of a woman with the habit of command. I obeyed at once and stood beside her, impressed by the elegant simplicity of her gown and the magnificent ruby at her throat and above all by the charm of her personality.

She went up the ladder without effort and perched in the uncomfortable seat I had vacated. It was almost half an hour before she rejoined me.

"You caught the strength and courage Verrocchio got into the features and the delicious green patina of the bronze," she said [and] ordered me to bring the picture and any other studies I had [to her hotel]. "I am Mrs. John L. Gardner," she turned to say, and was off.[10]

What Gardner saw was a young man who had, wrote Carter, "an enchanting personality," a gifted painter who would become one of her closest friends; more to our purpose just now is what Smith saw, but never painted, as it happened: an obviously wealthy woman, elegant, if in a very simple way, and both charming and imperious. That is exactly what another painter, also in Venice, the Swedish artist, Andreas Zorn, *did* paint and his much admired portrait of Isabella Gardner in her prime shows us just what Smith saw and was so instantly drawn to. Again the story, told this time by Carter, is a good one. Zorn, whose failures as a portraitist in depicting Gardner were making him an anxious house guest of his patron,

kept making little drawings and throwing them away, to be rescued by his hostess, and then one evening he found what he was seeking: Mrs. Gardner had stepped out into the balcony to see what was happening on the canal, and as she came back into the drawing-room, pushing the French window wide open with her extended arms, Zorn exclaimed: "Stay just as you are! That is the way I want to paint you." He went instantly for his materials, and then and there the portrait was begun. When it was exhibited in Paris the following spring. . . . a newspaperman wrote: ". . . if Mrs. Gardner's arms have made her famous in Rome . . . surely the painted ones will make her famous at Paris. . . . The figure is so graceful, so full of life, 'girlishness'–Mrs. Gardner was fifty-five at the time–"strength and beauty, the arrangement so dashing and so original . . . that it is sure to make a sensation."[11]

In oils or in words the characteristic exchange between Gardner and an artist was nearly always significant on both sides; for with her artist friends, Gardner tended to have the intellectual (and equally emotional) version of the more widely advertised hormonal experience of "love at first sight"–what someone once described to the writer Elizabeth Hardwick as "taking to someone more quickly than I can ever remember doing with anyone before."[12] Always an intense experience, it was invariably highly appraising on both sides. Let us continue to consider it from the artist's standpoint.

That Gardner was fine of figure and plain of face we have noted already. Crawford (assuming as most critics do that Mrs. Wyndan in *The American Politician* is, in fact, Mrs. Gardner) described her in more detail: she "might have passed for younger," he wrote, ". . . for she was fresh to look at, and of good figure and complexion. . . . There were lines in her face . . . but on the whole [she] was fair to see."[13] She was small, of medium or a little under medium height; in the words of Corina Putnam, the highly perceptive woman Joe Smith would later marry, the best feature of her famous figure was (as the review of the Zorn portrait suggested) "arms that were extraordinarily lovely."[14] Her complexion was delicate, "peaches and cream,"[15] said Carter, and her hair golden, though as she grew older it was more often called rusty or auburn. It framed rather a round, boyish face, the chin of which was "not quite straight . . . an irregularity," one critic reported, "that some people dare to admire,"[16] quite full lips and wide-set blue eyes. These seemed (when she was angry) like "blue icicles" to one person;[17] another thought them "a wonderful blue";[18] very "dark . . . bright and penetrating," was Crawford's take;[19] to Berenson they seemed extremely warm and sympathetic.[20] To Sargent they were at once strangely vulnerable and coolly appraising.

Overall, Corina Smith declared, there was in Gardner's face "strength of character rather than beauty."[21]

Appearance without prowess, always disappointing, was hardly Gardner's problem: all sources agreed it was Gardner in motion, so to speak, that was most to be conjured with: it was not just that physically she was as graceful as she was in her movements but Corina Smith recalled that "one of [Gardner's] greatest assets was a low-toned, richly modulated voice,"[22] an opinion agreed with by both Berenson and Carter: the former spoke of a "delicious caress" in Gardner's voice,[23] the latter of her "wonderful, rippling, musical laugh."[24] It may have been her most wonderful endowment—so much so that in her last years, well into her seventies, A. Hyatt Mayor, recalling fifty years later how hideous she had seemed to him as a boy, went on to say: "exactly how she was hideous I cannot now remember, but I do remember my shock at her wrecked features. And I as quickly forgot them when she began to speak: I can still hear her words, but even more clearly I hear her voice, a contralto that saturated her surroundings as effortlessly as a wood dove's call. The only utterance as compelling was Sarah Bernhardt's when just her whisper sent gooseflesh to the back row of the top balcony where I sat. Both women sounded supremely assured," and of Gardner's voice, Mayor insisted, a half century after her death, "even the recollection still commands me across so many decades."[25]

To grace and litheness of movement and so warmly sensuous a voice must be added driving energy: Henry James she invariably exhausted; even the much younger Berenson, who wrote: "she lives at a rate and intensity, and with a reality, that makes other lives seem pale, thin and shadowy."[26] Moreover, the result of all this was apparently a sense of her having cast some sort of enchantment: "though she was not beautiful, she produced the effect of beauty,"[27] wrote Carter, frankly baffled, as were so many. All Elsie De Wolfe could say was that Gardner was "a plain woman with a lovely body. Yet one never heeded her lack of beauty because of the radiant mentality and understanding heart behind it."[28]

◆

De Wolfe's attempt to explain the ambiguities of Gardner's stature by an appeal from her physicality to her character only deepens the ambiguities, however, rather than sorting them out. The high-strung youth, the delicate bride and grieving mother and love-lacking wife, the bold counterpuncher and scandal maker and precocious intellect, deeply emotional and greatly roused by love, and no less so by betrayal, the open-minded, boldly independent and Bohemian reformer, deeply religious and as deeply driven by–what?–this is not a personality easily understood or even simply described. In fact, if Smith's first impressions–elegant but simple, charming but imperious–were themselves somewhat antithetical, to be conducted into Gardner's psyche is to enter something like a room of many different antitheses. And for each, as it turns out, there is, so to speak, the same witness. Whereas anyone will seem to one person hot and to another cold, and so on, in Gardner's case nearly all her friends found her, alternately and often, both. Indeed, the people who offered the most admiring and friendly evidence about this very mysterious woman are the same people who relayed quite the worst report of her as well.

Carter, for example, did not hesitate to write, in print, that Gardner was a case of the old musical-comedy song–"I want what I want when I want it"–and nobody's inconvenience mattered. "That did not," he added, "prevent her being, when circumstances were propitious, exceedingly kind and considerate."[29] Nor was that the only contradiction he noticed: "fascinating as she was in her mirth," he wrote, "she could be terrible in her wrath"[30]–a range of reaction very much akin to what Elsie De Wolfe noticed: in the same place where she rejoices in Gardner's "understanding heart," De Wolfe goes on to say that Gardner "was both kind and generous, cruel and penurious. Hers was a type of mental sadism which sometimes expressed itself in sudden fury. I have known her to be guilty of astounding acts of cruelty," wrote De Wolfe, "and the next moment display a gentleness and a munificence just as astounding" (It was an echo, after all, of Sedgwick's observation that Gardner was "profoundly, sometimes ecstatically religious, and without worldly scruple").[31]

The same pattern emerges in the testimony of Berenson, after Gardner renewed her acquaintance with her old protégé, and also in the witness of his wife, Mary, who once described Gardner as "full of lies and charm and provokingness as usual,"[32] and another time positively railed against "her egotism [and] her malice."[33] But that did not stop her from also affirming with obvious sincerity on yet another occasion perhaps the finest thing ever said of Isabella Gardner, that "no one in the world is tenderer and deeper and more understanding than you, when you are really taken into a person's confidence . . . you have real miracles of kindly sympathy for grave human situations, and . . . unexpected healing lies in your hands."[34]

Bernard Berenson did not disagree with his wife.[35] Exasperated once by Gardner, he declared: the "secret of her perpetual youth is that she is a vampire and feeds on one young person after another!"[36]

Yet, soon after penning this, his biographer notes, when Gardner paid the Berensons a visit, Bernard was forced to admit that "she makes me feel she adores me, the wily old Circe. We sat out in the moonlight til nearly midnight, simply reveling in her society."[37] Moreover, in another place, Berenson seems to contradict his vampire theme. (It is, of course, a commonplace, genius always needing to be nourished and renewed by others' energy, and Samuels is certainly more sophisticated in referring to the sort of "emotional cannibalism" of any circle of artist-intellectuals.)[38] Wrote Berenson finally of Gardner: "she was the biggest and deepest and most fascinating nature I ever came across. She is so splendid that you can't ask too much of her. She always pays up, and more."[39] Maude Howe Elliott pushed out the boat even further, asserting Gardner's "rare power of *energizing* people [my emphasis]."[40] There's an oxymoron worthy of a paradoxical personality: a vampire who energizes her victims! Indeed, who is adept at "healing"!

Only one person was conspicuous among the close friends who wrote about her in never speaking ill of Gardner– Crawford! In *An American Politician* he has left of "Mrs. Sam" (i.e., "Mrs. Jack") a very different impression. She was, he thought, "really a very kind-hearted woman and a loving friend. That might be the reason why she was never popular. Popularity is a curious combination of friendliness and indifference, but very popular people rarely have devoted friends, and still more rarely suffer great passions. Everybody's friend is far too apt to be nobody's."[41] Similarly, only one characteristic among them all–Gardner's courage– seemed in the testimony of her friends to stand alone and without contradiction. She was never called a coward. She always faced the music, as it were, and did it well. "Win as though you were used to it, lose as if you liked it,"[42] her racing motto, was characteristic of her. And when in her last years severe physical trials came to her she earned from one Cowley Father the notable accolade: "You carry your cross as though it were a banner. That is splendid."[43]

In fact, Gardner's was a personality of extremes, contradictions; of which the most startling–that Gardner was on the one hand capable of great "gentleness" and on the other of a real "mental sadism"–already put by Elsie De Wolfe, may be the most important. Hardly less arresting was the fact that though she was a very honest woman, so trustworthy Carter recalled she "was as good as her bond"[44] and she herself claimed *never* to have betrayed a confidence,[45] she encompassed honesty (because perhaps she "knew instinctively," Corina Smith wrote, "the importance of being herself")[46] with the basest sort of vanity. Indeed, she was so vain it was the stuff (true in this case) of media legend. Witness one journalist's report: "The lack of portraits of Mrs. Gardner has often been a mark for comment. . . . She has been taken at various times in groups, but invariably the moment of exposing the camera coincides with some movement of Mrs. Gardner's so that the face is blurred."[47]

A third paradox: "You are always so kind & thoughtful to me, that it touches me very much," she once wrote Carter. "I am peculiarly sensitive to that sort of thing & *one's own efforts in that direction seem so often to miscarry*, that perhaps, although you may think it is silly, you may like to know that I feel all you do & thank you." She went on: "I really do feel sure that always my first thought & an abiding one is "others," *but I don't seem to have the knowledge which makes my thought of service* [my emphasis]."[48] This was a side of Isabella Gardner Maude Howe Elliott must have known well; yet Elliott, no sentimentalist, made a point of noting too that though Gardner was kind and caring and even vulnerable, her "leading characteristics [were] an iron will and immense ambition,"[49] using, of course, the gentlest words on a continuum that ranges from independent, bold, ambitious and willful through imperious, selfish, egotistical, and spoiled ("I want what I want when I want it"). Some examples that come to mind are telling. For example, Gardner had one of the first telephones. But though she could (and did often) use it to summon others, no one could call her for the simplest of reasons: she had no ringer on her phone. To reach Isabella Gardner you wrote–or telegraphed![50]

Just how imperious she could be is nicely illustrated by an anecdote of many colors–and as many variations, all on the same theme! Berenson, it seems, spending a week with her in Venice, receives no letter or message at all from anyone. Surprised and disappointed he inquires of his hostess: Isabella Gardner in this version "pull[s] open a drawer and shower[s] him with letters and telegrams," roundly scolding the younger man: "Your mail, indeed! Here's your wretched mail! Do you think of nothing but yourself and your mail? Don't you ever think of me?" It is a scene worthy of *Tosca*.

Another version, equally credible, puts one more in mind of Bernhardt. This time Gardner responds to the protest of Berenson (already widely known as a womanizer) with the highly provocative remark that there had, indeed, been a message from some other woman, but "it never reached you because I tore it up." Finally, there is a version worthy of our own Madonna, "the Material Girl" of the 1990s: this time Berenson confronts Gardner directly with his own suspicion that she has intercepted his messages, and she is described as explaining herself very coolly—and in only two words—"Of course."[51] Imperious, yes—and very possessive. One is suddenly very sympathetic to the young Crawford.

These several versions of the tale of Berenson's letters nicely introduce another and larger paradox: the "intensity of her deep emotional nature" and "soaring imagination"[52] (the words are Carter's), which contrasts so strongly with a quality Corina Smith thought "set [Gardner] apart from other women. . . . [an] idea of aloofness."[53] I think at once of how Carter answered a question in a radio interview many years later about why Gardner had been for so long deeply interested in a certain institution and then suddenly seemed to lose all interest: the departure from its leadership cadre of one of her dearest friends was the reason, said Carter: "No one took his place in her interests";[54] which is to say Gardner's interests were strongly people-driven. Yet in his book about her Carter seems to go to some lengths to document the opposite: that conviction took first place with Gardner and that ideas won out over people invariably:

> Mrs. Gardner could not have been the genius she was if she had not been independent in her judgment and firm in her convictions. More than once her honest expression of opinion did violence to an old friendship, but she could and did judge impartially, disregarding the personal element, the element of friendship, and, when she found it impossible for a friend to do so, her opinion of the friend suffered. On the other hand, she was perfectly capable of overvaluing the performance of one in whose success she was interested, and of trying to persuade her friends and the public to share her expressed opinion. Yet her own unconfessed opinion was probably accurate.[55]

Allied to this paradox was the fact that though she was deeply sincere in her convictions she was also, as so many guarded people are, an ironist. "Be nice to Molly [a mutual friend] and don't open any doors for her!!!!!" she admonished Berenson once. Another time, asked to receive a woman studying the question of women's suffrage, she retorted: "I hope I shall see the breezy Rag when she is here. Why not go back to the gar-den of Eden for the origin of female suffrage?" Women's issues, particu-larly, sparked her this way. She loved to repeat a story told her by a Japanese diplomat: "Someone asked him, 'Do you have strong-minded women in Japan,' meaning our odious kind," wrote Gardner, to which the envoy replied:

> "Oh yes, many, but I will tell you of one. A great warrior in [the Russo-Japanese war] was terribly torn between his country, for which he ought to give his life, and his mother who was old and could not live without his arm. A terrible, impossible position. What should he do? Distractedly he rushed out, distractedly he rushed back, to find his mother dead, a note saying 'I go to wait for you in the hereafter, where you will come to me, having given your life for Japan!!' Was not she strong-minded?"

This was, she thought, "a pretty tale," and so it is! So was that portrait of her by Sargent on which her report to Berenson was: "Even I think it is exquisite." Withal, Carter was not the only person who thought that Isabella Gardner, however sophisticated in one way, retained to the end an element of naïveté. Indeed, Jack Gardner was known to remark that Isabella Gardner had "never grown up."[56]

Gardner herself, however, once wrote to Berenson: "I am the sort of person who always believes at first, but from the moment I disbelieve faith is *dead*."[57] And it didn't take her long, as many astute men of affairs were quick to notice, including General Walker, MIT's president and a Washington insider if ever there was one, who shared much hard-boiled political gossip with Gardner. "What a power you have of understanding things!" he wrote her on one occasion: "All I ask is: Don't see through me; pray make this one exception."[58] Similarly, she mentored professors and congressmen as well as poets and artists: Congressman A. Piatt Andrew, the Harvard economist, once exclaimed to her at the end of one of his letters: "What a splendid counselor you are."[59]

◆

Over the field of her mentoring the same play of paradox is evident. George Proctor's testimony would seem to be that Gardner was in those roles capable of being quite challenging (he once referred to her "giv[ing] Clayton a dreadful 'talking to' [to] make him compose that piece which he promised,"[60] but at the same time Corina Smith, though she admitted she had "never been with a more stimulating companion [than Gardner]"—we have Bliss Perry's word for it that Isabella Gardner had a sense of humor and could tell a story—concluded that "all [Gardner's] assets considered, it was probably her infinite capacity to *listen* that provided a large measure of her attractiveness, and the real strength" she possessed as an antagonist.[61]

Antagonist! It was an odd word to have used, even if Corina Smith was thinking (as well she might have) of Gardner as a rival for her husband's attentions. And it was an odd gift for Gardner to have, to listen so well, if as Mary Berenson claimed, Gardner was always "dominating conversation, which concerned mostly herself."[62] But that was with Mary Berenson, whose ego some thought rivaled Gardner's own! I recall a comment of Christina Zwarg about Margaret Fuller (again and again, Fuller, like De Staël, comes to mind with Gardner) that may account for Corina Smith's choice of words. Zwarg writes of "Fuller's empathic responsiveness as her most powerful interpersonal skill. . . . she could be an extraordinarily attentive and engaged listener. . . . in her presence, ordinary defenses and decorum seemed to drop away."[63] Perhaps antagonist was the right word after all! Especially as Carter also thought Gardner also possessed "an extraordinary facility in 'focusing and unfocusing' her mind, or shutting up one compartment and opening another."[64] Wrote one reporter: "the man to whom she is talking is for the time being the only man in the room."[65]

That there was a real reciprocity in at least her more serious mentoring relationships, and that it was often romantic though not physically sexual, is apparent. The miracle always depends as much on the faith of whoever needs healing as on the healer! Consider these exchanges (many years later when they had become intimate friends) between Berenson and Gardner. She had taunted young Berenson: "It would be fun if you were on the sofa in this my room. We could throw pillows and ideas at each other."[66] Berenson, in another letter rather upped the ante, though admittedly at a safe enough distance, when after writing of a lady he was interested in: "Basta! If there is another I could desire it is you in moods I have seen you in, the intimate, tender esoteric Isabella, not the Mrs. Jack everybody has heard of. She too is fine, a stunner, but I do not long for her in my idyll."[67]

It is fascinating confession. Again, intimacy is not always physical: mapping the mind can be as intimate a bonding experience–and as sexually charged–as mapping the body. Possibly this is what happened between Gardner and Crawford. Probably too it is what happened between her and Joe Smith, about which we have a remarkably intimate witness in Corina Smith, who made a point of trying to comprehend the exchange between her husband and Belle Gardner. What happened, she said, as Joe characterized it, was that Gardner "had encouraged him to talk to her about his art ambitions *and had made him feel he could achieve them* [my emphasis–DST]."[68] No surprise there. But the surprise perhaps comes when Corina, having then put this question to Gardner herself, recorded that "her response was that, curiously enough, [Joe] had had *the same effect on her*."[69] When artistic fulfillment came to Gardner herself in her collecting and designing it was Joe Smith she turned to as her first choice as director of her gallery.

In Gardner's closest mentoring relationships the effect of her contradictory character thus emerges as rather different than in her overall society. Take the case of Loeffler, for instance. Though stimulated by her patronage–Gardner was one of the first to see Loeffler not only as a virtuoso but as the composer he wished to be and increasingly today is regarded as–Loeffler grew to feel at one point distinctly imposed upon by Gardner, who seemed to him possessive and only too willing to "show him off" in Ralph Locke's words, as "a kind of in-house virtuoso"[70] in the Gardner music room, all of this, of course, quite classic behavior on the part of humble but artful, trustworthy but vain, kind but cruel and rampagingly dominant Isabella! Loeffler (unlike Crawford?) was not one to suppress his feelings until it was too late to avoid an explosion; when he felt exploited[71]–indeed, at all times–his invariable principle, *La bonne franchise avant tout*/candor above all, secured their friendship. Loeffler, reports Locke, "spoke his mind when he felt offended or exploited," to which Gardner responded positively. When he began to feel as well that her kindness and generosity in letting him use her Stradivarius on several occasions was really more controlling than helpful, not to say artistically unempowering, she gave him the violin outright. And once on an equal footing, not just his art but their friendship flourished anew.

These contradictions in Isabella Gardner are not welcome. One of the reasons mapping the body is more popular than mapping the mind is that our fast-paced and reductionist world does not really take kindly to paradoxical people, who are inevitably demanding, after all, of our attention. Like the emperor who complains in *Amadeus* that Mozart had "too many notes," we all seek clarity, not ambiguity, and I think Victorians too, in Terry Teachouts' apt words, tried to evade "the Trollopian ... understanding–and acceptance–of the divided nature of men's souls."[72] Paradox is difficult. Of course, contradiction does yield contrast, and that is why Gardner (though unaccountably as yet undiscovered by Hollywood) is still much talked of today. Paradox also engenders mystery and enigma. Confronted, however, with so many contradictory qualities and character traits, most of us tend to assume that only some are real, that others are assumed, and at once fixate on which are which. And we make the further assumption, because we all know only too well how much quicker we all are to claim our virtues than their darker opposites, that it is the brighter of the contradictions that is phony, and that the person's darker traits disclose the *real* person underneath: Gardner was cruel; she only feigned kindness, we conclude, by way of cover; whereas the truth is that in the case of the paradoxical person *each* antithesis and *all* the contradictions are true and real. And for very good reason. In the words of that eminent psycho-historian, Peter Gay of Yale, "where there is paradox, a conflict often lies concealed."[73]

Jean Strouse points out in her biography of Alice James, to whom we compared Gardner in her early invalid period as a new bride, that Boston's leading neurologists had already come in advance of Freud by the 1870s to an understanding of nervous disorders that "emphasized conflicts within individuals who could not fulfill social norms, yet, because they had internalized them, could not consciously reject them." Two expressions were seen: "incapacitating physical symptoms" or "outbursts of emotion."[74] Previously I have identified these with two kinds of neurasthenia: Alice James' and Sarah Bernhardt's, or Gardner I and Gardner II! We have, moreover, already identified behind the expression the conflict. Though she had survived her sense of failing at the role demands of wife, matron, and mother (and this last more than once; recall Joe Junior), perhaps because in her heart she knew they were not for her, and indeed, had turned failure into triumph, so successful was she in the roles of muse and mentor, on another level she was still unsure of herself (having so internalized and made her own society's role demands) and deeply unfulfilled.

Her temperament must also be factored in here, and just as I have so pointedly compared Gardner's mentoring techniques to Margaret Fuller's, I want to sound an even bolder note in respect to Gardner's temperament: Gardner's was a "strong and flaring temperament"; she was "passionate for distinction" and for having her own way, and could be "willful" and "head-strong and high-handed as well as bold" and even "petulant" when she did not. Whatever image that description calls to mind, the words are Richard Brookhiser's in describing the temperament of George Washington![75] Where they differed, though, was that Washington read Seneca to calm himself; Gardner listened to Schubert or studied paintings. (Or had a cigarette.)[76]

She needed calm. There was the time she was annoyed with her husband's insistence they hire a courier to accompany them on a trip and the scene that resulted as they entrained at the Paris terminal was unbelievable. As Carter told it:

> It must be admitted Mrs. Gardner had a temper; no character approaching hers in strength ever lacked one. . . . The first spark was struck when Mrs. Gardner discovered that the courier had not reserved a whole car; [the second when she found her compartment] filled with pillows–white pillows–of every size and shape. Indignantly she asked the courier where they had come from; he had procured them hoping to increase her comfort. 'Never do anything you are not ordered to'–and with that she began throwing the pillows out [the window], with no thought of where they might land. There was an avalanche of pillows, one knocking off an officer's eyeglass, another hitting a Monsignor, and others astonishing lesser dignities. Mr. Gardner could not quiet her.[77]

Such a panic attack was rare, but even Carter's relatively smooth day-in-and-day-out experience of Gardner was never altogether easy. With a devastating candor he allowed in his biography of her that "to dominate others gave Mrs. Gardner such pleasure that she must have regretted the passing of slavery,"[78] while even so much an admirer as Corina Smith recorded that Gardner's speech could be characterized by "a startling frankness [and that she was] impatient with the commonplace and at times ruthless."[79] No less than Julia Ward Howe herself, who must rank with Norton as Gardner's leading mentor, testified to the intensity and volatility of Gardner's temperament and the effect it could have; warned that Gardner planned to attend a lecture Howe was giving on Aristophanes at the Concord School of Philosophy, that venerable lady offered to bring the lecture to Gardner herself if only she would stay away: "You must not go to Concord," Howe pleaded. "You would take people's minds off from their difficult themes and abstractions. You would play the devil with the *indifference* which is necessary for the pursuit of philosophy. My hair stands on end," Howe went on to her dear friend, "at the thought of the mischief you might work."[80]

Howe well understood the artistic temperament, which is what we are talking about: Not for nothing did Whistler inscribe a book: "To Mrs. Gardner–whose appreciation of the work of Art is only equaled by her understanding of the artist,"[81] or Carter try to explain that Gardner "comprehended [artists'] aspirations as well as their achievements."[82] He was, I think, more right than he realized, for Isabella Gardner was utterly frustrated and suppressed until she began through her roles of muse and mentor to suspect that the cause of social freedom and openness (what we would call today inclusivity) was a reflection of her innermost need *as an artist herself*, an artist who was, indeed, also something of an impresario.

Significantly, she was in respect of personality (though not temperament) quite similar to Sargent, one of whose biographers, Evan Charteris, confronted with that painter's conflicting character traits, described Sargent as "a continual paradox."[83] Similarly, Trevor Fairbrother is surely right to go further: "[Sargent's] conflicted social-sexual identity," he writes, "may be a key to the successful tensions within his art."[84] Sargent's inner conflict was different–he was gay–than Gardner's; but just as in Fairbrother's words, "Sargent's art is the best 'evidence' of his personality,"[85] so it is with Isabella Gardner. In fact, it is, finally, the only evidence, artist that she was.

Indeed, the only resolution possible of her paradoxical character is to be found in Gardner's own creative work, which fulfillment as collector and designer would depend hardly less for its genius on the problematic traits of her character and temperament than on the "good" traits. She had, after all, the weaknesses of her strengths. Indeed, Sargent, among the first to sense her forthcoming genius, may have been led to his insight by the very exercise of his art; if, that is, his sitter, Gardner, as some have suggested, really functioned as a kind of co-artist in the production of her celebrated portrait.

Certainly the suggestion is present in the testimony of Thomas Fox, Sargent's friend and McKim's associated architect at the Boston Public Library, who in his notes for some sort of lecture about the artist, tells the story that while at work on Gardner's portrait, Sargent, worrying about the background, stopped at one point and said, "as if a sudden inspiration had come to him, 'I know what it is'" to which Gardner replied: "Well, what is it?" Sargent said: "Why, a certain piece of Venetian brocade—but, unfortunately, it is on the wall of my studio in London." Gardner's turn: "Never mind that, Sargent, I knew exactly what would be proper background for my portrait when I decided to have you paint it, and I have *the other half of the piece* upstairs [emphasis added]. I will go at once and get it." Added Fox: "now that is a really good Sargent story because it is not only typical of him but also of [Gardner]."[86]

. Then, by way of explaining the matter fully, Fox concluded this excerpt of some part of a projected talk on Sargent with this reminiscence of his own.

> The painter and the subject were in many ways alike and had many artistic characteristics in common. A musician who was a friend of both [Sargent and Gardner] in the course of an evening's talk after the passing of both of the principals, told how Mozart once wrote a page of music to be played as a duet. There was an unusual feature of this composition, however, inasmuch as one musician began as usual and played forward while the other began at the end, so to speak, and played backward, and the result was not only good music technically but also pleasing to the ear. This incident was told to indicate the amount of imagination carried in the mind of the great musicians, but it also suggests the quality found to a large degree in the creator of Fenway Court.[87]

That climax—which is a tale of two parts: the assembling of her collection and the design and erection of Fenway Court to house it—is now upon us: madonna become not only muse and mentor but an artist in her own right; in fact, seductress—in the most telling and creative sense of that word. It is to claim a great deal for Isabella Stewart Gardner. But no less a cynic than Henry Adams, in a private letter to another woman who was his confidante, pronounced Gardner "quite the most remarkable woman I ever met, and yet she has no reason, *tant mieux!*"[88] So much the better indeed!

Part Three

Seductress

The artistic person . . . possesses . . . a "puzzling" ability—which Freud else-where says is a power of "genius" that psychoanalysis cannot explain—to mold the artistic medium into "a faithful image of the creatures of his imagination," as well as into satisfying artistic form. . . . [This] not only allows the artist to overcome, at least partially and temporarily, personal conflict and repressions, but also makes it possible for the artist's audience to "obtain solace and consolation."

—M. H. Abrams

10

In a Tempter's Garden

The Portrait of a Lady, Henry James' most characteristic masterwork, is notable for its famously independent protagonist, Isabel Archer. Her portrait, Leon Edel has written, now hangs "in the gallery of the world's classical fiction. She holds her head high; she possesses great pride, and there is a fierce shyness in her steady gaze."

It is, of course, Isabella Gardner's gaze, as Sargent painted it. And Edel himself asserts that

> Isabel Archer embodies a notion not unlike that of Isabella of Boston, with her motto *C'est mon plaisir.* . . . "I'm very fond of my liberty," Isabel says, . . . "I wish to choose my fate. . . ." Asked to define her idea of happiness she offers a vision of a journey into the unknown–"A swift carriage, of a dark night. . . ."

Henry James, however warily, had been watching closely enough! He had perhaps understood Isabella Gardner's so swiftly driven carriages after all; more than that, "Isabel speaks for a society," Edel continues, "in which a woman might claim full equality," and cites the reply to a remark of Isabel's by a male character who admits: "she does smell of the Future–it almost knocks one down."

That, surely, was Isabella Gardner too, whose promise was maturing rapidly by the early 1890s, when she was on the verge of something very like international repute, though few perhaps, beyond Sargent and James, saw it coming, or even for quite a while understood exactly what happened. For Isabella Gardner came late to fame and caught most people, who would not at first have known of her let alone associated her with Isabel Archer, by surprise, even those Bostonians who doubtless did recognize her in James' "A New England Winter."[1]

James, of course, did not leave it there either. The character of Mrs. Gareth, the fanatical art collector of The Spoils of Poynton of 1895, was easily associated with Isabella Gardner. And then, in the phase of Gardner's life now upon us, James would even make direct use of some of the paintings Gardner started to collect in "The Bel-donald Holbein" of 1901. Finally, through the (male!) character of Adam Verver, the public-spirited collector dedicated to bringing art to America, Isabella Stewart Gardner emerges as really the hero of that masterpiece of James' last years, The Golden Bowl.

However truly, as it turned out, James (like Sargent) intuited Gardner's life's course, it is almost certainly the case that she caught entirely off guard another man who was to play in the last and crowning phase of her life the most immediate and also most critical role, a man who would lend to Isabella Gardner's unfolding genius his own, and conspire with her to make them both famous wherever in the world the history of art is ever told.

It was in 1894 that Bernard Berenson, that slum child of penniless Jewish immigrants, who even in his brilliance had seemed after all one of Gardner's more problematic investments, emerged from their five years' estrangement to happily vindicate her ideas of a more open and inclusive mode of life, in fact to proffer the one thing needful for her coming triumph. (If estrangements were common in Gardner's life, in no small measure because she could be so difficult, so also were reconciliations, because knowing her could be so worthwhile.) "I venture to recall myself to your memory a propos of a little book on the Venetian painters," Berenson wrote her in March of that year, "which I have asked my publisher to send you." The failed literateur was evidently on the verge of becoming a historian and connoisseur of art! Why, as Ernest Samuels, his biographer, declares, Gardner was of all his old backers "the Boston patron whose good opinion Berenson . . . most keenly wished to regain" is not clear.[2] But from Gardner's point of view nothing could have been more timely. Always Gardner would be muse, mentor, and patron. But in the nineties she would emerge as collector, connoisseur, and designer.

As far back as in 1873 she had bought a small landscape by Jacque she later judged good enough to keep in her collection. But her early tastes had been too safe to be interesting: a Corot and a Courbet seemed to sat isfy. Besides, in the 1880s books were her focus, first editions and such recommended by Norton; what art she bought seemed to arise out of other interests, such as the need to furnish and adorn her new music room of 1880. It was only when Berenson first came to know her, in the mid-1880s, that she was beginning to venture more. Of her growing interest in contemporary painters–La Farge, Whistler, and then Sargent– Berenson might have known something, and that she had become a mod est collector of contemporary art, as well as of Jack Gardner's appoint ment as treasurer of Boston's Museum of Fine Arts in 1886. Thereafter it is hard to say–Berenson and Gardner had mutual friends, after all–but whatever intelligence reached either of the other we do not know.

Only two years after Jack Gardner's appointment as museum trea surer, his wife bought her first old master in 1888, the Zurbarán *Madonna and Child* brought back from Seville. But though she did briefly see Berenson that year at Bayreuth, they had been long estranged by the time of the key event of those years, the death in 1891 of David Stewart, from whom Isabella Gardner inherited her own (as distinct from her hus band's) fortune–a million and three quarters pre-1900 dollars–that she must always have hoped for in order to realize the dream, as it must by then have seemed, of her youthful time in Italy. Charles Eliot Norton having meanwhile focused her vision more closely, it began to resonate more and more with Ruskinian moral uplift, to which Isabella Gardner now dedicated herself.

For art this was to be a tremendous thing, so tremendous that it is easy to overlook its importance for Gardner herself. That she found her call ing in the first place was as important as whatever the calling happened to be. Gardner had discovered the one thing she would never be content with her second best in–the acid test of vocation–and had begun at long last to put herself in the way of real happiness: finding *what you feel you were created to do* (it is just another way of saying what you're called to do) is usually in the words of a contemporary Cowley Father, Russell Page, "a telling experience of God,"[3] as telling as may be possible for most of us.

These deeper meanings notwithstanding, this vocation, Gardner must have known, was likely to be as dangerous as stimulating. She now had half the Stewart fortune. But had she the knowledge, the skill; above all, *the eye*? Certainly she had the nerve! That much was clear from the way she dealt with Whistler in 1892 over *Harmony in Blue and Silver*. Of several versions, including a most unfriendly one by Mary Cassatt, Carter's is the best:

> Whistler agreed that she should have it, but characteristically could not bear to part with it. As Mrs. Gardner herself could not take it away, she asked Will Rothenstein, the painter, to go with her to the studio, making him promise at her command to carry off the picture. They had a delightful visit, admired everything, and, when they came to this particular *Harmony*, Mrs. Gardner said: "This is my picture; you've told me many times that I might have it, Mr. Whistler, and now I'm going to take it. Mr. Rothenstein, please take this picture down to the carriage." Off Mr. Rothenstein started, down the steep stairs, followed by Mrs. Gardner keeping Whistler safely in the rear, he protesting all the way down that the picture wasn't finished, he hadn't signed it. Mrs. Gardner invited him to come to her hotel to luncheon, come as often as possible—every day if he would—and sign the picture there. Whistler did turn up the next day, and begged to take the picture back to the studio, but Mrs. Gardner was firm, and eventually a butterfly [the artist's invariable signature] fluttered.[4]

Still, that was rather a genteel skirmish: larger forces hammer at collectors of old masters. Behold, Isabella Gardner that same year of 1892 on her first sally onto the battlefield, in a Paris auction house, her only adviser Ralph Curtis, her executive officer Fernand Robert, the prize Vermeer's *Le Concert*, chosen by Gardner at the preview. As relayed to Carter:

> Telling Mr. Curtis that they must not arouse the interest of others by looking [at the Vermeer] too long themselves, she left the gallery and went to place her order with her agent, M. Fernand Robert. Robert asked how high he might bid; as Mrs. Gardner was unwilling to set a limit, she told him to get her a reserved seat for the sale, and to keep bidding as long as she held her handkerchief to her face. . . .

when she arrived at the Hotel Drouot.... Mrs. Gardner took her
seat, not seeing Robert, but trusting he could see her, and when the
bidding on Number 31 started, she took out her handkerchief and
held it to her face.... The bidding went to twenty-five thousand
francs, the last thousands coming a little slowly; then, following
Mrs. Gardner's instructions, Robert bid twenty-nine thousand—and
got the picture.[5]

The last flutter of her handkerchief, her agent's last sudden bid as the
competition slowed, won the day. She was later told, she said, that both
the Louvre and the National Gallery wanted it, but thought it was not
etiquette to continue to bid against each other. Add to nerve, style—and
good luck! That day, unbeknown to anyone but the lady from Boston,
"the great era of art collecting and the taste for old masters in America,"
in Aline Saarinen's words, "were born with Isabella Stewart Gardner."[6]
Nor was hers an expensive debut. She paid six thousand dollars for the
Vermeer.

Yet Gardner knew well that most pictures weren't sold that way, but
through dealers of legendary duplicity who in the treacherous world of
the international art market could hardly be relied upon. As late as in
1900, eight years later, Louisine Havemeyer, a collector with far more
money than Gardner, and advised by no less than the painter Mary
Cassatt, would on a buying trip to Italy fall into the wrong hands and
come home with a bevy of spurious "Titians" and "Raphaels"; poor
Havemeyer, in her biographer's words, she "lived her entire life with
these illusions."[7] Gardner, in the far riskier early days of old master collecting, was far shrewder. The book Berenson had sent her to renew
their acquaintance, which suggested a wide-ranging sensitivity to all the
elements of collecting and connoisseurship, must have given her more
than one idea about how useful an alliance might be forged with her old
protégé. Though already committed to traveling in opposite directions in
1894—Gardner to Europe for a lengthy stay, and Berenson back to
Boston to sojourn with his family (now settled in suburban Roxbury,
where he would work on his second book), she renewed their correspondence.

For almost the only time in her life that I can discern, however,
Isabella Gardner was noticeably cautious, betraying perhaps her husband's counsel. She answered Berenson's letter pleasantly enough, but

she bided her time, finally deciding (probably, as Samuels suggests, as "a kind of test of Berenson's artistic judgment")[8] to send him in August photographs of two paintings recently offered her for his opinion of their worth. Berenson returned service smartly, in effect dismissing both pictures, and proposing instead an astounding coup: "How much," he asked, "do you want a Botticelli?"[9] It was a young man's move, bold enough to set any collector's heart racing, even a wary one. Of course, Gardner agreed the matter might be looked into! In Venice the following month she was still surely turning the thing over in her mind as her regular Venetian stay unfolded–it was during this visit of 1894 that Zorn painted her coming in from the balcony overlooking the Grand Canal, the fireworks visible in the background–and she must have been gratified that it was in her beloved Venice that it fell to her to make up her mind about pursuing a matter of such importance.

When in Europe Gardner ranged far and wide, of course, especially in aid of her musical interests, which never flagged. Always a besotted Wagnerite she went whenever she could to Bayreuth, where she met Cosima Wagner and heard singers trained by Wagner himself, even marching in 1886 with Cosima and the great Wagnerian singer Materna, at the head of Liszt's funeral procession. (Gardner's wreath, placed beside Queen Victoria's, was inscribed "*Hommage de l'Amérique.*")[10] At Ischl one year Gardner appears also to have enrolled Brahms in her circle (she was seen taking tea with him like old friends) and this year, 1894, after checking in on George Proctor in Vienna in November, it was the turn of Massenet, who when she finally reached Paris in December favored Gardner with a private recital of the piano score of his new opera, *La Navaraise.*[11] There, in the French capital, Gardner and Berenson would finally meet again. What is it Goethe said? "If there is something that you *think* you can do or even *dream* that you can, boldness has mystery and power and magic in it."[12]

By then Gardner must have realized how much was at issue, for in that very month of December 1894, when Berenson and Gardner remet, his second book, *Lorenzo Lotto,* came out, and the controversial issues of scholarship and connoisseurship it focused on–which were widely mooted: Berenson's future wife, Mary Costelloe, had explored them in an article in the influential *Nineteenth Century* magazine in May of 1894, "The New and Old Art Criticism," and then, more generally, the following year, in the *Atlantic*–were such that in considering any alliance with

Berenson, Gardner had to have known she would be associating herself with a position then on the cutting edge of the field. As Karl Meyer put it, the whole "perception of art changed as a result of an intellectual revolution most spectacularly personified by a single art historian, Bernard Berenson."[13] In retrospect, that sounds grand; in 1894 it can only have been alarming—or, perhaps, to Gardner, exciting!

Isabella Gardner would always feel, I believe, in accord with her friend Paul Sachs, the legendary Harvard figure who had so decisive an influence over the world of the American art museum, that (as Caroline Jones put Sachs' view) "the basis for judging quality [in a work of art] lay in an emotional understanding of the artist's message."[14] Wrote Sachs himself: "where there is [in a work of art] what is called *technique* and technique only, there is really nothing at all."[15] It was comparable, Sachs felt, to "a man [who] writes beautifully but unfortunately had nothing to say."[16]

Berenson's approach was fundamentally different: the authentication of a work as by a particular artist was his immediate interest. Building on the work of Giovanni Morelli, Berenson was advancing a new analytic method of art history which faced for the first time head-on the problem posed by the Renaissance masters who presided over studios where many assistants painted but the master alone signed, an analytic method which attempted to deal with this problem by focusing on a study of detail—characteristic treatment of fingernails, for example, or of drapery folds (a focus so much more easily sustained in the age of photography)—in an effort to differentiate the master's work from his assistants. At the same time, Berenson developed theories of "space composition" and "tactile values" that were to become so influential Leon Edel hardly exaggerates when he writes of Berenson's work spreading "through the art world like a new gospel, taking up the cult of beauty where Ruskin and Pater had left off." Finally, it was ultimately what Samuels calls "the psychology of artistic creation"[17] that concerned Berenson: the secret of our enjoyment of art, he contended, lay not in philosophy but in psychology. Influenced by William James, Berenson would become to art history, so to speak, what Henry James, the master of the modern psychological novel, would become to literature; significantly the *New York Times* praised Berenson's *Lotto* exactly for showing that figure to have been the "first psychological and therefore 'modern' painter."[18]

Nor was all this controversy just academic for Isabella Gardner. Not only were both Henry and William James friends of hers (Gardner was a member of the American Society for Psychical Research founded by William James), but even closer to home, as it were, Gardner can hardly not have known the highly negative views of her first mentor and cherished friend–and Berenson's old teacher–Charles Eliot Norton, about Berenson's revolutionary new analytic method. Isabella Gardner would be very much in the middle.

Much was at stake, therefore, in December of 1894 when Berenson, by "mere chance" as he thought, but as his biographer concedes, "powerfully assisted by Mrs. Gardner's resolute design,"[19] rendezvoused with his old patron in Paris. Samuels has recorded the event from the young man's perspective: "There was yet no hint that a momentous change in his fortunes impended. In mid-December he [reported to a friend of Gardner's] that 'this enigmatic lady is here,' [and that] 'she and I have been seeing some things together.'" Several days later, touring the Louvre with Gardner, he found himself "puzzled by a certain reserve in her manner. The enigma was solved the next day. She announced to him that she would buy the Ashburnham Botticelli, *Lucretia*.... Mrs. Jack had achieved her first great triumph.... she added emphasis to her gratitude by giving him a charming watercolor by Pissarro for Christmas."[20] Not quite her first, thank you–the Vermeer was that–but her decision to ally with Berenson certainly boded many more triumphs to come.

Years later Berenson called their meeting a "fatal moment."[21] He did not exaggerate. In the short run Gardner's patronage would free him of financial anxiety so he could study and write in more security; in the long run she would become, in Samuels' words, "his Maecenas and change the course of his life," virtually launching the career of one of the most notable scholars and tastemakers of the twentieth century.[22] However, all of this would prove distinctly a mixed blessing: if Gardner turned out to be "as she said, [Berenson's] too-willing Eve" even as he became "her too-willing Adam"[23] and proceeded all too eagerly to eat of "the apple of affluence which she offered him"–the words are his biographer's–both would pay a higher price in aid of all this than either foresaw.

The initial shocks came quickly. In 1895 Berenson, having examined an exhibition of Venetian art in London, declared that of thirty-three Titians only one was genuine; of eighteen Giorgiones he pronounced none authentic; the furor was immense. In the same year Charles Eliot Norton struck. "Evidently," Samuels wrote, "he had not been pleased that winter to see his prominent disciple, Mrs. Jack Gardner, adopt the immigrant upstart from Lithuania as her adviser in the purchase of art"; he therefore vented his wrath (on them both, really) in a "laboriously derisive" review of Berenson's *Lotto* in the April 1895 issue of London's *Athenaeum*. Scathingly, Norton wrote of the "ear and toe-nail school" of connoisseurship,[24] while Gardner, doubtless, secretly congratulated herself. What luck she had had! She was in the right place and with the right person at the right time. But she had also had the nerve to risk it! (Five years later when Havemeyer was so bamboozled by fakes, Cassatt knew little of Berenson and nothing of his theories!)[25]

Isabella Gardner found in Berenson not only a revolutionary specialist expert, however, but an inspired collaborator as a collector. Perhaps she guessed what we now know from his biographer: that among Berenson's "strongest desires . . . was to make Boston a world center of Italian art. In this aim Edward Warren was a dedicated collaborator."[26] Doubtless Berenson had his eye on compelling the respect particularly of the so cultivated (and bigoted) German Jews of Boston, just as Warren, who was gay, was sending a forceful message to whom today we'd call homophobes every time he gave Boston's museum another ancient Greek male nude.[27] But both were at the same time also sincerely dedicated to art! Similarly, Gardner wouldn't have minded at all people writing of her collection as the last audacity by which she would vanquish the Back Bay. Mixed motives only added spice to it all. But that was a smaller truth, perhaps, than the anonymous correspondent who wrote in a Boston paper: "the fine arts were [Isabella Gardner's] field and the home of her spirit, and this in a profound, personal and very unusual way; for it was neither as a practitioner nor as an amateur, nor as a collector, nor as a Maecenas that she dwelt with art. She did not patronize the fine arts . . . they were meat and drink to her."[28]

In the end, in a competition for art as fierce "as any that the Robber Barons of the time enjoyed in the world of high finance," wrote Samuels, "Gardner's passionate egoism and tyrannical individualism were a curious match to [Berenson's]" and their "drives to distinction, hers as chiefly collector, his mostly as connoisseur, did not so much complement each other as invite a genuine "rivalry of aspirations";[29] somewhat in the same vein as Gardner's "co-authorship" with Crawford, or her "co-artistry" with Sargent in the case of her portrait. Especially is this the case when it is remembered that Berenson's biographer concedes that it was "*her* dream [emphasis added, that] took possession of Berenson and inspired in him the most grandiose vision. That he should be the chief agent in . . . help-ing to create a great monument to culture in his beloved Boston, stirred his ambition as nothing else could have done. . . . It was a breath-taking challenge."[30] Isabella Gardner's greatest triumph of mentoring was the foundation of her role as a collector.

◆

Between 1894 and 1903, in just nine years, over a million dollars[31]–pre-twentieth-century dollars–would change hands before Gardner and Berenson were done, and the result would be the first and as it then was the greatest private art collection in America. Indeed, most of the master-works of the Gardner collection to which its founder lost her heart were secured in that first near decade of their partnership.

The Botticelli *Lucretia* of 1894 was a splendid catalyst. An important late work of that artist, the rape of that great Roman lady, whose virtue and courage in the face of her attacker, the tyrant of the day (so Livy tells us in his *Lives*) ultimately incited the rebellion that overthrew the tyrant and established the Roman Republic, was a tale even the mildest feminist could hardly not have responded to, and couched as it is by Botticelli in a manner at once so grand and so poignant, set against the resplendent architectural pomps of imperial Rome, it must have seemed irresistible. Similarly with the Rembrandt self-portrait acquired the next year, so Jamesian a Victorian as Gardner must have been fascinated by not the least insightful of Rembrandt's numerous self-portraits.

A third treasure of those years, purchased also in 1896, was a notable Francesco Guardi, veritably a dream of Venice. And if Berenson's keen identification with a great Boston collection of Italian art is recalled it is easier to understand his oft-made-fun-of enthusiasm: "Brava! A hundred times brava! I cannot tell you," he wrote Gardner, "how happy it makes me to think of your possessing that most glorious of all Guardi's."[32] How many times must Isabella Gardner have turned gratefully from the New England winter to this warming and limpid view of Venice suffused in the Italian sun, a dream as it must too often have seemed to her of the city of her heart, for which she forever pined,[33] she once wrote Berenson, and it was not entirely the undertow of depression of Crawford's absence. Then, very quickly, in 1896–so like Gardner was it that the only surcease for melancholy was high drama that she might herself have scripted it–so very early in her career as a serious collector, there came with the loudest of fanfares what would be the glory of her collection forever: Titian's *Europa*. "No picture in the world," Berenson declared with justice, "has a more resplendent history."[34]

Still today arguably the greatest Venetian painting in the New World (and that is one of the more reserved accolades Titian's *Europa* has accumulated: Rubens himself called it "the greatest painting in the world"),[35] this picture is one of a series of mythological studies sent by the artist to Philip II of Spain and intended, in turn, by Philip, for the leading collector of his age, Charles I, the Stuart King of England and Scotland, with whom, of course, Gardner of the White Rose strongly identified. It has, more popularly, come to be known as *The Rape of Europa*, for it depicts what I can hardly resist calling the most notorious "date-rape" of all time: Jupiter, no unimaginative deity as the legend has it, smitten as he was by the uncooperative Princess Europa, descends in the form of a friendly white bull to the shoreline where Europa and her companions are bathing. In this guise he delights and lulls the princess by his gentle lowing and other benign and neighborly gestures; so much so that, quite disarmed, Europa climbs trustingly on the bull's back–a mistake Jupiter is quick to act upon: the two are soon at sea, Europa clutching Jupiter's horns, her companions to say the least dismayed, Jupiter triumphant.

It is a world view, whether of men (or gods!) as sexual predators or women as their dupes, with which on the face of it one can hardly much sympathize with anymore. Nor does it matter much if Europa's expression is read as ecstatic or terrified. That is beside the point: evil is often keenly attractive at the beginning of things. Yet if no one would argue that a certain forcefulness in a lover's attentions is never welcome, the destructiveness on another level of any violence to the human person inevitably corrupts even the most ardently sought exchange on either side. Yet for Isabella Gardner, Titian's great painting had, I suspect, as many dimensions of meaning as her response, when Europa arrived, indicated: "no words!.. . . I am too excited to talk,"[36] she wrote Berenson. Even several weeks later she could only write: "I am breathless about the *Europa* even yet. . . . after two days orgy. The orgy was drinking myself drunk with *Europa* and then sitting for hours in my Italian Garden at Brookline, thinking and dreaming about her. Every inch of paint in the picture seems full of joy."[37] Even a month later she was still "having a splendid time playing with Europa."[38]

In the same breath, however, she gives us perhaps the most striking evidence of her lifelong ease with coupling the sacred and the profane when she adds that if Boston's "impossible Art Museum [whose timidity was a constant frustration to her] does not get the Giorgione (the Christ head, you know) please get it for me. I have seen the photographs and like it. They won't move quickly enough to get it, I fear."[39] To which Berenson, and no wonder in the wake of her orgies with *Europa*, replied rather incredulously that for all her Madonnas the Christ head was "somehow not the kind of thing I think of for you."[40]

Yet Gardner grew more insistent! In January of the following year she pined: "I hear that the Louvre has bought the [Christ head], which gives me a pang."[41] By February she reports to Berenson that "a little present. . . . is given to me for [the Christ head]. So I hope and pray and trust," she now implores Berenson, "that you can get it for me. Please try."[42] Seldom was she so revealing. And it is not surprising to discover that though the *Europa* would seem to have been the picture that most moved her based on the very full documentary record of her dealings with Berenson, in fact, it probably took second place in her thoughts to *Christ Bearing the Cross*. Or so at least we are entitled to assume from Carter's assertion after her death that the Christ head "remained [Isabella Gardner's] favorite picture"[43]–what a fascinating contrast between the power of inflicting suffering and the power of accepting it: *The Rape of Europa* and *Christ Bearing the Cross*. Wildly different from each other, they indubitably are; but the fact is that both pictures have also a great deal in common: if each contradicts the other so much that to enter fully into each is to reveal sharp underlying psychological conflict, each painting is also so much alike the other in the passionate and emotionally demanding (even exhausting) nature of its appeal that to revel in both is to reflect an underlying temperament of equal intensity. The paradox, of course, is Gardner's own: the "character" of the Christ head and of *Europa* is each very different; their "temperament" is exactly similar.

Another and scarcely less instructive kind of contrast arises when the Christ head is compared not with the *Europa* Gardner secured before it, but with the painting she next bought, the regal full-length portrait of the mid-1620s by Diego Velázquez, *His Most Catholic Majesty of Spain, Philip IV*. Full of the sort of associations Gardner reveled in–the Gardner *Philip* was carried off as loot once to Paris by Napoleon–she sought for him, she wrote Berenson, "new subjects" in the "new world."[44] Then: "His

Majesty is here! I have been unpacking him and trying to hang him all morning. . . . He is glorious. I am quite quivering and feverish over him. How simple and how great."[45] And how different from the Christ head. It was Philip and not Christ who Berenson pronounced "every inch a King."[46] But Gardner was fascinated alike by power temporal *and* spiritual. Had that not undone her and Crawford in some sense?

Philip IV, of course, had been a great lover of art. Though less interested in technique than subject, Gardner actually valued both. Witness two masterworks she acquired in 1897: one was mythological, though with religious overtones, the other a quite anonymous lady. *St. George and the Dragon*, magnificent and exotic in its jewel-like luster of gold and color, is the work of the fifteenth-century Venetian artist Carlo Crivelli; "a gorgeous thing" Berenson fairly sang to her, "more wonderful than any Japanese lacquer . . . resplendent in its gold background, its gold armor and brocade. . . . You never in your life have seen anything so beautiful for color, and in line it is drawn as if by lightning."[47] Gardner replied, as she put it, "without loss of an eyewink"[48] to secure it at once. And she rose also to Berenson's enthusiasm over *A Lady with a Rose*, "a lady so magnificent, so refined, with such exquisite hands that we must call her [Anthony] Van Dyck's *Mona Lisa*."[49] A delicately scintillating portrait, it did not disappoint: "the beautiful Van Dyck Lady salutes you," Gardner wrote back: "she has arrived and I am rejoicing over her."[50]

These first years of her life as a collector must sometimes have seemed to Gardner like the creation story from Genesis–1894: Botticelli; 1895: Rembrandt, Guardi; 1896: Titian and Giorgione and Velázquez; 1897: Crivelli and Van Dyck; and then in 1898 there would be a Rubens–his splendid portrait of *Thomas Howard, Earl of Arundel*–and yet another coup almost at the level of *Europa*: "You know, of course, all about the great Florentine banker and protector of the arts in the age of Leo X, BINDO ALTOVITI," Berenson wrote her in July 1898. "In his earlier years he was painted by Raphael. Later on when he was in the prime of his vigorous manhood, Benvenuto Cellini made a bust of him in bronze. . . . Vasari, altho' the personal enemy of Cellini, speaks of it with the greatest praise. In truth, ever since then," Berenson concluded, "and with every reason, it has passed as one of the world's greatest masterpieces."[51] In fact, Michelangelo himself, in a letter to Cellini, pronounced this bust most beautiful and one can easily imagine Gardner's hands trembling as she read Berenson's letter offering it to her. That Altoviti was an investment banker and a descendent of one of the wealthiest Florentine families of the day invited comparison, of course, to Jack Gardner, even as his progressive sympathies accorded somewhat with Isabella Gardner's, to say nothing of the fact that with all that Altoviti was a bit of a rogue, if a charming one, and was on that account all the more welcome to Gardner's collection as he himself would certainly have been to her table. Years later Berenson would pronounce the Cellini "the very greatest prize I have got for you."[52] But so fast and furious were the triumphs of 1898, it would only have been human nature for Gardner to have felt that the glory of that year of grace was that she had acquired and brought to the New World its first Raphael.[53]

It was no easy task even to decide on it. Raphael's *Count Tommasso Inghirami* depicts a sometime secretary to the College of Cardinals and the pope's chief librarian, altogether a star of the sixteenth-century papal court, a master alike of scholarship, stagecraft, poetry and rhetoric. But Tommasso had been both very fat and very homely, and on top of all that was wall-eyed. Yet Raphael had used these liabilities with consummate skill to play off against Tommasso's strengths, his wit, for instance, and his intelligence, and through a marvelous combination of pose and color and overall composition produced a picture no one would not admire.

But these aspects, color especially, and also the treatment of the cross-eyed glance, are beyond the possibilities of a black-and-white photograph! In despair, Isabella Gardner, her temper by no means improved for having lately broken her leg, fired off a letter at once fierce and pleading to Berenson. Her husband, she reported, had "taken the Raphael portrait into dislike and therefore says '*quite impossible*' for me to buy it."[54] Temporarily dependent on Jack Gardner because she'd exhausted the income during that period on her own fortune and needing a loan from him to tide her over until more of her dividends became available, Gardner felt cruelly trapped and helpless, lured by Raphael's great name and Berenson's urgent pleading but on the only evidence she had, the black-and-white photograph, not quite up to disputing with her husband as fiercely as clearly would be necessary. "I believe in you so much," she ventured to Berenson; "I don't like in the least to give up the Raphael without a kick (even with my plaster leg). So tell me again if I must have it. . . . I am in bed and nervous and sleepless and with much thinking. . . ."[55] The human cost of her already marvelous collection, the ideals behind it, the hurts to be redeemed, the arguments endured, the dreams dreamt and the treasure spent, were never so clear.

This is especially the case if these anxieties are seen in a larger context. To understand the strain Gardner was under it needs to be recalled that all these later triumphs of her life as muse, mentor, patron, collector, and, finally, as we'll see shortly, as designer, though they came more naturally to her and were, perhaps, more fulfilling, were hardly any less anxiety producing than her earlier roles as Back Bay matron, wife, and (twice) mother. Consider, by the way of comparison, for example, the brilliant Boston Brahmin modernist painter of the 1920s and 1930s, Margaret Sargent (a distant cousin of John Singer Sargent).[56] A patron of the arts (she brought both George Luks and Alexander Calder to Boston) and also a collector (of Gauguin as well as of Picasso; Boston's first, probably, in 1927), Margaret Sargent's work as a painter is increasingly admired today as well. But in her lifetime she had to give it all up: mental problems and a growing alcoholism were in her biographer's words "the inevitable result of conflict between art and female obligation [as wife, mother, and hostess] in upper-class, old family Boston."[57] And this was in the 1920s and 1930s. Isabella Stewart Gardner attempted to become her own person in a very similar way in the generation of Margaret Sargent's grandparents! If Isabella Gardner very often found herself "nervous and sleepless with much thinking," is it any wonder?

A month later Gardner was out of her cast but by no means at peace, for the Raphael was still a bone of contention: her husband, she stormed at Berenson, "says he hates it,"[58] which was definite enough, and *not* promising. Berenson himself, hardly less nervous, counseled extreme speed. Finally, a better purchase price disarmed Jack Gardner; it was only in November, however, in a customs shed on the Boston waterfront, that Gardner (having cajoled her way in) finally got the briefest peek at America's first Raphael: she was, she exulted to Berenson, "in the 7th Heaven of delight."[59]

◆

Isabella Stewart Gardner was not exaggerating. She took a very different view of things than would most, then or now. Whereas it would seem to nearly all that she was divesting herself of riches to assemble her collection, Gardner argued that she was *amassing* riches, or so at least she contended in a very frank letter to Berenson of 1898: "I look out as I write," she wrote from Beacon Street, "and see the rain puddling the snow and man and beast wallowing! Inside in this my boudoir, where I am writing, it is charming. Everywhere bits of Italy. Stuffs, pictures, frames and on a chair quite near me and the light, the little Cima *Madonna*. And downstairs, *I feel*, are all those glories I could go and look at, *if I wanted to!* Think of that. I can see that *Europa*, that Rembrandt, that Bonifazio, that Velázquez et al.–*anytime I want to*. There's richness for you."[60] Nor was this selfishness either. Rather, Isabella Gardner is pointing here to a key fact understood by only a handful of her friends.

One was Corina Putnam Smith, who as the wife of a well-known painter[61] had a wide acquaintance among American collectors; Smith thought that of them all only Charles Lang Freer, the Detroit collector, was comparable to Gardner in that both "seemed to derive the greatest satisfaction from *constant contact* [emphasis added] with their art possessions."[62] And it was Smith who elicited from Gardner the telling information that "when perplexed by an annoying problem" she liked to go and "sit quietly before a beautiful object"; added Gardner: "the problem tended to solve itself in the process." Which is not to say that her experience of the object was passive or even quiet. Consider the comparison she made to Berenson once in later life: "the doctor forbids any crowd. I couldn't even see the great [World Series] games. But I can always go and look at those wonderful stone carvings you got for me."[63]

What thought process she employed she never disclosed, but it cannot have been altogether different from her enjoyment of horticulture, about which Gardner was more forthcoming: "I shall be," she once wrote Berenson, "as silent as azaleas in flower. Do you *know* how silent they are? Come and sit on my little terrace [at Green Hill] where they all stand, in a cool, shimmering darkness made by the Japanese awnings over them, through which the sun only glints. They flower more densely than anything in the world, and each flower is silent. Perhaps!"[64] Paintings, too, are silent, perhaps! Gardner frequently seemed, out whatever window she was peering, her own or another's, to be painting pictures herself as much as writing letters–though, often, as befitted her musical ear, with a soundtrack after all: "a warm, wet December so far–but the trees are leafless and look like smoke"; "A violent and most beautiful snow storm yesterday"; "It is blowing a gale and tosses the sea about like jewels"; "My garden is riotous, unholy, deliriously glorious"; "The air from the sea under my window is absolutely delicious"; "the continuous *persua-*

sion of the sea is irresistible! Do you know the sound I mean?" Then again, she once shared with her collaborator a taste rather different than her well-known proclivity for the Madonna and Child: "I have such a foible," she confided to Berenson, "for Raphael's golden haired men."[65]

Poetry also seems to have figured in the equation, knitting together the strands. A wonderfully fugitive and telltale fragment exists of a sketch by Gardner of a picture by Turner along with a scrawled poem headed "Wilkinson wrote poem on Turner" and then, apparently, the verse: "Sky and water/bears a ship/slowly, repeating/each the other/soft and slow./Boy, boy/of [?]/sensitive heart/Turner became/the artist (light?)./Fairies dance/and make brocade/of clouds &/fire."[66] More academic studies also entered her thinking: among her notes about the *Europa* was this, marked by her as by Hazlitt:

> There is a gusto in the coloring of Titian. . . . his bodies seem to feel. This is what the Italians mean by the *morbidezza* of his flesh color. . . . Rubens makes his flesh colors like flowers; . . . Titian is like flesh, and like nothing else. . . . The blood circulates. . . . This is gusto: Van Dyke's flesh-color, though it has great truth and purity, wants gusto. . . . It is a smooth surface, not a warm moving mass. . . . The impression slides off from the eye, and does not, like the tones of Titian's pencil, leave a sting behind it.[67]

Sometimes she turned to her collaborator. "I am farming, gardening, etc., etc., and re-reading books by one Berenson," she wrote him once. Other times she applied to him directly: "I have given a great deal of time lately to studying pictures from the critical point of view" she announced on one occasion, complaining to Berenson that she could not "find at all the van der Weyden edges of things. Probably you won't have the ghost of an idea what I mean by 'edges.' I wish I could know the technical words to tell you in, for I want you to write to me on what points you found your belief in the authenticity of van der Weyden's *Annunciation*," she went on, rather flailing about: "What I call the edges in all of his that I know are so different. Do tell me that I may learn."[68] Nor did she confine herself only to the work of art as such; equally of interest, often, was the subject: having purchased a portrait as that of Isabella d'Este, Gardner promptly read John Cartwright's two-volume biography; "I am reveling in the Cartwright book. It is very interesting–but not exactly a literary production."⁶⁹ Berenson, who thought her Gardner's precursor, commanded: "read and tell me whether I am right."⁷⁰

Perhaps. But it is doubtful if that great lady of the Renaissance worked any harder than Gardner, who whatever the deepest well springs of her love for art, or the calming force it exerted in her life—or the personal triumphs it offered her—by no means merely signed a check and disappeared with her book or her thoughts into the garden and waited there serenely studying and thinking high and holy (or unholy) thoughts! She and Berenson were collaborators in the fullest sense, a team whose division of labor by no means favored Gardner.

She was hardly shy of letting her wishes be known: "let us aim awfully high," she wrote; "if you don't aim you don't get there."⁷¹ Nor was he shy: "I am not anxious to have you own," he assured her once, "braces of Rembrandts, like any vulgar millionaire."⁷² In fact, whether he proposed a purchase to her or she alerted him to something, both maneuvered so constantly to shape and give direction and focus to her collection that Samuels' phrase, a "rivalry of aspirations," is just right. Of the Gardner collection (not the museum) Gardner and Berenson were really co-founders! Thus Berenson once could write: "I have found ... what you yourself, when you were here last, urged me to find for you, a great Manet, if possible a portrait, and one worthy of hanging beside your Degas." Another time Gardner confided: "And now comes something from the back of my head and the bottom of my heart—a dream I have," forthwith proposing to Berenson a great task indeed. "But, oh, such tact, such diplomacy," she wrote, would be necessary: "So you see I put it into your hands. What do you say?" He replied: "Our dreams coincide perfectly." Alas, the painting proved elusive.⁷³

Right at the beginning of the process, Berenson's letter of appraisal and photograph in hand, Gardner's fabled "eye" comes into play. As long ago as in the late 1880s when she had allowed herself to be talked out of a bas relief she wanted only to learn from Professor Dyer that the Louvre had subsequently bought it, Gardner had remembered Dyer's insisting that "this certainly shows that you can trust your eye to pick out a good thing and leave a bad one.... you do not need to rely upon the advice of other people."⁷⁴ In Berenson's case, she often did, but as Berenson's own biographer points out: "more often than not she turned a deaf ear to [his] recommendations."⁷⁵ And sometimes, too, she followed up with a tart tongue! When Berenson protested that "a singular Lacuna in your taste is Watteau,"[76] Gardner would have none of it, firing back at once: "You have not in the least understood me vis a vis Watteau! I have not that 'lacuna,' *au contraire*, I like him very much. But," she went on, ". . . when it is a question of not money enough to go round don't you think there are others better for that price?"[77]

Occasionally she lost her temper: "I am not as stupid as you think I am. And you are as stupid as I think you are."[78] At other times, though, she could be intimate: "I have at this moment a cold in my head, my body, everywhere in fact–that makes me sure I like you very much or I should throw the inkstand at you instead of a letter."[79] And she was not without humor: "do bear my purse in mind and beat down the people who have what I want; for I *must* have the pictures! There's logic for you." Was ever spoiled such a virtue. Nor did she, for all her push and purpose, lack self-understanding, confiding once: "I suppose the picture-habit (which I seem to have) is as bad as the morphine or whiskey one."[80]

Such was her independence of judgment she more than once bought a painting on her own! Pourbus' portrait of the Infanta Isabella Clara Eugenia, for example, or Mantegna's *Sacra Conversazione*. "Here for years," complained Berenson, "I have been looking out for a Mantegna, and you who toil not, neither do you spin, have found one all by your-self."[81] But he learned soon enough that Gardner both toiled *and* spun. Though not always through Berenson! It was Charles Eliot Norton's son, Richard, who brought the Mantegna to her attention: Joseph Smith, Henry Adams, Andreas Zorn, Sargent, these and more helped her secure such treasures as the *Hercules* fresco by Piero della Francesca and the exquisite portrait of a Turkish scribe or artist, painted in fifteenth-century Constantinople.[82] And even when she accepted Berenson's advice, inspired as it often was, she kept a close rein on things: "Of course I want the Giotto–*that* there can be no question about! But the Rembrandt left me cold," she complained to him once, adding later, "Please in future . . . tell me about all at once, and let me choose. You know, or rather, you don't know, that I adore Giotto; and really don't adore Rembrandt. I only like him."[83] As it turned out the Giotto is today a glory of her collection; the Rembrandt is no longer a Rembrandt!

Once the decision was made and negotiations commenced, the burden did shift to Berenson, but Gardner's involvement hardly let up. In the case of the *Europa*, for example, the negotiations were in Carter's words "a test even of her unrivaled nerve."[84] Indeed, Berenson had only taken courage and hazarded the idea because he knew what she was prepared to pay for Gainsborough's *Blue Boy*, on which her heart was set at the time. "But she had seen the 'Blue Boy,'" wrote Carter, "and she had never seen the 'Europa.'"[85] When [Dr. Bode of the Berlin Museum, expecting a leisurely haggle], found that an American, and worse still a woman, had recklessly cabled that she would take the picture without argument, he was furious."[86] Yet Gardner could also be so tough a bargainer that Berenson was all but driven at times to distraction: once, he protested, he had worked like a slave to make possible a particular purchase, yet "this is my reward," he railed at her: "Dear Isabella, I wish I were rich *enough* . . . to make you a present of [it]."[87]

Such skirmishes between the two of them were nothing, however, compared to the "endless vendettas and the rivalries that seethed beneath the surface of the art world, in which no quarter was asked or given,"[88] in Samuels' words, and where Gardner and Berenson were united in relentless combat not only with sellers and dealers, whose interests were necessarily quite the opposite of buyers and their agents, but also with other potential buyers, formidable opponents that included the curators of great national museums like the Louvre and personages such as the Rothschilds and the German and Russian emperors, the last two of which could in the nature of things never be outspent and had therefore always to be outwitted, while all the while one eye at least had to be kept on the Italian government, so determined to staunch the outflow of the national patrimony by every possible means. Both Berenson and Gardner respected the Italian point of view. Told by Berenson that one seller "considers himself trustee of the pictures for Italy, and I must say I would more Italians had such feelings,"[89] Gardner was not without sympathy but frankly skeptical and kept her eye on her goal, replying bluntly: "kill the Giovanelli's for me. They are quite right, *if* [emphasis added] they are speaking the truth. Of course I think *it* ought never to leave Italy, unless it is to come to me! Don't you?"[90] He did indeed!

The result was that Gardner and Berenson literally, not figuratively, became international smugglers. Everyone–treating it rather as a sporting proposition–did it to some extent (including even the so scrupulous Henry Adams),[91] rationalizing the crime by the not entirely unfounded belief that left in Italy many of these pictures, very ill cared for as they were, would hardly survive. *Christ Bearing the Cross*, however, to cite one example, had been promised by its noble seller to the town of Vincenzia.

The reaction to its sale of the citizenry, already aroused enough by its noble seller on another matter to have staged a rock-throwing riot outside his palazzo, was a matter of concern. The picture was duly spirited out "in a blanket,"[92] but the *polizia* were on Berenson's doorstep before this play was ended, and it was only with difficulty that he defended himself from a charge brought against him by the authorities.

If the stress of getting a picture out of Italy fell mostly on Berenson, the stress of getting it into the United States fell always on Gardner. She was vigilantly watched and at varying times paid duties and fines of 150,000 dollars; and on another occasion, of 200,000, for the distinction between "private" and "public" collecting in Gardner's case was a shifting one.[93] And what if all this interfered seriously with what she could spend on art? American customs, not very Ruskinian, could hardly see Gardner's point at all. Especially as the public's access to the art she brought in was not at all clear. Indeed, the Italian authorities in attempting to keep their art in Italy, and the American authorities in attempting to keep it out of the U.S. proved in each case Gardner's most nerve-racking anxiety.

Nor was the day's work done when and if the painting finally arrived. "I was present at the opening [of the crate] at the Custom's [shed on the dock] so I know," she wrote Berenson once protesting the bad packing, that may well have damaged more than one picture, only the first of many aspects of conservation she had increasingly to deal with: "I found the back in a terrible condition," she complained once of another picture to Berenson, ". . . riddled and alive with worms! Of course I and Potter (who is a wonder) went for it and I hope the harm can be stopped." But not all restorers seemed so wondrous to her: "The Milan man's work," she admitted to Berenson, "is wonderfully amazing, but I never want that sort of thing"; his work seemed to her very overdone.

Then there was the matter of the frame. That of the Raphael portrait, Berenson lamented was "hideous. You must think out a frame," he wrote, suggesting something "flat-rimmed, simple, pale old gold," or, perhaps, "dark, deep purplish wood." Another time it was Gardner who was horrified: "the frame is a terror," she wrote; she was having "another made . . . that will not make the delicate little picture shriek and scream." It was, really, one thing after another! And at the end of the day, her fabled eye at rest, the jousting with Berenson over, the sellers satisfied, the other would-be buyers outwitted and the two governments flummoxed, the picture delivered, conserved (framed?), Isabella Gardner, beginning in her own circle, and rippling outward one hardly knew how widely into the intelligentsia and American popular opinion generally, took up yet another task, that of tastemaker–and to be art's private lover was a quite different task than becoming its public sponsor.

Elsie De Wolfe, knowing nothing of the anxious negotiations or of Gardner's private rapture over *Europa*, addressed only the public aspect of Gardner's acquisition when she wrote that she saw in Gardner's decision to risk the *Europa* as the centerpiece of her collection evidence that Gardner's was "one of the really distinguished figures of the last century. Her brain was far ahead of her time, and she had tremendous courage in advancing her ideas."[94]

The Red Drawing Room at 152 Beacon Street in the mid-1890s. Visible to the left is a self-portrait by Rembrandt. *Isabella Stewart Gardner Museum, Boston*

That Gardner knew the risks she took (and how many wished her to make a fool of herself in this last and most public stage of the matter especially) is clear in her reports to Berenson of how her end of things turned out. "Many came [to see *Europa*] with 'grave doubts'; many came to scoff"– the price alone, a hundred thousand dollars in 1896, invited ridicule–"but all wallowed at [*Europa's*] feet," she told him. "One painter," said Gardner, "a general skeptic, couldn't speak for the tears! All of joy!!!"[95]

Gardner's technique was faultless. For example, the purchase of Franceso Turbido's *Lady with a Turban* as a portrait of Isabelle d'Este, "the greatest and most fascinating lady of the Renaissance,"[96] as Berenson declared her to be, naturally excited Gardner. She had, to be sure, through Julia Ward Howe, real links to her Boston precursor, Margaret Fuller. And Gardner cannot but have been pleased that she was so often compared to Madame de Staël, so admired, despite her plainness, for her wit and intellect. But it was above all Isabella d'Este to whom Isabella Gardner seemed so entirely comparable. A notable patron of the arts and letters, who befriended artists and stimulated their creativity (both Titian and Leonardo painted her), Isabella d'Este was also a collector of the art both of her own time and of past eras; famed for her love of beauty and her critical taste, she was as well a sagacious politician and a great lady. *La prima donna del mondo*/the foremost lady of the world, as she was called, was given a worthy reception in Boston. Gardner reported to Berenson: "Isabella d'Este is here. She arrived safely and is most delightful. She and Rembrandt held quite a little reception this afternoon. I had some delicious music. When that was over, the devotees put themselves at the feet of the lady and the painter. They and the music–all three–had a great success."[97] According to Berenson, there was incense too. If it sounds as much a religious as a social event, so be it. Art and religion were sufficiently intimately allied for Isabella Gardner that her role as tastemaker was not unlike the preacher's.

And her influence was felt not only by collectors and curators but among contemporary artists as well. Of a most distinguished painter of the day, for example, Edmund C. Tarbell, Trevor Fairbrother has written: "the most telling influence on the evolution of [Tarbell's] interiors was Gardner's purchase of Vermeer's *Concert*."[98] What striking evidence of the importance of Gardner's role at the end of this last stage of the collecting process as tastemaker that this first coup of her life as a collector should have been so influential a creative spur to the work of so esteemed a contemporary master as Tarbell, leader of the Boston School, the legacy of which is with us yet in the work today of such fine artists as Robert Douglas Hunter.

Now it may well be argued that the Boston School was not very progressive, and Gardner herself, though on at least one occasion Tarbell was part of a group of artists asked to paint at Green Hill, did not ever collect his work. Yet if the smooth, suave surfaces of William McGregor Paxton, for instance, can be criticized as more Vermeer than Paxton, Tarbell himself, in the view of more than one critic, quite revivified Vermeer's aesthetic and without at all copying that master's technique; fusing Impressionism with the old tradition, Philip Hale thought. Tarbell's use of "opaque color laid on with a full brush" seemed also in Trevor Fairbrother's words, "unmistakably modern."[99] (Who else, Kenyon Cox demanded, since Vermeer, had "made a flat wall so interesting?")[100] Furthermore, in the best Boston tradition, not only was their contemporary art inspired by Gardner's collecting, but new scholarship too: the first American study of Vermeer, the work in 1913 of Philip Hale, came out of the milieu of the Boston School, which it may be mentioned also took much inspiration from the work of Gardner's protégé of the 1880s, Dennis Bunker.[101]

A perhaps crass but needful counterpoint to the preaching of various artistic causes concerns the fundamental matter of money. Just so fundamental a matter as paying for a painting posed a very real challenge to Gardner. She was only able to pay for the portrait of Isabella d'Este, for example, because of the winnings of her horse *Halton!*[102] And it was not entirely a case of her wonderful sense of black humor when she minuted Berenson typically in one case that her only recourse, she thought, would be "putting on my pearls and begging from door to door—no other clothes but my Rosalina point lace!"

Her worst financial struggles came in later years after Jack Gardner's death: "I sent for my business man this morning," she wrote Berenson: "We almost came to blows." That was in 1899. A year later she was still reporting "a stormy interview with my business people," and within a month: "I have had to have another man put in charge of my own fast diminishing property," and something of her force of character emerges in her next sentence: the new man, she reported, was "arranging *hard* to send the money." On the other hand she could also cajole: "if I could fire Swift's imagination by showing the photograph [of a painting] to him, perhaps he could twist out more money." But it was often a depressing business: "all my hopes," she admitted once, "are on George Gardner's arranging something, and my insides feel that he won't." Finally: "But I don't give up so easily. . . . Brookline [her house at Green Hill] is to let, and if someone would only take it I could get some money."[103]

Even at the height of her purchasing power, in the mid-1890s, with Jack Gardner at her side, it was an anxious business raising sums hard-head Yankees could hardly be expected to understand her need of. In fact, Gardner's expenditures were mounting so precipitously by century's end she had, as she wrote Berenson in 1898, so little money in hand that "the only chance would be to have Mr. Gardner lend."[104] Usually this was not a problem, as Jack Gardner took a lively interest in the collecting of his wife, who was, after all, a millionaire in her own right. But soon enough, events conspired to suggest to him that his wife's increasing financial problems were accounted for not only by her superb taste and keen eye, but perhaps also by the dishonesty of Bernard Berenson, whose money problems were far worse than Isabella Gardner's.

If she had after all, very little money, really, for the work she had taken up ("with tears streaming down my face, because I haven't [J. P.] Morgan's money, I do up the photographs to return"[105] was a characteristic lament repeated in substance by Gardner to Berenson time and time again) Berenson, for his part, was still a poor scholar, often financially strained. On at least one occasion it is known that only a three-thousand-dollar check of Gardner's saved Berenson from an overdraft of over two thousand dollars.[106]

Berenson received in the first place from Gardner a very low 5 percent commission.[107] There was also the matter of the necessity of payments by him to various dealers to guarantee him first refusal, or, perhaps, to hold a picture for a certain period of time. Moreover, because Gardner was so tough a bargainer, Berenson found it easier to quote her a price high enough that if necessity required he need never ask her for more and, indeed, might be able to ask for less. Finally, he was vulnerable, to some extent because of Gardner's very low commission, to the temptation of taking an additional commission from the seller or even from the dealer, a fact Gardner might have guessed was likely but that Berenson never discussed with her; in fact, he was operating, Samuels admits, "on the razor's edge of probity." Jack Gardner, nobody's fool, found out.

Worse, Richard Norton, the son of Charles Eliot Norton, neither of them Berenson's friend, weighed in to confirm Jack Gardner's suspicions, writing, for example, to Isabella Gardner in 1898 that Berenson was dishonest. "He is as you must know a dealer. Well, there are only one or two honest Fine Art dealers in the world and Berenson is not one of those."[108] Norton added that when he had recommended works to Gardner "I have never, as you yourself know, made one single *centisimo* in the business. This is the only right way of doing such work for it leaves me free as the winds of heaven."[109] It was the privilege of the patrician that the son of North End immigrants could hardly lay claim to.

Though she loyally stuck up for Berenson, Isabella Gardner had really no choice but to write to her collaborator that September in the strongest possible terms: "there is a terrible row about you. . . . vile things have been said to Mr. Gardner. . . . *They* say (there seem many) that you have been dishonest in your money dealings. . . . Hearing this Mr. G. instantly makes remarks about the Inghirami Raphael you got me. He says things I dislike very much to hear. . . . I'm sure that you have enemies. . . . Every word I write seems cruel and unnecessary. Forgive the sound of the words and look beneath them for my truly friendly motive."[110]

Berenson could hardly honestly do otherwise than insist he felt "no animosity"[111] toward Jack Gardner; but in Samuels' words, he was "overcome with remorse and fear." His wife described him as "almost suicidal,"[112] and Samuels concedes that "in view of [Berenson's] panic it is unavoidable to say his financial arrangement plainly would not have borne disclosure."[113] There is no way around it. Writes Samuels: "[Jack Gardner's] accusations were not entirely without foundation."

Another of Berenson's biographers, however, has frankly pointed out that "the moral price Berenson had to pay for the larger and larger sums of money he was making was one that continued to weigh on his mind all his life."[114] Especially was this true as it impacted on Isabella Gardner, for if he had played Adam to Gardner's Eve only too well, "the fact that he owed her everything," as Meryle Secrest put it, "including his gratitude, did not make it easier"[115]–for him *or* for Isabella Gardner, who found herself seemingly thwarted on all sides at the end of 1898 when, in Samuels' words, Berenson was "providentially relieved from the need of allaying Mr. Gardner's suspicions by his sudden death"![116]

Felled at the cruelly young age of sixty-one by a stroke at one of his clubs on December 10, John Lowell Gardner had been, whatever else he was or was not, Isabella Gardner's most insistent admirer and most trusted lifelong adviser, and second only to Berenson himself, her collaborator and confidant in the matter of the forming of her great collection. No wonder Isabella Gardner admitted to "mental confusion,"[117] in the midst of yet another loss that must have been keenly felt.

All things considered, however, the loss was in certain respects clarifying. Not only was the triangle with Berenson eased, but so was a much more long-standing one.

◆

What was it Gardner had caused to be painted on to the tilework of her bathroom: "Think much, speak little, write nothing." It is one possible explanation for why–despite widespread gossip in her lifetime and beyond–hardly any trace at all exists a hundred or so years later of Isabella Gardner's supposedly fabled secret love life, which if rumor was and is to be believed rivaled in her day that of Pamela Churchill Harriman in our own.

Only once have I felt a surmise take form that somehow persists: the biographer of the brilliant and handsome Italian composer Ferruccio Busoni notes that there is no evidence of an affair between him and Isabella Gardner even though such affairs were by no means uncommon for Busoni, who did from time to time meet Isabella Gardner in Europe– and, it must be added, even though Gardner lent Busoni at his request the then enormous sum of a thousand dollars, a gift that could be seen as indicating a relationship closer to devotion than patronage.[118]

Significantly, this possibility arises in the Old World. But even there Isabella Gardner could hardly have led much of a double life. Jack Gardner, of course, could easily without trace have sought sexual companionship either at home or abroad in time-honored ways, and have maintained, for example, a mistress (as many of his class did) in Boston's South End, a diverse residential quarter[119] that had its respectable enclaves adjoining the Back Bay. Edwardian house party mores, however, the only context for a lady to have such an affair, not only hardly prevailed in Boston, but for an American lady in her husband's company were rather problematic abroad as well. Especially for someone as increasingly well known in fashionable transatlantic circles as Isabella Gardner. True, Gardner burned many letters to her. But someone, somewhere, would have written of this or that affair of Gardner, not to her, but to someone else (rather as Ralph Curtis wrote to Gardner about other women's affairs). Yet not one such letter has surfaced in a century and a half! There are only suggestive observations like Carter's about how fearful Gardner's friends were of the publication of whatever. And there is the other painted tile Isabella Gardner imbedded in her bathroom tilework: "Secret of two secret of God; secret of three secret of all"!

It is possible, of course, that like Margaret Fuller, Gardner was driven for much of her life by erotic energy she gradually learned to focus on art.[120] More likely, however, Isabella Gardner, faithful in one way to Jack Gardner, was faithful in hardly less important ways to her great and as it turned out her abiding love—Frank Crawford. Not just her bathroom mottoes are at hand. Gardner's commonplace book, the closest thing to a diary, emotionally, we have, offers clues as well. It was there after all (and of whom else than Crawford?) she had written that "indifferent souls never part; only passionate souls part, and return to one another because they can do no better."

A relationship may end well if it is, so to speak, fulfilled—which is to say in the minds of both people, who mutually agree to part. Thus the amicable divorce, not unknown. But neither Gardner nor Crawford could very well ever have been at peace in that way about their relationship's ending. For Gardner it had been a savage hurt, and for Crawford at best a cruelly inept defensive retreat which as he matured he would have been less and less happy about. Crawford, proud and stubborn man that he was, and by then a famous novelist as well, found the courage to make the first move, even if it did take ten years and was rooted in his growing desperation and depression of the nineties, which he must have guessed only Gardner could ease. It speaks even better of him that he made a second overture when Gardner did not reply. It is much more difficult to ask for and accept forgiveness than to give it. His courage, indeed, may well have sparked her forgiveness, which really did cover Isabella Gardner in glory, for it was evidently not grudging; she forgave Crawford wholeheartedly, herself now older and wiser and more aware doubtless of her own faults.

In 1892 Isabella Gardner and Frank Crawford were soul mates again, and just as *To Leeward* reflected the emotional crisis of his departure from Boston in 1883, so did another of his novels, *Casa Braccio*, relate to his return to America—and, in a very real sense, to Isabella Gardner. So at least Crawford's biographer argues, noting that the character of Paul Griggs, always Crawford's "fictional representative," speaks in *Casa Braccio* both of his near-suicidal state and of the only light he saw–"the truest [friendship] that ever was between man and woman"–clearly him and Isabella Gardner.

How immediate and intimate was their rapprochement is clear from his three-week siege in a New York hospital the next year. His biographer declares that "not even [Crawford's] wife knew that he was there, but he informed Mrs. Gardner, who visited him several times."[121] In 1894 Gardner had resumed her old role of reading the uncorrected proofs of Crawford's books, and letters from him to Gardner exist (though none from her to him; Crawford burned them all; she merely cut out certain passages) right through the 1890s into the 1900s, all making very clear that the alpha male who had bailed out on the middle-aged married woman in 1882 and made the conventional, upwardly mobile, age-appropriate marriage had discovered, for all his worldly success, that however demanding and difficult Gardner could be, the devotion, loyalty, and faithfulness of her love, once so inconvenient for him, was a rare commodity in the real world, and worth laying claim to after all. "I often think of you," he wrote to her in 1893, "when I am all alone, and know how much alone I am."

By 1895 they appear to have reestablished what became again a most cherished intimacy: he even wrote her that he thought "we shall read out Dante this year."[122] How close their renewed relationship was emerges in a letter of his of December 1894, which also discloses its continuing complexities, and how much more alert Crawford had become to them with a greater maturity. He knew himself much better now. And he knew now what love was.

You wrote me a very kind letter some time ago. Yes–I know that you wish to believe well of me, and that you take my defense, when you hear me abused by your friends. But with me, whether in writing or in talking, you show that in spite of the best intentions the belief itself will not really come. I do not in the least blame you for that, and I am honestly grateful to you for taking my part, though it is quite useless, as you have no doubt discovered. But I did not mean that you wished to think evil of me–you cannot help it. That is all, and I suppose that you have every reason on your side. Besides,

appearances and public opinion are often against me, because I am
rather indifferent to both, and the world never forgives indifference.
If you like, we will say no more about it.

Gardner, if in 1882 she had been the wronged one, had nonetheless
subsequently waxed and not waned; the stronger of the two as it turns
out, though devastated by their parting, she survived it better. Crawford,
for his part, grew increasingly suicidal in the mid-1890s (despite his great
success, "sadness, even bitterness, is creeping upon him" wrote Maude
Howe Elliott; Crawford had separated from his wife after only seven
years, in 1891) and only his renewed friendship with Gardner sustained
him through his increasing melancholy.[123]

Jack Gardner's feelings about all this, or if, indeed, he knew of it in the
first place, we cannot know. In one letter to Isabella Gardner, Crawford
suggests the real problem was Mrs. Crawford, not Mr. Gardner.
("Madame's behavior," he wrote, "has put a stop to my staying in any of
your houses. I *cannot* stand the idea of stopping under your husband's
roof, when I cannot even have you to dinner in my own house.")[124]
Perhaps as they approached sixty Jack and Belle had made their peace
with each other about poor Crawford. Theirs, after all, was a good marriage in its way. Isabella and Jack Gardner's union was not, as Meryle
Seacrest believed, that of an "eternal adolescent, ravenous for an adoring
circle of admirers" to an "indulgent father [figure]."[125] On the other hand,
it was not quite what Arlo Bates imagined in 1888 in *The Puritans*, where
both Jack and Isabella are cast as amiable cynics who served each other's
purposes, he struck by her grit and her style (he calls her "a devilish hum-
bug" at one point; but adds: "you do manage to get a lot of fun"),[126] she
only "free" so long as her activities amused her husband. Bates' was an
affectionate caricature but still a caricature, no truer than Seacrest's. In
fact, Isabella Gardner gave focus and direction to her husband's life as
much as in different ways she did to Berenson's or Crawford's. She was,
in the end, as much muse and mentor to Jack Gardner as she was to anyone, while he in turn gave her always the strong wall to grow against her
paradoxical character and artistic temperament needed.

I think of a tale by Edith Wharton, who in the next generation was
most insightful of many concerns common to women in both generations, a tale called "The Fullness of Life," in which a woman dies and
upon meeting the Spirit of Life in Paradise confesses to never having

known "that fullness of life which we all feel ourselves capable of know-ing." When the Spirit queries her about her feelings for her husband, she offers what Shari Benstock calls "the most famous [image] in Edith Wharton's fiction," the one about "a great house of many rooms for many purposes," at the heart of which, writes Wharton, is "the innermost room, the holy of holies, [where] the soul sits alone and waits for a foot-step that never comes." Yet when the Spirit offers the woman eternity with a "kindred soul"–in other words, a Crawford figure–the woman, free now and older, prefers to wait for her husband; she would not "feel at home," she says, "without him."[127]

The image is so apt for Gardner, famous as she was for her own "great house of many rooms" and especially for her small boudoir at Beacon Street, where she and Crawford read their Dante, a room artfully described by T. R. Sullivan in 1891:

> Lunched today with Mrs. J. L. Gardner, in her boudoir, which might be called "The Chamber Over the Gate." It is filled with rare and beautiful things from every clime. Above the wainscot is a frieze of portrait-heads, early Italian, thirty in all. A Dutch landscape, all gold and red and brown, is let into the wall over the fireplace. The hang-ings are priceless–Chinese and Indian from imperial looms. A little Bartolozzi print in one corner once belonged to Byron. There is a laurel from Aruga, a bit of San Francesco's miraculous tree, etc., etc., "Everything here is a remembrance," said the hostess, who was arranging orchids. . . .[128]

And so with Jack Gardner. As it happens Christ Bearing the Cross had just come before Jack's death and before it there would always be violets.

◆

More than violets–there would be a museum! For whatever reason–did she sense likely opposition from her in-laws?–Isabella Gardner moved decisively after her husband's death, with almost unseemly haste, to make her vision a reality–a vision Jack Gardner (like Bernard Berenson–though for different reasons!–Isabella Gardner's magnetism was like that) had so made his own that while the form it finally took, Fenway Court, would be overwhelmingly Isabella Gardner's, the idea was also impor-tantly not only Bernard Berenson's but Jack Gardner's too.

The Rembrandt self-portrait, the first picture–so Isabella Gardner told Carter–bought with a museum in mind,[129] had been offered to her by Berenson in January of 1896 in a letter in which Gardner's collaborator mentioned "your gallery," an idea we know he had put earlier to Gardner because Berenson had written beforehand to his future wife, Mary Costelloe, that "Mrs. Jack seems delighted with my dream of her gallery and hints at wishing it to be realized."[130] Whether or not Gardner had incited Berenson previously with her own youthful dream, confided to Ida Agassiz, in 1858 is not known. Probably she would have unfolded her own idea first (and gradually!) to Jack Gardner. In whichever event by July of 1896 Isabella Gardner was writing to Berenson quite openly of "my Museum."[131] Note that the words are always "gallery" or "museum," *not* "house," although its location was originally residential Beacon Street, where Willard Sears, who had already designed a summer house for the Gardners in Maine,[132] was set to work on an attached building in the midst of the Back Bay town house block the Gardners lived in.

Whoever sparked whose vision of the Gardner Museum, it was Jack Gardner who took the most decisive hand in shaping it, as Corina Putnam Smith documented. It seems one night, at dinner with the Gardners, Smith heard this significant conversation between Isabella and Jack Gardner:

> She interrupted him as he referred to the advantage of a site with open space around it, permitting light from windows on four sides of the building. She told him not to be "practical," or he might tempt her to invent a new system of lighting. To him, apparently, this was a warning signal. The subject was dropped and other matters were discussed.
>
> Unquestionably, they were on the best of terms. Obviously, she relied on his judgment . . . she remarked seriously to Joe that no one knew better than he how Jack had encouraged an Isabella Stewart Gardner collection.
>
> Her husband showed inordinate pride in her ability and achieve- ments and, as I was to learn, was pleased at the admiration she aroused in all men of distinction.
>
> I have remembered as a final scene of that unforgettable evening his eloquent appeal to her imagination in urging her to create a Venetian palace out of barren waste land.[133]

Within two weeks of Jack Gardner's death, and with no warning at all to her architect, already at work on plans for the Beacon Street building, Isabella Gardner bought a large tract of land in the Fenway, a new and just then beginning to be developed area adjoining the Back Bay which took its name from a park recently laid out there by Frederick Law Olmsted. If whether her museum was to be on the site of the Back Bay town house or in the Fenway was Jack and Isabella Gardner's last argument, Jack had won.

◆

If it was over Berenson, however, Jack just as certainly lost. A further fracas about Berenson's wheeling and dealing blew up in May of 1899, and "again Bernard fell into an almost suicidal despair, not knowing how to appease her wrath,"[134] for Isabella Gardner herself threatened to sue this time; not Berenson of course, but a particular dealer whom she settled on more or less frankly as a scapegoat. She had signaled her displeasure. But as clearly made as her decision for the Fenway was her decision for Berenson; in fact she most likely sympathized with him all along; certainly she wrote to him some years after the affair, when they were on more intimate terms, with evident understanding: "Dear old man, [it was a term of endearment, he was just over forty] I will not have it that you should ever be that odious thing, 'a social lounger and money grubber.' Take a brace, for love of me."[135] And then, in another letter: "nothing matters except that you have to make money! That is really desperate and horrid. You are not that kind; and should always be under the shower of gold! I think I'm that kind too."[136] In her sixties as the new century dawned, more focused now on art, her husband dead, Crawford back in Europe again, Gardner increasingly found in Berenson more of a soul mate than ever she had expected, joined as they were in a truly great undertaking.

Berenson was proving after all to be an inspired collaborator: Paul Clemen, the eminent professor of art history at Bonn University would assure Gardner: "you have now the best private collection in the world– not the largest, but the noblest,"[137] documenting Berenson's later boast to Gardner: "We may between us have made one or two mistakes, but we have brought together masterpieces of a beauty, of a splendor, and of a harmony, that nothing in the last 20 years can touch. This is pretty universally granted,"[138] he concluded, enclosing a news clipping from the

Times of London singing his and Gardner's praises. A similar news clipping (perhaps the same one; it is not identified) in the Gardner scrapbooks takes a similar line: "The collector must, of course, in modern times have large sums. . . . but this is not enough. He must have the experience of an antiquary and the quickness of a tiger. He must be at the same time an impassioned votary and a big business man." Gardner, the report goes on, was such a one, but above all, she was an "unusual combination in a single person of a rare gift for beauty and an equally remarkable knowledge of the world." The writer continued, "*I mean the instinct of whom to trust* [emphasis added]." In Gardner's case, the report concludes, it was "her fortunate alliance with Mr. Berenson, whom she . . . first befriended as a poor scholar,"[139] that assured the success of her efforts. Yes, Gardner had an eye, nerve, all the rest of it. But one must not forget by 1900 that Berenson was the greatest connoisseur of Italian Renaissance art in the world;[140] in no small measure thanks to her patronage. And for his part, if Berenson was quite sincere (if not too shrewd) in his belief that his financial needs would never corrupt his judgment, it must be said that, overall, the glory of the Gardner Collection goes far to document his own genius.

Although Isabella Gardner resumed collecting promptly enough after Jack Gardner's death, a certain darkening of vision overall is newly discernible: the paintings bought in the years just after Jack's passing were preeminently religious pictures, such as Rembrandt's magnificent *Storm on the Sea of Galilee* of 1633. This work, which depicts the drama of St. Luke's tale of Christ rebuking the wind in the face of his disciples' anxiety in a great storm that is all but engulfing their boat, is a study of calm (Christ's) in the midst of great turbulence and it appealed at once of course to Gardner. So did Botticelli's *Madonna of the Eucharist*: lyrically beautiful but in a very tense sort of way, this appealed doubtless for a different reason, perhaps because, in Samuels' words, "The pleasure one gets from Botticelli is really an exquisite high-strung pain."[141]

Then there was Simone Martini's *Madonna and Child with Four Saints*. First called to Gardner's attention by Richard Norton, by then at the American School of Classical Studies in Rome, this glorious five-fold altarpiece was secured for Gardner by Berenson in 1899. A "dazzling" work[142] (the word is Berenson's) of the Sienese master–five panels of richly colored shimmering figures against a lustrous gold background–it so entranced Berenson that he confessed to Gardner he had "bitterly regretted" parting with what "would have been a joy forever to me, and at a price I easily could afford. . . . I had an awful struggle with myself," he concluded, offering to "joyfully" pay her a thousand pounds for the altarpiece, if she was willing to part with it.[143] She wasn't. Instead, told by Berenson he was pursuing a Fra Angelico–"at last I have my hook in a work by this angel which I hope to land safely"[144]–she reached out promptly for *The Death and Assumption of the Virgin*, a superb picture of about 1432.

Not content, she celebrated the first year of the new century with two triumphant acquisitions. Knowing how dearly she sought a Giotto, when Berenson produced for her that year *The Presentation of the Infant Jesus in the Temple*, a work by that legendary master over five hundred years old when Gardner bought it, Berenson could be forgiven for rather a flourish: "I am not going to insult you by talking to *you* about Giotto," he wrote, but he could not help boasting that Giotto's work was "a rare thing for any of the collections of the world to boast of."[145] Forthwith he matched the one coup with another for what seems to us now rather a finale of this nine-year period: a *Pietà* of about 1501–02 by Raphael; "a jewel" it seemed to him, "of the most exquisite delicacy." Again, the photograph simply couldn't be depended upon, and there was "not a moment to delay." But Berenson knew his patron: "use your imagination" he roared![146] She did, though "in fear and trembling. My trustee may kill me."[147]

Financially, it was more difficult for her now Jack Gardner was gone, as she confided in Berenson in 1900:

> You see the way with my money is this–I had two fortunes–my own and Mr. Gardner's. . . . The income of mine was all very well until I began to buy big things. The purchase of *Europa and the Bull* was the 1st time I had to dip into the capital. And since then, those times have steadily multiplied. . . . Woe is me. The income from Mr. Gardner's fortune is about half what it was before his death, owing to the trustees' changing everything to perfectly sure investments that give very little return. . . . I don't care particularly to tell my private affairs to those whose business it is not. The outside world seems to have got an idea that I have millions. . . . Probably much of the misunderstanding comes from the way I spend my money. I fancy I am the only living American who puts *everything* into works of art and music; I mean, instead of into show, and meat and drink. I wish they would understand, and leave me in peace.[148]

At about the same time she thus explained what would be the increasingly spare lifestyle of her late middle age, she made rather a point of defending it. Her philosophy of life, she wrote Berenson, had become "very simple," amounting more or less to "seeing and doing only what is beautiful. I thank the Lord I am not as other men are, who bother about the Dreyfus case [referring to the anti-Semitic scandal of the time in France] and climb mountains. . . . I am quite content," she continued, "*au niveau de la mer*. Perhaps if you come here, I may convert you."[149]

That, sent from the Palazzo Barbaro in Venice, or this from Green Hill, her Brookline estate–"The grape vine that holds this house in its embrace is in flower. Do you know the odor, pervading, inebriating! It comes in at my window"[150]–do seem dangerously self-absorbed. Yet, looked at more closely, such letters surely disclose Gardner's perennial need for calm in a life driven by her nervous energy. In even the simplest things she was ever an enthusiast: "I am just going out for a drive; my little bay pair are waiting at the door"[151]; one letter to Berenson begins rather lazily in May of 1899: "I have been giving chickweed to the mocking bird, and trolled about with the fox terriers," she continued, concluding this relaxing agenda with news of her drive's *purpose*: she was "now starting on a hunt for a new variety of lilacs"![152]

Berenson's response to her disclosure of her philosophy and her finances was a warm one: "I have always more than suspected that you were really spending all your fortune on works of art," he wrote, and a year later he returned to the subject, writing to her with unusual eloquence:

> Please do not think that I regard your purse as bottomless, or fail to recognize the dose of heroic effort and real sacrifice incurred in arranging your purchases. A miracle that continues forever ceases to startle. . . . Yet the enlightened person fails not to continually admire. And I am in a state of perpetual admiration of your courage, your determination, your readiness to sacrifice anything and everything to your purpose. Although in a humble degree, I am myself enough of the same family to appreciate and adore the person who can live for an end. And the end really is a splendid one. At this eleventh hour you are gathering together a collection which in many respects will rival those that generations and the resources of Nations have brought together. Nor is the end yet I hope. . . . *Courage mon amie*, and good luck.[153]

These were heartfelt salutations for all Berenson's interest in the matter and to understand how much they must have meant to Gardner, it
needs to be remembered how shy Isabella Gardner was in disclosing her
intended public benefaction. Indeed, other than to Berenson, only once
did she take anyone else into her confidence: Edmund Hill, the horticul-
turist and an old friend, to whom she explained herself years later and
only when she felt misunderstood enough to need to explain her penurious lifestyle by making a defense that while it by no means obscured her
egoism (for which, praise be; nothing would have happened without it!),
disclosed also the altruism she rather hid but which, like Freud, she
insisted was the only mature adult goal of youthful egoism. "My position," she wrote to Hill in her plainspoken and never at all literary way,
"is not quite what you think. Years ago I decided that the greatest need in
our Country was Art. We were largely developing the other sides. We
were a very young country & had very few opportunities of seeing beautiful things, works of art, etc. So I determined," she went on, "to make it
my life work if I could. Therefore, ever since my parents died I have
spent every cent I inherited (for that was my money) in bringing about
the object of my life. So, you see for my personal needs I cannot possibly
sell any work of art. I economize as much as possible with the income of
Mr. Gardner's money left to me. The principal I shall never touch. I economize with the income because what I save goes to the upkeep of my
ideal project."[154]

Not only was "the object of [her] life" as she conceived it in the 1890s
quite unsuspected by anyone except Berenson, but precisely because she
hid her developing altruistic goals Gardner herself contributed to widespread misunderstanding of her purposes. Apparently fundamental philo-
sophical differences with Gardner as art collector and tastemaker led
even some friends to question and even to condemn what she was doing;
as it turned out risking alienating her old friend and mentor Charles Eliot
Norton in the matter of Berenson and his new theories of connoisseurship was only the beginning. More formidable was Henry James, who, if
he was increasingly fascinated by Isabella Gardner personally, was also at
first rather alarmed with her collecting activities, as these began to dominate her life to the exclusion of all else. Leon Edel's observation is perti-
nent: "Isabella took her place in the pattern of James's days and years,
and fixed her image in his work: for if one of his great themes was the
chase of the American girl for the husband, another was the chase of the
wealthy American for the artifacts of Europe."[155] James' biographer

acknowledges "American shrewdness in the gathering in of Europe's treasures"[156] and in another place declares that it was, indeed, Gardner who offered James the type of the ardent American "collector" swooping down on Europe for great spoils.[157] But for James, however useful for his work was this theme, which he exploited to the full, the New World's exercise of capitalist power could fairly be compared with the Old World's exercise of military power, which is to say that looting was loot-ing, whether of Constantinople by Venice or of Venice by Boston–and that it was a form, after all, of rape.

It should not surprise, therefore, that in 1894, in his notebooks, those diary–like journals of James wherein we can now read his mind some-what, Isabella Gardner appears most importantly, but also now most harshly considered, not so much as a queen but as a spoiler, for what James wrote he feared above all was "the deluge of people, the insane movement for movement, the ruin of thought, of life, the negation of work, of literature, the swelling, roaring crowds, the 'where are you going?', the age of Mrs. Jack, the figure of Mrs. Jack, the American, the nightmare–the individual consciousness–the mad, ghastly climax . . . The Americans looming up–dim, vast, portentous–in their millions–like gath-ering waves–the barbarians of the Roman Empire."[158] James had not fled from America to Europe only to see Europe–above all, his much loved Venice–looted of her treasures and sent back to–of all places–America.

On the other hand, Venice's own splendors *were* largely looted from elsewhere, and Byron was hardly wrong to think Americans "the appro-priate heir[s] to Venice's ancient republicanism."[159] American artists par-ticularly were also drawn to Venice. Between 1860 and 1920, nearly a hundred American artists are known to have worked in Venice, despite its lack of an established art school or any sale galleries. And they brought significant gifts, including a unique vitality. Only in the work of some of these Americans, Margaretta Lovell has written, do "we recog-nize something we miss in that of their European counterparts, and that is, curiously, the clear, frank irreverent note of modernity."[160] In turn, she continued, having Sargent, Whistler, and Prendergast chiefly in mind, "Venice provided the occasion for their most innovative work, work touched more clearly with the stamp of modernism than that produced in far less archaic environments."[161] Truly, Gardner and her circle by no means languished, or even, in our sense, vacationed in Venice. They lived there, taking much but giving much back, conscious perhaps of Arthur

Symon's elegy: in Venice by the late nineteenth century he wrote: "the masque or ballet ... is over. The scenery is still there, the lights have been left on; only the actors, the dancers are gone";[162] a perfectly reason-able assertion, not meant to disparage contemporary Venetians (Gardner was very active in the artistic and social and charitable life of the city) but a frank acknowledgment of the fact that Venice no longer was at the center of historical events and its splendid art and architecture were thus rather stranded in a certain historical sense. Gardner and her friends wrote in the event a charming historical afterword from their point of view (a new chapter from ours) to Venice's long history. And by no means an unworthy one! More than one Venetian guidebook today takes proud note of how the Palazzo Barbaro was the scene of a painting by John Sargent, how it inspired a novel by–of course–Henry James and also a certain famous American museum created by–Isabella Stewart Gardner![163]

It was when James saw Fenway Court that his restless perspective on Gardner finally settled down. James saw that Gardner herself, whatever would be the case with others who followed, had not been on any kind of rampage after all, and that her collecting had, indeed, "composed itself into a set form, a museum mold," in Edel's words, "as [James himself] had imagined in his creation of Adam Verver and his dream of an art center in an American city." Then, at last, James understood. So, indeed, did Berenson. William Vance has noticed "how the fulsome language of sycophancy that Berenson employs to address his benefactress in the early years ... are converted ... [after he saw Fenway Court] into the sincere language of high respect for an astonishingly vital individualist and bold achiever." Thus, in *The American Scene*, James finally paid Isabella Gardner an extraordinary homage, writing now without reserve of her "unaided and quite heroic genius"[164] in the design of Fenway Court. It was, truly, Isabella Stewart Gardner's apotheosis.

11

———— •◦• ————

The Age of Mrs. Jack

The light was somewhat dimmed in the courtyard, giving a bluish hue to purplish walls, yet it was as fresh and clear as full moonlight. The softly out-lined silhouette of a singer showed [in] the Venetian window, and his song, carried on ethereal waves of sound, created an exotic atmosphere. . . . It seemed as if it were being sung by a gondolier or someone in the higher story of a house by the waterways of Venice while our boat drifted on and on. We were moving quietly and slowly from one room to another. . . . We were all in evening dress. The trailing of the ladies' gowns . . . set the leisurely pace . . . as if we were in a procession, while the echo of the song became fainter and fainter. . . .

. . . The procession [continued] round the cloisters. The moonlight effect became paler, as if a sheet of frost had covered all the plants in the court-yard. . . . My eyes closed for a moment. Someone must have shivered, causing her satin dress to produce a gentle noise. All of a sudden, two huge doors flew wide open. Straight in front of us, a big fire was blazing and crackling in an enormous fireplace. Our eyes opened wide. . . . Nothing could have been more appreciated than [the] warmth [of this fire] after the chilly night air, nor more dramatic than the way it burst upon us. . . . in Mrs. Gardner's tradition.[1]

"PROBABLY UNIQUE IN the Western world" is the way W. G. Constable, in his *Art Collecting in the United States*, describes "the Isabella Stewart Gardner Collection as it is seen today."[2] So remarkable is the

Gardner Museum in strictly artistic terms! But it is doubly remarkable, unique twice over: what other work of art and architecture of the last century stands solely in the name of a woman, a woman whose life and work culminated in envisioning the collection, leading in its assembling, designing the building and founding the institution? There never has been anything anywhere quite like the Isabella Stewart Gardner Museum, a charter for the incorporation of which was duly issued to its founder and six others chosen by her on December 19, 1900.

Rumors had already begun to circulate freely in Boston and New York. "WHIM OF A WOMAN," trumpeted Boston's *Herald.* In London the *Daily Telegraph* would speculate on whether Gardner's gallery would be a private affair or given to the City of Boston. Even so far afield as Kansas City, the *Times* of that city would dedicate a half a page on September 22, 1901, to Gardner's plans: "countless conjectures" were reported, "... and wonderful are the stories." Kansans were evidently enthralled. Gardner was described as "America's most fascinating widow." The building was said to be an Italian palace she'd bought; once shipped to America, stone by stone, it would be rebuilt here, again stone by stone. People have done such things after all. At least one report got one thing right–someone in a Florida paper noticed that "the Boston woman who is getting columns upon columns of free advertisements out of her love for privacy is a genius in her way."[3] Gardner had learned well the art of scandal standing at the doors of concert halls where her pro-tégés were performing, handing out programs. One of the first figures of the fast-approaching media age, she learned too how to let the news-papers do it for her!

Meanwhile, at her harbor-front storage warehouse, Gardner's accumu-lated treasure–her European trips since 1896 had been dedicated as much to buying medieval choir stalls and architectural fragments as to old mas-ters or contemporary paintings–was being unpacked by the founder her-self! Astonished enough I imagine by the presence of a woman in such a venue, her helpers–artist friends and laborers–were the more astonished by her directions: "the cases were stacked high but the unpacking did not begin at one point and proceed methodically around the room; in each instance," Carter was told, "Mrs. Gardner decided what case should be opened next; if it was at the bottom of a pile those on top must be lifted"–no small labor as all these crates contained marble columns and such–"and placed at one side.... As each column, capital, and base was unpacked, she indicated the place in the storeroom where it should be put." Her helpers, wrote Carter, absorbed wonderingly the fact that the design of the court arcade was all in her head: "when the labor was over, [the bases, columns and capitols in the warehouse] were all arranged as she wanted them to stand at Fenway Court"!⁴ To be sure, at the building site, her "working architect," as she called Willard Sears, was marshaling men and materials even as foundations were being laid and walls were rising. But Sears really functioned more as Gardner's clerk of the works, for she was on site nearly all of the time herself, and it was very clear who was in charge.

It was contentious work, riven as the construction process so often is by the too-frequent cross-purposes of designers, contractors, and work-men, and exacerbated as well by class and sometimes ethnic conflicts. In this daily struggle Gardner was often at a loss. Sears' construction diary records one crisis after another in 1900–01 with the various trades. Gardner at one point was so provoked as to have called the chief stone-cutter "a liar" and fired him;⁵ then John Evans, a much respected architec-tural sculptor (Richardson's own), told Sears in consequence "he would not be bothered with her any further." Some time later it was the floor layers, whom Gardner ordered off the site "for mimicking her when she spoke to them for not working." Then there was the electrical foreman; again dissatisfied, Gardner called him "a thief" and fired him. Matters finally reached such a state that a strike was threatened. This was an era, afterall, of labor unrest, and Gardner was not very progressive at all in such matters. Still, she rallied her forces and faced everyone down. Bliss Perry recalled a lunch with Annie Fields and Sara Orne Jewett at which Gardner regaled him and them and the novelist William D. Howells with "a most entertaining account of her struggles with the Italian workmen [building Fenway Court], . . . how she had fought the workmen and con-tractor down on the matter of wages, and bluffed them out of a threat-ened strike." Perry was vastly amused; Gardner, he wrote, "had a keen sense of humor, and there was in truth something exhilarating in this pic-ture of a lone Yankee woman subduing the insurgent sons of Italy by sheer pluck and will power." But this was classic Gardner, the paradoxi-cal, two-sided figure remembered so well by Elsie De Wolfe. "Mr. Howells laughed a little with the rest of us," Perry wrote later, "but as we got into the cab [after lunch he] broke out in bitter denunciation of the arrogance of wealth." Howells, recalled Perry, had been American consul in Venice; "himself none too rich in worldly goods," he greatly "admired and loved Italian workmen."[6]

That Gardner did too, but, as usual, in her different way, accounts for another construction story, this time relayed by Carter: "among the employees of the contractor was an Italian, Teobaldo Travi, who showed such an interest in [the old columns and capitals and such] that had come from his native land and handled them with such affectionate care that Mrs. Gardner gave him official supervision over them." Bolgi, as he was soon nicknamed, invariably accompanied all the materials from the warehouse to the building site; Isabella Gardner had discerned a kindred spirit in an Italian laborer as quickly as in an author or a painter.

And in the event Gardner also thereby alleviated much of her labor problems, for Bolgi became a bridge between her and the men. Gardner marshalled tact as well as bravura after all in solving her problem: "many a workman," Carter recalled, "was saved from losing his job by Bolgi's explanation that a column was broken when it arrived."[7] To Sears, who acted, in effect, as her executive officer, Gardner soon added Bolgi, who became her sergeant-major, and showed at once a power of imagination that explained Gardner's choice: a cornet player, he devised a system of so many toots for the mason and so many for the plasterer and so on, and "as the building progressed, [Gardner] would clamber all over it with Bolgi at her side, cornet in hand."[8] Gardner's labor problems dissipated. And Bolgi ended up her faithful major-domo for a quarter of a century at Fenway Court.

If in the design and construction of the Gardner Museum Isabella Gardner was always the central figure, as she always had been in the forming of the collection, it was as well the case that the government remained her most vexing enemy; in the case of construction in the form of building inspectors. Although she did agree to have her marble columns tested for crushing strength, and allowed where utterly necessary a certain use of steel reinforcement, she was forever "fighting with [Sears] and [the] city government because I won't have 'steel construction'–so I may have to end by having nothing," she wrote Berenson; "oh my poor bubble, who will prick it?"[9] Certainly no building inspector. To each and every one, according to Carter, she declared "slowly and impressively," the same thing: if Fenway Court was to be built at all "it will be built as *I* wish and not as you wish."[10] Indeed, she never bothered even to file plans with the city, or to get a building permit as required by law. Three quarters of a century later, an official of Boston's building department would admit to Gardner archivist Susan Sinclair that the Gardner Museum was still "the joke of the department. No plans had been submitted and no permit issued,"[11] except for a small shed near the building site. Who, indeed, would have dared.

If Gardner's anxious and arrogant perfectionism was inevitably disruptive to the construction process, it was a situation, after all, in which she was at a considerable disadvantage, both as a woman and as an amateur, with none of the experience of Sears and the various workers. Furthermore, she had every reason to be skeptical of their understanding of her design concept, which was to say the least unusual. At one point, for instance, Gardner was so frustrated trying to explain to a highly skilled woodcutter who had produced beautifully smooth ceiling beams that while she found no fault with his skill it was not what was wanted in a room designed as a setting for medieval art, that Corina Smith recounts how Isabella Gardner at sixty-two years of age proceeded "to mount a very high ladder, axe in hand, to show the expert at work exactly how she wanted the surfaces to look."[12] Similarly, when her explanations to the painters of the court walls of the effect she wanted

Isabella Gardner mounting a ladder during the construction of the Gardner Museum, ca. 1900. *Isabella Stewart Gardner Museum, Boston*

John Singer Sargent, *Isabella Stewart Gardner*, 1888.
Isabella Stewart Gardner Museum, Boston

James Abbott McNeill Whistler, *Mrs. Gardner in Yellow and Gold*, 1886. *Isabella Stewart Gardner Museum, Boston*

Anders Leonard Zorn, *Mrs. Gardner in Venice*, 1894. *Isabella Stewart Gardner Museum, Boston*

John Singer Sargent, *Mrs. Gardner in White*, 1922. *Isabella Stewart Gardner Museum, Boston*

did not produce the desired result, she ordered a pail of white paint and one of pink paint to be brought, then climbed upon the staging, and "with a sponge dipped first in one pail and then in another began smearing the wall, [yielding] a charming variation in color."[13]

There was a further dimension to Gardner's excruciating attention to detail which Sears surely recognized: it was a necessary creative counter-point, even a corrective, to the hard-boiled assurance of her arrangements at the warehouse. Isabella Gardner seems to have sensed that in design the value of many first thoughts is found in the second thoughts they generate. Carter, for example, was plainly flabbergasted to observe that "even in the foundations [Gardner's] personality expressed itself, for the . . . dressed stone which [Sears] had planned to have show above ground . . . she substituted a course of undressed bricks of varying height, so that the brick building does not appear to rest upon a layer of stone, but to be knit into it."[14] It was an example of how fiercely she insisted on controlling everything. Another was Sears' note: "Mrs. Gardner changed her mind in regard to the arrangement of the triple arch windows at the west end of the Gothic Room today after they had been built part way up, and had them rebuilt."[15] Similarly, Sears recorded at another point that "she decided to make the basin of the fountain in front of the Court staircase leading to the Dutch Room smaller than first intended and she had Mr. Nichols lay out the marble pieces for the rim on the Music Room floor."[16]

In like manner, Corina Smith once found Gardner "busily engaged in sorting and arranging according to the plan she wished used on the walls"[17] two thousand or more Mexican tiles. No one recorded coming upon Gardner contriving the door surround of the Gothic Room with Italian Romanesque and Gothic fragments, but it was surely achieved in much the same way. It is only by studying the photographs of the dealers' ensembles of such fragments and Gardner's own ensembles that some sense of her design process emerges. Isabella Gardner hardly ever explained anything of what she was doing. The only very general evidence is that of Corina Smith, who (for moral support, doubtless) Gardner often brought with her: "she gave me the privilege more than once during the crucial stage of construction of 1902 of seeing her in action," wrote Smith, who recalled that Gardner "was on the grounds all day. . . . the construction, as well as the architectural blueprints, was a complete expression of herself."[18]

It was a role, moreover, her architect was used to! The famous firm,

Cummings and Sears, of which Willard Sears had been a partner until 1890, when the senior partner left practice to take up architectural writing full-time, was dominated by Cummings, the designing partner, as the minutes of the Boston Society of Architects of the 1880s show,[19] and after the firm's breakup Sears on his own designed relatively little–a Back Bay apartment house, a riding club in the Fenway near Gardner's, and the Pilgrim Monument at Provincetown were his (not very) major works of those years. Indeed it was modest alterations at Green Hill and a small summer house in Maine for the Gardners that occasioned their first sustained connection. Sears, used enough to being a second-string player, knew Gardner well enough to know what he was getting into when she asked him in 1896 to put pen to paper. Recall the basis on which Carter would be chosen to be her first museum director: "I was not to have any ideas of my own," he remembered ruefully.[20] Sears apparently was chosen on the same basis; as all involved in Fenway Court have testified, the ideas were Gardner's from first to last.

That Isabella Gardner was her own architect has hardly been subsequently acknowledged, however. As modernism has increasingly captured the critical mind in this century, since the building's completion, moreover, so "historicist" a design as Fenway Court's didn't matter anyway: when America's leading architectural historian in 1954 wrote a guide to Boston architecture, hardly anyone cared that he attributed the design to Sears; the Gardner Museum's "architectural interest," Henry-Russell Hitchcock wrote, was "negligible"![21] Even Gardner's admirers tended anyway to think of the building as more a case of art and interior decoration than of architecture. And the enormous gulf between the field of interior design, which began to come into its own just at the turn of the century, and that of architecture, was seldom bridged then. A designer like Ogden Codman, though he would design many complete buildings was refused membership in the American Institute of Architects in the 1900s because he was considered a decorator. Even more to the point it was just as Fenway Court was being built that Lois Lilley Howe was admitted a member of the same institute, of which she would be the first woman elected on her own to the rank of Fellow.[22]

Howe, whose firm Howe and Manning, established in 1913, was then one of just four architectural firms in America founded and managed by women, was a graduate of MIT, the only school of architecture in New England that admitted women until the founding of the Cambridge School

of Architecture and Landscape Architecture. Significantly, it was a graduate of Radcliffe College, where Gardner was so early a supporter of its
first president, Elizabeth Cary Agassiz (who was herself bowled over by
Fenway Court, pronouncing it "a new standard of ideal beauty, largeness
of conception . . . and grace of expression")[23] that got the Cambridge
School going in 1915, when women were still denied admission to
Harvard's graduate schools of architecture and landscape architecture.
Moreover, one of Gardner's close friends and protégés, Martin Mower,
was one of the first four members of the Cambridge School's faculty.

Interestingly, the biographer of one of his students, and one of the
school's most notable graduates, architect Eleanor Raymond, cites as the
most immediate background for these female architectural pioneers the
work of women literary figures who in their books in the late nineteenth
century "constructed imaginary towns and dwellings . . . as extensions of
their fictional characters. In particular, Edith Wharton's work . . . based
upon the author's framework of aesthetic principles formulated through
her knowledge and writings on architecture."[24]

Never was there a better example of how authors always seem to survive historically as so disproportionately influential–Wharton's and
Codman's *The Decoration of Houses* comes to mind. Yet it is rather careless
not to say cruel for architectural historians not to notice that Isabella
Gardner didn't, like her acquaintances, write about it; Gardner did it![25]
Certainly she wasn't an architect formally trained in the usual appren-
ticeship tradition of those days, much less educated in the modern sense
then emerging. Nor was Gardner a literary figure like Wharton whose
writings gave young women ideas. But in the sense of the fine old term
"gentleman architect" (like Lord Burlington or Charles Bulfinch) Isabella
Gardner was, perhaps, America's first "lady architect." Indeed, her old
friend, Bishop Grafton, suggested her achievement at Fenway Court
warranted an honorary degree from Harvard![26] Alas, such recognition
had to wait for the next generation–when, in fact, it was Edith Wharton
who was so honored–and not by Harvard, but by Yale!

If Gardner is scarcely credited even today as she should be as Fenway
Court's architect, she is not either accorded the distinction that is unarguably hers of being America's proto-interior decorator. An exception to
this neglect is found in the work of Isabele Anscombe who, in her history of interior decoration, notes that Elsie De Wolfe, generally
acknowledged to have been the first interior designer in the modern

sense (in whose wake followed figures like Syrie Maugham and Sibyl Colefax in England) was a great admirer of the design of Fenway Court, and that, while Gardner was "in no way a professional," she was the only woman whose design work influenced greatly De Wolfe's own pioneering work in this field.[27]

To thus rank Gardner as virtually America's first interior designer is no small thing, but it would be more generous and more accurate to acknowledge that Gardner's achievement at Fenway Court was one not only of decoration but of architecture; indeed, an inspired unity of both and more. But not even Anscombe's view is universal. Significantly, Isabella Gardner does not figure in Beverly Russell's recent study *Women of Design*. The book opens quite appropriately by detailing the career of De Wolfe (who founded her firm in 1907) while the (literary!) work of Edith Wharton and the architectural work of Julia Morgan arise immediately, as does (within a paragraph or two) the design work of Florence Schurst Knoll, herself a student of Eliel and Eero Saarinen and Mies van der Rohe, carrying the tale, in other words, well toward the post-World War II era. Nowhere does there appear the name of Isabella Stewart Gardner.[28]

◆

The evening so long awaited . . . finally came. The guests all agog entered Fenway Court . . . and found themselves in a small lobby; at the right was a dressing room for the ladies . . . in the small coat-room for men at the left . . . there [was] little to gratify eager curiosity. . . . the guests entered the rather narrow, rather high, pure white Music-Room with . . . a horseshoe staircase leading up to the balcony at the rear. On the landing at the top of the horse shoe stood Mrs. Gardner, dressed in black, her diamond antennae waving above her head; up the stairs the representatives of Boston's proudest families climbed to greet their hostess, and then—except the chosen few, perhaps possessing less family pride, whom she invited to sit in the balcony—they climbed down the other side, some of them inwardly fuming, but most of them amused at the homage Mrs. Gardner had exacted of them. . . . she herself sat alone in a high Italian chair on the landing while fifty members of the [Boston] Symphony Orchestra . . . performed [Bach, Mozart, Chausson, and Schumann].

When the music was over, a great mirror in one corner of the hall was rolled back and the guests were admitted to the court. No one was in the least prepared for the fairy beauty . . . it was overwhelming. Here, in the very midst of winter, was "a gorgeous vista of blossoming summer gardens. . . . There was intense silence, for a moment broken only by the water trickling in the fountain; then came a growing murmur of delight . . . the guests pressed forward to make sure it was not all a dream." From the eight balconies [around the court] hung round flame-colored lanterns, brilliant and yet soft globes of light in the lofty court, and through windows and arches came the flickering gleam of myriad candles. The whole scene was indescribably beautiful. . . . The thrill of it was beyond words. The next day . . . William James [wrote of the evening as] "a Gospel miracle."[29]

That the author of *The Varieties of Religious Experience* should have caught the religious resonance of an apparently only social evening, an evening Wharton's biographer called "the party of the decade, perhaps even of the century," is not surprising. The only student of Gardner's life since Carter to feel similarly about Fenway Court explained it thus: "the creation of the beautiful environment," Aline Saarinen rightly declared, was for Gardner, "an act of virtue. A basically religious woman, she warmed to Norton's belief in the moral stature of art."[30] Indeed, the Isabella Stewart Gardner Museum was Ruskinian to its core, and, taken as a whole—painting, sculpture and the minor arts in organic relation to overall art and architecture—it is I think true to say that if there is a Ruskinian style of art and architecture, Fenway Court is its unrivaled masterwork anywhere.

But it is also distinctly modern in being edgier, almost double-edged. Consider, to take just one example, the relationship between the

 photographic studies of the male nude in Isabella Gardner's scrapbook and the (more daringly conceived!) ensemble of frag-

Marble fragment of a Greco-Roman torso of a kneeling male figure over a pool flanked by two Putti. *Isabella Stewart Gardner Museum, Boston*

ments of sculptures–including full frontal nudity–in the fountain under the cloister staircase; from yet another perspective how homoerotic that ensemble must have seemed to so many of Gardner's friends. There are depths often quite unsuspected to the Gardner Museum; Ruskinian moral uplift is by no means the extent of it, and by itself does not quite ring true.

The trouble with that kind of uplift, of course, in Wendy Lesser's words, is that "the kind of art that transparently works at having a beneficial moral effect mostly isn't as good as the dodgier kind."[31] The whole secret of Fenway Court, however, is that it is dodgy–bohemian, really, in the then widest meaning of the term. Frequently irritating to scholars, violating as it does so many weary conventions of museum theory[32] (that pictures should always be hung at eye level, for example), and often willfully off-putting even ("it is my pleasure" declares Gardner),[33] Fenway Court is a place at once of joy, even of fun ("the very thought of it is such a joy," she wrote Berenson; and another time, "shan't you and I have fun with my museum?") and yet also demonstrably as much as anything else about *anger* (think of Henry Adams' confidence to Elizabeth Cameron: "Mrs. Gardner hates a picture gallery almost as much as I do"!) and even madness (think of Henry James, in his notebook: "the figure of Mrs. Jack ... the individual consciousness–the mad, ghastly climax.")[34] Fenway Court, finally, has as much to do with an edgy modernism as with uplifting Ruskinianism. That is why even a century later the Gardner Museum hardly seems to have exhausted its capacity to stimulate the alert psyche in a way museum curators seldom understand.

That first night more than one visitor probably also found its overall architectural concept a little unnerving. Just as Fenway Court is no gaudy Victorian millionaire's "castle" (it was Aline Saarinen who pointed out that in Isabella Gardner's bathroom there was no "swan bathtub in the manner of Chicago's Potter Palmer"[35]–instead there are very Bostonian admonitory mottoes printed on the tilework) so too in Isabella Gardner's "museum" there were no windowless, top-lit galleries, which she "abhorred," or monumental staircases, or any of the atmosphere of a classroom, or, indeed, a museum!

Instead, there was, almost at once, a three-story-high court and sculpture garden that was a tour de force, at once very simple in conception but strikingly original. The building's mysterious, severe exterior that had so mystified so many journalists, was at once explained: different as the

The great court of Fenway Court, the Isabella Stewart Gardner Museum, is the first such sculpture garden in an American museum (Photo by David Bohl, 1993). *Isabella Stewart Gardner Museum, Boston*

climate of Venice is from that of New England, where neither was there any Grand Canal, Gardner had had the inspired idea of turning the Venetian palazzo, so to speak, outside–in; what would have been in Venice the principal Canal facade was to be found, quadrupled, on each side of a huge interior court, itself so splendid with flowering plants the Grand Canal was nowhere missed; especially as the court permeated all– every floor opens onto and overlooks it and from every gallery sight and sound of it (the splash of its fountain), even scent of it, is pervasive. Even today and even for the hundredth time, the mind's eye conjures in this court a modern American descant on Verdi's triumphant cry at the open- ing of *Othello*, echoed in Norton's own words to Ruskin: "for splendor in life, for the union of beauty with strength, elegance with force, luxury with self-control, Venice and the Venetians of old were never matched in history."[36]

Looked at more closely, the architecture of the court and its surround- ing galleries celebrates much more than Venice and even that at one remove and quite imaginatively. There is, for instance, in the ground-floor cloisters, where grayish stone detail is set in dark brick walls, a Ruskin Gothic feeling very like the chancel of the Church of the Advent, a quite deliberate feeling, moreover, for Sears . . . noted in his construction diary that Gardner had "originally intended to have [the cloisters] plastered, but has now decided to leave a brick finish."[37] More American and more "modern" in its resonances is the turn-of-the-century arts and crafts aes- thetic that is so widely felt throughout Fenway Court's galleries because of the work of Henry Chapman Mercer, that remarkable archaeologist- tile maker who "transformed the art of the ceramic tile in America" in Cleota Read's words, "elevat[ing] it from a prosaic form of decoration to a medium of plastic expression capable of conveying original and com- plex ideas."[38]

Because Mercer's work is comparable to that of the greatest names in the turn-of-the-century American arts and crafts movement–Tiffany, Stickley, Bradley, Stone, the Koralewskis, and Grueby (the two last named of which, ironworkers and tile makers, also made their contribu- tion to Fenway Court), it is especially of interest that a contemporary magazine report claimed Mercer's famous Doylestown, Pennsylvania, fac- tory and studio "practically came into being because [of] Mrs. Gardner," a view Mercer's biographer calls "exaggerated," but surely not by much; for "Mercer's first major order for a floor incorporating Castle Acre tiles,"[39]

Read admits, came from Gardner. Probably she was charmed by the way Mercer incorporated into his design the nice contrast of *worn* medieval tiles: by glazing only the recessed part of the tile's design and leaving the clay exposed on the raised portion "he breathed new life into the old tile designs"[40] in a way that appealed not only to Gardner. She was, in fact, as one of Mercer's earliest clients, in very good company. Other early orders came from architects Julia Morgan and Irving Gill. Here again a larger pattern of patronage is disclosed, for Mercer was not the only important American arts and crafts figure Gardner helped. Another was Hugh Robertson, much praised then as now for his glaze experimentation. When he was forced to close the Chelsea Keramic works outside Boston, it was Gardner and eight others (including close friends like Joe Smith, Sarah Jewett, and Clipston Sturgis) whose financial backing in 1891 enabled him to keep afloat, ultimately as Dedham Pottery.[41]

It was through another distinguished arts and crafts artist, Sarah Whitman, that Gardner first met Mercer, in Venice in 1894, and through J. Templeman Coolidge, Mercer's classmate at Harvard, that she learned of the tilework of this brilliant young bachelor, of whom Gardner became so enthusiastic a patron she went to Doylestown herself to establish what became a long-lasting relationship. A letter of hers to Mercer of April 1901 documents how close was her control of yet another aspect of Fenway Court's design: "all miscalculations are forgiven and forgotten. 1st: go ahead with hexagons (No. 29–#260) for 2nd floor corridor with washboard according to sketch No. 1 (counting 15 little bricks to every foot, with glazed squares fleur de lis & castle, hotel de Cluny) #31."[42]

That Gardner could so skillfully fuse Ruskin Gothic and American turn-of-the-century arts and crafts into an overall Venetian aesthetic that was itself a fusion of the medieval and the Renaissance shows her gift for architectural synthesis. So does the fact that she may well have annexed the American Classical Revival as well, for I feel the likeliest source for the Gardner's court was the Boston Public Library, where in 1895 McKim, Mead, and White did nothing very extraordinary in endowing that splendid Italian Renaissance building with an equally splendid court-yard, but where, whether deliberately or not, they achieved quite an unusual and, indeed, almost magical effect by not paving the courtyard as a Renaissance court certainly would have been, but endowing it instead with lawns and plantings. The result—a New England green, so to speak, in an Italian palazzo court—may well have suggested to Gardner the horticultural aspect, hardly then exampled, of her own court. It reflected, after all, a passionate interest of Isabella Gardner who was a keen lifelong, hands-on gardener ("I am always in the garden, planting and trimming,"[43] she wrote Berenson once), who in 1891, for instance, won a medal for her Japanese iris from the Horticultural Society and was very interested as well in garden design. Her garden at Green Hill was, in fact, called by *Country Life* in 1902 "one of the finest examples of Italian Garden design in this country."[44] Certainly it was one of the first. Not for nothing was Julia Ward Howe's nickname for Gardner "kipoura," derived from the Greek word for gardener.[45]

Fenway Court's "greensward," a word more suggestive of New England greens than Mediterranean patios, was in 1900 noticed by at least one critic, and it was, significantly, the same observer who also glimpsed the fact that like Sargent's contemporary watercolors of Venice, Gardner's "Venetian" court was as new American as old Venetian. "Its modern brickwork is decoratively consonant with the antique fragments," that critic wrote, going on to point out that "the steel ribbing of the glass canopy above the court serves to remind one that Pittsburgh is nearer to our time and clime than Venice."[46] These ribs, be it noted, were quite frankly expressed and are an integral part of the disciplined geometry and clarity of the court, key aspects of why the court is as much modern American in feeling as medieval Venetian. Indeed some of its features even then were as significant for being "Ruskinian" as for being medieval Venetian: eight of the court balconies are from Venice's legendary Cà d'Oro, for example, the palazzo which figured so importantly in perhaps the most famous of Ruskin's books, *The Stones of Venice*.

In detail as in the larger elements of style this same kind of synthesis pervades Gardner's design. It is also true that to no small extent because it was so pioneering in concept, the design is flawed: if the medieval and Romanesque sculpture Gardner included in Fenway Court, for example, was according to Walter Cahn, "the first to have been brought to this country;" it was also true, Cahn thought, that Gardner had collected unevenly, "often with more enthusiasm than discrimination."[47] But there was as well a strength of that weakness. Gardner's use of detail generally was so enthusiastic as to yield a wonderfully exuberant experience. Indeed, not just doorways and fountains, but the whole building as Gardner designed it was conceived of in a very real sense as a fantasia, so to speak, of detail—an architecture of fragments. As that unusually perceptive critic Aline Saarinen so aptly writes of the 1890s and 1900s: "the eclectic architects of the time were using the vocabulary of the Gothic and Renaissance to make, at its best, a new style" (the Classical Revival Boston Public Library, a very original use of the classic style, is a good example). Saarinen, perhaps because she is a woman, was not afraid to assert that Gardner "went them one better, for she used bits of old architecture to create her own style."[48]

Nor before the triumph of modernism did the architectural profession, so slow to credit Fenway Court to the right designer, disdain the achievement itself. The Gardner Museum, palatial in scale, not domestic, and with no "household" aspect at all, was no house museum. Rather, it became the prototype of a new building type, the private collector museum, examples of which include Beauport in Gloucester, Massachusetts, as well as Hammond Castle nearby, the Frick Museum in New York, the Walters in Baltimore, and the Norton Simon and Getty Museums. Nor was that the extent of its influence: as a courtyard museum type, the Gardner's design was the background of the designs of such as the Detroit Art Institute and Harvard's Fogg Museum, the unbuilt design by Cram for the Currier Gallery in Manchester, New Hampshire,[49] and Cram's earlier masterpiece of museum design, Boston's Museum of Fine Arts' Japanese Garden Court. Finally, the influence of Gardner's design is evident in several of Cram's church designs, most notably St. Anne's Convent Chapel outside Boston (where many of the antique fragments were Gardner's own gifts), and most important of all, in the design by Allen and Collens, the Boston architects, of the Cloisters in New York.[50]

Well might Joe Smith claim he had never known any other person who possessed the "sense of proportion, rare artistic taste and an instinct for construction" necessary to the achievement of Fenway Court, as well as the "patience and gaiety of spirit . . . [and] determination." Above all, he thought (harking back, perhaps, to her warehouse ensembles), it was Gardner's "extraordinary gift of having the image of the building so clearly in mind that she knew exactly where each purchase was to be placed which explained her success." "Only in this way," wrote Smith, "could a detail become an integral part of the structure her genius was to make a reality."[51] Moreover what was built into the fabric were not the only "fragments." Every picture, every statue, every chair needs to be seen in the same way; the sculpture garden in the court, for instance– quite aside from the unusualness of its "greensward"–is "the earliest," in

Mary Cornille's words, "of its kind in an American museum."[52] When the public was first admitted to Fenway Court, the February after Gardner's January opening, it was to experience a truly unprecedented kind of "built fantasy."

Several critics saw this at once. Within a year or two of its opening Mary Augusta Millikin would write of Isabella Gardner's work that "its appeal is not to the archeologist, the historian, and the collector. It is, rather, a creation." Similarly Sylvester Baxter in the *Century* felt bound to make the same point before it was too late: Fenway Court, he wrote, "is Italian in all its essentials. . . . Yet it is like no one building that ever stood either in Italy or elsewhere. . . . Every element that has entered into it has gone to produce *a new form* [my emphasis]."

◆

If Isabella Gardner was extraordinarily secretive about her thought processes in designing Fenway Court, she was equally secretive about the design of her installations, hardly ever touching on the subject, doubtless because it would have taken the joy out of it for herself and visitors to have done so. Yet Carter is surely right that "the visitor in a sense experiences her creating pleasure. . . . aware that it was not an easy task, . . . conscious of the effort and the labor, but always of the joy in work and the exhilaration of success."[53]

Architecture and art cohere beautifully. The plan of galleries on both the upper floors is the same. The west side of the court is always the stair hall, long and narrow and tight to the court windows so that the feeling is always one of ascending and descending almost within the court. At its top each staircase points to a small anteroom (the first gallery) and then to a great *salone* beyond that on both floors, the chief feature of the court's north side. Progressing around to the south and back to the stair hall, the sequence of galleries unfolds in ways both obvious and complex, relating space and contents intimately. The first-floor galleries for contemporary art are small, low-ceilinged, informally decorated modern (which is to say, Edwardian) rooms, while the upstairs galleries for Renaissance and Baroque art are large, richly decorated, high-ceilinged galleries. Relationships also disclose themselves from gallery to gallery. The Early Italian Room on the second floor, architecturally an anteroom to the Raphael Room, reflects the evolution of art both rooms celebrate; nor does the Veronese Room on the third floor just happen to lead into the

Titian Room. More interesting is that both the anterooms to the big *salones* are so different: the Early Italian Room is a very sparse and plain anteroom–bare white walls above a wood dado–not at all like the anteroom upstairs, the Veronese Room, which is quite the most richly decorated in Fenway Court with its lustrous gilded leather wall covering and elaborate ceiling. Understanding comes when you try to imagine early Italian paintings on their rich gold ground on gilt leather walls!

Everything seems to revolve around these two pairs of anterooms and great *salone*; having established that splendid center, there is elsewhere no sense at all either of any forward sequence or, indeed, chronological time. Rather, there is a sense of traveling backward, if in any direction at all, of being drawn back, so to speak, in the sense, at least, of going deeper and deeper into–what? Gardner's own psyche? History? Art? It is hard to say. Having traversed the whole sequence of all the galleries–and all the glories of the Renaissance–the last one is the Gothic Room! Like the adjoining chapel, moreover, this room is dedicated primarily to sacred art. Yet here it is that her own famous portrait by Sargent is to be found, as if emerging out of its secret, storied past, somewhat of a modern haunting of the Middle Ages.

If on the other hand one considers Gardner's individual installations and ensembles throughout the museum, there are a whole range of possible explanations of more or less interest. In the Raphael Room, that painter's *Pietà*, for example, like *Christ Bearing the Cross* in the Titian Room, are both placed on a low table with a chair before it; not much of a puzzle now we know how Gardner "calmed down." Nor is this only self-referential. For

The Raphael Room, looking toward the fireplace. *Isabella Stewart Gardner Museum, Boston* all her horror of "open days," Gardner had so intuitive a feeling about these things that it was her favorite picture, *Christ Bearing the Cross*, according to Morris Carter, that turned out to be the public's favorite as well.[54] Gardner–it is a secret too long obscured!–was a popularizer as well as a tastemaker; that's what Carter meant when he wrote that her arrangement of art at Fenway Court violated so many museum theories, and was in fact often irritating to scholars, though for the general public he observed Gardner's arrangements were a delight, even "a source of ecstatic pleasure."[55] Then again the Christ head is so placed that from its chair Gardner could see both it and Titian's *Europa*. That was, perhaps, a more sophisticated taste.

A curator who has studied Gardner's arrangement in detail is Hilliard Goldfarb. He notes that Gardner placed Lorenzetti's *St. Elizabeth of Hungary* on an easel against a French chasuble, the pattern of which picks up the floral elements within the basket the saint is holding, for example; and that in the case of Botticelli's *Madonna of the Eucharist*, "Gardner clearly appreciated the painting's luminous colorism, placing in front of the work a fragment of a mid–fourteenth-century glass mosque lamp whose enameled colors and gilt correspond to those in the Botticelli." Objects, in other words, are related according to form and color and technique more than by period or place. Consider her installation of the *Europa*. It is not surprising that in proximity to it she would place a watercolor attributed to Van Dyck after a Rubens copy of the version of *Europa* at the Prado, but she also set off her great Titian with two eighteenth-century Venetian consoles, on one of which a seventeenth-century putto is, as Goldfarb notes, "set on its side to mime the poses of Europa and the putti [in the painting], its feet in front of an enamel platter, the design of which suggests the splash of water."

Nor does that by any means exhaust the matter. As a young woman Gardner was as we have seen an eager client of Charles Frederick Worth, the controversial Paris dress designer to the Empress Eugénie, whose low-cut gowns for Gardner so shocked Boston, and it is surely no accident that Gardner chose to set off the *Europa*, Titian's masterwork, with a length of pale green and silver figured silk, a textile originally the skirt of a dinner gown made by Worth for her. Still shocking, Isabella Gardner had learned subtlety: though how many got her point is a matter of conjecture: for years the catalog of the museum said nothing! In the most recent edition, it is noted that the "color and tassel pattern of

Worth's silk material [can be seen as] complementing the [Venetian] tables under *Europa*, while completing the approach to the wall is a mid-sixteenth-century Persian carpet, roughly contemporary with the painting [acquired through Sargent] that dominates the room and picks up the many colors found in the Titian."[56]

To my mind her most audacious stroke, however, was to place in proximity to Titian's sixteenth-century *Europa*–celebrated, after all, as are the greatest works of the Renaissance–the twentieth century *Europa* of her friend Paul Manship, the greatest American sculptor of the Art Deco style. That young American, moreover, was by no means the least of the artists for whom Gardner even in her late seventies would always be both mentor and muse ("There is," Manship wrote to her in 1918, "no inspiration in the world to me like that of being with you");[57] indeed, Manship's *Europa* was a gift to his patron.

Gardner's proclivity for bringing together seemingly divergent things extended as well to larger conceptions. In the Dutch Room, for instance (where Manship's *Diana* was once the center of the whole room before she moved it, perhaps because the refectory table it was on got so much

The Titian Room, looking toward Titian's *Europa*. In the foreground is *Christ Carrying the Cross*, now attributed to the Bellini Studio. *Isabella Stewart Gardner Museum, Boston*

use)[58] Gardner arrayed in the gallery she was most apt to use for enter-taining a company of historical portraits sufficient to stimulate any party: Sir William Butts, whose depiction by Holbein along with that of his wife hangs to the left of the fireplace, was physician to the English queen Mary Tudor, whose portrait from the studio of Anthonis Mor hangs on the other side of the fireplace. Mary was the wife of Philip II of Spain, whose daughter by a later marriage was the Infanta Isabella Clara Eugenia, later Archduchess of Austria, a portrait of whom by Franz Pourbus II shares this room with a masterful portrait, *The Earl of Arundel* by Rubens, of whom the archduchess was a patron, and also with *A Lady with a Rose* by Van Dyck, who was Rubens's most famous pupil. Thus Gardner brought her guests into touch with a notable company of old masters who keep company here with a fair enough sampling of royal and imperial pomp, power, and genius to give even the most learned and critical Bostonian something to think about.

Switching gears from personalities to different media, this historic gathering in the Dutch Room makes for an interesting comparison with the gatherings in the Blue and Yellow Rooms and the Long Gallery of

The Dutch Room, looking toward the court. Interiors and installations such as this designed by Gardner greatly influenced the work of Elsie De Wolfe, who pioneered the new field of interior decoration in America. *Isabella Stewart Gardner Museum, Boston*

then contemporary figures Gardner admired and in some cases knew, and who are depicted in portrait photographs. As Pam Mathias Peterson has pointed out, Gardner's enthusiasm for photography was typical of her generation (she and photography were born, after all, only a year apart); what was not typical–in fact, was very original–was the *use* Gardner made of photography in Fenway Court. Instead of tucking away her portrait photographs into albums, she displayed "her miniature portrait gallery,"[59] as Peterson calls it, in cases in the museum, that are hardly less stimulating assemblages than her old masters.

Often the relationship between individual works of art can also be a rewarding study. When Gardner hung Baccio Bandinelli's self-portrait, thought then to depict Michaelangelo, directly beside the Cellini bust Michaelangelo so highly praised, she had one thing in mind; when she agreed with Berenson on hanging together three character studies of middle-aged women by, respectively, Pollaiuolo, Manet, and Degas, it was something else, though not very different perhaps from the idea behind her array on a bookcase in the Long Gallery of three small animal sculptures intended to show three differing conceptions or treatments of a similar subject: the nineteenth-century bronze rabbit by Antoine Las Baryne is entirely naturalistic; on the other hand the old gilt bronze Venetian lion is very abstractly handled and is highly stylized; while the nineteenth-century gilt cat by Emmanuel Fremont is a little of each. Yes, Gardner was an animal lover.[60] And, of course, this is all very eclectic.

But eclecticism on so vast a scale is something more. In fact, the secret of Gardner's design concept at Fenway Court is that she was an inspired matchmaker–of works of art, actually, more than of people, the possibilities in art being greater, especially given her apparent fascination with time-warps like the placing of her greatest modern portrait, her own by Sargent, in the Gothic Room, or the startling juxtaposition like the display of a fifteenth-century Russian icon, *The Assumption of the Virgin*, with a twentieth-century silk design painted by Isadora Duncan's brother, Raymond, which bridges–perhaps transcends–centuries. In another fashion, so does the way Gardner set Domenico Tintoretto's sixteenth-century painting, *A Lady in Black*, against a tapestry thought to be of the eighteenth century: the result is an unusual visual experience, impossible, obviously, in the sixteenth or seventeenth centuries, and highly characteristic of Gardner's installation design. The two landscapes of painting and tapestry spoke to each other perhaps in her mind's eye.

Equally characteristic was the way with great wit and whimsy she used two seventeenth-century Sicilian iron bed-heads as railings between the columns of the second-floor stair hall: or the way she pulled the court, so to speak, into the gallery, and the viewer into the picture, in her habit of placing before Zurbarán's *Doctor of Laws* a bowl of nasturtiums to point up the bright orange red of the lawyer's academic hood. Moreover, it is characteristic of Isabella Gardner that the mosaic center-piece of the court shows at its center the face of Medusa—the ugly and terrifying woman of classical mythology whose look turned people to stone!

That she was trying to create an effect whose origins in her mind's eye did not always correspond with her resources is also clear. Her imagina-tion must often have got ahead of her possessions. For example, the two lanterns to either side of the Isterian stone reredos in the west cloister: one is almost a thousand years old, dating from the ninth, tenth, or eleventh century; the other is not yet a hundred years old today and was, in fact, brand new then, when Gardner ordered the reproduction in aid of her desired installation.[61] Nor is this the only reproduction, and frankly called such in the catalog, in Fenway Court. She was also not above some artful chicanery in achieving her effects: two capitals of the cloister arcade evidently displeasing her, she had Bolgi "antique them by burying them in tobacco leaves."[62]

Particularly imaginative is the presentation of paintings and textiles; John Coolidge noticed that "a wall of disparate small paintings will be drawn together by hanging a splendid cope below them;" even more interesting, that "a fireplace will be framed by velvet curtains in such a way that on entering the room the visitor sees two Raphaels brilliantly illuminated but does not see the window that provides the illumina-tion"[63]—which is to bring up Gardner's fascinating use of *light*. It is not just that the Veronese Room, for example, is small and the Titian Room beyond large; the Titian Room is also quite bright, the Veronese Room very dark.

She was confronted, of course, with the harsh New England light. Just as fashionable churches all over Boston suffered from stained glass designed for the much softer English light, so might New England's glare, Gardner must have worried, overturn her effect of Mediterranean court and palazzo. She could never have quite the glorious light of Italy, she knew, in Boston, but still, New England light might nonetheless be persuaded to gentler effect: major pictures, for instance, are placed beside a window and at right angles to it: thus the Giotto, the Masaccio, the Fra Angelico, the Vermeer and, of course *Europa* and *Christ Bearing the Cross* are beautifully lighted. Nor was that all of it: brilliantly, Zorn's *Omnibus*, for example, is so placed that the (always moving!) light falls on it so as to reinforce the striking diagonal light in the painting itself of a (presumably mostly moving) streetcar.[64]

Other effects were equally imaginative. Gardner's use of lace overall to soften light, for example, was noticed as early as in the 1900s by at least one critic, who wrote of the court's "mullioned windows backed by the witchery of pale, gray lace,"[65] and here I have often felt she was somewhat playing on an allusion in *The Stones of Venice*, where Ruskin likens the intricate window tracery extended across Venetian palazzi facades like the Cà d'Oro to a "colossal piece of marble lace." Within, she also used lace well, particularly in the Veronese Room, where the way the richly dark seventeenth-century gilt leather wall coverings attract, hold, and soften the light, is enhanced, Goldfarb notices, "by placing gossamer lace curtains in the windows and a case of antique lace in the corner." It is, he writes, a "glistening space," and an even more striking effect strikes him in connection with the *Europa*. "No place better captures . . . the subtlety of [Gardner's] eye . . . than does the Titian Room . . . [where she surrounded *Europa*] with Venetian furnishings and glassware opposite the marble entry portal at a height where the natural morning sunlight streaming in through the Venetian window casements would match the lighting in the painting."[66]

Gardner's most telling lighting effects, however, were to be seen at night, especially, of course, when the building was en fete for a great event. On such nights Gardner hung from the balconies of the court round flame-colored Japanese lanterns–"brilliant and yet soft globes of light," Carter called them–"that suffused the whole court with a soft light, punctuated by all the many flickering candles visible through the arched openings."[67] And not only the court. Walter Whitehill recalled serving as acolyte at Gardner's Christmas midnight Mass one year and how the "Gothic Room, lit only by candles, with great logs blazing in the fireplace, was, like the view into the court, unforgettable."[68] It was an effect to be expected of the woman who once wrote Mary Berenson of a day in Rome: "my day ended, after dark, with a visit to [Cardinal] Merry de Val [Secretary of State to Pope Pius X] in the Borgia Rooms [of the

Vatican, decorated by Pintoricchio]. They looked their best, they were
wonderfully lighted, and the whole thing was middle ages and mystery.
Great dark walls, Swiss guards, black priests, and his eminence, with
many red splashes by way of cap, sash, etc."[69] No better documentation
exists of Gardner's artful eye.

Her friend Nellie Melba's description in her memoirs of Gardner's
own chapel and its adjoining galleries at Fenway Court comes at once to
my mind: imagine "a long Italian gallery, dimly lighted . . . [with] a hint of
marvelous pictures in the dusk. We all gather . . . Mrs. Gardner . . . lights
a taper. Very slowly, she walks down the gallery in silence, while we
wait . . . and then we see her gravely light two little candles in front of an
altar at the far end."[70] No less unforgettable was the overall effect,
thought Melba, in gallery after gallery: "at night [Fenway Court] was lit
with hundreds of candles, and the first effect one had on entering it was
that of darkness so thick that none of the pictures could be seen.
However, one had not," she recalled, "been in [a] room five minutes

The Chapel at the end of the Long Gallery, dominated by Henry Adams's stained glass.
By the terms of Gardner's will the Cowley Fathers offer a requiem mass here in her memory every year. *Isabella Stewart Gardner Museum, Boston*

before every picture became clearly visible in its smallest detail."[71] Today, when we rush to turn up the light, we lose that marvelous effect of the eyes adjusting to low light, in which, slowly but surely, objects soon enough disclose themselves, and in specially revealing ways. It was apparently an effect Gardner depended upon, and which prompted one insightful visitor to Fenway Court to exclaim about: "the massing of the candle-light and the bigness and mystery of spaces and objects as they died away into darkness."[72] Isabella Gardner's was, finally, an architecture of darkness.

And never more beguilingly so when even the candles were put out and the fires had died down, and Fenway Court was lit only by moon-light. Often, after dinner and some music, when Gardner would lead her guests on a tour, it was thus: "we made a little procession," she wrote Berenson, "and wandered . . . the moon pouring down into the court. I think everyone was pleased."[73] Probably, as Carter remembered of another such tour, they "carried candles for light."[74] It must have been an unforgettable experience, and all the more so as the chatelaine of this fairy tale landscape left no sense unappeased. Very early on, an unusually knowing newspaper report about Fenway Court remarked on the fact that although there was hot air heating, Gardner preferred open "huge fires, . . . kept going all the time." She kept, furthermore, a variety of "incense cones and all sorts of fragrant and pretty burning woods to throw on them; . . . a delicious odor of the forest"[75] was in consequence everywhere noticeable. Then too, there was the scent of the flowers in the court, where Gardner also kept birds, seen perhaps only now and then in flight, their birdsong was more or less constantly heard.[76] Built fantasy indeed!

All these effects, whether of light through lace or moonlight in the court, taken as a whole and in conjunction with her various ensembles of paintings and textiles and statuary and flowers as a part of an overall architecture of fragments (meaning by fragments all the individual works of art) constitute, it must be clear, *one single, organic work of art in and of itself*. It was always Carter's defense in later years when some change or other was mooted, to remind whomever that "a work of art does not need constant change or addition in order to remain alive." The vital thing, he insisted, was "the vision which the artist has"; if it is common-place, the world will pass by; if it is great, "the world will stand breath-less."[77]

In his simple way, Carter so often got it right. Gardner's work, so striking in its melancholy beauty, in its uncanny feeling for the modern mind's almost cinematic need for shifting focus and cross cutting and double vision–at once so rich and so lucid, a dialogue between Old World decadence and New World vitality–is such that the world is not soon likely to pass it by. But it does require of the visitor a knowledge of what I think Richard Klein meant when he wrote (in quite another con-nection) of "the morality of connoisseurship," which in his linking of it to Jewish culture's "stern discipline of moral restraints" and its avoidance of

The North Cloister of Fenway Court at the main entrance. To the right is Isabella Gardner's Majordomo, Teobaldo Travi ("Bolgi"). *Isabella Stewart Gardner Museum, Boston*

"excessive prudery or asceticism," reminds us of Bernard Berenson's part in all this. A key to understanding the Gardner Museum often overlooked is what Berenson himself all but invented–connoisseurship. And Klein's definition even Berenson could not have improved upon: the connoisseur, Klein writes, "places between himself and the focus of his desire the little distance of knowing appreciation." Isabella Gardner not only insisted on that little distance but time and again in the way she persuaded works of art to relate to each other and to the viewer she made that experience of the little distance truly, as Berenson would have said, life enhancing.

It is, however, worth noticing that for all her debt to Berenson, Gardner's achievement was different than his, he having been aided so much more ably by his wife Mary than ever Isabella Gardner was by anyone. Wrote William Vance:

> without Mary [I Tatti, Berenson's villa-museum in Florence] would never have come into existence. The same can be said of Berenson's publications and fortune. Mrs. Gardner's achievements were more truly her own. While she . . . needed the advice of Berenson and others, . . . the driving force and final decisions . . . were entirely hers.[78]

12

———•◦•———

Stairway of Jade

No WONDER SO many people dreamed of Fenway Court. "I shut my eyes close," wrote Elsie De Wolfe, "to shut in all the beauty . . . of your beautiful things and shut out all the *banalite* and sordidness of our incred-ible present."[1] Similarly, the Frederick Winslows, a young Bostonian cou-ple: "you led us with your magic lamp," Mrs. Winslow wrote, "I dreamed of Fenway Court all night."[2] Sargent, too, confessed it was often in his mind. Even Ralph Curtis had his dreams of the place.[3] Most movingly so did the famous Irish playwright, of whom more soon, Lady Gregory:

> Last night I dreamed that I was going into [Fenway Court] and you were waiting there & welcomed me, & I awoke with a sense of well-being, and of all the beauty that had been around me–I had been dis-couraged when I lay down, troubles about the theater chiefly, & my own work, & wondering if all I had done had been worth while–So I was comforted by thinking of what a great work you have done, . . . and I thought I must go on trying to get at least some beauty into our theater that might comfort tired minds in the same way.[4]

No better memorial of Isabella Gardner as muse *and* creator exists. And what such a letter surely meant to her, we can infer from the fact that Gregory's letter was found in Gardner's copy of Yeats' *Poems*

Written in Discouragement. "People do seem to hate me! Why?", she queried Berenson. And then recovered herself at once: "But it can't be helped, so must be endured. At any rate I shall always go straight for my goal."[5] To which Berenson replied that she had answered her own question: "So this Lady of the Fens knows after all *why* she is hated. Everybody is in the measure that he goes straight for his own goals . . . "[6] More pejoratively, his wife agreed, pointing out that it was, for example, "part of [Isabella Gardner's] nature to be intensely selfish, and to wish to be the *one and only*–it goes with her superb achievement,"[7] Mary Berenson concluded, seeing truly that the Gardner Museum owed much to Gardner's strengths, but hardly less to her weaknesses.

"I fancy no one is quite so alone in the world as I, or with no one to care,"[8] wrote the chatelaine of Fenway Court to Berenson in 1904; and again, later: "You ask if I am happy? Oh I want to be. And when I don't feel alone, I am."[9] But she was often alone for all her friends. Crawford admitted that it was when he was alone he most often thought of her. Who else but Crawford could she have meant when she wrote in her occasional book: "We have all a sufficiently hard battle to fight in life and we fight it a great deal better from feeling that we have a wall of friendship which we stand up against & have only to think of the foe in front of us."[10] Crawford had torn that wall down and left her cruelly exposed. Ever loyal, Gardner had helped him rebuild it for the both of them, without recrimination. However, in the early 1900s significantly in the wake of Jack Gardner's death, Crawford's and Gardner's intimacy had faltered again, and what turned out to be their final act must have been a strain, for Crawford, though only in his early fifties, was dying. As late as in 1903 an interviewer could still describe him as "broad shouldered" and "athletically built,"[11] but he suffered from a progressive disease of the lungs and from terrible asthma. They saw each other for the last time in 1907: "his main object in going to Boston was to see Mrs. Gardner once more," Crawford's biographer declares, and asserts that at fifty-three, "Crawford still felt the charm which Mrs. Gardner, even at the age of sixty-seven, continued to exert over his intellect and his emotions."[12] They did resume their correspondence (now, Crawford wrote, there was no longer any need to write to him through his publishers), but what passed between them can never be known; Crawford burned all her letters before he died on April 9, 1909.

That was Good Friday that year. Isabella Gardner would have known from Julia Ward Howe by the next day. Gardner, who had written Berenson on the ninth that she'd had "a bad fever for a week or so–and no end of worries and anxieties,"[13] including the recent suicide of Loeffler's brother, was already and understandably depressed. Now she could not very well even trust herself to send condolences. On Easter morning Julia Ward Howe spoke about Crawford's life from the chancel steps of Boston's Church of the Disciples. Gardner, perhaps, was at the Advent. Wrote Crawford's biographer: "What Mrs. Gardner at Fenway Court felt or thought about [Crawford's] death, she kept to herself; but even had she wished to comment, there was scarcely anyone in his family to whom she could have revealed her feelings."[14] Or, indeed, in her late husband's family.

That sort of repression, of course, exacts a price. Isabella Gardner, as noted before here, had been for years neurasthenic, a disorder George Beard concluded was rooted in "conflicts within individuals who could not fulfill social norms. Yet, because they had internalized them, could not consciously reject them."[15] Beard's definition coincided with Gardner's life development as we've discussed it here exactly. So did one of the commonest symptoms of the disorder Beard noted: neuralgias, treatment for which it is known that at least once, in 1894, Gardner sought at Langen-Schwalback baths in Germany. "The Germans in particular made *Nervositat* their own," writes Peter Gay, who rather deprecates the sort of "resort physicians ... who addressed the troubling matter of painful nerves"[16] at such places, and, to be sure, in a letter recently discovered (significantly, in the Cowley Fathers' archives), Isabella Gardner admitted of going there for "my neuralgia cure" that "the very thought of it I hate."[17]

Seventeen years later, in 1911, she was still complaining to Berenson that she had been "really ill for six weeks, a bad, dizzy head, and take digitalis and lie still"[18] and on another occasion admitted, "the stupid fact is that I have a bad head and have had one *always* more or less. *No worries* is the main thing; as I have worries and cares quite incessantly, it goes back on me now and then. ... The doctor says it [bad head] comes from a heart not over strong."[19] It was a common (and very vague) diagnosis (just the year before, in 1910, Henry James, back in Boston, had complained of "fainting attacks and heart palpitations" as well as of "episodes of nerves")[20] and increasingly at the dawn of the age of Freud and Jung it was no longer the baths that were sought for a cure but a psychiatrist.

Thus James in 1910 in Boston sought treatment from James Jackson Putnam, William James' colleague and perhaps Freud's chief American disciple.[21]

James would probably have shared all this with Isabella Gardner, whom he saw much of at this time and she also knew William James, of course, and probably Putnam too, and most certainly Morton Prince, the third of the trinity of neurologists who were among the leaders of what was called "The Boston School" of psychotherapy, which has been called "a small circle in Boston between 1890 and 1909 [which] developed the most sophisticated and sensitive psychotherapy in the English-speaking world."[22]

Prince, who lived in a splendid Beacon Street town house, Gardner was, in fact, closely involved with socially. That does not mean, of course, she was the patient of the founder of the *Journal of Abnormal Psychology*, the first devoted solely to psychotherapy in English. But the overall field arose in her intellectual life as much as its effects appeared in her psyche life, for Berenson and she corresponded about Prince's influential book *Disassociation of a Personality*, which Berenson asked her to quiz William James about.[23] It is perhaps also significant that Prince was connected with Tufts Medical School, to which, rather than Harvard, Isabella (as opposed to Jack) Gardner's known attending physicians after 1900 were attached. Did Isabella Gardner follow Henry James' example and seek psychiatric treatment? No conclusive evidence exists either way. The record is clear, however, that whether or not Gardner was Prince's patient, Prince was in a very real sense Gardner's! Under a cloud at one point, and accused of marital and financial infidelities, Prince's and Gardner's mutual friend, Mary Berenson, wrote Gardner to relay the intelligence that "[Dr. Prince] wants *you* to understand more than anyone else."[24] It is a nice point whether so famous a muse and mentor as Isabella Gardner would have been a better doctor or a better patient.

If this is not quite the picture posterity has of Isabella Gardner's life in her new palazzo it is necessary to understand that even for its creator and founder Fenway Court, for all its glory, was distinctly a mixed blessing.

In the first place Gardner found the strain of running (and living in) an art museum—even one that was only open to the public a few weeks every year—considerable. Never the easiest person to get along with, "open days" reduced her to a nervous wreck, and the innumerable tales of her anxious watchfulness and sometimes outright rudeness to an equally nervous public are sad to remember and perhaps–as she always made amends later when she could–best overlooked.[25] One story, though, is too typical and too funny to overlook: it seems an old lady persisted despite many polite remonstrances by attendants, in poking virtually everything she came upon with a cane, finally driving an exasperated Isabella Stewart Gardner to blasphemy: "Jesus Christ, Madam," she is reported to have cried, "this is no menagerie!"[26]

Reaction to Fenway Court was also not universally admiring. Some have even hated it. Charles Mount, one of Sargent's biographers, called it, "an oversized green house"; the "demented fancy" of a "shallow mind."[27] Mary Berenson was once driven to call it a "junk shop" of art "ravished" from where it belonged, the "horrid" result of "snatching this and that away from its *real* home."[28] She was identifying, presumably, more with the citizenry of Venice than of Constantinople–or her husband's beloved Boston! More to our point, though, and more serious, in another mood, Mary Berenson told a sad tale of old Back Bay: declaring Fenway Court to be "a work of *genius*," Mary Berenson observed, however: "you can't think how disgusted people have been since, at hearing us say so. They do so long to hear evil of her and her works. Half a dozen people have taken us confidentially aside and said 'Now tell us what you *really* think of it–you are quite safe with us!' and they *ought* to pardon her anything for the beauty of it and her generousness in making it to leave to Boston. . . . Yet all they think of is envy, and small spites; and she remains a very lonely and unloved person. We really adore her, in a way, and stand up for her everywhere, *not* 'in a way,' but all round."[29]

So did Henry Adams, who helped her find the stained glass she put up as a kind of reredos behind the altar of her chapel. Adams' praise doubt-less made up for much:

Knickerbocker Club, 9 Feby: 1906
My Dear Mrs. Gardner,

You have given me a great pleasure and greater astonishment. You will not feel it strange that I should write to thank you for it. Not that I know what to say that could be new to you, but that you can have no objection to hearing the same things said and re-said.

As long as such a work can be done, I will not despair of our age, though I do not think any one else could have done it. You stand quite alone. Only I must admit that no one has ever done it before you, though many have tried. If I were obliged to treat it like the scientific gentlemen of our world who preach Evolution, I should have to say that your work must be classed as a tour-de-force—no Evolution at all—but pure Special Creation in an adverse environment. You are a creator, and stand alone.

Creators are so rare as to have no atmosphere to live in, but must create it all. You would have been almost equally alone two thousand years ago. America is a terribly pathetic picture to any one who wants something else, but it is hardly worse off than Germany or Sweden or Russia or England have nearly always been; only the reasons are different. We are not quite so stupid and impenetrable as some. We can, in a certain proportion—say one or two in a hundred—feel what you do and have done.

All the same, this living with one or two in a hundred—or a thousand—is living in rarefied air. The effect of an hour with you is that of the Absolute—vertigo—loss of relation—absence in space, time and thought. It is peace, repose or dream, rather like opium; but the return to air and dust is painful. It hurts me. I feel as though you must need something—not exactly help or flattery or even admiration—but subjects.

I bring you the only offering I can, which is thanks.

Ever truly yours,
Henry Adams[30]

◆

"Repose or dream," when the founder was in residence Fenway Court quickly became what we'd call today a performing arts center. It was Isabella Gardner's usual response to criticism: to up the ante! People who mistake Fenway Court for a house museum because the museum's founder provided an apartment for herself on the top floor and made limited use for daily life and entertaining of some of the lovelier galleries, misunderstand Gardner's purposes. A projection of her own experience of art, and somewhat hostage to what Paul Goldberger calls "the fallacy

of physical determinism"[31] (but it would be very risky entirely to surrender the idea that our environment helps refine or coarsen us!), the
Gardner never was, at least in its founder's lifetime, the usual museum
experience. A popularizer Gardner in part might be, but one with almost
impossibly high standards and unreasonable expectations, who though
herself mute (because she cultivated no literary gifts) Gardner can only
be understood through Fenway Court itself. Fortunately, though, much
of her underlying philosophy *was* expressed in words by yet another brilliant and handsome young bachelor of Gardner's circle, Matthew
Prichard. An Englishman, a graduate of Marlborough and New College,
Oxford, described once as the "strong, virile element" in Ned Warren's
band of gay scholar-collectors, Prichard in the 1900s became a close
friend and strong influence on Gardner after his appointment as assistant
director of Boston's Museum of Fine Arts and, historically, an articulate
spokesman for her point of view.

A wonderfully gifted, forceful, and persuasive man possessed of
many attributes Gardner sought in a man (a Dantesque profile and an
athletic body among them) and a few she obviously worked around (he
was distinctly a misogynist) Prichard was best known for having waged
at the Museum of Fine Arts what has been called the battle of the casts.
Likening those plaster reproductions of classical sculpture to the player
piano and insisting on the distinction between "data mechanically repro-
duced" and "originals [which] are works of art," which alone belonged,
he felt, on public display, Prichard insisted that it was "not for education" anyway that the visitor ought to go to a museum. Rather, it ought
to be, he declared, for "inspiration and the pleasure of exercising our
faculties of perception,"[32] a purpose in which plaster casts could hardly
figure.

It was a view close to Gardner's heart, and not only at her own
museum: she was also known to have worked "hand-in-glove with the
younger members of the [Boston] museum staff, actively and enthusiastically supporting their radical ideas," as Carter put it. In aid of these she
essayed various "Isabelline tactics" (the term is Walter Muir Whitehill's)
including "keeping [a member away from a critical] Building Committee
meeting by the bait of luncheon at Fenway Court"![33]

At that so much more personal museum no such tactics were ever necessary—"I fear everything must be done by one person,"[34] Gardner once
wrote—nor were there any casts! There was instead a philosophy

Matthew Prichard, an etching by Henri Matisse of 1914
given to Isabella Gardner
by Prichard. *Isabella Stewart
Gardner Museum, Boston*

Prichard articulated in a mere three words–"joy, not education." That
was the Gardner Museum's chief purpose. We cannot know, so averse
was Gardner to putting pen to paper, what role her design concept at
Fenway Court played in Prichard's formulation of the rather unusual philosophy he and Gardner shared, and through which Prichard so greatly
influenced Boston's Museum of Fine Arts and thereafter American
museums in general, but the affinity between Prichard's words and
Gardner's design concept and certain views of Henry Adams, who was a
long-standing influence on Gardner, may be significant. Adams was, he
wrote in *Mont-Saint-Michel and Chartres*, as Ernst Scheyer has pointed
out, "trying to get on the way [to Chartres] not technical knowledge; not
accurate information; not correct views either on history, art or religion;
not anything that can possibly be useful or instructive; but only a sense
of what those centuries had to say, and a sympathy of their ways of saying it," a view of art and history that certainly resonates at Fenway
Court. Wrote Adams, whom Gardner had known by the opening of her
museum, for twenty years, "the world is not a schoolroom or a pulpit, or

a stage." That is perhaps the context of his ecomium to Isabella Stewart Gardner–"you are a creator, and stand alone."

If Adams likely influenced Gardner, and Gardner probably influenced Prichard, it was Prichard whose profession museum administration was and who gave most widespread effect to those ideas. And Prichard, for all his emphasis on joy, not education, understood this in a new and quite interesting way, as I believe did Gardner. Thus he advocated such revolutionary ideas according to Carter as "lectures to the public by [a museum's] staff, guides in the galleries, [and] exhibition and study series,"[35] all new to American museums in those days. I am reminded of what Gardner once said of the Louvre: "–if I could only take hold! Some things are so wonderful–and yet badly presented. . . . strength of mind they do need–and taste."[36] And by presentation I doubt she meant just physical ensembles; or that she disagreed with Prichard (who lived for a time in Fenway Court's guest suite, allowing him and Gardner much time together) when he told her of his conviction "that the museum of the past was found in the church, and the museum of the future must consist of a [similar?] combination of all branches of art. You cannot enjoy music without pictures and you cannot enjoy pictures without music, and so on."[37]

Was he not expressing, after all, the guiding principle of Fenway Court (all he left out was horticulture) as it developed under Gardner's hand? Indeed, in the most natural way Gardner had artists living in her guest suite, and liturgies in her chapel while the sculpture-garden was an ongoing horticultural show, and the Music Room was hardly ever quiet. Moreover, she all but anticipated as well the theme parks of our own day by dressing for the part! Remembered Carter: "while I was sitting in the cloister, Mrs. Gardner came by [on her way to Mass] dressed as much as possible like Mary Stuart."[38]

In 1908, for instance, a noted Italian actor of the day, Ermete Novelli, gave two plays at Fenway Court: Gardner's guests included the lords spiritual and temporal insofar as Boston could muster such things (the governor of the Commonwealth and the Roman Catholic cardinal archbishop), to say nothing of a distinguished contingent from Harvard led by William James. Another time there was a "duologue" by Sir Charles Wyndham and Mary Moore–"Mrs. Hilary regrets." In 1906 Amherst Webber's opera *Fiorella* was performed. Dancer-choreographer Ruth St. Denis also appeared at Fenway Court. Nor was the action always in the Music Room. In December of 1908 "a little French Christmas play" was

performed in the Gothic Room so successfully it was repeated the following year.[39]

An event which stood out for all who were present was Nellie
Melba's concert of March 1905; afterward, Carter reminisced, "while the
guests were wandering through the cloisters and galleries, which were
illuminated [in the usual way], Melba stepped out of the Dutch Room
where supper was served, and, standing on the landing above the fountain in the court, sang again. Never was music so lovely."[40] The
Australian superstar, as we would call her today, wrote later in the year
to Gardner to say that she would "never forget that evening" and how
glad she had been to "be invited by this wonderful woman who had built
this beautiful palace and done *so much* for art in America."[41] It was a close
relationship, Melba and Gardner. Similarly vital women, whose gifts
could never for some excuse their "unfeminine" aggressiveness, they had
understood each other. One day Gardner would give to Melba a yellow
diamond which had been much admired by the King of Cambodia when
Gardner wore it during her Eastern tour of 1883.

Far and away the most notable artistic work-in-progress of Gardner's
own time at Fenway Court was Loeffler's *Pagan Poem*. Its first performance, for two pianos and three trumpets, occurred in 1903. Then,
October of 1907, came the world premiere, also at Fenway Court, of the
full orchestral version, performed by the Boston Symphony Orchestra,
which also gave the public premiere that November in Symphony Hall.
The premiere at Fenway Court earned rave reviews. It was, wrote the
critic for *Harper's*, "the most original, imaginative, and significant piece of
orchestral writing that has come out of America."[42] That was, to be sure,
more enthusiastic than critical, but the success of the work played a big
part in Loeffler's acceptance as an American composer of note. A musical fantasy of dramatic and exultant spirit, it moved Gardner deeply: "it
really was tremendous," she wrote Berenson.[43] But the best part of it all
seems to have been the rehearsal week, the time in its history I'd like to
have passed at Fenway Court above all. Wrote the pianist Heinrich
Gebhard:

> The five or six rehearsals for this performance were rare events.
> They were all in the evening from 8:00 till 11:00 o'clock. Mrs.
> Gardner, at the height of her powers, was always present, and there
> were four or five distinguished guests present each time.... John

Singer Sargent was in America at that time.... And Okakura, the great Japanese connoisseur of art, was here supervising the wonderful new Japanese collection [at Boston's] Art Museum. Sargent and Okakura were with us at these thrilling evenings, and everybody was much excited over the trying out of the trumpets in various parts of the [court].

... After each rehearsal Mrs. Gardner regaled us with a late supper in the Gothic Room, and how unforgettable this was in these marvelous surroundings, with the brilliant conversation between Sargent, Loeffler, and Okakura, and Mrs. Gardner's great charm of personality, her delicious speaking voice, and her unequaled talent of narrating.[44]

Sargent too played his own characteristic part in the ongoing cultural feast that was Fenway Court. According to Melba he "loved staying with [Gardner] more than with anyone else in the States, and once he got inside [Fenway Court] nothing would drag him out,"[45] a thing the painter's rather lonely and wistful letters to Gardner from London in later years seem to bear out: "at the risk of boring you with my daily notes I again seize the typewriter," he once wrote, "to tell you that my thoughts are often at the Palazzo, sometimes in the clear-sounding court, sometimes in the boudoir, or in the Gothic Room."[46] It was in the last named room at Fenway Court that Sargent painted Mrs. Fiske Warren, a picture now in Boston's Museum of Fine Arts. He painted Gardner again too, in the court, leaving her face this time a mysterious blank.

Drama, dance, opera, music secular and religious, liturgy and lectures and horticulture and painting and, always, connoisseurship–all played their part in a kind of presiding trinity which quickened Fenway Court: *art and religion* (including music) were Gardner's muses; *social freedom and creative design* her causes; and *artists and intellectuals* her friends and co-workers, whether painters, authors, musicians, gardeners, poets, teachers or even dancers and athletes (she did at least once have a sporting exhibition in the Music Room–of jujitsu). Certainly art and religion never disappointed as muses, nor social freedom or creative design as causes, and a surprising number of artists and intellectuals proved also worthy friends. It was a peculiar dance, life at Fenway Court, where most adjusted their masks carefully. Nor was it just a rather more erotic venue than most for whatever: Fenway Court was no more an affair of a parade of unrelated concerts and such than of haphazardly chosen paintings.

There was, for example,–as between what one saw and what one heard at Fenway Court–a discernible unity of design concept and a deep, underlying and very personal consistency, a consistency, as the music critic William Apthorp saw when he wrote Gardner: "your Music Room"–and in the 1900s Back Bay Boston boasted a good many of some splendor–"is the one place of the sort where you are not reminded of 'music in the parlour' (which I abominate) nor of a 'concert' (which I

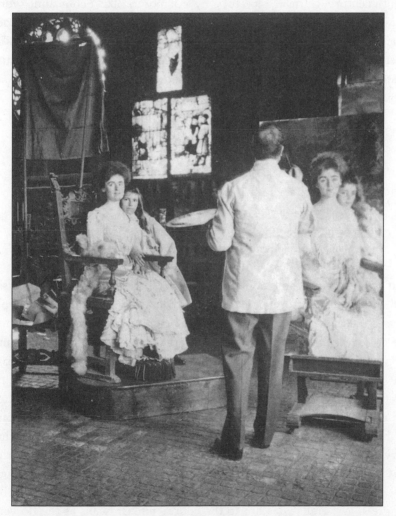

Fenway Court was a center both of the visual and the performing arts in Gardner's lifetime: John Singer Sargent painted Mrs. Fiske Warren and her daughter in the Gothic Room in 1903. *Isabella Stewart Gardner Museum, Boston*

enjoy merely professionally). You ought to give a course of lectures at the Lowell Institute on Artistic Atmosphere. You know more on the subject than anyone else."[47]

Exactly what he meant is hard to explain, though Gardner's musical programs paralleled her arrangements of paintings and such in reflecting a clear underlying design. Ralph Locke's analysis concludes that for the most part there were usually at her concerts four types of music heard: established eighteenth-century classics by Bach or Mozart; mid–nineteenth-century German repertory by composers like Schumann; work drawn from the newer French school (Chausson, for example) and, finally, the work of contemporary composers she was encouraging like Loeffler. As well, music historians have been quick to notice an unusual mixing of different performing forces characteristic of musical events at Fenway Court. Of one concert, Locke has written:

> A lengthy piece for piano and symphony orchestra (including solo English horn and three offstage trumpets), some songs for soprano with piano accompaniment, and a work for women's chorus, solo soprano, viola d'amore obligato, and piano. . . . [a] diversity, impractical in normal concert life, [reflected something that] must have felt quite natural in Mrs. Gardner's Fenway Court, [so notable for Isabella Gardner's] love of juxtapositions.[48]

It was just such thoughtful contrasts, both of different kinds of music and of differing performing ensembles, that surely explained Apthorp's praise of Gardner's music. Moreover, if her "love of juxtapositions," for example, was just as evident in the programs of music at Fenway Court as in her ensembles of painting and other works of art, it was also apparent in Gardner's horticultural presentation in the museum court. Everywhere there is the hand of the matchmaker. Characteristic was her use of the South American nasturtium: "no saccharine white carnations for her, nor garlands of pink sweetheart roses, but instead, the olé of this fiery flowery vine" was what Isabella Gardner chose to festoon the museum's court. Indeed, she created waterfalls of nasturtiums, their "opulent orange blossoms and elegantly etched water-lily like leaves" a striking green and orange descant to the court's pinkish walls as the flowers spill over the third-floor balconies, dropping dramatically down for a distance of two stories. Though her favorite flower was the modest violet, for the museum's dramatic court Gardner chose the more fittingly theatrical flower; "she loved the look of them," Gardner archivist Susan Sinclair has written, "cascading down." Indeed, as so often happened Isabella Gardner's own art sparked another's and the painter Arthur Pope, entranced with Gardner's unusual arrangement of nasturtiums, actually painted one of the cascades in 1922.

All of this, it can surely now be seen, constituted a richly interrelated overall multimedia work of art that proceeded evidently from the mind of one creator. Is not Fenway Court imbued with Isabella Gardner's courage, her passion, egotism, willfulness, and daring? Is it not the tangible expression of her almost unbridled imagination and deep emotional nature, so needful of love, so alert to beauty, so full at once of striving and energizing and of healing and serenity—words heard before here? And above all, in music as in her installations of paintings and in her horticulture, is not the overall architecture expressive exactly in its love of thoughtful juxtaposition, not just of Isabella Gardner's artistic temperament but of her paradoxical character? And therein lies the heart of its appeal: always in art, whether it may be the beauty and menace of Norse art, for example, or the innocence and decadence of the American Gothic Revival in its last stage, the force of thoughtful contradiction provokes to the most worthwhile experience.

And so the pilgrims came, and from distant climes indeed. Distinguished visitors to Boston now made it their business, of course, to seek admission to what was already one of the great museums of the world. Ever a lover of French music, Isabella Gardner welcomed the composer Vincent d'Indy, showing him around herself. He had much in common with Gardner. So did Sir Rabindranath Tagore, the Indian philosopher and poet and Nobel laureate, who also visited Gardner, evidence that she had not lost her taste for more multicultural experiences.[49]

Not that Boston itself was not stimulating in this golden era, as it seems to us now, fielding a great number of figures of interest. There were Sunday lunches at Fenway Court with Santayana and the Berensons and the Morton Princes (*there* was a company of moderns!).[50] There was also yet another brilliant young man, A. Piatt Andrew, the Harvard economist and congressman who with Henry Davis Sleeper, a pioneer interior decorator whose Gloucester house, Beauport, was so indebted to Fenway Court, was the leader of a discreet gay colony in Gloucester on Boston's North Shore. This colony included the famous inventor-engineer John Hays Hammond, Jr., his own Hammond Castle another homage to Gardner's work, and in Gardner's life Andrew and Sleeper figured increasingly in the early 1900s. ("*Louise* with Mrs. Gardner," Andrew's diary records one night in 1912, "supper after [the opera] in Dutch Room . . . with Mr. And Mrs. Arliss, Edvina, Marcoux, the Loefflers, etc., stayed at Vendôme with H.D.S.")[51] And, too, there were Gardner's tête-à-tête dinners with friends both old and new: "there's Russia and England and all in between but one must come to Fenway Court for anything so beautiful as dining in the cloister,"[52] wrote the Harvard art historian Thomas Whittemore, of whom more soon. Nellie Melba also had pleasant memories of Fenway Court's cloister, recalling how she and Gardner used to have their after-dinner coffee in front of *El Jaleo*.[53]

And by herself?–"I read William James and continue to smile"[54] she wrote enigmatically to Berenson. As often as not she was in the garden, "grubbing in the earth, which I love."[55] Or similarly occupied above-ground: she had been, she once shared with a correspondent, "trailing

Notice the expression on the face of Henry Sleeper (*far left*) as Gardner shares a confidence with him at a picnic in Gloucester in 1910. *Isabella Stewart Gardner Museum, Boston*

vines in the Monk's Garden [at Fenway Court] all morning";[56] fascinated to observe that "the sun uncurled the leaves whilst I looked."[57] Her public, as opposed to her friends, thought they knew better, of course, and the most exotic of lifestyles was imputed to her. There were, for instance, "the legends of her baths"! As Cleveland Amory, who should have known better, put it: "during hot weather she had a habit of ordering [her servants away] after which she would take to her fountain [in the court] and sit for long periods of time, striking elaborate poses"[58]– presumably in the nude! We have, have we not?, come full circle. And, again, it is ultimately as beside the point, these legendary baths, as whether or not she had posed for Whistler (or anyone else) in the nude. Certainly a long-standing friend, having in mind the mosaic pavement in the court's center, associated then with the Empress Livia, wrote to Gardner once, not of his dreams of Fenway Court, but of Gardner's own as he liked to imagine them:

> With one part of your philosophy, to do and to love the beautiful, I am one. The sensation is the same, I think, wether [sic] one listens to the Mondschein sonata, or looks at a picture painted by the "fiortu-nato garzon," or at a white eagle soaring high above lake Nyasa in the approaching twilight, to catch the last rays of the disappearing sun. You live up to your ideal–le culte du beau. Perhaps you were Petronius, the arbiter Elegantiarum, in a former incarnation. On a warm summer night you must sleep on Livia's pavement; you will remember many things.[59]

Loeffler's pagan poem resonated in Fenway Court all the more for Gardner's own pagan sensibilities. Indeed for all the rumors of Isabella Gardner disporting herself on tiger skins in front of the *Europa*, we have Joe Smith's word for it that while she certainly did have a tiger skin, it was *he* that adorned it: "soon I shall be home," he wrote her once, "and sitting on the tiger skin, in front of you, up in the beautiful room at Fenway."[60]

She was as outrageous a Christian, of course, as she was a pagan. Imagine having a private Christmas midnight Mass in one's own chapel, rather than going to church! Actually, though, Gardner may have been trying by example (as was her wont!) to get that ball rolling too, for the Advent had no Christmas Eve midnight Mass then (which is why the

The Chinese Loggia led originally toward a staircase into the darkness of the Buddha Room. *Isabella Stewart Gardner Museum, Boston*

The Buddha Room. *Isabella Stewart Gardner Museum, Boston*

parish's rector was free to come to Fenway Court) and did not dare to introduce the custom into Puritan Boston until after Gardner's death.[61] Moreover, she was not only the aesthete: she also observed Christ's natal day on at least one year we know of with a dinner "for waifs and strays."[62]

From our perspective today, however, whatever the artistic dimension of all this, it seems, whatever else it was, rather crossing the line to incorporate a particular religion's place of worship and liturgical service into what was intended to become a public museum, though, of course, Italian studies can't leave out Catholicism. But much more to this point is the fact that few realize today that Gardner's original conception was much more daringly multicultural. Curiously–or, perhaps, not!–just as Gardner's role in the gay, Jewish, Irish Catholic, African-American and feminist communities has been subsequently obscured, so too the only important interior of Fenway Court which has been dismantled and destroyed since Isabella Gardner's death[63]–during the directorship of Rolin N. van Hadley who took advantage of a technicality in Gardner's will–was Gardner's Buddhist Temple. Every bit as splendid as her Anglican chapel, it too was fully used religiously, though in its own way. Thus Gardner once announced to arriving guests who found her coming out of this room that she had, indeed, been "communing" with her great gilded Buddhas.[64]

One part of it may be said to remain (awaiting the restoration some day of the whole?) and that is the great eleventh- or twelfth-century gilded Kuan-Yin who looks down the Chinese Loggia from what was the entrance of the Buddha Room to the Spanish chapel, and the painting of the Virgin Mary. These two–the *Virgin of Mercy* from the studio of Zurbarán, the first old master Isabella Gardner acquired, and the Compassionate One of Buddhism, may well carry on the most profound dialogue at Fenway Court. And thereby hangs more than one tale.

◆

Though by all accounts brilliant enough when en fete and lit up for some great event, once night had fallen, Fenway Court must have been in the ordinary way almost as dark inside as was the Fenway and its largely undeveloped and deserted streets outside. By day, of course, the sun flooded into Gardner's plant-filled court through its lofty skylights. However, as has been noted before here, though opened in 1903,

Fenway Court was not lit by electricity. Nor was there gas illumination in the main galleries. Until the time Gardner died in 1924, evenings at Fenway Court were no brighter than in Venice 500 years before, which brings to mind a particularly poignant memory of Harold Nicolson, formed when he was a boy in Morocco, where his father was British minister in the early twentieth century. James Lees-Milne, Nicolson's biographer, has written:

> There was no electric light in Tangier [in the 1900s]. When asked out to dinner (Nicolson's) father rode and his mother was carried in a sedan chair, preceded by a servant bearing a lantern. Harold too would set out . . . on horseback, the flickering beams of the servant's lantern falling, now upon some iron-studded door in a blank wall, now upon a street fountain spluttering upon colored tiles, and now upon a rat scuttling from an open sewer. His horse would pick its way cautiously . . . Suddenly a door would open in the silent street, disclosing a small courtyard, with a lamp hanging from a colonnade, its wick smoking angrily across the arches.

Nicolson was quick to notice, his biographer remarks, that "the lamp was shaped like the lamps used at Pompeii," but it was only in later years, "recalling these evening scenes in Tangier [that Nicolson] realized it was not the glamour of the East which that smoking lamp suggested to him. It was the life [two thousand and more years earlier] of Rome and even Athens."[65] Similarly, so must more than one visitor to Fenway Court, finding their way along its candlelit cloisters, whether to Gardner's apartment on the top floor, or to one of the state rooms or even to the guest suite below, have felt (all the more keenly for needing to somewhat watch their step), that though in Boston in the 1900s they were being pulled gently back many centuries at Fenway Court to the era of the Italian Renaissance.

Chatelaine and guest alike, unless for some great occasion, invariably came and went by the side door on Palace Road. (A nice touch, that; if Fenway Court was a palace it was a New England palace; New Englanders, though they like to have a front door, hardly use it.) And while Bolgi, Gardner's major-domo, would always be on duty to greet a dinner guest, and someone would usually wait up if Gardner were dining out to usher their so often late returning mistress into the elevator that reached her rooftop aerie, it is unlikely such courtesies were extended to whoever was occupying the guest suite. Nor to that person's guests either; so for the most part rather a varied cast of characters regularly came and went both by day and night from Fenway Court, largely unannounced.

What a setting for a play (but who should write it?)–Isabella Gardner coming and going from her penthouse; her guests going to and from some gathering in one of the galleries; the occupant of the guest suite and his guests in turn back and forth; the whirl of Gardner's bird-cage elevator; the thudding shut of the heavy wooden guest suite door with its heavy fifteenth-century ironwork and "speakeasy" grate through which visitors could be identified; Bolgi sometimes there, sometimes not; candles lit and replaced, fires built, then burning down; perhaps after dinner music from the Dutch Room; always the burble of the courtyard fountain–all these comings and goings so often quite independent of each other, but just as surely in another way (as Henry James would have put it; *there* perhaps is our playwright) so most intimately linked in the presiding mind of the great lady whose refuge and shrine this was. Fenway Court, world-class museum, grand ballroom to New England, Gardner's own theater and the Shangri-la of so many artists, was hardly any the less a fin-de-siècle apartment house, and one worthy of Arthur Schnitzler's Vienna. Or Henry James' Boston. For as we have come to know in previous chapters the cast of characters at Fenway Court–not least the habitués of Gardner's bachelor guest suite (WAG, Sargent, Prichard, Carter and Piatt Andrew–gay blades all!)–it is clear such a cast would have been worthy of either author.

Neither in novel or play, however, did James or even Schnitzler ever create a character quite so exotic as the young man, also an occasional occupant of Gardner's guest suite, who comes to mind immediately the subject arises of Fenway Court by moonlight: Okakura Kakuzo.[66] Just out of his thirties in 1904 when he first met the mistress of Fenway Court, by then well into her sixties, Okakura was a striking and graceful figure, a man with just the range Isabella Gardner liked, proficient in all the expected refinements of a Japanese gentleman, mental and physical, from poetry writing and flower arranging to fencing and jujitsu.

A student in Japan of Ernest Fenollosa, the Harvard scholar who pioneered the study of East Asian art, Okakura had served in the 1880s as interpreter for Fenollosa and his New England friends–Sturgis Bigelow and Sylvester Morse—on their buying trips to the island empire for the Boston Museum, and after graduation Okakura became with Fenollosa the head of a new Fine Arts Academy established in Tokyo. Subsequently director of the New Art School, Okakura was ultimately the inspirer of the Nippon Bijitsuin or Hall of Fine Arts at Yanaka, intended to forcefully counter Japan's Europeanization of the time and spearhead the revival of the country's indigenous arts. Perhaps most important, Okakura was instrumental in the passage of the law of Kokutiv, or National Treasures, by which in 1884 all the remaining ancient art of Japan was registered and its export forbidden.

Fascinated by the Far East for generations, Bostonians, long drawn to East Asia not only by the money to be had there (the Gardner fortune, after all, like so many in Boston, had been made in some measure in the China trade) but by the surely unexpected but nonetheless striking affinity of the richly figured art of China and Japan for the sparse, attenuated elegance of New England's neo-classical parlors, had established Boston by the 1900s as one of the leading centers in the West of Asian studies. Indeed, it was Okakura's considered judgment that the

collections of his friends Fenollosa, Bigelow, and company, collections that had themselves awakened Japan to the value of its own artistic patrimony, had endowed Boston's Museum of Fine Arts with art so grand he did not hesitate to assert that it held "the pre-eminent place among the Oriental collections of the world."[67] Of all this in 1910 he became curator. Artist as well as scholar, critic and connoisseur, activist and

Okakura Kakuzo. *Isabella Stewart Gardner Museum, Boston*

reformer, he was, too, philosopher and poet. Okakura, among Gardner's circle, was less comparable to Berenson, perhaps, than to Charles Eliot Norton and John Singer Sargent combined. Okakura was, after all, one of Japan's foremost art critics and educators, sometimes called the "William Morris of Japan." He hardly needed anyone's patronage. That he learned to value both her friendship and inspiration says much for Isabella Stewart Gardner.

It was the artist John La Farge, who was well acquainted in Japan, where he and Henry Adams had traveled extensively, who seems first to have sensed the importance Okakura might be going to have for Gardner, writing to her before the young Japanese's first visit to Boston in 1904 that not only was Okakura "the most intelligent critic of art . . . that I know of," but that "his very great learning in certain ways is balanced by his perception of the uselessness of much that he knows. I think he is one of the very few persons whom you should not miss enjoying."[68] So well did John La Farge evidently know Isabella Gardner! And thereafter we have Morris Carter's word for it that "whenever [Okakura] was in Boston [he and Gardner] were much together. Each understood the other and stimulated the other."[69]

It is not difficult to imagine the themes which fired their friendship; they are those of Okakura's three books of this period: The Ideals of the East with Special Reference to the Art of Japan came first, in 1903, followed the next year by the Awakening of Japan; then, in 1906, The Book of Tea disclosed to its fullest Okakura's uncanny gift of being able to interpret the art of the East to the West, and vice versa, echoes of which I think still resonate between the two merciful figures of the Chinese Loggia at Fenway Court, a dialogue, moreover, apt to the nature of his influence on Fenway Court, almost none of the art of which he helped Gardner acquire, but all of which he helped her to understand better.

This is more important than might seem at first glance to be the case, for there is more far Eastern art in the Gardner Museum than most realize. Thus Walter Denny writes: "The visitor standing before the painting of The Storm on the Sea of Galilee may perhaps be excused for overlooking a ritual bronze Chinese beaker of the Shang dynasty standing nearby, even if that vessel with its polished olive-black patina and stark, archaic grandeur was created over two and a half millennia before young Rembrandt began to listen to Bible stories at his mother's knee."[70]

Something of the same thoughtfulness, even wit, such as one senses in

Gardner's ensembles of Eastern art seems evident as well in Okakura's rejoinder to Gardner after she had given him a white Angora kitten:

> Dear Mrs. Gardner:
>
> Our name is Kowun, which means the "Lonesome Cloud." It also signifies "The Gift by Favor," and again the "Messenger of Bliss"—all these we hope are appropriate titles symbolic of our quality and high descent. We have discarded names like "Haima" which suggests the snowy realm of India, "Mishio," the crested foam, "Sogettse," the frosty morn, because our coat at present is far from being immaculate white.
>
> Kowun (they may call us Kotan in moments of tenderness or even Kochan if they are silly) may have reference to the Ode by Tao-Ying-Ming which begins:
>
> > "All Things
> > on Things are supported;
> > I, the lone-some Cloud,
> > Resteth on none by myself."
>
> We delight in the name, for we are not lonesome. We, like a cloudlet in the sky, curl, unfurl, and swirl on in immense glee. We sleep beautifully. Our only lament was over some hairs singed in snuffing a candle with our tail.
>
> With homage and humble greetings to the seat of the Honored One
>
> > We remain your most obedient,
> > Kowun and Okakura Kakuzo[71]

Okakura got perhaps even closer to the heart of the affair when, back for a while in Japan in 1911, having had to leave Kochan behind in the care of Dodge Macknight, he sent back this message—to Kochan!

> Dear Kochan,
>
> Ages have passed—are you changed any? Swans sailing across the ocean have brought tidings of your whereabouts and I am glad that fate has dealt kindly with you.

When you left I have felt the loss deeply—My breast has missed your nightly tread, the table was suddenly large without your prowling presence. Even now I write with your picture before me. You have killed all the cats in the world for you are alone,—the only one dear to me.

Have you caught your first mice yet? Did he taste nice? Perhaps you enjoy chasing squirrels, there is great pleasure in the quest of the unattainable. You and I know that wonder is the secret of bliss and that with reason comes the death of the beautiful.

I hope you that made the acquaintance of the feline feminine—treacherous things who pretend to understand you and has only claws to match their eyes. Be cautious of forming friendship with tomcats—even of the best sort. They can teach only what they acquired through pain; you must learn all through the gate of gladness. Be courageous, for bravery is the key into life. Never be ashamed of yourself—Think of your high lineage and under whose protection you were brought to me—

Kochan! are you lonesome? Loneliness is the lot of many worthier than you or me—

With the best greetings

Your friend
Kakuzo

P.S. I am sending you a small parcel of Japanese Catnip—and hope that it may agree with you.[72]

It is hard to imagine Isabella Stewart Gardner as lonely in the ordinary way. But both Crawford and Jack Gardner were dead; and we have seen that she twice admitted loneliness to Berenson. There are many kinds of loneliness. One may have many friends but no soul mate or spouse or lover, for instance—exactly Gardner's situation—especially after Crawford's death in 1909. And there is no doubt of the depth of her relationship with Okakura thereafter or of its importance. Mary Berenson quoted Gardner as saying after the Japanese poet's death that she might have "gone to her grave with her hard heart and selfish character if it had not been for ... Okakura," who was "the first person, she said, who showed her how hateful she was, and from him she learnt her first lesson of seeking to love instead of to be loved."[73]

Of course, this is harsh. But Gardner had more than a little to reproach herself for over the years. Especially with respect to Jack Gardner and to some extent with respect to Joe Junior, and even insofar as Crawford was concerned (she was much older after all, yet hardly without blame) Isabella Gardner was hardly above reproach. Doubtless she came to understand Martin Smith's sage observation that "wherever intimacy is present there is attraction and pulling back. Love has its shadow side of exasperation."[74] But intellectual understanding is not emotional acceptance. And in her seventies Isabella Gardner was very fortunate to have found in Okakura a man who it seems could give her peace of mind, indeed, to touch her the more deeply, I believe, because they met after the creative crest of Gardner's life, her design of Fenway Court, which for all that it was trivialized, tipped her hand, so to speak, and elevated her to a sphere—lonely enough, I'm sure—where it needed someone of Okakura's depth, not to be enthralled, or even overcome, but to understand.

That he did that and more is certainly the impression of a poem he gave Gardner on the occasion of her birthday fete of 1911, at which a protégé of Okakura's, a Japanese dancer, mimed Japanese legend. At party's end Okakura gave her "The Taoist":

> She stood alone on earth—an exile
> From heaven. Of all the immortals
> She was the flower.
> Time receded in reverence at her approach.
> Space bowed the way to her triumph. The wind
> brought to her its untrammeled grace, the air
> lent to her voice the balm of its own summer.
> Blue lightning swept in her glances, clouds
> draped the flow of her queenly train.
> Infinity asked of Wonder:
> "Below and above, in my wanderings amongst the
> stars, hast thou heard the name of this fearless
> Spirit, who laughs with the thunder and plays
> with the storm, whom fire burneth not because she
> is fire itself, whom water quelleth not for she
> herself is the ocean?"
> Quote Wonder: "I know not."

Glory to the Nameless! sang the swaying
pines of the forest.
Glory to the Nameless! echoed the billows of
the sea.
On the birthday
of the Presence[75]

1911

Other festivities at Fenway Court centered on Okakura himself, including what one might almost call the near-sacramental apotheosis of their friendship, which brought together both the intellectual and the more strictly artistic aspects of their relationship, in the Japanese tea ceremony, a subject (a cult, really) not without interest even on the eve of the twenty-first century. After all, nearly 100 years after its first publication, Okakura's *Book of Tea* is still in print and widely read. And in this case certainly there is a clear link between book and reader and author and their friendship. As Gardner wrote to Berenson: "I am still full of the sentiment and flower of the great Tea Ceremony, the 'Chano-yu,' which was performed here yesterday at 5 PM (candlelight) by Okakura."[76] But it was only three years later, again to Berenson, that she wrote: "Okakura has gone, which I mourn daily." And then, in 1913, quite suddenly, at only age fifty, Okakura was dead.[77]

When Mrs. Gardner and others honored him with ancient Shinto rites the gossips of the Back Bay had yet another field day. But in the long run, it was perhaps most important that in life Okakura Kakuzo's finest English poems were addressed to Isabella Gardner, while it is very likely that the Buddhist Temple of 1914 Gardner designed at Fenway Court was, in turn, her own memorial to him, and not less worthy.

◆

Gardner's Buddha Room was one of six new galleries, some of which had been in Gardner's mind since 1902, that she designed in her seventy-fourth year, carving them out of her two-story Music Room: the East Cloister, the Spanish Cloister and chapel, the Chinese Loggia, the Buddha Room and on the second level her new Music Room, called the Tapestry Room, itself designed to display ten splendid sixteenth-century Flemish tapestries Gardner bought in 1903.

In all this later work at Fenway Court in its second decade Gardner labored hardly less mightily than she had the first time round. "I am so busy putting up Chinese doors and asphalting them—at this moment, my hands are black with the asphalt"[78] she once wrote Berenson, taking her usual hands-on approach. Another time she reported that she had "measured and looked and contrived for the two days to find a place" for a twelfth-century French Romanesque portal.[79] (Finally she installed it in

The Spanish Cloister, designed by Gardner as a setting for Sargent's *El Jaleo*. *Isabella Stewart Gardner Museum, Boston*

the Spanish Cloister, amid seventeenth-century Mexican tiles, as eclectic and unlikely an ensemble as it is effective.) A number of important pieces were bought in connection with this later work, most notably a magnificent carved Chinese stele ("I am overcome by the wonder of it," she wrote Berenson. "Magnificent! Of course I can't quite realize it," she wrote), for the Chinese Loggia; a series of three great gilt Buddhas from Yamanaka's, the famous import house, for the Buddha Room, and, finally, the glory of the Spanish Cloister, *El Jaleo*.[80]

The installation of that painting by Sargent, a masterpiece of his early years, and, indeed, the design of all these new galleries, extended

Gardner's experiments with lighting so as to successfully compass electricity. The subject had long interested her. She had once protested to Jack Gardner she might have to "invent a new system of lighting" for her prospective museum; in 1897 an "electrician" is mentioned in a letter to Berenson as part of her plan to better light the *Europa* in her Beacon Street town house, in connection with which Gardner took the occasion to complain "you have no idea how difficult it is to arrange artificial light satisfactorily."[81] At Fenway Court, however, early electrical fixtures apparently disappointed and were rejected. I suspect it was Sargent who in the 1900s revived her interest when he asked her advice about electric lighting of his Boston Public Library murals. "We tried an experiment last night," the painter wrote her, "and we are going to do it again," inviting her to come to the library late one night after its closing to give her opinion of his design for lighting,[82] an interest which according to R. H. Ives Gammell, a Boston painter, arose out of the fact that, "being a great admirer of Wagner, [Sargent] had no doubt [seen] the tricks of stagelighting" Wagner used and sought to annex them. Moreover, wrote Gammell, Sargent well "knew the spell exerted by dancers glimpsed in the dim light of Spanish taverns and Arab cafes."[83] Certainly nothing is clearer than that even within many of his paintings Sargent was fascinated by the idea of catching and holding such an effect of light, above all in *El Jaleo*, which may have been no little part of why Gardner contrived to secure that picture for her collection with unusual bravado even for her. The painting was a gift to Gardner famously made on the spot when she showed its then owner (her admirer, admittedly), T. Jefferson Coolidge, the Spanish Cloister she had brazenly designed for it! He gave it to her at once.

It was a triumph which doubtless emboldened Gardner to try it a second time in aid of the Tapestry Room upstairs with Paul Sachs, the distinguished Harvard professor and connoisseur. According to John Coolidge, who had the story from Sachs himself:

In 1916 or thereabouts she had considered the acquisition of a Spanish primitive but had not made up her mind. Meanwhile it was purchased by Paul Sachs, who had just moved to Cambridge from New York. Shortly Mrs. Gardner gave a highly select dinner party in his honor. Toward the close of the meal she remarked quietly: "Mr. Sachs, I understand you have just bought a Spanish primitive.

Turn around. Don't you agree your painting would go very well over the fireplace?" Then she laid her right hand on the table and continued: "You know, this hand could hold a stiletto. If you tell me what you paid for your painting I will send you my check in the morning." Today it hangs over the fireplace and does look very well.[84]

The primitive in question, "a chilling gold and tempera panel,"[85] in Goldfarb's apt words, of St. Michael, is really as stunning if less dominating a climax to the Tapestry Room as El Jaleo is to the Spanish Cloister on page 258, even as the manner of her acquisition of both pictures is striking documentation that even nearing eighty years of age Gardner had not lost the nerve that had been so key in the first place to building America's first great collection of old masters. Nor did she flunk the opportunity that El Jaleo offered to try her hand after the manner of Sargent at the library at the vexing task of electrical illumination of pictures.

Her design was an inspiration: behind and under a "proscenium" arch such as topped all stages of those days, she set back the painting, treating El Jaleo as itself a smaller stage, while where footlights might have been expected at the bottom of the larger stage she placed a row of concealed electric lights. She treated the "proscenium arch," moreover, as a scalloped, Moorish one. The effect is wonderful: somewhat after the then fashionable "tableaux," the effect is to create the illusion the dancer is really there and in motion (close your eyes; then open them!), so dramatically do the "footlights" enhance the internal light of the painting. The idea Gardner had earlier used with natural light in the case of Zorn's The Omnibus, now proved even more effective with electricity.

Gardner and Sargent, I suspect, were not the only artists involved in this triumph; a third may have been Joseph Urban,[86] an architect and stage designer from Vienna who came to the Boston Opera in 1911. Influenced by Adolphe Appia, a revolutionary Wagnerian set designer (that Sargent, Gardner, and Urban were all besotted Wagnerites is significant), Urban "drew on the work of familiar European painters, but his use of color and lighting were like nothing Americans had ever seen. . . . He preferred soft, diffused light, and frequently worked,"[87] John Dizikes notes, "with a stage-within-a-stage, . . . concentrating and expanding illusion." Given that Gardner was a devoted ticket holder to the Boston

Opera in this period of her lighting experiments, the fact that she was influenced by this man whose work in Boston so stunned it has been called "a revolution in the setting and lighting of the American stage,"[88] seems highly probable, especially as her correspondence has lately documented the fact that Gardner and Urban were friends, she having asked him and his family to the Christmas Eve midnight Mass in 1914.

If the Spanish Cloister reflects perhaps a train of thought Urban's ideas started in Gardner, the same may be true of the Buddha Room nearby, which, like the Spanish Cloister and Chinese Loggia, stirred Maude Howe Elliott to the belief, as Elliott put it when she came "to see Mrs. Gardner's new additional rooms at Fenway Court," that the "new rooms seem to me the best."[89] For if *El Jaleo* was theatrical, the Buddha Room verged on the sort of high drama that would soon come to be found (though with reproductions, of course, not original art like Gardner's) in the movie palace. Isabella Gardner was ever the popularizer! And again light was key, light very much as Urban used it, to the effect of the Buddha Room, an almost entirely subterranean chamber reached by a broad flight of stone stairs at the end of the Chinese Loggia. Indeed, the Buddha Room's placement and feeling seems very much in the spirit of one music critic's report of Urban's set and lighting design for *Pelléas et Mélisande*, a modern French opera Gardner would not have missed, centered on "a subterranean chamber [that led up to] a high, narrow, shadowed grotto. . . . the grotto glimmered blue," the critic continued (Urban's work was often thought "suggestive of Maxfield Parrish's unreal, poetical landscapes"), "until the startling moment when the moonlight's probing finger touched it."[90]

Darkness and moonlight. Significantly, though in the Spanish Cloister Gardner showed she could deploy electrical light brilliantly, in the Buddha Room she showed how with equal brilliance she could eschew all light utterly: Elliott's description of the Buddha Room was that it was "rather awful in its dark thrill, like a tomb."[91] Thus in her final work at Fenway Court, Gardner worked fundamentally with light and with darkness, actually with chiaroscuro and achieving what could almost be called the effect of no architecture at all!

No wonder Okakura seems close at hand. For it was by moonlight he himself saw Isabella Gardner. And it was that moonlight, as it fell on the court's walls, that prompted Okakura's wonderful poem to Gardner, "The Stairway of Jade."

The One,
Alone and White.
Shadows but wander
In the lights that were,
Lights but linger
In the shadows to be
The Moon
White and alone.
The stars have dissolved
To make a crystal night.
Fragrance floats
Unseen by flowers,
Echoes waft,
Half answered by darkness.
A shadow glides

The West Cloister, ca. 1903. *Isabella Stewart Gardner Museum, Boston*

On the stairway of jade–
Is it a moonbeam?
Is it the One?

In the Abode
of Solitary Shadow?[92]

There, in the shadow–for the mind's eye (at Fenway Court supremely) sees not less clearly–there *is* a staircase of jade, and if not everyone can see it, so much the better. One is grateful for the ambiguity that obscures her and Okakura in this perhaps deepest of Gardner's storied relationships. Finally, of Isabella Stewart Gardner's own mind's eye Van Wyck Brooks was perhaps more insightful than (as has been thought) unkind when he wrote of "innocent eyes that . . . wore no veils."[93]

13

The New Woman

EVEN AS ISABELLA Gardner was initiated by Okakura into ancient serenities not previously known to her, in these her final active years, stretching into her seventies, between the turn of the century and the First World War, she by no means disengaged either from the rapid pace of change in the Western world in the 1900s. Indeed, it all thrilled her– aviation, for instance: the three historic "Harvard-Boston Aero Meets" held at Squantum just outside Boston in the years just before the First World War fascinated her; and though the 1910 meet is the only one it can be documented she attended, she must have been especially inter- ested in the 1912 meet, "notable as the first in the United States at which women fliers were seen," including Boston's Harriet Quimby, who just the year previously had become "the first woman to obtain a pilot's license in the country." Just as had been the case when Gardner enrolled in Norton's lectures at the time women's education was starting at Har- vard, so Gardner's only lament about the meet she is known to have attended was that an important engagement at the other end of the state the same day meant she had to decline the offer of one of the pilots to go up with him to experience herself the new marvel of flight.[1]

The modernism of the future author of *The Waste Land* also interested her, and she was more than welcoming to the new generation that made their way to her. Thus, for example, T.S. Eliot's signature appears twice in Isabella Gardner's guestbook in 1912, when he was still a graduate student at Harvard. There is also significant correspondence between Eliot and Gardner after Eliot settled in England. They had many mutual friends–Santayana, Okakura, Prichard–and much in common across the spectrum of the arts. In one letter to Gardner, Eliot wrote eloquently of arts more visual than literary, in this case of the sculpture of Henri Gaudier-Brzeska and Jacob Epstein and of the central African art one or two figures at a recent exhibition had put him in mind of, Gardner having perhaps shared with Eliot her interest in the primitive and in the sculpture of Paul Manship, of which more soon. In another letter Eliot touched on more literary matters, promising to send Gardner a copy of *Blast*, rather a notorious and distinctly avant garde little magazine he clearly thought would amuse her and in which he expected a few of his own forthcoming works would appear.[2] He also sent her one of his early poems, probably *The Love Song of J. Alfred Prufrock*, published in 1915 in *Poetry* magazine, of which, interestingly, Gardner was a subscriber. He shared too with her his interest in the work of the modernist painter Wyndham Lewis, who with the poet Ezra Pound was much involved in Vorticism, a movement in the visual arts which Bergonzi has called "a real attempt to foster a native English version of cubism and futurism."[3]

New words in Gardner's lexicon, but one gets a real sense in Eliot's letters of the kind of outpourings of young genius (so like Berenson three decades earlier) Gardner so often fostered. In one letter of 1915 Eliot essays a wide-ranging discussion of his literary hopes and ambitions (it could have been Henry James thirty-five years previously) bringing Gardner up to date about his recent marriage, his decision to live in England, and his increasing shift in focus from philosophy to poetry. He concludes with the sort of frank request that implies Isabella Gardner's interest in the young poet's work, alluding to Ezra Pound's suggestion his brother would be seeking soon on Eliot's behalf interviews with the editor of the *Atlantic* and with Amy Lowell–and, indeed, with Gardner. Could she help?[4] Though it is not known how Gardner replied (only Eliot's letters to her survive) there can be little doubt she did her bit to help the far away but brilliant young man. Both Lowell and the *Atlantic* editor were friends; the latter, indeed, had been a classmate at Harvard of Joe Junior.

None of this should amaze. In respect to music especially Isabella Gardner's taste had always been sophisticated; a Wagnerite, for example, when that was to be on quite the leading edge of the era. Whereas Julia

Ward Howe would liken *Tristan* in 1890 to "broken china" (breaking, presumably), and her niece Maude recalled Howe's friend and Boston's leading musical figure of the era, John Sullivan Dwight, describing Wagner's music (as some might today the hardest rock) as "wanton cacophony," Gardner was already in 1888 presenting Wagner in her Music Room.[5] Indeed, she helped to sponsor a lecture by Walter Damrosch introducing the revolutionary composer's work to Boston, and was herself a guarantor of the Boston Musical Association, dedicated to the performance of contemporary music. In fact, "musical events of a strikingly missionary nature," in Ralph Locke's words, that occurred in Gardner's Music Room over the years included an early performance in this country of Arnold Schoenberg's D-Minor Quartet[6] and yet another lecture by Damrosch, this time on Debussy's *Pelléas et Mélisande*,[7] evidence that as Locke notes, Gardner's taste in modern French music might properly be accounted "somewhat advanced" for its time.[8]

Certainly she took by contrast no known interest at all in the rather grand but very conservative Boston group of composers of the time, people like George Whitefield Chadwick and John Knowles Paine, not even in their well-known female colleague, H. H. A. Beach. Instead, the composer Gardner served most ardently as patron and mentor was Charles Loeffler. Distinctly numbered "among the non-traditionalists, the avant-garde," writes his biographer, Loeffler was noted for playing with the Boston Symphony Orchestra the American premieres of works by composers like Max Bruch, Saint-Saëns and Edouard Lalo, while Loeffler's own music, known eventually for advanced harmony, was so widely perceived as modern and decadent he was once called by the *New York Sun* "the blond musical Verlaine of Boston."[9]

That Gardner herself was seen by Loeffler as avant-garde is also evident. She was among the first to see Loeffler as not primarily a virtuoso but as a composer, and when he dedicated his *Divertimento* to her, it was, he said, because "no conventionality" was to be looked for in it and that "it may stir your imagination by astonishing your ears"[10]–all apt reasons for a dedication to a patron like Gardner, apt to like what he called the most "original and the best work I have done."[11] It was no idle remark. How much this composer depended on Gardner is clear in his query to her about another work of his: "Is there any hope of your wanting to hear those Rhapsodies later? You know I write for the few, almost 'en une de quelqu'un.' I don't know why, but it is so. . . . Naturally I always hope for your interest in my doings. And I consider myself lucky to have you on my side."[12] Interestingly, furthermore, the patronage Gardner showed Loeffler, he, in turn, extended to Gabriel Fauré himself. Building on Gardner's publishing contacts, Loeffler helped Fauré get his music published and edited the Boston Music Company's issue of Fauré's sonata for violin. Grateful, Fauré dedicated to Loeffler his second cello sonata.[13]

Loeffler, the composer most intimately associated with Isabella Gardner, was notable also in his later years for his fascination with jazz; so much so that his wife once complained to Isabella Gardner that at the winter garden of the old Hotel Westminster in Copley Square Loeffler thought the jazz orchestra so good he couldn't tear himself away typically before the early hours of the morning. Nor was this only an affair of a moment. "Duke Ellington's trumpeters," according to a friend, could throw Loeffler into "ecstasies." Loeffler, moreover, numbered among those who studied with him the distinguished jazz musician Leo Reisman. And Loeffler was there when the soloist of Reisman's orchestra was George Gershwin, whom Loeffler became a good friend of and admired hardly less it would seem than Stravinsky. Indeed, Loeffler incorporated jazz elements into his own compositions, most notably in *Clouds*, his chief work for jazz orchestra, and in what he originally called *la princesse nègre*, the third movement of a partita where Loeffler's use of African-American themes, in which he and Gardner had long been interested, scandalized traditionalists. To the everlasting shame of the Gardner Museum, after Gardner's death when Loeffler's partita was played there, the controversial jazz movement was omitted. Loeffler, who was present, may have been deferring to the woman who commissioned the piece, Elizabeth Sprague Coolidge. But it makes clear how important was the founder's guiding hand; once Carter moved upstairs, as it were–the touch was inevitably much less sure, and never sure enough to court scandal–which Gardner, far from ever being troubled by, of course, knew well how to use to her cause's advantage.

In painting and sculpture too Gardner's taste in contemporary art was not quite what might have been expected.[14] Always a leader, never a follower, she invariably charted her own and individualistic way. Never in the first place much engaged by Impressionism, for example, even when it was quite the leading edge–and despite the fact that back in the 1880s, as Erica Hirschler points out, Denis Bunker, who was then quite in the vanguard of the American Impressionist movement, painted in Gardner's own greenhouse a picture, *Chrysanthemums*, that has been called "among the first impressionist pictures painted in this country"–Gardner, perhaps because she disdained to compete either with Berthe Palmer on the one hand or the far more serious collector, Louisine Havemeyer, on the other, just wasn't very interested–beyond, that is, one lone Childe Hassam. Nor did visiting Monet at Giverny in 1906 with friends change her mind; even the urgings of Sargent himself that she acquire one of Monet's Rouen Cathedral pictures were to no avail.[15] There are no Monets at Fenway Court.

Nor were there any of the works of the leading Boston School painters. Perhaps Isabella Gardner felt much as did Margaret Sargent two genera- tions later, that "the women [painted by that school in their exquisite sig- nature interiors] as contemplative dreamers were often nothing of the kind. . . . Tarbell's *Mrs. C* [for example, was] actually Blanche Ames, . . . an illustrator, botanist and suffragist."[16] Whether or not Gardner, of an ear- lier generation, was as much offended by the misrepresentation as Sargent, it is most likely Isabella Gardner agreed with Henry James that Impressionism lacked "emotional complexity,"[17] which would also explain Gardner's similar disinterest in the much admired academic traditionalists of the Boston School (despite the influence of her Vermeer on their work), a disinterest moreover, that mirrors her equally dismissive attitude, already noted here, for the rather parallel academic music of the Boston Classicists school of composers.

That neither Impressionism nor the Boston School aroused Isabella Gardner's interest does not mean, however, that beyond Whistler or Zorn and Sargent she did not probe. Trevor Fairbrother has explained better than anyone the surprising (to some perhaps) direction Gardner's taste took in her last years in terms of contemporary art. Gardner and her circle, including such influential figures as the Harvard teacher and col- lector Denman Ross, constituted, Fairbrother writes:

> a cultural intelligentsia that exercised broadly based hedonistic stan- dards in selecting the local artists they encouraged . . . their exten- sive network of European acquaintances included such figures as Henry James, Whistler, and Berenson . . . their local circle specifi- cally did not include teachers at the Museum School–Tarbell, Benson, Paxton, and Hale–who must have seemed too parochial. . . .

the artists in the Gardner–Ross group . . . were perhaps more sophisticated and more forward-looking . . . [than] the "Tarbellites."[18]

Perhaps it should be called the Sargent-Berenson-Gardner-Ross group
because Gardner's disinterest for the Boston School surely reflects also
the advice of Sargent, with whom after 1910, when he was much in
Boston working on his murals for the Museum of Fine Arts, Gardner
spent a great deal of time, and to whom she would naturally have given
her ear with respect to contemporary work as much as to Berenson. One
does not have to dignify the petulance of some defenders of the Boston
School about Sargent and Gardner to credit the fact that Sargent may
well have advised Gardner to eschew the Tarbellites as "too bourgeois"
and to be more "forward looking" in her collecting. Certainly Mary
Berenson was clear enough on the subject, writing to Gardner once that
she and Bernard were not impressed by "the dreary waste of Tarbell and
other mediocrities."[19]

Actually it would have been characteristic of Sargent, rather than being
negative about the Boston School, to have been simply more positive about
other directions open to Isabella Gardner. We know now, for instance, that
Sargent made an effort to introduce Gardner to the work of George
Hallowell. A student at one time of Charles Eliot Norton, later trained as
an architect and a member of Ralph Adams Cram's circle, Hallowell, who
(according to Cram) Sargent called "the painter with the greatest power and
promise in America," studied at the School of the Museum of Fine Arts in
Boston under both Tarbell and Benson. But Hallowell was distinctly more
bohemian than bourgeois. And he struck out in a very different direction as
a painter from either of his teachers, and though only one of the three early
Hallowells Gardner bought may be said to reflect his mature gifts,
Hallowell's shadowed, dark, disturbing canvases of shattered trees and
vivid landscapes and aggressive lumbermen, his lurid colors and vivid hues
and turbulent Byronic temperament, were about as far removed from the
genteel elegance of the Boston School as was possible. In a recent appraisal
of his work, T. Leah Lipton writes of Hallowell's harmless enough sounding painting, *Upstream*, as a painting "as contemporary as the maelstrom of
Bosnia, . . . [or] the firestorm of AIDS."[20]

Eschewing conventional gentility as Gardner did, it is no wonder
Sargent recommended Hallowell to her, for he was not unlike the contemporary painter Sargent knew Isabella Gardner apparently admired

second only to Sargent himself, Dodge Macknight, whom Sargent may also have recommended to Gardner. His seascapes and landscapes were, in fact, not unlike Sargent's own work in his wonderful late period watercolors of the Rocky Mountains, which Gardner not only collected, but in one key instance herself commissioned Sargent to paint.

So drawn to Macknight was Gardner that she bestowed provocatively on him (by no means the Boston painter most would have chosen for such an accolade) the honor of the only gallery at Fenway Court named after a living painter, and so the Macknight Room would remain. A student in Paris in the 1880s, thereafter Macknight traveled widely throughout Europe, attracting the attention not only of Sargent, in whose London studio Macknight reportedly exhibited in 1890, but of Vincent van Gogh, whom he met in Paris, and who invited both Macknight and Gauguin to join him in an artists' colony at Arles where Macknight, however, could never be persuaded to stay. Indeed, they were hardly dissimilar artists. Critics at first found Macknight's work, as they did both Van Gogh's and Gauguin's, strident; Macknight's palette "shocking and distasteful"; his intense colors "savage"—one critic spoke of "Macknightmares"![21] Yet Albert Gallatin, the great collector of modern art, went so far as to call Macknight "one of the American masters of the medium [of watercolor],"[22] and Gardner's friend, Denman Ross, also much respected Macknight's work. Gardner first bought his work when he was still considered very controversial, in 1890, and the Macknight Room was no whim: set aside in 1915, by then she owned a great many of his pictures, her estimation of his work having evolved over a quarter of a century, doubtless to his benefit! By then they had, in fact, become good friends and Macknight often asked for the help of Gardner's eye in hanging his shows in the 1900s, when he began at last to achieve conspicuous success.

It must be said, however, that if Gardner agreed with those who thought the Tarbellites too academic and bourgeois and was herself more forward looking in her tastes, she seems also to have agreed with those who on the other hand found too radical that most gifted, perhaps, of all Boston's painters then, Maurice Prendergast, the "Yankee Giorgione"[23] as Van Wyck Brooks was so aptly to call him. Possibly, though, Gardner eschewed Prendergast in deference to his established Boston patron, Sarah Choate Sears. To be sure, Sears and Gardner's joint patronage of Bunker and Macknight seemed amicable enough, but both those painters were personal friends of Gardner's; Prendergast, for whatever reason, was not. Gardner once told Berenson that in collecting she wished to avoid rivalry and never wanted to seem to compete with another collector, instancing no reason, though no one who knew Gardner could have failed to notice her desire always to stake out first and hold her own turf. Perhaps she came to feel "rivalry" with another patron as distasteful as with another collector, particularly in the case of a friend, as Sears was. In this case it would have been especially complicated, for Sears was herself an artist, whose work Gardner thought highly enough of to add to Fenway Court's collection.

Because Sarah Sears was married to J. Montgomery Sears, reputedly Boston's richest man, she tended to be portrayed in the more sensational newspapers as a rival of Gardner. Actually, however, they were more friends than rivals; and it may even have been the case that Gardner may somewhat have mentored Sears, who was a generation younger. Despite her high-profile marriage, Sears was very straightforward–a very "simple, unaffected and unpretentious person" in Berenson's words[24]–who suffered, moreover, about as tragic family losses as did Gardner, and was also so gifted a painter and photographer (as well as a serious patron and collector) as to have been really quite more interesting to Gardner than the usual Back Bay matron. Certainly they exchanged many gifts and kindnesses, and Sears also is known to have esteemed Gardner's work as collector and designer as much as Gardner esteemed Sears' painting. It is telling that when Sears and Sargent happened to discover a new "Bohemian" restaurant to their liking in Boston, the younger pair at once reported their find to Gardner and invited the older woman to join them there the next night.[25]

Though the painting by Sears Gardner bought, *Gladioli* (executed in 1915), exhibits in Erica Hirshler's words a "distinctly modernist aesthetic,"[26] thus documenting again Gardner's own rather advanced tastes even at seventy-five, Sears that year was only fifty-eight, and her relative youth surely explains what were by then her more adventuresome patterns than Gardner's of patronage and collecting. Sears not only patronized Prendergast: uniquely in Boston, she collected the work of Cézanne, one of whose pictures Sears lent to the famous Armory Show of 1913 that was the herald of Modernism in America. If that was to steal a march on Gardner, the older woman was to have her day, however, because of the happy thought of the celebrated art historian Thomas Whittemore,[27] a Boston-area native and Tufts graduate who later studied and taught at Harvard, and finally achieved fame for uncovering the famous mosaics of Hagia Sophia in Istanbul. Brilliant, engaging, unmarried, probably gay, a devout Anglo-Catholic (a friend, in fact, of Harold Peto, he of the Advent reredos), despite a thirty-one-year age difference, Whittemore and Gardner were so close that his letters to her would embarrass lovers: "from the blue of my heart," he wrote her once, "I think of you in your garden of singing waters in the path of the moon, and am, yours, T."[28] Meanwhile it transpired that Whittemore was a friend of both Isabella Gardner and Henri Matisse.

One of the "founding fathers," in H. J. Janson's words, "of twentieth-century painting,"[29] Matisse was much admired by Whittemore, who possessed a painting which marks in Hilliard Goldfarb's words "a critical moment in Matisse's transition from a more traditional painting style to the looser, more brilliant colorism of his Fauve period,"[30] *The Terrace, St. Tropez*, which Whittemore forthwith presented as a gift to Isabella Gardner in 1912. Remembering that fourteen years before *Count Tommasso Inghirami* had been the first Raphael to come to America, this gift of the Matisse gave an extraordinary range to the Gardner collection, carrying it forward to the cutting edge of twentieth-century modernist art.

That this wonderful picture was a gift may seem at first glance to lessen Gardner's vision or volition. But Gardner's own few purchases in this period were hardly very traditional. She bought several works by Leon Bakst, the brilliant young designer of the sets and costumes of Diaghilev's Ballet Russe, and it was during this period that she extended her patronage to perhaps the greatest American Art Deco sculptor, Paul Manship, several of whose works she bought, while also becoming the young man's muse and mentor. Furthermore, it is not very likely that so close a friend as Whittemore would have given her anything, especially anything so grand as *The Terrace, St. Tropez*, that Gardner did not covet. Nor was Whittemore the only friend to give Gardner a Matisse! In the absence of imagining a plot to madden Gardner by forcing her into collecting several works by an artist not to her liking (not too plausible an idea!), it must be said that there is every reason to believe Isabella Gardner liked Matisse! In fact, many letters survive documenting her timely interest in this modernist master: "Matisse is very lively: I was in his studio yesterday," Gardner learned in 1913; then, a year later: "Matisse made a little etching of me the other day. . . . The prints are only to be 15 in number. . . . [I] have mentioned you as one of my friends to whom I intend to offer ... this little gift."[31] Matthew Prichard, another mutual friend of Gardner and Matisse, was as good as his word, and so another Matisse entered the Gardner collection–this time as a principal feature of Isabella Gardner's writing desk.

Such were the storms of Modernism, however, no Picasso was forth-coming from Prichard! Gertrude Stein might desert Matisse for Picasso; Prichard didn't, writing Gardner: "I said nothing, but Picasso remains for me what he was to Okakura, who said, remember: 'I stretched out my mind toward [his paintings] and I touched nothing.'" Berenson (to whom the Steins also introduced Matisse's work, which Berenson told Gardner intrigued him) did not disagree, and it is clear that Gardner's chief artistic advisers were all united in understandable efforts to sway her, famous collector that she now was, to this or that part of the newly discovered land of Modernism.

On the other side of the question of Picasso was one of that master's earliest and most influential champions, the English critic, artist, and scholar, Roger Fry, whom Gardner knew well enough to have "dined with ... last night at a little Italian restaurant," as she reported to Berenson in 1907. Fry's own opinion of Gardner is clear in the words Virginia Woolf attributes to him about "the wonderful and eccentric Mrs. Gardner who has made the most remarkable [art] collection of modern times and is altogether a woman of extraordinary force of character."[32] But Fry, of course, famously argued the merits of Picasso *and* Matisse–and of Cézanne, Gauguin and Van Gogh as well–and it was really therefore all the more seemly that in the end it was, so to speak, Matisse himself who introduced the influence of Picasso into Fenway Court in his *Nude Seated on a Table*, probably done in 1907, the year after the artist first became interested in African art. Certainly Karen Haas argued persuasively that one can see in this work of Matisse not only the effect of Cézanne but "the charismatic influence of Picasso," who had exchanged paintings with Matisse in 1907 and was then at work on his famous *Demoiselles d'Avignon*, itself dependent on Matisse's *La Joie de Vivre*.[33]

That pairing, as it happens, was then hanging in the Paris apartment of Gertrude Stein, about whom Gardner was also curious, and kept up to date both by Prichard and by Berenson, to say nothing of Whittemore. Nothing is clearer than that Gardner's friends were following her lead in all of this–including Sarah Choate Sears, who also gave Gardner a Matisse *Nude Seated on the Ground*, done in 1908–9, a work Gardner in turn lent to Boston's Museum of Fine Arts for exhibition when it mounted the first American museum show of Matisse's work in 1911.[34] Gardner was in all this distinctly progressive. Her "displaying of works by Matisse at this early date is particularly noteworthy," notes Haas, for at that time even "in New York galleries and collectors could accept . . . only barely. . . . the Ash Can School and the European avant-garde."[35] There is also little doubt Gardner understood fully what she was doing. Witness Prichard's remark to her in a letter of 1922: "By the bye the Luxembourg [Museum in Paris] has bought one of Matisse's paintings, thus the French accept him about fifteen years after your approval!"[36]

Macknight, Manship, Bakst, Matisse–a search for common ground here could become wide ranging indeed. One line of thought, though, stands out: that Van Gogh found Macknight interesting, and that so many critics found Macknight's work "shocking" and "savage," suggests that there was a strong aspect of the "primitive" about the kind of modern work Isabella Gardner was drawn to. After all, the modern sculptor Gardner seemed attracted by, who most influenced not only Gaston Lachaise (whose work in turn greatly influenced Picasso's first Cubist sculpture) was Paul Manship, of whom Walker Hancock has written that though the art of the Italian Renaissance meant much to Manship, he was "the beginning of a revolution. . . . [his work] the first noteworthy instance of an American sculptor turning to an earlier, more primitive art for a fresh realization of the properties of his medium. . . . Since that time almost every primitive art from the palae-olithic to that of the African Negro has been explored."[37] It is a significant commentary on Isabella Gardner's growth that whereas Elizabeth Sussman feels one of Gardner's old advisors, Charles Eliot Norton, would have "paled to see"[38] Manship's work, Gardner's new acquaintance of the 1900s, Paul Sachs of Harvard's Fogg Art Museum, would in subsequent years become notable for innovative installations there that included a gallery of Maya and other "primitive" work that was "the first permanent installation in any museum to present [such work] as *art* rather than ethnographic artifact."[39] Why do I emphasize this proclivity of Isabella Gardner for the primitive and the archaic? Because Guy Davenport has well described twentieth-century "Modernisn as a re-discovery of the freshness of the archaic," citing by way of example "Picasso and T. S. Eliot scramb[ling] to gaze at the [prehistoric] Lascaux cave paintings." And it is in this sense that Isabella Gardner may be definitely characterized as drawn to and a par-

ticipant in the modernist movement with which she is usually unthink-
ingly thought to have had no sympathy.[40]

We know, in fact, that Gardner was interested in the sculpture of
Jacob Epstein and painter Wyndam Lewis' "native English version of
cubism," for it is most unlikely in a letter seeking a favor from Gardner
that the young T. S. Eliot, who had called on her at least twice, would
have raised subjects that would have offended or bored her. And the fact
is, the traditionalists have historically rather hijacked Isabella Gardner in
so far as our understanding of her taste and influence is concerned. Yes,
Gardner through her Vermeer greatly influenced contemporary traditionalists, but so also through her Matisse she had an equally strong
influence on modernists, an influence, indeed, that also extended past her
death into the late 1920s and 1930s. Certainly John Walker, later Director of the National Gallery in Washington, recalled when he was a Harvard undergraduate in the 1920s that while there was no Picasso in
Boston to console him, there *was* Isabella Gardner's Matisse.

To carry this line of thought perhaps a little too far, it is also true that
the first director of the Museum of Modern Art in New York, Alfred H.
Barr, was a graduate of the Harvard museum course taught by Gardner's
close acquaintance, Paul Sachs, three of whose other students founded in
1928 the Harvard Society for Contemporary Art, "the first [society] to
be designed as a model for the modernistic museum in America" in
Elizabeth Sussman's words. And, characteristically, Isabella Gardner,
dead four years in 1928 when the society was founded, was an influential force not only among the society's faculty trustees but among the student founders as well. Gardner had a "younger mind" at eighty than most
of her contemporaries at twenty! Two of the society's trustees were well
known to her, Paul Sachs, a close acquaintance, and Arthur Pope, a
friend, while two of the student leaders were as ardent admirers of
Gardner and her vision in the 1920s as ever Berenson or Sargent had
been in the 1890s: Lincoln Kirstein, later the founder of the New York
City Ballet and the great patron of Balanchine, wrote that he much
admired "the romance of Fenway Court"; while John Walker, his fellow
modernist, admitted that "as an undergraduate I loitered so many days in
Fenway Court that the circle of Isabella's friends and/or lovers whose
portraits, photographs and letters surrounded me might have cried 'La
Belle Dame sans Merci' hath thee in thrall."[41]

Isabella Gardner lived to be in a very real sense a modernist after all, but one most comfortable at the more conservative end of the modernist continuum, with artists like Bakst and Manship and Macknight. It is a clear pattern in her taste: in music not Chadwick or Payne *or* Ives, but Loeffler; in painting not the Boston School *or* Picasso, but Matisse. Yet Alfred Barr pronounced Matisse along with Picasso, Braque, and Klee "the four great painters of [the twentieth] century." And any who think it going too far to emphasize the Modernism of Gardner would do well to consider the fact that the first Matisse to enter an American museum was Isabella Stewart Gardner's.

Yet Picasso matters more at the Gardner Museum than just his influence on Matisse's drawings there suggests. Bearing in mind how significantly Gardner's work at Fenway Court influenced not just Elsie De Wolfe but that other pioneering interior designer, also Gardner's friend, Henry Sleeper, whose extraordinary assemblage of interiors at Beauport, north of Boston, was nationally influential, I like very much this insight of architect Robert A. M. Stern:

> At the same time that Braque and Picasso were developing their technique of collage, using artifacts ... to create two- and three-dimensional works on canvas of great plastic and narrative complexity, Sleeper proceeded to develop similar techniques on the architectural level. ... To proceed through [Beauport's] rooms is to walk through Sleeper's mind ... eccentricity is elevated to the level of genius. Its dense assembly of artifacts from different eras telescopes time in an effort to render history readable in a moment's glance.

Now it is exactly for this quality that Beauport is indebted to Fenway Court, of which, indeed, Gardner named Sleeper a trustee, evidence of how truly his work at Beauport moved her, showing an unusual understanding of what she was trying to do at Fenway Court with her "architecture of fragments"—a technique that in turn illustrates how alert Gardner was to modern currents of thought in her late-middle and early old age in her sixties and seventies. So alert that I believe in the light of recent scholarship, not only of my own, a dramatic reinterpretation of the design concept of the Gardner Museum is timely.

Consider Hugh Kenner's analysis of William Everdell's *The First Moderns*, where the author identifies, first in mathematics and physics, then in music (such as the work of Debussy), and, finally, in the literary work of

Joyce, Pound, and Eliot particularly, the key concept of twentieth-century Modernism: in *Ulysses*, for instance, Kenner writes of the "discontinuity among [Joyce's] 18 episodes–each invokes a new hour, a new place, often new protagonists and a new narrative voice." Now, I would say pretty much the same thing of the Gardner Museums galleries! Indeed, when Everdell notes how in the work of many including Joyce "emotions superimpose themselves . . . and succeed themselves . . . without predictability, logic, or coherence," I think at once of long-standing, though small-minded (usually curatorial) complaints about the Gardner's "eclectic jumble." Like the music of Debussy or the poetry of Eliot–to cite two of the artists Everdell focuses on who Isabella Gardner admired–the design of Fenway Court is a striking example in its own field of Modernism's key theme of discontinuity as Everdell defines it, even as it is also a brilliant example of Modernism's key technique of collage.

The significance of this is far-reaching, for Donald Barthelme is correct, I believe, in characterizing collage as *the* art form of the twentieth century: "The confusing signals, the impurity of the signal," he argues, "gives you verisimilitude." What Kenneth Tynan says of "Waiting for Godot" is equally true of Fenway Court: It has "no plot, no climax, no denouement, no beginning, no middle, and no end." And that, Morris Dickstein concludes in the case of "Waiting for Godot," is to take "modernism just as far as it could go."

To overlook this achievement of Gardner's is fatal and it is the reason not everyone gets it at Fenway Court. Just as those puzzled by the artistic mix will usually miss the "edgy modernism" I've already touched on, so those who worry about the "rigidity" of a "dead" museum, where nothing (according to Gardner's will) may ever be moved, will often also miss the fundamental fact that it is precisely the modernist "discontinuity" of the Gardner's galleries that challenges the thoughtful visitor to risk a highly personal *reintegration* of all the art's meaning. And that very modern experience, the purpose of the mix so brilliantly staged by Isabella Gardner, has always been–years before the term was ever heard of–supremely *interactive.* That is why the Gardner museum is like no other.

Gardner, by the way, did take in the controversial Armory Show of 1913, with its works by Gauguin, Matisse, Picasso, Kandinsky, and Brancusi, but as usual her dislike of writing–no letters at all, even to Berenson, survive from that year–impedes any conclusive knowledge of her response. We know of her attendance only through Piatt Andrew's diary, itself a highly laconic affair (all he noted on March 12 was, "visited the international cubist and futurist exhibition with Y [Isabella]. Went to opera. . . . "), but the fact that she and Andrew made a special visit to New York to see the show ahead of its Boston appearance does indicate Gardner's characteristic enthusiasm for new ideas.[42] Certainly she did not act on her chance to buy a Picasso! On the other hand, of the etchings by Matisse she owned, two date from the year after the Armory Show.

When all is said and done, however, the most telling image of Gardner as very much a woman of her time is disclosed by a note to her from John Sargent in London: "I feel very homesick for Boston," he wrote, "and at loose ends. . . . I wish we were dining tonight at the Copley Plaza and going to see Charlie Chaplin." What an evening: Isabella Stewart Gardner, John Singer Sargent–and Charlie Chaplin.[43]

◆

"I should like to live forever, if I were well."[44] So wrote Isabella Gardner in 1908, roused by the eighty-ninth birthday of Julia Ward Howe (by now America's Queen Victoria). Herself sixty-eight that year, on the cusp of late middle age and early old age, Gardner doubtless saw in Howe's vigorous last years yet another inspiration from her old friend and mentor of nearly fifty years by 1908. Howe's birthday, like the British Queen's, approached (in Howe's jubilee years especially) the status of national holidays; of one such celebration Howe's biographer reported that whether in town or country, east or west, "one and all wanted Mrs. Howe, suffragists, women

Julia Ward Howe. *Isabella Stewart Gardner Museum, Boston*

ministers, Unitarians [or] uplifters of every description."[45] Amen.

This was *not* the kind of company Isabella Gardner kept; nor, proba-bly, would such bluestocking do-gooders have easily welcomed her. And they would have been somewhat taken aback, I suspect, to learn that at the luncheon held on the actual birthday by the Howes, one of seven friends invited (along with such hoary heavyweights as Edward Everett Hale) was that apparently frivolous and scandalous Isabella Gardner. Surprised, too, they would have been at the intelligence that Howe and Gardner were, in fact, the leading spirits—along with the artists Sarah Choate Sears and Martha Sills, the novelists Margaret Deland and Sarah Orne Jewett, and Mrs. Barrett Wendell and Mrs. J. Templeton Coolidge—of a women's luncheon club called only "It," the meaning of the name of which would doubtless have not only surprised but shocked them, unaware as many may have been of the coded discourse of the day. Notes Gardner archivist Susan Sinclair:

> In *Unlocking the English Language*, Robert Burchfield records that the use of "it"—which stands for sexual intercourse—was long part of "the secret language of the Victorian period." In 1915, the romantic novelist Elinor Glyn was credited with coining the term "it" to describe sex appeal. Dorothy Parker, writing facetiously in the *New Yorker* in 1927, bemoaned not having read Mrs. Glyn: "I did not know that things like *it* were going on. I have misspent my days, when I think of all those hours I flung away reading Henry James and Santayana." The members of Gardner's club may not have been as sexually emancipated as Eleanor and Dorothy, but they were more than several steps ahead of them in appropriating "the word."[46]

If Howe's and Gardner's closeness discloses Howe was not the stereo-typical grandmother many thought (nor, for that matter, was Queen Victoria!), it also underlines a fact noted before here when Gardner's feminist altar screen at the Church of the Advent was our focus: Julia Ward Howe was magisterial in forever "ridiculing the pretentious man-sions, ostentatious parties, and cultural poverty of the nouveau riche"[47] and given that Gardner *was* a scion of new money, Howe would hardly have sustained so long and intimate a friendship with Isabella Gardner had Howe thought of her as the flamboyant hostess in the Newport-type "palace" in the Fenway Gardner is so often advertised as today. The bond between Howe and Gardner discloses the fact that though Gardner was neither a suffragist nor a bluestocking, both women were partners in the women's movement. In fact, the Gardner-Howe relationship probably centered on women's issues in the most fundamental ways.

All her life especially welcoming and caring of brides newly arrived in Boston from her native New York because Gardner was uniquely alert to the ramifications of such a transfer, she shared with Howe a bond that we too easily forget a century and more later: each of them in her own generation had made this fateful journey and each had paid a much dearer price for doing so than either could have contemplated. In Howe's case her grim Bostonian husband turned out to be implacably opposed to his wife's expression of her literary and political gifts, and as her public life was the more honored her private life was made in consequence the more miserable. Isabella Gardner—and perhaps Julia Ward Howe too!—must have learned more than one lesson, and, perhaps, applied it so as to shape somewhat the very different sort of marriage the Gardners had forged, where Jack had always been supportive of Belle's expression of her gifts in her increasingly more public life as patron of the arts, collec-tor and tastemaker. Beacon Street neighbors for many decades, Julia and Belle had surely much to talk of on both sides, if, that is, one can judge from Howe's "outpouring of poems and plays, with their recurring motifs [of] violent love, betrayal [and] suicide [that if they] puzzled Bostonians"[48] then do not at all puzzle us now, not in the post-post-Freudian era. (Henry Adams's wife Clover's tragic suicide comes again to mind. As Eugenia Kaledin points out it was "an angry reminder that society failed to value adequately brilliant women.... There was nothing left for [Clover] to do when [Henry Adams] sat down to write."[49] It was a situa-tion Howe very nearly found herself in too. But not, happily, Gardner.)

There was also a more public dimension to the way women's issues linked Howe and Gardner, for as William L. Vance has observed, once arrived in Boston, Howe's "immediate model was Margaret Fuller":[50] hence Howe's domain, the mid—nineteenth-century world of the Radical Club and such, out of which came her considerable biography of Fuller of 1883. In it, writing of what Joan von Mehren has characterized as Fuller's fierce call for women "to raise themselves out of their condition of dependence to one of self-reliance,"[51] Howe completely associated her-self with Fuller's famous book of 1845, *Women in the Nineteenth Century*, "the subversive message of [which] coupled with [Fuller's] unconventional personality" sparked bitter attacks, in von Mehren's words, and was not without controversy for Howe even as late as in 1883. Howe, wrote von Mehren, was "a Fuller champion."[52] So too it followed that Howe should be as much a champion of Isabella Gardner, as unconventional and subversive in her era as several comparisons here have underlined, as Fuller had been two generations earlier.

Gardner, a very different sort of character from Howe, did not take Fuller or Howe as her model in that sort of immediate way. Rather, such was Gardner's wide-ranging historical imagination one must look much further afield; indeed, we have considered already a few of those models in the saints she chose to figure in the Advent altar screen, and the rest are very evident in those women (though it would be a mistake to entirely overlook the men) whom Gardner chose to represent in her collection, especially those who figure in it only for themselves—in a manuscript or letter, for instance, where the matter is not complicated by some other mediator's artistry.

As there are historical Isabellas in the high altar screen of the Advent, so also Gardner bought several paintings for her collection as depictions of historical Isabellas. But amid many men—including Bismarck, for example!—a number of women in Gardner's collection of manuscripts, books, and letters may well be singled out. Interestingly, the dominant figures are either artistic—George Sand, Elizabeth Barrett Browning, Christina Rossetti, George Eliot—or political, including the Hapsburg Empress Maria Theresa, Queen Christina of Sweden, Mary, Queen of Scots, and Catherine de Médicis. In every case they were considerable achievers, as were those other historical figures in Gardner's collection of portrait photographs of contemporaries actually known by Gardner, such as Howe, Bernhardt, and Annie Fields.

That aspect, that all are remembered today chiefly for political or artistic or literary achievement, and not for their progeny, is at once rather striking when one considers the hardly arguable analysis of Anne Higonnet that "the most pervasive and persuasive factor specific to the arts [has always been] the exclusively masculine concept of genius." Higonnet points out that "the assumptions underlying genius are most clearly exposed in . . . Honore de Balzac's 1837 *Le Chef d'Oeuvre Inconnu*, Nathaniel Hawthorne's 1860 *The Marble Faun*, or Kate Chopin's 1899 *The Awakening*," in each of which, "against the conflicted values of activity, imagination, production and masculine sexuality are pitted the similarly indivisible values of passivity, imitation, reproduction, and feminine sexuality. Men create original works of art; women recreate themselves in their children."[53]

But not Gardner's models nor, of course, Gardner herself; though Higonnet goes on to suggest that in Gardner's era the way "women found diverse and multiple detours around the artistic domains forbidden to them" was noteworthy: it involved, she writes, a strategy whereby "female artists incorporated high art by men into projects with domestic origins," citing by way of example Edith Wharton's early book with Ogden Codman on interior decorating, Gertrude Jekyll's gardens for Sir Edwin Lutyens, and Gardner's creation of Fenway Court, which Higonnet characterized as "model[ing] a public institution on a private home."[54] This is only very loosely true; Fenway Court is *not* a house museum any more than the great mansions of Newport are cottages. Nonetheless, if one means by domestic the often quite grand scale of the apartments of Venetian palazzi, and by institutional the palatial enfilades of, say, the Louvre, Fenway Court is certainly more domestic than institutional in feeling. Moreover, Kathleen McCarthy makes the point that however domestic (i.e., feminine) its roots, "rather than being a purely 'feminine' creation, Fenway Court anticipated the institutional designs of some of the nation's wealthiest and most ambitious twentieth-century *male* connoisseurs [my emphasis]."[55]

In doing all this Isabella Gardner had indeed "skillfully transgressed the prerogatives of men,"[56] true, also, of course, of all Gardner's models. Some–George Sand, for instance–famously dressed as a man. As in fact did Gardner's contemporary, Rosa Bonheur, one of the women artists Gardner collected in an age when changing gender roles made an artistic career more likely for women. Other women artists represented in Gardner's collection include the sculptors Anna Coleman Ladd and Anna Hyatt Huntington, the painter Francesca Alexander, as well as people already touched on here, including Sarah Choate Sears and Sarah Whitman, from the last of whom Gardner commissioned the splendid ornamental marble escutcheon on Fenway Court's facade which announces "The Isabella Stewart Gardner Museum in the Fenway–MDCCCC." That this is the work of a woman is surely no more an accident than the predominance of women saints in the Advent reredos.

It was in music, however, that Gardner was most conspicuously a patron of women, most importantly, perhaps, in the case of the legendary Australian soprano Nellie Melba, of whom Gardner early became a mentor. It was William Whitney, the New York collector, who asked Isabella Gardner to take Melba under her wing, writing to Gardner of his hope that Melba's success in New York would be repeated in Boston: "she has been told the same thing by everyone–'Mrs. Gardner'–'Mrs. Gardner'–'Mrs. Gardner.' She is the one who takes talents by the hand and marshals them to the front–so they all say. Well," continued Whit- ney, ". . . George Haven and I have made a point of helping Melba demon- strate herself here, and we want you to be kind to her there–she is to be at The Vendôme after Wednesday."[57]

Lest such patronage seem too much only like lion-hunting (to which Isabella Gardner was hardly averse, but it is only a small truth, best lost in the larger one), it is equally important to note her less conspicuous efforts on behalf of women artists. Gardner played a leading role in launching the Manuscript Club, a group dedicated to offering a sympathetic hearing not only to contemporary local composers–a rare enough breed then (one was E. A. MacDowell)–but as well to *female* local composers, an astonishingly avant garde idea. The first concert of the club, in fact, was in Gardner's Music Room, and led off with a work by Clara Kathleen Rogers, who typically for the day had been forced to study piano and singing at the Leipzig Conservatory because composition as a field of study was then closed to females. Furthermore, of the five composers represented at

that first concert, *two* were women; the other being a student of MacDowell's and George Chadwick, Margaret Ruthaven Lang, who five years later was to be the first woman composer in the United States to have work of hers performed by a major symphony orchestra, Boston's.[58]

A major force and influ- ence both in the women's movement and in modern American dance, Ruth St.

Dame Nellie Melba. *Isabella Stewart Gardner Museum, Boston*

Denis also appeared under Gardner's patronage at Fenway Court, where she danced her first work, "Radha," inspired by Hindu dance movements. Yet another manifestation of Gardner's interest in native and folk music of all kinds, it was the sort of *succès de scandal* Gardner delighted in, provoking such newspaper reports as: "'Cold Roast' Boston sat up and took notice . . . yesterday in Fenway court and rubbed its eyes at the spectacle of a barelegged maiden who put the Persian dancers on the Midway to shame. . . . they gasped."[59]

Not content, Gardner aided women musicians in terms of performance opportunities as well by serving for twelve years as sponsor of another and also rather advanced club–the Orchestral Club of Boston.[60] Open to women as well as to men, its orchestra included an unusually large number of women (seventeen of the first violins alone, for instance), one of whom, the saxophonist Elise Coolidge Hill, commissioned a composition from no less than Debussy himself.

Music and literature often kept good company at the Palazzo Gardner, and Gardner in feminist mode was no less likely to explore one as another. Thus Georgette Le Blanc, the wife of Maurice Maeterlinck, once appeared at Fenway Court, creating almost as much stir as Ruth St. Denis with much less effort. She was described as:

> clad in long, trailing robes of mole-colored satin with cascades of lace at her throat and veils floating from either shoulder, her luxurious golden hair kept under restraint in an elaborate headdress. Tapestries framed the small stage on which she sat in a high-backed chair beside an ancient table on which rested a curious ewer. She curved herself into a corner of the chair and declaimed pensively. Then she came upright in it and declaimed intently. She leaned over it and declaimed confidentially. She stood high above it and with upraised arm declaimed passionately. Occasionally she strode about, as one under nervous stress, but still declaiming.[61]

More intimate occasions, such as Gardner's luncheon for Paul Bourget, are also of interest in this connection as showing that at Gardner's table women literary figures like Annie Fields and Sarah Orne Jewett and Edith Wharton noticeably met the French novelist on an equal footing with such male lions of the era as Alexander Agassiz and Thomas Bailey Aldrich.

Missing on this occasion but often prominent in Gardner's circle were

Maude Howe Elliott. *Private Collection*

two poet friends, Louise Imogene Guiney and Amy Lowell. Of Guiney something has already been said. Of Lowell, a much more "modern" poet, the leading light of the notorious "Imagist" movement and more or less openly lesbian, we know comparatively little of her relationship with Gardner. Rather as in the case of Father Hall, the little we do know is, however, suggestive. That it was not just a social but an artistic and literary relationship seems clear from the poet's writing at one point to Gardner that she found it "very agreeable to read [her] 'New Poetry' to so sympathetic a listener,"[62] and such comments of Gardner's as her warm salute of 1916 to Lowell: "Thank you. You have opened doors for me I thought were blank walls."[63] That both practical women used each other is also clear. When Lowell declared to a confidant that Gardner would make "an excellent advertising agent . . . nothing could be better,"[64] it sounds a bit crass. But Lowell promoted poetry of a certain kind, Gardner art of a certain kind. That they stimulated each other artistically was a matter of course.

A similarly warm relationship was Gardner's with Lady Gregory, the Irish dramatist. Gardner's Irish (and even republican though not anti-British) sympathies, touched on before here, naturally attracted her to the appearance in Boston in 1911 of Dublin's Abbey Theater. The centerpiece of the Irish renaissance, as it is so often called, a literary movement of which Gregory and poet William Butler Yeats were the leading lights, along with George Bernard Shaw and John Millington Synge, the Abbey production of Synge's *Playboy of the Western World* was so widely misunderstood as anti-Irish that Boston literally braced itself for a reprise of the near riot that marked the play's production virtually everywhere, from Dublin to New York to Philadelphia, where the cast was actually arrested for attempting to put on an "immoral" play![65]

Bostonians were not in the event disappointed. Witness Doris Kearns Goodwin's story in *The Fitzgeralds and the Kennedys* of how troubled at the opening was the young Rose Fitzgerald, whose father was then mayor of Boston. "Blushing and squirming" in her seat, offended by aspects of the highly realistic play but far more embarrassed by the audience's tumultuous response, and "not knowing how to respond, Rose turned her eyes [to] where Isabella Stewart Gardner was seated. . . . Gardner [being regarded] as an arbiter of taste." Continued Goodwin: "As the tension and tumult mounted, the people sitting with Mrs. Gardner were overheard discussing the advisability of retiring. . . . But Mrs. Gardner insisted on remaining. . . . and to every boo and hiss that floated down from the balcony she responded with a clapping of her hands in praise. . . . And when the curtain closed she led her friends," Goodwin reports, "in a standing ovation, making it absolutely clear that she, for one, believed it was a 'splendid play.' 'It was a great success'; she announced in the lobby, her face wreathed in smiles. 'I enjoyed every minute of it.'"[66]

Years later, wrote Goodwin, Rose Kennedy (as she became) "confessed that in her mind she knew Mrs. Gardner was right" that night. What the mayor's daughter didn't know was that Gardner was not content to lead an ovation. Recalled Lady Gregory later, "that evening at the Plymouth Theater [Mrs. Gardner] came round to my box, shoulders erect, treading lightly, disclaiming the assaults of age (I think she must have been then seventy or over [seventy-one actually]). She was full of praise . . . and I felt at once it was not an acquaintance I had made but a friend."[67] A figure of speech, perhaps, but Gregory was right, and as it turned out Gardner was able to mentor even this distinguished woman through a very difficult period, assisting the playwright to drum up sponsorship for the Abbey's Washington run, for example, and, most important, helping the playwright herself over rather a hurdle, as Susan Sinclair writes:

> Lady Gregory, who had a fear of public speaking, discovered to her dismay that on tour in America she would be called upon to make frequent "remarks." This she was loath to do. . . . she preferred the prospect of a formal speech. . . . if it were incumbent upon her to speak she wanted to say something substantial. Her new friend, Isabella Gardner, provided the opportunity "and offered [for her] first trial the spacious Music Room at Fenway Court.". . . The lecture on 19 October 1911 was . . . a success. Lady Gregory wrote Mrs. Gardner the same evening: "You have been so good to me—today means more than you can know—a new faculty discovered."[68]

Though the playwright admitted it was "strange to discover a gift so late in life,"[69] Gardner had opened up for her something of a new world. Both plain of face but brilliant of mind, forceful and high-spirited, they had much in common and formed a lasting friendship, evidence very much like that of Maude Howe Elliott and Elsie De Wolfe and Nellie Melba that though Gardner did, indeed, as the old saying has it, love a man, she could and did both love and mentor women. In fact Gardner was very much the "New Woman," as Piatt Andrew saw when in 1910 he implied that she was "utterly emancipated,"[70] a phrase that may well explain why she didn't seem to care, for example, that she couldn't vote. I'd like to suggest this was characteristic of a mind set Gardner shared with, of all people, Emily Dickinson—of whom Gardner's friend and ally Amy Lowell, after all, at about this time, was the first real serious champion.

It is a comparison odd only at first glance. Consider Karl Keller's observation. Dickinson, he writes, "had more to offer than the New England bluestockings thought a woman should offer: wildness."[71] True also of Gardner, that is why Julia Ward Howe had been in such a panic about the likely effect of Gardner's presence at Howe's projected philosophy lecture in Concord. Consider too, again in Keller's words, Dickinson's relationship to "the New England tradition of dissent"; her "resistance to Puritan tradition"; and that while one can hardly imagine Dickinson as a schoolteacher or a nurse, it is "not hard on the other hand to imagine her, though, as a performer of some sort, or as a hooker."[72] And so Gardner. The volitional aspect of prostitution being suspect, courtesan might be a better word than hooker (all the more so in Gardner's case, considering her admiration of Madame de Pompadour!). But when Keller writes of how nineteenth-century progressive reform definitions of womanhood "did not allow for the anomalous and flamboyant and could not have excited Emily Dickinson very much,"[73] Gardner again comes very much to mind.

Of all the models for a liberated woman proposed by American writers during Emily Dickinson's lifetime, none of them, not even those by her circle of literary friends, was written as if the authors knew anyone quite like *her*. . . . she was beyond them all. . . . herself, that is, magic, ... haughty, everything. Instead of contemporary America, she had, she said, a "Republic of Delight. . . ."[74]

For Gardner it was no different, if less literary and more visual. Gardner's work in art, like Dickinson's in words, "was meant to express," in

Keller's words, "the beauty of power-through-flamboyance. That too was a form of liberation—one that has not been recognized as a reformer's method, a means of change and challenge, an alternative model for feminist that was not well appreciated and was usually condemned outright in the liberationist literature of her time."[75] (Julia Ward Howe, significantly, was unusual in not condemning it.) And did Gardner not appreciate this form of liberation? In Boston she all but invented it! The conventional feminism Howe championed involved causes (like women's suffrage) that were—in some of Keller's most beautiful words about Dickinson (and to my mind about Gardner)—"too small for [her] cosmology . . . and at the same time too large for the scale of her anxieties and fantasies."[76] It is a somewhat similar point to that made by Simone de Beauvoir that confronted by "clubs, magazines, delegations, movements" and such "the most intelligent women . . . like Mme. de Stael and George Sand, remained apart from these movements while fighting their own battles for freedom."[77] So with Emily Dickinson and Isabella Gardner.

Fascinating in their similarities, Gardner and Dickinson are hardly less interesting in their differences. Dickinson was decidedly not, for instance, the "New Woman." Gardner was. Writes Kathleen McCarthy:

> An early harbinger of the "new woman," [Gardner] was both admired and abhorred for her unwillingness to bend to more traditional female roles. . . . She stormed the male citadel of culture and taste *in her own way, on her own terms* [my emphasis], setting the stage for a string of individualistic women. . . . Gardner frightened and fascinated. . . . Her career was a premonition, a signal of . . . female individualism that began to accelerate with the opening decades of the twentieth-century. . . . Gardner would use her museum as a novitiate for the "new women."[78]

Gardner, like Dickinson, was more not less of a feminist, just as she was in a sense more not less of a modernist. Like Dickinson, like Howe, Isabella Gardner was a rebel more than a hedonist, an altruist more than an egoist. But Gardner's genius was not words, and her motto—it is my pleasure—has been widely misunderstood. Dickinson, a master of words, brooked no misunderstanding: "I took my Power in my Hand–/And went against the World–/'Twas not so much as David–had–/but I was twice as bold-."[79]

14

End Game

A JAMESIAN STORY, only timely to tell now: "The Beldonald Holbein," which Henry James wrote in 1901, seems to at least one scholar "to turn on the character, personality, and art possessions of Isabella Stewart Gardner." As the story unfolds, Lady Beldonald, an American who seeks to conquer London, provides herself, not for the nicest reasons, with "a female foil to set her own Titianesque beauty in relief." However, in Adeline Tinter's reading of the story, "the little, old, plain elderly relative, Mrs. Brash, is the more aesthetically compelling of the two women"; in fact she comes to personify a Holbein portrait, which Tinter identifies as Holbein's portrait of Lady Butts in the Dutch Room at Fenway Court. Writes Tinter:

> The painter who recognizes the Holbein in Mrs. Brash is a Frenchman, Paul Outreau, ... a sort of in-joke reference to [Paul] Bourget. *Outreau* means the same as *outre-mer*, that is, across the sea ... *Outre-mer* was the account Bourget published in 1895 of the trip to the United States in which he met Mrs. Gardner. Upon the discovery of the living Holbein, there is "the light of admiration in Outreau's expressive face". . . . He exclaims "How beautiful this old lady is. . . ." Outreau wants to take her to Paris, for there, the narrator says, "they do see . . . more than we; and they live extraordinarily. . . . She was, in short, just what we had made of her, a Holbein

for a great museum. . . . this living Holbein. . . . was indeed a Holbein
for a great museum, the Gardner Museum."[1]

It was in *Outre-mer*, of course, that Bourget had discussed at such
length Sargent's famous portrait of Gardner, and rather uncannily Henry
James' story points toward the other great portrait that John Sargent
painted of Isabella Gardner near the close of her life, in 1922. A hardly
less masterful image of her at eighty-two than his earlier portrait of her at
forty-eight, it depicts, really, Gardner's end game, and for that reason is of
the two Sargent portraits, in my view, "more aesthetically compelling."
End game is a harsh term, of course, but one a sportswoman and a
Christian, and Gardner was both, would have appreciated.

In a very real sense Gardner's end game began in the first place with
her move into Fenway Court, when she was only in her early sixties, for
the whole idea of establishing her legacy was fraught with intimations of
mortality, and, moreover, readying her museum for the future had a
slowly cumulative sort of limiting effect that forced Gardner far more
than her health did to slow down: "it was a strange spot, that palace of
hers in Boston," an out-of-town paper ruminated, "where her own [top
floor] living rooms were so bare and all the rest so magnificent. . . . Under
an imported ceiling illustrating the more unprintable scenes from Ovid,
she sat [until] well past eighty, . . . And there she defied, as from behind
impregnable breast-works, time, care, dullness and all prosaic things."[2]

It was, at first, the contrast, so to speak, that carried the day. "In two
days, I have lost an inch around the waist, between a plain spare diet and
freezing cold. She [Gardner] is a person who cares absolutely nothing for
physical comfort, so long as she has fresh air. She eats dried toast . . .
[and] flourishes upon it."[3] So wrote Mary Berenson to her family as early
as in 1903, adding a week later that Gardner "saves up all her old candle
ends."[4] Elsie De Wolfe's testimony is similar:

> The first time she asked me to stay with her I was invited only for
> the night. At dinner she noticed that I did not eat meat, that in fact I
> ate very sparingly. The next day, commenting on this, she said, as I
> was such an inexpensive guest, she would like to have me stay with
> her for as long as I was to be in Boston. Once when she was our
> house guest, after she had left we found one of her silk stockings.
> There was not a single space in the entire foot that had not been

darned. My Scotch soul rejoiced at her thrift, particularly because in
so many other ways she put her money to such splendid use.[5]

Increasingly, even her large-scale entertaining was affected. Clayton
Johns swore she entertained the Thursday Evening Club, a venerable
Boston dining club, with no fires in the dead of winter: "She had," he
reported, "put the last touch to her decor with a frieze of eminent
Bostonians"![6] That was to be not only witty but insightful: never interested in food or drink, once Fenway Court was done, Gardner was
indeed more and more concerned with saving for its endowment, the
background, no doubt, of a reportedly less than friendly exchange
between her and Edith Wharton[7] (who distinctly *was* interested in the
pleasures of the table) at Fenway Court's opening when the repast
seemed to Wharton not up to snuff! If it is hard to imagine an intelligent
woman like Wharton having that sort of response to the Gardner
Museum, it is not difficult at all to imagine the contempt such a response
on such a night would have drawn from Isabella Gardner. Gardner
always begrudged money spent on food or wine! And now she grew
more and more miserly. So much so that when Augustus Saint-Gaudens
asked for her help in behalf of the American Academy in Rome, she fired
back: "I have done, at great sacrifice and cost and single handed for
America what no school in Rome could ever do."[8] And now she needed
to endow it. Who, pray, could argue with that?

The First World War when it came—just after her final creative surge
in designing the new galleries at Fenway Court—also naturally depressed
her. Not the least of Gardner's counter-cultural tendencies was that for
all her love of the fiercest of sports, she really seems to have been something of a pacifist. Of the Civil War it is impossible to discover her feelings; in those days and on that subject she had guarded her tongue. Of
the Spanish-American War, however, she was quite direct: "I loathe this
war. . . . I think it is such an unrighteous and dishonorable war. . . . I hope
the Jingoes will be sent and made to do the fighting," she wrote
Berenson, "and I hope they may be killed the first day. Teddy Roosevelt
is going—Praise the Lord!" It was, she thought, "a war of a bully."[9] In fact
she hardly met a war she thought worth it, and was hardly less clear
about the First World War: she incurred widespread displeasure in
sticking up for the German-born (and admittedly pro-German) conductor
of the Boston Symphony, Dr. Muck, who when he was arrested,

absurdly, as a spy, Isabella Gardner, to public outrage, visited in jail.[10] (Wrote Muck to Gardner from imprisonment: "of all our many friends in Boston at least one has stood by my poor, haunted wife and . . . it was you who so openly demonstrated your feeling toward us."[11]

Gardner vented her spleen to Berenson, who was strongly pro-Allies: "I am pro only one thing and that is peace," she wrote him. "I am running two ambulances [in the American Field Service in France, founded and led by Piatt Andrew] and have given one, besides running it (financially I mean) but I will not give money for ammunition and I will not make money (as people are doing to the bursting point) by owning stock in war weapons." Bluntly, she told him: "I call it blood money—now you know my creed."[12] It was, I suspect, with a kind of desperate pleasure the night the First World War ended she dined with Martin Mower and then got into her car and essayed an "exciting tour through the packed downtown streets" with him to see the excited crowds celebrate the Armistice.[13]

It was the sort of thing she'd always done, like going to Symphony wearing a hatband inscribed "Oh You Red Sox,"[14] or, refusing to drag out her faithful old chauffeur to bring the car around to the opera house or to Jordan Hall after a concert to drive her the few blocks home. Instead she'd stride off all alone up the street! In her seventies, in evening dress and wearing a fortune in jewels, she'd either walk the few blocks back to Fenway Court, or take the Huntington Avenue streetcar. The one concession the by now legendary Mrs. John L. Gardner would make to rank and safety was to let the doorman at the opera house ring the night watchman at Fenway Court. Either he or Bolgi would be on the lookout for her, perhaps walking down to the street in front of Fenway Court with a small lantern to guide her home.[15]

Alas, the first year of peace was the last year Gardner spent whole and well. As if with foreknowledge she used her time well, beginning to surrender her long habits of dominance. In March she wrote finally to Joe Smith, now greatly enmeshed in the Boston Museum's Egyptian collections, to say that though it was a wish she had "long cherished," she had concluded she could not very well expect him to be her museum's first director: "I cannot clip your wings and tie you down. It was cruel to you to think of it. You are made for other things," she wrote, "you always have my deep affection."[16] Gratefully, he replied: "I was proud and always shall be that I was your choice, but realization of your plans meant my coming for service when the light and spirit of the wonderful Treasure

House had gone out of it. It was that fact ... that made me so seldom speak to you of the future."[17] Morris Carter was the perfect choice to take his place.[18]

Morris Carter. *Isabella Stewart Gardner Museum, Boston*

"It is quiet, cool and comfortable here," Gardner wrote about this time, having sold Green Hill in the family, and settled into Fenway Court now the year through for as many as remained to her. "My upstairs little corner bedroom has the south and the west wind galing through.... I sleep with my hair blowing! And my cloister life below is very pleasant.... Here, the only thing that will cause my death are the servants," she wrote: "I have four women, one a wretched cook, two of them old cripples I keep on to help them (they do little or nothing), and the fourth woman is everything." One light there was, though: "my life is saved daily by Bolgi"; her major-domo never disappointed; he was, she wrote, always "a comfort. And my doctor allows me to have coffee with hot milk every afternoon, and that is a spree!"[19] Her life was contracting: "2 rooms. A bedroom for me and the little room on the first floor [the present Macknight Room], which will be my living room. I shall eat in the cloister. I think it will all be cool enough, and it will make a money difference."[20] And all the while upstairs there was the first of all the great collections of Old Masters in America to buy her every comfort had she but raised her hand. Riches indeed.[21]

Carter installed, her art was secure; only her other muse remained to claim her attention, for art and religion would keep close company with her to the end. Thus at a time when she was scrimping everywhere for her museum's endowment she gave to the Cowley Fathers, in April of 1919, so princely a gift, with which to buy the remaining land necessary and then to start building their monastery along the banks of the Charles in Cambridge, that the then superior, Spence Burton, wrote to acknowledge the society's debt without reserve:

How can we ever thank you adequately for your great goodness to us.... Land on the River in Harvard neighborhood is scarce and high priced. With the $25,000 my parents gave me we were able to buy half the lot and to secure an option on the rest. Your money we hope will buy it. [In fact it also enabled them to build the first part of the monastery complex.] Our hearts are so full of gratitude.... We pray that many generations of devoted Religious [i.e., monks or nuns] will venerate your memory as a foundress of their monastery.[22]

It was a gift from Isabella Gardner that enabled the Cowley Fathers to begin the erection of their monastery on the Charles River near Harvard. *Isabella Stewart Gardner Museum, Boston*

Time Magazine would go further. In a story about the laying of the cornerstone (in 1936, many years after Gardner's death) of the center-piece of the monastery complex, the Conventual Church of St. Mary and St. John, *Time* devoted hardly eight lines to Mrs. Caspar Burton, in whose memory the church was given, and to her son, Spence, the then superior of the order, while the Society of St. John the Evangelist itself and architect Ralph Adams Cram were dispatched in nineteen more. Eighty lines, however, were devoted to Isabella Gardner, even though she had been dead more than a decade and her gift to begin the monastery had been made nearly a quarter of a century earlier. *Time* rea-soned, as most would, that a monk's inherited family money in the nature of things must go to his order, and that Gardner ought rightfully to be considered the founder of the monastery of the American congregation of Anglicanism's oldest monastic order for men.[23] It is a view the Cowley Fathers would take no exception to today.

Art and religion both satisfied, 1919 wound down uneventfully enough to Christmas, with its usual Mass and other festivities. But now her legendary good health began to give way. In 1912 when she was seventy-two Henry Adams could write that "of all our old set ... [Isabella Gardner] is by far the youngest and spryest" (even if he did add she'd become "a wrinkled old fairy"). Six years later Adams could still write he found Gardner "more magnificent than ever ... not in the least disturbed by twenty-four hours railroad journey."[24]

But even for Isabella Stewart Gardner the toll old age takes of us all began to be evident. Not very long after this time, after the end of the war, Arthur Johnson, a close friend of Gardner, described her rather sadly to Edward Weeks, then an editor of the *Harvard Advocate* of which Johnson was a trustee. Gardner, Johnson said, was living quite "alone, frail and aging, in a small room on the ground floor of the Court." Unlike Berenson, whose own interests led him too often to misunderstand Isabella Gardner's penury as womanish timidity, Johnson, whom Gardner had appointed one of the first trustees of the Gardner Museum, knew, as he told Weeks, she was living so simply because she was "conserving her income for the endowment of the collection." But Johnson still clearly felt Isabella Gardner, like so many old people (she was nearly eighty in 1918), was feeling neglected and depressed: "she has moments of despondency; the other night her housekeeper found her wandering in her nightgown on the second floor, dangerously close to the balcony," Johnson told Weeks worriedly. The servant, doubtless concerned that there was neither gas illumination nor electric light on the second floor of the museum and perhaps that night little moonlight either, had telephoned Johnson, he said, "in alarm [and he had] hurried to the court: 'Mrs. Gardner,' he said, 'you'll get pneumonia! Come to bed.'" The chatelaine of Fenway Court was doubtless glad of the attention, but left no doubt that she thought Johnson, as we would say today, distinctly uncool; nightgown, indeed! "I never in all my life caught a cold in a ball dress," she retorted, allowing herself nonetheless to be led back to her bedroom.[25]

Vintage Gardner, to be sure, but the incident (perhaps not the only one) must have been disturbing for those who cared at all for her and in a very real sense it may have been seen as not without its good side when late in 1919 she suffered a catastrophe the effect of which was on the one hand to distinctly restrain and perhaps protect Isabella Gardner, while on the other hand challenging her (as setbacks always did) to marshal her still formidable resources, in this case in aid of revitalizing life itself.

Curiously, that catastrophe also involved Arthur Johnson; for it was after what Carter called a very "merry evening" at Johnson's house (Sargent also had been a guest) that Gardner returned to Fenway Court only to suffer a serious stroke.[26] Never again would she regain the ability to walk; or, indeed, without difficulty, to write. She was seventy-nine, and now paralyzed on her right side, very differently placed indeed when in April of 1920 Spence Burton kindly wrote again to say Cowley had not forgotten that "tomorrow is your birthday and . . . the anniversary of your great gift to us. On that day we shall always have a Mass for you. . . . Tomorrow morning the Mass will be . . . at our Lady's altar before your Madonna."[27] Still today, every year on her birthday the Cowley Fathers say a Mass for her at Fenway Court.

In her last years Gardner grew even closer to these monks. Though she would always be drawn to the flamboyant liturgical and musical life of the Church of the Advent, as opposed to the more austere and monastic "plainchant" liturgy of the Society of St. John the Evangelist (increasingly less involved with the Advent over the years, their work more and more centered on their mission church of St. John's, Bowdoin Street), Isabella Gardner's liturgical and musical tastes were not to be confused with other aspects of her religious life. Though the Advent's clergy continued to preside at Fenway Court services throughout her lifetime, Gardner had good reason, it would seem, to be drawn to the more sophisticated ministry of the Cowley Fathers after the arrival as rector of the Advent in 1902 of William Harmon van Allen. An archconservative ascetic, scandalized by cocktails before dinner and even professional sports on Sunday, van Allen was inclined to be strong-minded and even testy in his admonitions, and he apparently attempted to rebuke Gardner for causing scandal in the 1900s, perhaps because she continued to receive Crawford. Whether the rebuke was a public or a private one or whether or not it included the refusal of absolution or communion, is not clear, but Gardner's godson, Kenneth Conant, told me that he thought thereafter Isabella Gardner ceased regularly to attend the Advent, and drew closer to St. John's, Bowdoin Street. (Indeed it was about this time that St. John's erected the high altar reredos with its altarpiece by Martin Mower, a work I have suggested elsewhere was, like the Advent's reredos of twenty years earlier, the gift of Isabella Gardner.) All of which is rather a fitting, and classically Freudian, finale to my theme here of the various tales of Gardner doing penance for her sins, washing the Advent's front steps and such being a case of Back Bay Boston projecting sins real and imagined onto her, for van Allen himself was eventually to become involved in a considerable scandal: accused of pedophilia, he responded by abruptly resigning the Advent's rectorship and leaving the country.

Interestingly, the Cowley Father Isabella Gardner became closest to after the stroke which paralyzed her in 1919, Father Frederick Powell, who brought her communion for the next five years every two weeks and was accordingly probably her last confessor, was also shadowed by ill repute; not only did Powell, one gathers, not suffer fools gladly but as the founder of an order of nuns (St. Anne's), he was in a position for a celibate only too likely to seem problematic to some. But if Powell was both a gifted and a complex man that may well have made him more effective a spiritual adviser to the "serpent of the Charles,"[28] as Berenson once called Isabella Gardner. Was Powell, adroit as he was, perhaps, at courtliness, flattering Isabella Gardner when he wrote to her: "You know—no, you do not know—how much I love you?" Certainly he seemed sincere as well as insightful when he told her: "You have kept what so many lose as they grow up—simplicity and vision. We get wise with so many little details called facts and we lose the great view." Perhaps, really, he was thinking of himself when he wrote Gardner once: "Most of us, as we grow up seem to walk into a fog that hides all or nearly all the real things and stuffs up our eyes and ears. It might be called the cotton-wool of age."[29] In whichever event Powell was always direct enough: "a friend writes to ask me," he told Gardner, "if life ever looked sad and wearisome to me. *Ever!*" It was thus that he sought always to strengthen Gardner, gallantly but truthfully. "Don't allow yourself," he warned her forthrightly, "to think that your soul is not prospering."[30]

Indeed, as always, Isabella Gardner, even paralyzed, was waxing more than she was waning, ever a survivor. What was it Nietzsche said? That which does not kill you will strengthen you. While this is not, of course, applicable for a Christian to the unquiet conscience we all have for our self-serving and dishonorable deeds, it is true enough for the onslaughts of the impersonal forces of fate the inbuilt logic of the cosmos too often randomly or not hurls at us; and while we know Gardner had a some-what Nietzschean view of some things (witness her speech to Coudenhove about sacrifice and merit) there is no evidence at all on the other hand that she was the sort to rail at a "God of evil" for smiting her for any reason including (as more than one Back Bay matron undoubt-edly opined) her sins. Unable to alter the hand dealt her in old age, she knew what she could affect: how she played it. And what Isabella Gardner had left to give, she gave. "When you have to be in Boston," she wrote Powell when he had been feeling under the weather, "you can sit in my garden with Max the Squirrel! Please do. My love and rejoicing that you are better. Affectionately, Isabella." She even named her garden the "monk's garden."[31]

Powell responded in kind: "your kindness is pure, entire, pearl-like for roundness and completeness," he wrote her; "there is no rough side to it as when a crystal is broken off and given."[32] If it was true, and Crawford

The Monk's Garden at Fenway Court. *Isabella Stewart Gardner Museum, Boston*

once–and Loeffler–might have quarreled with Powell, it was very much what Okakura would have hoped for in his leading of Isabella Gardner to the serenity she does, indeed, in her last years, seem to have attained.

Serene she was; calm, never! For an invalid in her eighties she lived in the "roaring twenties" rather a full life. She loved automobiles. In the mornings she demanded to be driven about by her faithful chauffeur, and not just through parks; she also loved the bustle of the downtown streets. In the afternoons she would read (mostly detective stories) in the monk's garden at Fenway Court, her decrepit dog Roly, by her side. Inside the museum she was carried about in a gondola chair; she even made a few last purchases; most notably a Madonna and Child by Giovanni Bellini, and that Art Deco prize, Manship's *Diana*, both bought in 1921. She also bought a number of watercolors by Sargent, who professed "shock at your extravagance" and protested "the sums that you lavish on water colors that have 'no moral lesson in their chiaroscuro'. . . . How did you elude the vigilance of your nurses?"[33] More practically, he relayed to her that the manager of the Hotel Lenox yearned to send her over a consoling risotto but "hadn't dared." Sargent asked if he might. He did.[34]

Sargent remained faithful. Another was Proctor: her true knight and loyal to the end, he often came to play for her. So too did Loeffler, who would organize groups of two or three to come and perform, for example, Bach's concerto for two violins and piano: "I will be in the music room on Thursday a little before half-past eleven," she wrote Loeffler eagerly (by Carter's hand) "and need not say how anxious to hear you and Gebhard. As it will be my first ball," she wrote, "I do not suppose [this was just after a bad period] I shall be allowed to listen more than half or three quarters of an hour–probably half an hour is wiser. But what a joy for me!"[35] Her first ball! Isabella Gardner was irrepressible. "Was-a-bella," as Curtis rather cruelly called her, had still a life–and a tale to tell.[36]

She was, in fact, conducting her last "affair," if not with Father Powell, then with old Count Hans Coudenhove, as her dashing young cavalier of forty years previously had become, with whom she corresponded ardently. In 1922, eighty-two and all but physically helpless, she wrote the count:

> . . . I haven't a horse or anything now, but I am trying to keep up my courage. I'm quite an invalid, but cheerful to the last degree. I think my mind is all right and I live on it. I keep up a lot of thinking and am really very much alive. I live in one house, everything else having

been sold. This house is very nice, very comfortable, and rather jolly. It is on the outskirts of Boston, not in the country. I have filled it with pictures and works of art, really good things I think, and if there *are* any clever people I see them. I really lead an interesting life. I have music, and both young and old friends. The appropriately old are too old–they seem to have given up the world. Not so I, and I even shove some of the young ones rather close.[37]

Reports of any detail of callers on Isabella Gardner at Fenway Court are remarkably few after her stroke, but they confirm her assertions. One such, by the future editor of the *Atlantic Monthly*, Edward Weeks, is especially interesting because he recalled that

> Mrs. Gardner received us in the little room which had become her home, surrounded by her favorite watercolors by Sargent and Dodge Macknight. She reclined on a chaise longue, under an ermine robe. One arm in its lace sleeve gestured us to our chairs. Tea was served, and knowing of her affection for them, I spoke of Colonel A. Piatt Andrew and Harry Sleeper and of their leadership of the [American] Field Service [in France], but my mind was only half on what I was saying. To my right and close to where she lay stood a tall brass urn, filled to the brim with hand-written letters, elegant stationery of every tint, ripped in half. I could not help reading their salutations–"Dearest Belle"–and my editorial instinct was silently pleading, shouldn't some be saved, surely they had a story to tell? But I lacked the nerve. My one meeting with that gay withered spirit told me with what imperviousness she was discarding the past.[38]

There was, too, a last, touching visit from Berenson described by Alice De Lamar, who pulled no punches. Conducted by Bolgi into the courtyard, in the center of the patio Berenson and his friends saw

> a large table and several large Renaissance chairs. On the table, there seemed to be a clutter of tins of biscuits, cartons of grocer's prod-ucts, magazines, bottles and jars. As always, with the old and infirm, there were medicines and pills. In a sort of throne chair beside the table, wrapped in an ermine robe and chiffon scarves, was what appeared to be a mummy carved in ivory wearing a somewhat disor-

dered, yellowing, white wig piled high on the head. The face had as many wrinkles as an aging chimpanzee or a withered orange.... Mrs. Gardner was a sort of "Folle de Chaillot," and indeed a strange and frightening sight. Only the famous pearls she wore had not changed with the hand of time. Her dentures probably were giving trouble when she talked, but she managed to hold out a parchment bird's claw to greet B.B.[39]

Berenson, having introduced his friends, shortly produced a series of paintings–by Mantegna and Fra Angelico–he had brought to show Gardner. Her face, as Ernest Samuels tells the story, "lighted up," and as each of the paintings was shown her "she gratefully scanned them through her lorgnette." So deeply touched, Samuels wrote, that "tears stood in her eyes," the formidable old woman–"too paralyzed now to be able to show the way her treasures should be viewed–said, "Go upstairs. . . . see everything and take plenty of time."

It was this "mummy carved in ivory" that Sargent asked to paint in 1922. And nearly thirty-five years after his notable first portrait of Gardner at forty-seven his portrait of her at eighty-two is no less iconic but vastly more loving and penetrating. If eyes were ever windows to anything Isabella Gardner's here surely document the spirit's triumph in the face of the body's death. Never mind her wasting and crippled body; to meet the steady knowing of her regard is, for all its sphinx-like quality, a very modern experience. If James was right to call Sargent's first por-trait a Byzantine Madonna we may rightly call Sargent's second portrait a Jamesian Madonna. She was clearly dying. And whatever it meant, on her face, as Corina Smith observed, there was, indeed, "a marvelous expression of elation."[40]

Even now she could inspire, not only a painter of Sargent's stature–for all that he had long since sworn off portraiture–but a poet of the caliber of John Wheelwright, a poet of the next generation furthermore, who was not even in her circle, being a few years too young and also probably too militant a Marxist and too extreme a modernist to have felt comfort-able there. But Isabella Gardner still mattered in the 1920s even to a Marxist! Because of his parents' relationship with Gardner (the Gardners and the Wheelwrights were both Brahmin families with artistic inter-ests), Wheelwright had grown up very much aware of Isabella Gardner and had strong enough views about her that sometime (the exact date is unknown) between 1914 and 1930, between ages sixteen and thirty-two he wrote a poem about her by turns harsh, respectful, cruel, and yet insightful and very penetrating, even understanding.

He trotted out all the old stuff ("Sandow received her and her friends stark naked"); he was judgmental ("She bore false witness at the Custom House"); he maligned her ("She took as lovers Boston's leading citizens") and he cruelly caricatured her (at the opera)–"poking her magentaed hair and ostrich plumed/monkey face at them between box curtains." Nor did Wheelwright hesitate to find fault even with her genius: "An evil Boston woman loved the Virgin/with merely nearly mediaeval marvel," he wrote, brilliantly, adding: "When she grew old, she stuck together a junk shop. . . ." *That* was Fenway Court, the source, doubtless, for Lee Simonson's witticism of many years later that the Gardner Museum *was* a junk shop, a junk shop gone to heaven!

But Wheelwright also saw what Isabella Gardner had to contend with: "women whose power depended on each other/said she was not a 'lady' that no 'lady'/with any moral sense, could leave cards on her./But she kicked up rubied heels, and thanked the Lord"–of which last the poet, also Anglo-Catholic, clearly approved. Nor was Wheelwright much more impressed with the men in Gardner's life, though there was a little homo-sexual self-loathing typical of the post-Freudian mind-set (the poet was also gay) in the way Wheelwright couched what was still meant chiefly, I think, to be understanding of Gardner, the inevitable counterpiece, he wrote, of one event after another, "while Men crossed and uncrossed their legs all evening,/like bees who cluster round a honey cluster." Notice that though Wheelwright ridiculed as well how Gardner in her last years, husbanding her resources for her museum's endowment, "lived off canned baked beans and cold corn beef," the poet was after all an artist too and saw truly how Isabella Gardner was, indeed, "Fed by her interior court's interior life."[41] And so she was, until the day she died. It was enough.

On July 8 of 1924 she became very ill and though she was long in dying, the end came peacefully at just short of eleven o'clock in the evening on Thursday, July 17. The following Monday the Cowley Fathers celebrated the first Mass of requiem in the Spanish Chapel, outside of which stood her coffin, open, but her body covered with "a thin, dark purple silk pall, so that you saw the outline of her head and hands. When finally it was closed, violets (her first choice) being out of season, her coffin was cov-ered with a cross of white roses and white heather." So too, she commanded, in her directions, "the enclosed piece of Tartan ribbon to be tied on the cross somewhere *inconspicuously*. . . . I do not want to be looked at . . . I should like to have a small piece of white heather by my hands."[42]

It was a fine and sober Boston funeral, though at the Church of the Advent, of course, which marshaled all its pomp and splendor. The three hymns were the same sung at Jack Gardner's funeral: "Jesus Lives, Thy Terror Now No Longer Death, Appall Us," "Ten Thousand Times Ten Thousand," and "Abide with Me." But as William Endicott reported to Sargent it was all very solemn and simple; "nothing dramatic about it,"[43] he insisted; except, perhaps, that as her body was carried out of Fenway Court to its final rest, there between the court and the main entrance was Isabella Gardner's very Italian major-domo (it was not a position so far as is known replicated elsewhere in the New England capital!). Bolgi, doubtless vulgar enough to some, was a brave sight that would have won Gardner's heart: with his tall staff and cocked hat, resplendent in gold-embroidered livery worthy of the Medici, there he stood as she was borne out past him.

Like the founder of Fenway Court he was never one to hang back. And he was enough in love with her (so many had been) to tell her favorite niece, Olga Monks, after Isabella Stewart Gardner's death, that "he often thought he heard her calling him."[44]

Not only Bolgi, and not only then.

◆

Among the last of those Isabella Gardner mentored, on the cusp of seventy, was T. S. Eliot, some of whose work of those days, of course, she knew. It is unlikely she knew even the earliest work, however, of Eliot's much loved and esteemed friend, that extraordinary Anglican poet, novelist, and theological writer Charles Williams. I suspect, however, that Gardner shared the belief Williams articulated so forcefully in the next generation, that we can never bear our own burdens successfully; someone else must; and we in turn can only bear another's—it is life's secret, which the self-absorbed never see—an exchange, mirroring as it does the Golden Rule in a distinctly modern, psychological way, that may ground the most enduring and productive of human relationships. Surely this is the exchange that enabled so much in Isabella Gardner's life, empowering her to triumph over an ambiguous marriage, her son's death, a devastating and never fully resolved great love of her life, her nephew's tragic suicide, and all the suffering it disclosed to her not just of Joe Junior but of so many of her protégés during what was by all accounts a strenuous, anxious, and rather lonely life of considerable triumph nonetheless. Even Okakura died young. Isabella Gardner outlived them all in every sense.

I am reminded of Bruce Metzger's words about the Book of Revelation, the dramatic imagery of which appealed to Gardner. "The profound religious insight that lies behind [that book's] kaleidoscopic pictures ... is that ... men and women worship some absolute power," Metzger writes, and "in the last analysis, it is always a choice between the power that operates through inflicting suffering, that is, the power of the beast, and the power that operates through accepting suffering, namely the power of the Lamb."[45] Gardner's paradoxical personality may have seemed to veer from one to the other (never mind De Wolfe's comparison of her kindness and her sadism: were not her favorite pictures *The Rape of Europa* and *Christ Bearing the Cross*?). Finally, however, without at all neurotically seeking out suffering (far from it!), Isabella Gardner identified, not with the power of the beast, but with the power of the Lamb—which perhaps only Crawford and Okakura and Powell saw her at close enough range to know.

What was it John Jay Chapman said about Gardner's "native buoyancy"? And the way it "seemed to make her float on the waves of moral controversy if they rose; for her soul's interest lay in other directions."[46] In fact, in the homely old phrase of the New Englander—so apt thus to cloak the most transcendent truths—Isabella Gardner, a New Englander herself in the end, made the best of it. And her best not only involved brilliant sallies against Elizabeth Young-Bruehl's "four prejudices" of America's twentieth-century—anti-Semitism, racism, sexism, and homophobia—but a significant influence on the life and work of a number of the leading artists, musicians, and literary figures of her era; and, finally, an artistic epiphany of her own of world rank in the design of Fenway Court, perhaps the outstanding triumph anywhere of the Ruskinian ideal of the moral stature of art.

So she triumphed, if not always gracefully, certainly courageously. And hardly selfishly either in the end. Among the most formidable figures of her time in her field, and a pioneer in the emerging role of women in America in the twentieth century, it is only to be expected that Isabella Stewart Gardner left us more than one legacy; for was she not always twice as bold?

Notes

The following abbreviations are used in the text:

ISG: Isabella Stewart Gardner

BB: Bernard Berenson

FMC: Francis Marion Crawford

JSS: John Singer Sargent

MC: Morris Carter

MB: Mary Berenson

HJ: Henry James

HA: Henry Adams

MHE: Maude Howe Elliott

GMA: Gardner Museum Archives

SSJEA: Society of St. John the Evangelist (Cowley Fathers) Archives, Cambridge, MA

SSJE: Society of St. John the Evangelist

ISG&FC: Morris Carter, *Isabella Stewart Gardner and Fenway Court* (Boston: Houghton, Mifflin, 1925)

H/L: Rollin N. van Hadley, *The Letters of Bernard Berenson and Isabella Stewart Gardner* (Boston: Northeastern University Press, 1987)

DAB: Dictionary of American Biography (New York: Scribners)

CHAPTER ONE: Reverie

1. Oscar Wilde, quoted in Richard Ellman, *Oscar Wilde* (New York: Random House, 1988), 3.

2. Corina Putnam Smith, *Interesting People* (Norman, Okla.: University of Oklahoma Press, 1962), 157, hereinafter Smith, *Interesting People*.

3. MB to ISG, May 22, 1923, H/L, 659.

4. ISG to BB, October 24, 1922, H/L, 652.

5. See MC, *ISG&FC*, 246; Edward Weeks, *My Green Age* (Boston: Little, Brown, 1973), 107, hereinafter Weeks, *Green Age*. See also note I/16 below. ISG is also known to have asked some of those she wrote to burn her own letters. Note T. Jefferson Coolidge's assurance to her in a letter of April 26, 1884 (GMA), that "I destroy your letters in obedience to your command."

6. Exceptions that come at once to mind—the Catherine Palace at Tsarskoe celo, for instance—will always be seen to fail in one category or another.

7. BB to ISG, July 16, 1921, H/L, 632.

8. MC, *ISG&FC*, 12, 52; Theodore Roosevelt, *Ranch Life and the Hunting Trail* (New York: Century, 1888; Scribners reprint, 1926), 329.

9. Lord Byron, *Childe Harold's Pilgrimage*, quoted in Margaretta M. Lovell, *Venice, the American View* (San Francisco: The Fine Arts Museums, 1984), 11, 9, v, hereinafter Lovell, *Venice*.

10. ISG to BB, July 29, 1902, H/L, 296.

11. Virtually the only source for ISG's early life is MC, *ISG&FC*, 3–22. For the tavern-owning grandfather see court records, November 2, 1919, Kings County, N.Y., Courthouse, administration papers granted to Ann Smith, cited in Louise Hall Tharp, *Mrs. Jack* (Boston: Little Brown, 1965), 320 n 18.

12. MC, *ISG&FC*, 15.

13. Ibid., 11.

14. Ida Agassiz to ISG, March 8, 1923, GMA.

15. Lovell, *Venice*, 11.

16. MC to W. C. Endicott, March 7, 1930, GMA. MC writes that Bolgi told him of ISG's destruction of the Bible.

17. MC to Mr. Morse, December 16, 1925, GMA.

18. MC, *ISG&FC*, 22.

19. John L. Gardner, Sr., to the president of Harvard College, July 5, 1856, Harvard University Archives.

20. In the GMA are an atlas, *Atlas Universel de Geographie* (A. Brué, Paris, 1858), inscribed "John L. Gardner Jr., Paris, 1858," and the *Handbook or New Guide of Rome and the Environs According to Vast and Nibby* (Rome, 1857), inscribed "John L. Gardner, Hotel d'Angleterre."

21. Isobel Anderson, *Letters and Journals of General Nicholas Longworth Anderson* (New York: Lund & Edinburgh, 1942), 124, hereinafter Anderson, *Letters*.

22. MHE, *Three Generations* (Boston: Little, Brown, 1923), 379, hereinafter MHE, *Generations*; A. J. Phillpot, unidentified newspaper clipping, GMA. Gardner served on a number of boards of trustees of firms in which he was a

significant investor, including Calumet & HeclaMining Co., and the Chicago, Burlington and Quincy Railroad. For his investments with his father see Frank Augustus Gardner, comp., *The Gardner Memorial* (Salem, Mass., privately printed, 1933), 200–1. John L. Gardner, Jr. was also a trustee and member of the Finance Committee of the Suffolk Savings Bank as well as treasurer of Boston's Museum of Fine Arts. His occupation in the modern sense is hard to pin down. He first appears in the Boston Street (Business) Directory in 1859, when he is listed as in business at 22 Congress Street, the same office address as his father, John L. Gardner, Sr., and George A. and Joseph P. Gardner, brothers of John Junior. Although George and Joseph are listed as merchants, neither John Senior or John Junior are categorized at all. For the *Puritan* see MC, *ISG&FC*, 102.

23. John L. Gardner, Jr., academic record, Harvard University Archives; Anderson, *Letters*, 34.

24. Coolidge to MC, GMA. For a discussion of "illegitimacy" in Edith Wharton's world, comparable to Gardner's, see Benstock, *Wharton*, 10, 18.

25. MC, *ISG&FC*, 128.

26. ISG to Julia Gardner, February 28, 1859, quoted MC, *ISG&FC*, 18.

27. Julia Gardner, John L. Gardner's sister, married Joseph Randolph Coolidge, whose mother, Eleanor Randolph, was a daughter of Thomas Mann Randolph of Tuckahoe, Virginia, and a great-granddaughter of Thomas Jefferson. Eleanor Randolph took up residence in Boston after 1826, but naturally there were always many Southern connections.

28. See *Boston Daily Advertiser*, 9. 10, July 14, 1863, cited Tharp, *Mrs. Jack*, 331 n 19.

29. Alexander W. Williams, *A Social History of the Greater Boston Clubs* (Barre, Vt.: Barre Publishers, 1970), 24–28.

30. For John L. Gardner's clubs see the 1899 Boston Social Register, published the year after his death. In addition to the Somerset he also belonged to the Tavern, the (Brookline) Country Club, St. Botolph Club, the Myopia Hunt Club and the Exchange.

31. Barbara A. White, ed., *Wharton's New England* (Hanover, N.H.: University of New Hampshire Press, 1995), viii, 9; MC, *ISG&FC*, 83. For Julia Ward Howe see Laura Richards and MHE, *Julia Ward Howe* (Boston: Houghton, Mifflin, 1915), hereinafter Richards/Elliott, *Howe*; and Paul S. Boyer, "Howe, Julia Ward," *Notable American Women* II (Cambridge, Mass.: Belknap, 1971), hereinafter Boyer, "Howe"; ISG to MHE, March 27, 1884, quoted MC, *ISG&FC*, 83.

32. Edward Chalfont, *Better in Darkness* (Hamden, Conn.: Archon Books, 1944), 46; hereinafter Chalfont, *Darkness*.

33. Henry Lee Higginson to ISG, December 12, 1898, GMA; Bliss Perry, *Life and Letters of Henry Lee Higginson* (Boston: Atlantic Monthly Press, 1921), 284, 437; see also Anderson, *Letters*, 195; MC, *ISG&FC*, 25–26.

34. John Jay Chapman, "Mrs. John L. Gardner," *Boston Evening Transcript*, July 18, 1924, hereinafter Chapman, "Gardner."

35. Nathan G. Hale, *Freud in America*, vol. I of *Freud and the Americans* (New York: Oxford University Press, 1971), 121, hereinafter Hale, *Freud*.

36. MC, *ISG&FC*, 23, 24. John L. Gardner, Jr., is listed in the Boston Street Directory as resident at 152 Beacon Street from 1859 to his death in 1898 with the omission of a few years when he and ISG traveled. For the apartment hotel see *ISG&FC*, 23.

37. Jean Strouse, *Alice James* (Boston: Houghton, Mifflin, 1980), 105, hereinafter Strouse, *James*.

38. Peter Gay, *Education of the Senses* (New York: Oxford University Press, 1984), 164–65, hereinafter Gay, *Education*.

39. Shari Benstock, *Edith Wharton* (New York: Scribners, 1994), 57, 58, hereinafter Benstock, *Wharton*.

40. Gay, *Education*, 231, 233.

41. Leslie A. Vensel, ed. *Aescolapian Boston* (Boston: Paul Dudley White Medical History Society, 1980), 11. Dr. Henry Jacob Bigelow (Harvard Medical School, Massachusetts General Hospital, 1846–86) was the son of Dr. Jacob Bigelow of the same two institutions, called the "apostle of anesthesia" (in Joseph E. Garland, *Every Man Our Neighbor* (Boston: Little, Brown, 1962), 22, and the father of William Sturgis Bigelow, called (in *ISG&FC*, 50) by ISG "(my (our) doctor's son)."

42. Yvone Knibiehler, "Bodies and Hearts," Geneviève Fraisse and Michelle Penot, eds., *A History of Women in the West* (Cambridge, Mass.: Belknap, 1993), 333.

43. MC, *ISG&FC*, 25, 27.

44. Gay, *Education*, 235.

45. MC, *ISG&FC*, 25.

46. Mrs. John Amory Lowell to Augustus Lowell, n.d., quoted in Louise Hall Tharp, *Mrs. Jack* (Boston: Little, Brown, 1965), 36–37 and 331n4 (of Chapter 4); The whereabouts of the original is unknown. Tharp thanks George Peabody Gardner for permission to publish the letter, sent her, she records, by Mrs. Harey H. Bundy.

47. MC, *ISG&FC*, 27.

48. Ibid., 29.

CHAPTER TWO: **The Capacity of Enjoyment**

1. MB to ISG, May 22, 1923, H/L, 659.

2. MC, *ISG&FC*, 52.

3. Ibid., 90.

4. Ibid., 226–27.

5. Ibid., 226–27; MHE, *Generations*, 379; Smith, *Interesting People*, 154.

6. Smith, *Interesting People*, 153.

7. Ibid., 154.

8. MC, *ISG&FC*, 33.

9. Ibid., 34.

10. Ibid.

11. "Religion: Cowley Fathers," *Time* (August 24, 1936), 42.

12. "Saunterings," *Town Topics*, December 1, 1887, quoted Tharp, *Mrs. Jack*, 109.

13. Henry J. Bigelow to ISG, n.d., quoted MC, *ISG&FC*, 30.

14. William Sturgis Bigelow to ISG, n.d., quoted MC, *ISG&FC*, 143–44.

15. Maude Howe Elliott, *My Cousin, F. Marion Crawford* (New York: Macmillan, 1939), 122, hereinafer Elliott, *Crawford*.

16. MHE, *Generations*, 378–79.

17. MC, *ISG&FC*, 29–30.

18. Clara Rogers, *The Story of Two Lives* (Norwood, Mass.: Plimpton Press, 1932), 35–36; hereinafter Rogers, *Lives*.

19. Margaret Chanler, *Roman Spring* (Boston: Little, Brown, 1934), 119, hereinafter Chanler, *Roman Spring*.

20. Rogers, *Lives*, 35.

21. MC, *ISG&FC*, 33-34.

22. MC, *ISG&FC*, 143–44.

23. ISG's leonine exploits are "documented" in various unidentified newspaper clippings in the GMA. (One identified clipping is from the *Boston Post*, February 2, 1902.) See also MC, *ISG&FC*, 160–61.

24. Walter Terry, *Miss Ruth* (New York: Dodd, Mead, 1969), 50.

25. Jane Smith, *Elsie De Wolfe* (New York: Athenaeum, 1978), 168, 286. The origin of the elephant story may be a planned ride by ISG on one at a fete planned by Joseph Lindon Smith at the Larz Anderson estate in Brookline, for which see, Tharp, *Mrs. Jack*, 81. ISG, of course, also rode elephants in Cambodia.

26. Arthur Gold and Robert Fizdale, *The Divine Sarah* (New York: Random House, 1992), 174–75, hereinafter Gold/Fizdale, *Sarah*.

27. BB, *Rumor and Reflection* (New York: Simon & Schuster, 1952), 14.

28. Gold/Fizdale, *Sarah*, 120.

29. Ibid., 121, 122.

30. MC, *ISG&FC*, 32.

31. R. B. Lewis, *The Jameses* (New York: Doubleday, 1991), 474; MC, *ISG&FC*, 32.

CHAPTER THREE: On Pilgrimage

1. M. H. Abrams, *A Glossary of Literary Terms* (Fort Worth, Tex.: Harcourt Brace, 1993), 133.

2. John D. Wade, "Grafton, Charles," DAB, IV, 470–71. See also Andrew Mead, "Sawdust and Incense," *The Beacon* 6 (Michaelmas, 1988), 8.

3. Betty Hughes Morris, *A History of The Church of The Advent* (Boston: privately printed, 1995), 32, hereinafter Morris, *Advent*; see also MC, *ISG&FC*, 49.

4. Ibid.

5. Mary Catherine Louise, *The House of My Pilgrimage* (Boston: privately printed, 1966).

6. I attribute ISG as donor of the Advent high altar on the basis of the two "Isabellas" which appear in its reredos.

7. F. A. Walker to ISG, March 1885, GMA.

8. Morris, *Advent*, 201–2. Her source is verger Joseph Hunting.

9. Smith, *Interesting People*, 160; Tharp, *Mrs. Jack*, 141 and 336 n. 4; Morris, *Advent*, 201.

10. ISG's travel diary, GMA.

11. For 152 Beacon Street see Arnold Lewis, et al., *The Opulent Interiors of the Gilded Age* (New York: Dover, 1987), 131 (a reprint of G. W. Sheldon, *Artistic Houses of Boston* (New York: D. Appleton, 1883–84), vol. II and T. Bentzon, *Les Américaines chez elles* (Paris, 1893), 113, quoted in R. G. Saisselin, *The Bourgeois and the Bibelot* (New Brunswick, N.J.: Rutgers University Press, 1984). Henry James also depicted 152 Beacon Street in "A New England Winter," his short story of 1884.

12. Van Wyck Brooks, *Dream of Arcadia* (New York: Dutton, 1958), 114, hereinafter Brooks, *Arcadia*.

13. Christina Zwarg, "The Storied Facts of Margaret Fuller," *New England Quarterly* LXIX (March 1969), 139, hereinafter Zwarg, "Fuller."

14. Elizabeth Cary Agassiz to ISG, June 18, n.y., GMA.

15. Charles Moore, "Norton, Charles Eliot," *DAB*, vii, 569–72. Leslie J. Workman, "My First Real Tutor," *New England Quarterly* 62 (December 1989), 571, 580, hereinafter Moore, "Norton," hereinafter Workman, "Tutor."

16. Maureen Cunningham, "The Dante Quest," *Fenway Court*, 1972, 19, hereinafter Cunningham, "Dante."

17. Ibid.

18. Workman, "Tutor," 574, 580.

19. J. C. Levenson, et al., eds., *The Letters of Henry Adams 1858–1892* (Cambridge, Mass.: Harvard University Press, 1988, vol 11) 235–36, hereinafter Levenson, *Adams Letters*. For a discussion of ISG's three nephews see M. A. De Wolfe Howe, *John Jay Chapman and His Letters* (Boston: Houghton, Mifflin, 1937), 35–36.

20. Chapman, "Gardner."

21. Leon Harris, *Only to God* (New York: Athenaeum, 1967), 62.

22. HJ, quoted MC, *ISG&FC*. No source is given. See also MC, *ISG&FC*, 48–49.

23. Fred Kaplan, *Henry James* (New York: William Morrow, 1992), 243; hereinafter Kaplan, *James*. See also Leon Edel, *Henry James* (New York: Harper & Row, 1985), hereinafter Edel, *James*; and Sheldon Novick, *Henry James* (New York: Random House, 1996), hereinafter Novick, *James*. Edel's work is a condensation of his five-volume *The Life of Henry James*, each volume of which is separately cited here as appropriate. For the European "cathedral pilgrimage," see MC, *ISG&FC*, 49–51.

CHAPTER FOUR: The Awakener

1. Benstock, *Wharton*, 169.

2. Ibid., 49.

3. Ibid., 51.

4. Edel, *James* (Cambridge, Mass.: Belknap Press, 1975), IV, 265–66.

5. Leon Edel, *The Conquest of London* (Philadelphia: Lippincott, 1962), 382, hereinafter Edel, *Conquest*.

6. For F. Marion Crawford see John Pilkington, Jr., *Francis Marion Crawford* (New York: Twayne, 1964), hereafter Pilkington, *Crawford*; see also Brooks, *Arcadia*; and Elliott, *Crawford*.

7. Elliott, *Crawford*, 90.

8. Pilkington, *Crawford*, 31.

9. Ibid., 102.

10. Ibid., 102, 90.

11. Edel, *James*, 275.

12. Ibid., 276.

13. Elliott, *Crawford*, 92.

14. Edel, *James*, 276.

15. Leon Edel, *The Middle Years* (Philadelphia: Lippincott, 1962), 41, hereinafter Edel, *Middle Years*.

16. Edel, *James*, 242.

17. Ibid., 678.

18. Edel, *Middle Years*, 20.

19. Benstock, *Wharton*, 197.

20. Leon Edel, *The Master* (Philadelphia: Lippincott, 1972), 201, hereinafter Edel, *Master*.

21. Ibid. See also 325.

22. Kaplan, *James*, 399.

23. Pilkington, *Crawford*, 46.

24. Ibid.

25. Ibid., 102, 42.

26. Ibid., 25, 29, 36, 40–41.

27. Ibid., 36–37, 25, 29.

28. Cunningham, "Dante," 25.

29. Brooks, *Arcadia*, 207.

30. Douglass Shand-Tucci papers, Box G (correspondence), closed collection, Boston Public Library.

31. FMC to ISG, n.d., GMA.

32. Horace Gregory, *Amy Lowell* (New York: Thomas Nelson, 1958), 16, hereinafter Gregory, *Lowell*.

33. For FMC's and ISG's trips to New York see Pilkington, *Crawford*, 47. The poem is signed and dated: "FMC, 13 May, 1882," GMA.

34. The valentine is undated, GMA.

35. Walter De la Mare, Introduction, *Love* (New York: Morrow, 1946), 51, hereinafter De la Mare, *Love*.

36. Pilkington, *Crawford*, 192.

37. Gore Vidal, "The Political Novel from Darius the Great to President Chester Arthur," Gordon Poole, ed., *Il Magnifico Crawford* (Sorento Crawford Memorial Society, 1988), 41–42.

38. Brooks, *Arcadia*, 211.

39. MC to Mr. Morse, December 16, 1925, GMA.

40. FMC to Louisa Terry, March 26, 1882, quoted Pilkington, *Crawford*, 47; Samuel Ward to Julia Ward Howe, March 23, 1882; both Houghton Library, Harvard University.

41. "Saunterings," *Town Topics*, December 8, 1887, quoted Tharp, *Mrs. Jack*, 134.

42. Chanler, *Roman Spring*, 119.

43. Karl Maria Rilke, quoted De la Mare, *Love*, 11.

44. The photograph is unsigned and undated but the inscription is in Crawford's hand. GMA.

45. P. J. Pierce, *Edmund C. Tarbell and the Boston School of Painting* (Hingham, Mass., privately printed, 1980), 59–60.

46. Pilkington, Crawford, 64; FMC to MHE, May 17, 1983, quoted Pilkington, *Crawford*, 64.

47. Marsilio Ficino, *The Letters of Marsilio Ficino* (London: Shepheard-Walwyn, 1978), quoted Thomas Moore, *Soulmates* (New York: HarperCollins, 1994), 208.

48. Charles Anderson, Introduction, *The Bostonians*, by Henry James (New York: Penguin, 1984), 9.

49. R. D. Godder, Introduction, *The Bostonians*, by Henry James (Oxford: Oxford University Press, 1984), vii–viii.

50. HJ to W. D. Howells, quoted Van Wyck Brooks, *Howells, His Life and World* (New York: Dutton, 1959), 142.

51. Pilkington, *Crawford*, 70; Jackson Lears, *No Place for Grace* (New York: Pantheon, 1981), xviii.

52. FMC, *To Leeward*, quoted Pilkington, *Crawford*, 70. Arlo Bates attempts a variant explanation of events in *The Puritans*, 115. Of the ISG character of Mrs. Wilson he writes: "Mrs. Wilson in the early days of her married life had tried to make her husband jealous by allowing the desperate attentions of a single lover. She never repeated the experiment. The lover went abroad to recover from the sting of having been made hopelessly ridiculous. . . . Fortunately she had married for love, and no woman loves a man less for finding him able to control her. In these days Mrs. Wilson amused herself by having a troop of admirers." His view does not ring true.

53. ISG to Lilian Aldrich, March 20 [1907], Houghton Library, Harvard University.

54. ISG, *Commonplace Book*, 214, GMA.

55. ISG to BB, June 11, 1924, H/L, 667: "Divorce," ISG wrote, "is really on the rampage; America is worse than ever."

CHAPTER FIVE: **Jamesian Perspectives**

1. Anne Higonnet, "Representations of Women" in Genevieve Fraisse and Michelle Perrot, eds., *A History of Women in The West*: IV (Cambridge, Mass., Belknap Press, 1993), 306–18. For the feminist interpretation see M. H. Abrams, *Glossary of Literary Terms* (Fort Worth, Tex.: Harcourt, Brace, 1993), 236.

2. HJ, quoted in MC, "Gardner Museum," 55, 147. MC refers to a letter of ca. August 1901 I have not been able to locate.

3. *ISG&FC*, 173.

4. All that follows is drawn from ISG's travel diary and letters, quoted *ISG&FC*, 59–88.

5. Rose Macaulay, *Pleasures of Ruins* (London: Thames and Hudson, 1966).

6. Martin L. Smith, SSJE, ed., *Benson of Cowley* (Cambridge, Mass.: Cowley, 1980), 10–11.

7. *ISG&FC*, 59.

8. Edel, *Middle Years*, 112.

9. Edel, *James Letters*, 11, 384.

10. *ISG&FC*, 121. MC's figure, $2,750,000.00, now believed by Gardner archivist Susan Sinclair to have been incorrect. It was nearer $1,750,000.00 For David Stewart's business affairs see Ibid., 8–9.

11. For Sargent see Stanley Olson, *John Singer Sargent: His Portrait* (New York: St. Martin's Press, 1986), hereinafter Olson, *Sargent*; Evan Charteris, *John Sargent* (London: William Heinemann, 1927), hereinafter Charteris, *Sargent*; David McKibben, *Sargent's Boston* (Boston: Museum of Fine Arts, 1956); Trevor J. Fairbrother, *John Singer Sargent and America* (Ph.D. dissertation, Boston University, 1981; New York: Garland, 1986), hereinafter Fairbrother, *Sargent and America*; and Trevor J. Fairbrother, *John Singer Sargent* (New York: Abrams, 1994), hereinafter Fairbrother, *Sargent*.

12. JSS to ISG, n.d. [1886?], GMA.

13. For Whistler see Stanley Weintraub, *Whistler: A Biography* (New York: Weybright and Talley, 1974).

14. Olson, *Sargent*, 141.

15. *ISG&FC*, 104.

16. For Zorn's portrait, see *ISG&FC*, 147; for Bunker's see Erica E. Hirshler, *Dennis Miller Bunker and His Circle* (Boston: Gardner Museum, 1995), 26–27, hereinafter Hirshler, *Bunker and His Circle*. See also Michelle Facos, *Swedish Impressionisms* (Boston: Gardner Museum, 1993).

17. Paul Bourget, quoted in Fairbrother, *Sargent and America*, 105–6.

18. Fairbrother, *Sargent and America*, 104.

19. *ISG&FC*, 105. *The Boston Transcript* review (January 30, 1888) all but ignored the Gardner portrait; reviews in *The Boston Journal* (February 4, 1888) and *The Boston Traveller* (February 8, 1888), on the other hand, found the Gardner portrait highly noteworthy, even eccentric. See Fairbrother, *Sargent and America*, 136.

20. In the nature of things, the "Crawford's Notch" witticism is not documentable, explained perhaps by Jack Gardner's threat to horsewhip its author if it was! That threat itself is also documentable only through the oral tradition, which may be said to have climaxed in Tharp, *Mrs. Jack*, 134–35. Tharp herself serenely attributes the witticism to *Town Topics* without venturing either date or quotation, insisting piously that "*Town Topics* printed it but in terms too vulgar even for a scandal sheet." A search of the complete run of *Town Topics* being

impracticable (in the absence of any index), the witticism stands rather than falls, however, on the basis of ISG's rule, oft quoted here, that one should never spoil a good story. An echo is perhaps found in Bates, *Puritans*, 210, where the ISG character tells an admirer: "if my husband . . . were here he would horsewhip you."

21. Fairbrother, *Sargent and America*, 104.

22. HJ made this pronouncement sight unseen (on the strength of an account of the sole exhibition of the portrait at the St. Botolph Club in Boston by a Lady Playfairs) in a letter of February 22, 1888, to a Miss Reuble, Houghton Library, Harvard University. Its first appearance in print appears to have been by Paul Bourget in his *Outre-mer* (Paris, 1895), vol. I. Bourget's text on the subject is quoted in Patricia Hill, *John Singer Sargent* (Abrams/Whitney Museum, 1986), 95.

23. *ISG&FC*, 107, 110–11.

24. A. R. Tinter, *The Pop World of Henry James* (Ann Arbor, Mich.: UMI Research Press, 1989), 108–9.

25. HJ, "Venice: An Early Impression," in Richard Howard, ed., *Collected Travel Writings, The Continent* (New York: Library of America, 1993), 337.

26. Kaplan, *James*, 320–21, 387–88. See also n. 35 below.

27. Olson, *Sargent*, 86.

28. F. Hopkinson Smith, *Gondola Days* (Boston: Houghton, Mifflin, 1902), 157.

29. Edel, *Middle Years*, 324–25.

30. Ibid., 326–27.

31. Ibid.

32. Kaplan, *James*, 321.

33. Rachel Brownstein, "What Henry Did," *Boston Globe*, November 3, 1996.

34. Novick, *James*, xiv. "Why should we suppose," Novick queries aptly, "that [James] accomplished so many miracles of imagination?"

35. Curtis to ISG, n.d., GMA. With respect to Curtis' sexual orientation see his letters to ISG of July 18, 1911, and March 30, 1917, in which he claims the openly gay poet Jack Wheelwright as a friend, and a letter to ISG of November 13, 1894, in which he expresses his liking for Robert Hichens' *The Green Carnation*, for the homosexual significance of which see Shand-Tucci, *Boston Bohemia*, 65, 335. GMA.

36. Curtis to ISG, November 13, 1894, GMA.

37. Curtis to ISG, November 13, 1894, GMA.

38. Coudenhove to ISG, n.d. GMA.

39. T. Jefferson Coolidge, *The Autobiography of T. Jefferson Coolidge* (Boston: Massachusetts Historical Society, 1923), 182.

40. *ISG&FC*, 128.

41. See pp. below for an outline of ISG in James' fiction.

42. Edel, *The Master*, 121.

43. Robert Coles, *The Caught Image* (Chapel Hill: University of North Carolina Press, 1954), 80; Edel, *The Master*, 215; F. O. Matthiessen and Kenneth Murdock, *The Notebooks of Henry James* (New York: Oxford University Press, 1947), 322.

44. Stephen Donadio, *Nietzsche, Henry James and The Artists' Will* (New York: Oxford University Press, 1978), 192.

45. None of JSS's biographers have explored the nature and extent of his relationship with ISG in any detail.

46. See Eleanor Palfrey, *The Lady and the Painter* (New York: Coward-McCann, 1951).

47. Ellery Sedgwick, *The Happy Profession* (Boston: Atlantic Monthly Press, 1946), 60–61, hereinafter Sedgwick, *Profession*.

48. All JSS's biographers agree he was not in or around Boston during the summer of 1887 or that of 1888.

49. Charles M. Mount, *John Singer Sargent* (New York: Norton, 1969), 131–32.

50. Joseph Lindon Smith, *Tombs, Temples and Ancient Art* (Norman, Okla.: University of Oklahoma Press, 1956), 118, hereinafter Smith, *Tombs*.

51. See below.

52. Fairbrother, *Sargent and America*, 268 n. 15.

53. Olson, *Sargent*, 107.

CHAPTER SIX: Figure in the Carpet

1. George Proctor to ISG, n.d. GMA.

2. Jeffrey Richards, "Manly Love and Victorian Society" in J. A. Mangdis and James Walvin, eds. *Manliness and Morality* (New York: St. Martin's Press, 1987), 108.

3. Ralph Waldo Emerson to Thomas Carlyle, July 31, 1846, quoted Joan von Mehren, *Minerva and the Muse* (Amherst, Mass.: University of Massachusetts Press, 1994), 235.

4. *Harvard College Class of 1882, Secretary's Report*, vol. iii (Boston: April 1890), 37–38.

5. Sox, *Bachelors*. Sox's source for the friendship of Ned Warren and Joe Junior is Osbert Burdett and E. H. Goddard, *Edward Perry Warren* (London: Cristopher, 1941); Alan Simpson, *Artful Partners* (New York: Macmillan, 1986), 51.

6. Robert Gathorne-Hardy, *Recollections of Logan Pearsall Smith* (New York: Macmillan, 1950), 112, 114.

7. Hasty Pudding Club Alligator Records, 1848–58 (March 1857), Harvard University Archives.

8. Ernest Samuels, *Henry Adams* (Cambridge, Mass.: Harvard University Press, 1989), 17, hereinafter Samuels, *Adams*.

9. Chalfont, *Darkness*, 513; Ernest Samuels, *Henry Adams: The Major Phase* (Cambridge, Mass.: Belknap Press, 1964), 72, 157; W. H. Jody, *Henry Adams* (New Haven: Yale University Press, 1952), 79; Ernest Samuels, *Henry Adams: The Middle Years* (Cambridge, Mass.: Harvard University Press, 1958), 58 and indexed under Dwight; Ernst Scheyer, *The Circle of Henry Adams* (Detroit: Wayne State University Press, 1970), 82, 167.

10. HA to John Hay, March 4 [1888], as quoted Levenson, *Adams Letters*, III, 102.

11. HA to Lucy Baxter, November 4, 1890, quoted Levenson, *Adams Letters*, III, 223.

12. HA to R. D. Rae, 5 December 5, 1891, quoted Levenson, *Adams Letters*, III, 581.

13. Ernest Samuels, *Letters of Henry Adams* (Cambridge, Mass.: Belknap, 1982), II, 641.

14. Roger Austin, *Genteel Pagan* (Amherst, Mass.: University of Massachusetts Press, 1994), 126–27. Dwight's papers are in the Massachusetts Historical Society.

15. T. Sullivan to ISG, August 31, 1892, GMA.

16. Barbara Hardy, review of Kate Miller's *Sexual Politics*, *New York Times Book Review* (October 6, 1996), 96.

17. T. Dwight to ISG, September 18, 1892, GMA.

18. Ibid., September 18, 1892, GMA.

19. Ibid., December 15, 1908, GMA.

20. Ibid., n.d.

21. John McCormick, *George Santayana* (New York: Paragon, 1988), 119.

22. Shand-Tucci, *Boston Bohemia*, 207–9.

23. T. Sullivan to ISG, August 31, 1892, GMA.

24. Ibid., May 16, 1892, GMA.

25. Ibid., March 9, 1889, GMA.

26. Thomas Russell Sullivan, *Passages from the Journal of Thomas Russell Sullivan* (Boston: Houghton, Mifflin, 1917), 97–98, hereinafter Sullivan, *Journal*.

27. For Bunker see Erica E. Hirschler, *Dennis Miller Bunker* (Boston: Museum of Fine Arts, 1994), hereinafter Hirschler, *Bunker*; Hirschler, *Bunker and His Circle*; Shand-Tucci, *Boston Bohemia*, 230–31, 208–9, 210, 226, 425.

28. Olson, *Sargent*, 145.

29. *ISG&FC*, 103.

30. T. Sullivan to ISG, n.d., GMA.

31. *ISG&FC*, 89.

32. Hirschler, *Bunker*, 16.

33. Shand-Tucci, *Boston Bohemia*, 492 n. 104.

34. "Saunterings," *Town Topics*, 36 (November 12, 1896), quoted Shand-Tucci, *Boston Bohemia*; Karl Miller, *Doubles* (London: Oxford University Press, 1967), 241.

35. WAG's letters from Greece to ISG are in the GMA. For Amory Gardner see Frank Ashburn, *Peabody of Groton* (Cambridge, Mass.: Riverside Press, 1967); Shand-Tucci, *Boston Bohemia*, 232–36.

36. For Johns see Clayton Johns, *Reminiscences of a Musician* (Cambridge, Mass., Washburn & Thomas, 1929), hereinafter Johns, *Reminiscences*; Shand-Tucci, *Boston Bohemia*, 210, 229–30; for Adamowski see Shand-Tucci, *Boston Bohemia*, 21, 211, 230.

37. For Loeffler see Ellen Knight, *Charles Martin Loeffler* (Urbana, Ill.: University of Illinois Press, 1993), hereinafter Knight, *Loeffler*.

38. For Gericke see H. Earle Johnson, *Symphony Hall, Boston* (Boston: Little, Brown, 1950), 32–47, hereinafter Johnson, *Symphony*.

39. Johns, *Reminiscences*, 74.

40. Morris Carter, *Reminiscences* (Boston: privately printed, 1964) 53–54. See also Johnson, *Symphony*, 75–78, hereinafter MC, *Reminiscences*.

41. See below.

42. Ralph P. Locke, "ISG: Music Patron and Music Lover," unpublished paper, Eastman School of Music, dated August 7, 1989, 31, hereinafter Locke, *Gardner*, GMA.

42. Martina Weindel to Susan Sinclair, October 8, 1994.

43. F. Busoni to ISG, November 5, 1894, GMA.

44. For Tirandelli see *ISG&FC*, 128–30, 146, 148, 154, 160.

45. Locke, *Gardner*, 33; see also Knight, *Loeffler*, who does not, however, comment on any role of ISG's in Loeffler's relationship with Schirmer.

46. Shand-Tucci, *Boston Bohemia*, 210.

47. Locke, *Gardner*, 24, 27.

48. GMA.

49. *ISG&FC*, 121. See also Bradford Washburn to Virginia Felton, August 8, 1996, GMA.

50. Quaintrance Eaton, *The Boston Opera Company* (New York: Appleton-Century, 1965), 108–9, hereinafter Eaton, *Opera*.

51. See below.

52. Johns, *Reminiscences*.

53. *ISG&FC*, 123, 145–46, 148.

54. George Proctor to ISG, [1897?], GMA

55. George Proctor to ISG, n.d., GMA.

56. Robert Martin, *The Homosexual Tradition in American Poetry* (Austin, Tex.: University of Texas Press, 1979), 112.

57. C. Loeffler to Evan Charteris, January 30, 1926, quoted Charteris, *Sargent*, 147–48.

58. Hirschler, *Bunker and His Circle*, 11.

59. See color plate.

60. For Coolidge see Harold J. Coolidge and Robert H. Lord, *Archibald Cary Coolidge* (Boston: Houghton, Mifflin, 1932). For ISG's influence: 11, 32.

61. Peter Gay, *Tender Passion* (New York: Oxford University Press, 1987), 206, 212, hereinafter Gay, *Passion*.

62. Shand-Tucci, *Boston Bohemia*, 232–36.

63. James Gifford, *Dayneford's Library* (Amherst: University of Massachusetts Press, 1995), 116–17, 121–23.

64. Shand-Tucci, *Boston Bohemia*, 492–93 n. 110.

65. Arthur J. Monteney Jephson wrote of his adventures in Africa with Stanley in *Emin Pasha and the Rebellion at the Equitor* (New York: 1890).

66. *ISG&FC*, 57; Ellmann, *Wilde*, 180–84.

67. A. Jephson to ISG, January 30, 1890, GMA.

68. A. Jephson to ISG, May 15, 1891, GMA.

69. A. Jephson to ISG, February 8, 1901, GMA.

70. ISG to BB, December 18, 1900, quoted H/L, 238. See also ISG to BB, December 4, [1900], 237.

71. BB to ISG, April 1901, quoted H/L, 255. See also Samuels, *Connoisseur*, 355.

72. ISG to BB, February 1901, quoted H/L, 248.

73. ISG's personal library, with its card catalog, still exists at Fenway Court.

74. Poèmes (Paris, 1896), 182, quoted Martin Creen, *The Mount Vernon Street Warrens* (New York: Scribners, 1989), 115.

75. Shand-Tucci, *Boston Bohemia*, 52–53, 139–40, 468 n. 147.

76. Ibid., 52, 468 n. 147.

77. Ibid., 154.

78. Unidentified newspaper clipping, February 2, 1902, GMA.

79. *ISG&FC*, 12.

80. For Gardner's athletic ability see Crawford's poem, p. below.

81. Unidentified newspaper clipping, February 13, 1906; see also "East Meets West," 38 n. 44, both GMA.

82. *ISG&FC*, 144.

83. Ibid., 12.

84. ISG to BB., December 1898, quoted H/L, 161. For Haughton see *ISG&FC*, 13.

85. Pilkington, *Crawford*, 25.

86. "Jack Sheehan Reflects Upon Old Prize Fighting Days," *Boston Herald*, April 11, 1926. A clipping found among ISG's papers also documents her ongoing interest in the sport: "Dempsey Wins," "Fight Extra" of *Boston Evening Record*, July 2, 1921.

87. ISG to BB, May 3, 1905; H/L, 364. See also Michiko Kakutani, "Making Art of Sport," *New York Times* Magazine, December 15, 1996.

88. John Boswell, *Christianity, Social Tolerance and Homosexuality* (Chicago: University of Chicago Press, 1988), 25.

CHAPTER SEVEN: Diversities

1. Peter Brooks, review of Julia Kristevas' *Time and Sense, New York Times Book Review*, May 19, 1996, 39.

2. Leaving aside Rollin N. Van Hadley's passing reference to BB's "Hebraic [conscience]" in H/L, xxiv, the only hint in Hadley's biographical essay that BB was Jewish.

3. For a complete treatment of the subject see Jonathan Sarna and Ellen Smith, *The Jews of Boston* (Boston: Combined Jewish Philanthropies of Greater Boston, 1995), index.

4. Samuels, *Bernard Berenson, The Making of a Connoisseur* (Cambridge, MA: Belknap Press of Harvard University Press, 1979), 218, hereinafter Samuels, *Connoisseur*. For another view of BB's sexuality see David Sox, *Bachelors of Art* (London: Fourth Estate, 1991), 22.

5. Samuels, *Connoisseur*, 33, 39.

6. Colin Simpson speculates in *Artful Partners* that the Gardners may have paid BB's term bill from the beginning.

7. For ISG's lifestyle generally see MC, *ISG&FC*, 52.

8. Jean and Kahlil Gibran, *Kahlil Gibran and His World* (Boston: New York Graphic Society, 1974), 206–23. McCormick, *Santayana*, 359–60.

9. George Santayana, *The Last Puritan* (New York: Charles Scribners, 1936), 24.

10. See H/L, 224–25, 417, 653.

11. For the Carney benefit see unidentified newspaper clipping, n.d., GMA; for the Knights of Columbus see W. O'Connell to ISG 19 November 19, 1912, GMA.

12. James M. Curley, *I'd Do It Again* (Salem, N.H.: Ayer Co., 1991), 133–34. Curley writes of ISG's "feud with the Brahmin snobocricy" and asserts ISG favored him with a campaign contribution.

13. ISG to Olga Monks [1921], GMA.

14. ISG wrote Andrew on December 27 (GMA) that she was "inwardly disturbed by the political situation" and that she could "only hope and pray you and Gussie will not tear me to pieces." The pro-Curley letter postdates the literary legislation battle.

15. Andrew Gray, "A New England Bloomsbury," *Fenway Court* (1974), 4.

16. Jack Beatty, *The Rascal King* (Reading, Mass.: Addison-Wesley, 1992), 134, 135–36.

17. Henry Cabot Lodge to ISG, January 29, 1918, GMA.

18. ISG to BB, May 16 [1898], quoted H/L, 137.

19. *ISG&FC*, 89.

20. See below Chapter 12.

21. MC, *ISG&FC*, 247.

22. *ISG&FC*, 89.

23. Knight, *Loeffler*, 218. Ibid., 34.

24. Unidentified newspaper clipping, GMA.

25. *ISG&FC*, 56.

26. Henry Adams to Elizabeth Cameron, December 11, 1898, quoted Levenson, *Adams Letters*, vol. iv, 633.

27. Chapman, "Gardner."

28. Ibid.

29. Unidentified newspaper clipping, n.d., GMA.

30. *ISG&FC*, 91.

31. Johns, *Reminiscences*, 69–70.

32. George Santayana, *The Middle Span*, vol. 2 of *Persons and Places* (New York: Charles Scribner's, 1945), 121, 124–26, hereinafter Santayana, *Middle Span*.

33. John Jay Chapman, quoted Walter Muir Whitehill, *Museum of Fine Arts, Boston: A Centennial History* (Cambridge, Mass.: Belknap Press, 1970), 11–12.

34. H/L, 3.

35. BB to ISG, March 11, 1894, quoted H/L, 38.

36. Samuels, *Connoisseur*, 39.

37. Ibid., 40.

38. McCormick, *Santayana*, 38.

39. Ibid., 361.

40. Ibid.

41. ISG to BB, December 13, 1897, quoted H/L, 110.

42. ISG to BB, January 12 [1898], quoted H/L, 117.

43. BB to ISG, Easter Sunday [1898], quoted H/L, 132.

44. Santayana, *Middle Span*, 125.

45. Brooks, *Indian Summer*, 438.

46. Bates, *Puritans*, 412.

47. Samuels, *Adams*, 405.

48. See Eugenia Kaledin, *The Education of Mrs. Henry Adams* (Amherst: University of Massachusetts Press, 1981), hereinafter Kaledin, *Mrs. Henry Adams*.

49. Samuels, *Adams*, 405. BB also felt, with less reason probably, that Henry James was anti-Semitic. Edel, *The Master*, 378.

50. Samuels, *Connoisseur*, 429.

51. Samuels, *Adams*, 405.

52. Ibid., 446.

53. Wendy Lesser, "The T. S. Eliot Problem," *The New York Times Book Review*, July 14, 1996, 31, hereinafter Lesser, "T. S. Eliot."

54. Fairbrother, *Sargent*, 94.

55. Martin L. Smith, "Who Do You Say That I Am?" in *Nativities & Passions* (Cambridge, Mass.: Cowley, 1995), 25–29. Lest I seem to be reading current thought back into past understanding, note William James's letter to Henry of June 21, 1899: "It is like the Dreyfus case—one cannot mention it in general company, but it works all the worse within" (I. Sknoskelist and E. M. Berkely, eds., *William and Henry James: Letters* [Charlottesville: University of Virginia Press, 1997], 375).

56. Samuels, *Connoisseur*, 9–10, 67–69.

57. BB to ISG, August 24, 1887, quoted H/L, 5.

58. Samuels, *Connoisseur*, 8–10.

59. BB to ISG, August 24, 1887, quoted H/L, 5.

60. Samuels, *Connoisseur*, 286.

61. Sarna, *Jews of Boston*, index.

62. *ISG&FC*, 234.

63. Eileen Southern, "Johnson, J[ohn] Rosamand," Stanley Sadie, ed., *The New Grove Dictionary of Music and Musicians* (London: Macmillan, 1980), ix, 680; Edward G. Perry, "Negro Creative Musicians," *Negro* (New York: Continuum [reprint], 1997), 221.

64. Margaret Sherman, "Party Honors Roland Hayes," *Boston Globe*, report of event of June 3, 1967.

65. ISG to Mrs. Arthur Foote, March 3, 1884, Houghton Library, Harvard University.

66. Calvin Tomkins, *Living Well Is the Best Revenge* (New York: Viking, 1971), 28–29, 20.

67. Henry E. Krehbiel, *Afro-American Folksongs* (New York: Schirmer, 1914). Inscribed: "gift of Gerald Murphy, May 14, 1921," in Carter's hand. A thank-you note from the Murphys notes their performance at Fenway Court and ISG's "wish to know more of these spirituals," GMA.

68. For a discussion of the influence of black and African-American folk music on Dvorak, see Robert Bagar and Louis Biancolli, *The Concert Companion* (New York: McGraw-Hill, 1947), 239–42.

69. Percy Grainger to ISG, November 1915, GMA.

70. Knight, *Loeffler*, 234, 235, 236.

71. Adelaide M. Cromwell, *The Other Brahmins* (Fayetteville, Ark.: University of Arkansas Press, 1994), 57.

72. Mark A. Duffy, ed., *Episcopal Diocese of Massachusetts, 1784–1983* (Boston: The Diocese, 1984), 64, hereinafter Duffy, *Massachusetts*. Father Powell writes of St. Augustine's Camp in Foxborough in a letter to ISG of November 20, 1923, SSJEA.

73. Sister Catherine Louise, S.S.M., *The House of My Pilgrimage* (Boston: Society of St. Margaret, n.d.), 69.

74. Duffy, *Massachusetts*, 669.

75. Fairbrother, *Sargent*, 142. For *The Nude Study of Thomas E. McKeller*, 141–44.

76. Information supplied by Eldridge Pendleton, SSJE, Cowley's archivist.

77. *ISG&FC*, 234. Andrew does not call ISG directly "utterly emancipated," but strongly implies it by suggesting only such women could be invited to the performance.

78. Interview with William Coe and Peter Liberman of St. John's, Bowdoin St. Their sources are in the SSJEA.

CHAPTER EIGHT: The White Rose

1. Bates, *The Puritans*, 303, 306–24. For ISG's Anglo-Catholicism generally see Douglass Shand-Tucci, "Ralph Adams Cram and Mrs. Gardner," *Fenway Court* (1975), 27–34.

2. Shand-Tucci, *Boston Bohemia*, 183, 230, 316–22, 330, 350, 373.

3. Van Wyck Brooks, *An Autobiography*, (New York: E. P. Dutton, 1965 ed.), 107.

4. John Reed, "A Female Movement," *Anglican and Episcopal History* 57 (June 1988), 200.

5. David Hilliard, "UnEnglish and UnManly," *Victorian Studies* 25 (Winter 1982), 181–210.

6. Ibid., 164.

7. Estelle Jussim, *Slave to Beauty* (Boston: Godine, 1981); Shand-Tucci, *Boston Bohemia*, 39–45 et. seq.

8. Henry G. Fairbanks, *Louise Imogene Guiney* (New York: Twayne, 1973); Alice Brown, *Louise Imogene Guiney* (New York: Macmillan, 1921); Shand-Tucci, *Boston Bohemia*, 35–39.

9. Shand-Tucci, *Boston Bohemia*, 13–29.

10. Peter J. Gomes, "Beautiful Buildings, Beautiful Music, Beautiful Men," Boston Book Review (March 1996), iii, 22.

11. This is perhaps George and Peto's only American work.

12. Graeme Moore, "Renaissance D'Azur," *Country Life*, July 7, 1988.

13. Henry James to ISG, October 20, 1887, GMA.

14. Ibid., March 18, 1888, GMA.

15. Kaplan, *James*, 453–54.

16. There is a file on Mower in the Fine Arts Department of the Boston Public Library (Research Library).

17. Lincoln Kirstein, *Mosaic* (New York: Farrar, Straus & Giroux, 1994), 164–69.

18. Martin Green, *The Problem of Boston* (New York: Norton, 1966), 146–47, 153, 154.

19. Unidentified newspaper clipping, n.d., GMA.

20. There is, so far as I can discover, no contemporary documentation of this; however it is so characteristic of ISG I have included it.

21. *ISG&FC*, 107.

22. Robert W. Gleason, SJ, Introduction to *The Spiritual Exercises of St. Ignatius of Loyola* (New York: Doubleday, 1964), 10, 12, 17; hereinafter Gleason, *Ignatius*; See also W. H. Longridge, SSJE, *Ignatian Retreats* (London: A. R. Mowbroy & Co., 1926), hereinafter Longridge, *Ignatian*.

23. See above.

24. Robert Speaight, *Eric Gill* (New York: P. J. Kennedy, 1966), 99–100.

25. Longridge, *Ignatian*, ix; Gleason, *Ignatius*, 18, 19, 25.

26. MC, *ISG&FC*, 167.

27. Bates, *Puritans*, 121, 52, 200; MC, radio interview, January 16, 1936; MC, *Reminiscences*, 37–38.

28. George L. Richardson, *Arthur C. A. Hall* (Boston: Houghton, Mifflin, 1932) 24, 32–39. See also "Hall, Arthur C.," *DAB*, IV, 117, and Shand-Tucci, *Boston Bohemia*, 187–93.

29. Ibid., 5.

30. Ibid., 41.

31. Arthur C. A. Hall, *The Hidden Life of the Heart* (Boston: Joseph George Cupples/Back Bay Bookstore, 1882).

32. A. Hall to ISG, January 31, 1888, GMA.

33. Coudenhove to ISG, March 5, 1918, GMA.

34. McCormick, *Santayana*, 124.

35. Alexander Zabriskie, *Bishop Brent* (Philadelphia: Westminster Press, 1948), 199.

36. Santayana, *Middle Span*, 126. See also (for exceptions, mostly having to do with spouses, male and female, of ISG's close friends) H/L, 468, 598, 218.

37. Frances Weitzenhoffer, *The Havemeyers* (New York: Abrams, 1986), 145, hereinafter Weitzenhoffer, *Havemeyers*; Samuels, *Connoisseur*, 425.

38. Sedgwick, *Happy Profession*, 170–71.

39. See Shand-Tucci, *Boston Bohemia*, 187–93. See also Linda Dowling,

Hellenism and Homosexuality in Victorian Oxford (Ithaca, N.Y.: Cornell University Press, 1994).

40. Lawrence D. Mass, "Still Closeted After All This Time," *Harvard Gay & Lesbian Review*, 111 (Fall 1996), 47.

41. Simone de Beauvoir, *The Second Sex* (New York: Vintage, 1989), 130, here-after Beauvoir, *Second Sex.*.

42. Hans Urs von Balthazar, quoted John R. Kevery, "Assumption of the Blessed Virgin Mary," Ave (July-August, 1996) LXV, 39–42.

43. Paul Robinson, review of Elizabeth Young-Bruehl, *The Anatomy of Prejudices, New York Times Book Review*, May 19, 1996.

CHAPTER NINE: A Paradoxical Character

1. *ISG&FC*, 139–40.

2. S. Foster Damon, *Amy Lowell* (Boston: Houghton, Mifflin, 1935), 103. Damon also links Lowell's increasing notoriety with "The absurdities demanded by a public whose appetite had already been whetted by the gossip about Mrs. Jack Gardner," 264.

3. *ISG&FC*, 31.

4. Rogers, *Two Lives*, 149.

5. Marquess of Queensbury to Lord Alfred Douglas, April 1, 1894, quoted Ellman, *Wilde*, 417.

6. *ISG&FC*, 31. See also Weintraub, *Whistler*, 188.

7. Unidentified newspaper clipping, n.d., GMA.

8. This exchange occurred in class between an American student and John Macquarrie, Lady Margaret Professor in Divinity in the University of Oxford.

9. For Joseph Lindon Smith see under his name, Erica Hirshler, "Artists' Biographies," Trevor J. Fairbrother, et al., *The Bostonians* (Boston: Museum of Fine Arts, 1986), 226, hereinafter Hirshler, "Artists' Biographies."

10. Smith, *Tombs*, 8.

11. *ISG&FC*, 128, 147.

12. This exchange occurred at a dinner party given by Robert Bell Rettig in Castine, Maine, one evening in the early 1990s.

13. F. Marion Crawford, *An Amercian Politician* (Boston: Houghton, Mifflin, 1885), 8, hereinafter Crawford, *Politician.*

14. Smith, *Interesting People*, 153.

15. MC, *ISG&FC*, 25.

16. Unidentified newspaper clipping, n.d., GMA.

17. Tharp, *Mrs. Jack*, 345.

18. MC, *ISG&FC*, 25.

19. Crawford, *Politician*, 8.

20. BB to ISG, in a letter I cannot now locate.

21. Smith, *Interesting People*, 153.

22. Ibid., 153.

23. Samuels, *Connoisseur*, 307.

24. MC, *ISG&FC*, 30.
25. A. Hyatt Mayor, "Mrs. Gardner Comes to Call," *Fenway Court* (Boston: Gardner Museum, 1972), 40.
26. BB to Mary Berenson, September 1897, quoted Samuels, *Connoisseur*, 286.
27. MC, *ISG&FC*, 25.
28. Elsie De Wolfe, *After All* (New York: Harper Bros., 1935), 102, hereinafter De Wolfe, *After All*.
29. MC, *ISG&FC*, 128.
30. Ibid., 26.
31. De Wolfe, *After All*, 102.
32. MB to H. W. Smith, October 29, 1905, quoted Barbara Strachey and Jayne Samuels, *Mary Berenson* (London: Victor Gollancz, 1983), hereinafter Strachey, *Mary Berenson,* 147.
33. MB to her family, December 24, 1920, quoted Strachey, *Mary Berenson*, 236.
34. MB to ISG, May 13, 1914, quoted H/L, 521.
35. ISG was, it must be recalled, as between BB and his wife, the third party of a shifting triangle.
36. Ernest Samuels, *Making of a Legend* (Cambridge, Mass.: Bellknap Press, 1987), 36, hereinafter Samuels, *Legend*.
37. Samuels, *Legend*, 37.
38. Samuels, *Connoisseur*, 235.
39. BB, as quoted by MB to ISG, May 1914, quoted H/L, 521.
40. Elliott, *My Cousin*, 94.
41. Crawford, *Politician*, 20. Maude Elliott notes that this novel "vividly recalls[s]" ISG and 152 Beacon Street, *My Cousin*, 93.
42. MC, *ISG&FC*, 144.
43. Powell to ISG, October 21, 1923, SSJE Archives.
44. MC, *ISG&FC*, 150.
45. ISG to BB, December 7, 1916, quoted H/L, 592.
46. Smith, *Interesting People*, 153.
47. Unidentified newspaper clipping, n.d., GMA.
48. Carter, *Reminiscences*, 45–46.
49. Elliott, *Generations*, 94.
50. MC radio interview, 20.
51. For the three versions see Samuels, *Connoisseur*, 359; Nicky Mariano, *Forty Years with Berenson* (New York: Knopf, 1966), 85; A. Hyatt Mayor, *Archives of American Art Journal* 32 (19), 14.
52. MC, *ISG&FC*, 129, 107.
53. Smith, *Interesting People*, 157.
54. MC, radio interview, January 16, 1936, 3.
55. MC, *ISG&FC*, 45–46.
56. ISG to BB, March 4, 1910, May 2, 1904, October 24, 1992; H/L, 467, 334, 652; MC, *ISG&FC*, 34.
57. ISG to BB, December 13, [1897] quoted H/L, 110.

58. F. Walker to ISG, n.d., quoted *ISG&FC*, 92.
59. A. P. Andrew to ISG, Spring 1908, quoted *ISG&FC*, 234.
60. George Proctor to ISG, n.d., GMA.
61. Smith, *Interesting People*, 156.
62. MB, quoted *H/L*, 242.
63. Zwarg, "Fuller," 137–38.
64. *ISG&FC*, 112.
65. Unidentified newspaper clipping, GMA.
66. ISG to BB, February 1898, quoted *H/L*, 123.
67. BB to ISG, January 1907, quoted *H/L*, 393.
68. Smith, *Interesting People*, 130–31.
69. Ibid., 131.
70. Ralph P. Locke, "Charles Martin Loeffler," *Fenway Court* (19), 30–37.
71. Ibid., 30.
72. Terry Teachart, review of Patrick O'Brien's *The Yellow Admiral, New York Times Book Review*, November 3, 1996, 9.
73. Gay, *Education*, 392.
74. Hale, *Freud*, 59. For a discussion of this in Alice James' life see Strouse, *Alice James*, 106.
75. Richard Brookhiser, "A Man on Horseback," *Atlantic Monthly* (January 1996), 50, 56.
76. That ISG did smoke is documented in Coudenhove to ISG, July 27, 1924, GMA.
77. MC, *ISG&FC*, 164–65.
78. Ibid., 26. Corina Smith also calls ISG "ruthless," *Interesting People*, 153.
79. Smith, *Interesting People*, 153.
80. Julia Ward Howe to ISG, August 23, 1887, GMA.
81. MC, *ISG&FC*, 90.
82. Ibid.
83. Evan Charteris, quoted Fairbrother, *Sargent*, 142.
84. Ibid.
85. Ibid., 8.
86. Thomas A. Fox, "Notes on JSS," Sargent/Fox Papers, Boston Athenaeum, Box 11, Folders 29, 39.
87. Ibid., 38.
88. HA to Elizabeth Cameron, August 25, 1906, quoted Levenson, *Letters*, IV, 26.

CHAPTER TEN: In a Tempter's Garden

1. Edel, *James*, 258, 259, 260, 262; Adeline R. Tinter, *The Museum World of Henry* James (Ann Arbor, Mich.: UMI Research, 1986), 199.
2. BB to ISG, March 11, 1884, *H/L*, 38; Samuels, *Connoisseur*, 187.
3. W. Russell Page, SSJE, interview, October 1996.
4. MC, *ISG&FC*, 135–36.
5. Ibid., 134–35.

6. Aaline Saarinen, *The Proud Possessors* (New York: Random House, 1958), xxiii.

7. Weitzenhoffer, *Havemeyers*, 139–40.

8. Samuels, *Connoisseur*, 193.

9. BB to ISG, August 1, 1894, quoted H/L, 39.

10. MC, *ISG&FC*, 101.

11. Ibid., 146, 148.

12. I am indebted for this quote to Bradford Washburn.

13. Samuels, *Connoisseur*, 185; Mary Logan, "The New Art Criticism," *Atlantic Monthly* (August 1895), 214; Karl Meyer, *The Art Museum* (New York: Morrow, 1979), 177.

14. Caroline Jones, *Modern Art at Harvard* (New York: Abbeville Press, 1985), 32, hereinafter Jones, *Modern Art*.

15. Paul Sachs, "Tales of an Epoch," quoted Jones, *Modern Art*, 32.

16. Ibid.

17. Samuels, *Connoisseur*, 210.

18. Ibid., 211.

19. Ibid., 194.

20. Ibid., 267–68.

21. Ibid., 308.

22. Ibid., 194, 187.

23. Ibid., 308.

24. Ibid., 213.

25. Weitzenhoffer, *Havemeyers*, 139.

26. Samuels, *Connoisseur*, 358.

27. For Warren see Walter Muir Whitehill, MFA, 142–71.

28. Unidentified newspaper clipping, GMA.

29. Samuels, *Connoisseur*, 239.

30. Ibid., 239–40.

31. Samuels, *Legend*, 2.

32. BB to ISG, December 18, 1895, H/L, 45.

33. ISG to BB, July 29, 1902; H/L, 296.

34. BB to ISG, May 10, 1896; H/L, 55.

35. MC, *ISG&FC*, 157.

36. ISG to BB, August 25 [1896]; H/L, 64.

37. ISG to BB, September 19, 1896; H/L, 66.

38. ISG to BB, September 11 [1896]; H/L, 65.

39. Ibid.

40. BB to ISG, September 22, 1896; H/L, 67.

41. ISG to BB, January 1, 1897; H/L, 72.

42. ISG to BB, February 25 [1897]; H/L, 79.

43. MC, "Gardner Museum," 147.

44. For the Velázquez see Samuels, *Connoisseur*, 247–48.

45. ISG to BB, February 8 [1897]; H/L, 75.

46. BB to ISG, November 9, 1896; H/L, 69.

47. BB to ISG, November 24, 1897; H/L, 102.
48. Ibid.
49. BB to ISG, January 10, 1897; H/L, 73.
50. ISG to BB, April 13, 1897; H/L, 82.
51. BB to ISG, July 6 [1898]; H/L, 142.
52. BB to ISG, October 18 [1898]; H/L, 156.
53. There are two versions of Raphael's portrait of Tommasso Inghirami; the other is in the Pitti Palace in Florence. Which Raphael painted more of is a continuing controversy of a sort widespread among art historians. Recently, for example, a picture ISG bought (over BB's objections) as a Botticelli, and later thought not his work, has now again been attributed to Botticelli.
54. ISG to BB, February 23 [1898]; H/L, 125.
55. Ibid.
56. For Margaret Sargent see Honor Moore, The White Blackbird (New York: Viking, 1996).
57. Ibid., 6.
58. ISG to BB, March 3 [1898]; H/L, 127.
59. ISG to BB, November 7 [1898]; H/L, 159.
60. ISG to BB, January 20 [1898]; H/L, 120.
61. For Joseph Lindon Smith see below.
62. Smith, Interesting People, 141.
63. Ibid.; ISG to BB, December 7, 1916; H/L, 592.
64. ISG to BB, May 17 [1901]; H/L, 256.
65. ISG to BB: December 2, 1895; April 6 [1898]; July 29 [1900]; June 24 [1898]; July 18 [1898]; September 24, 1898; H/L, 43, 133, 224, 141, 145, 154.
66. Fragment, GMA.
67. Fragment, GMA.
68. ISG to BB, July 25, 1903, July 9, 1907; H/L, 319, 400.
69. ISG to BB, June 17 [1903]; H/L, 317. See also Julia Cartwright, Isabella D'Este (New York: Dutton, 1905).
70. BB to ISG, May 3, 1903; H/L, 315.
71. ISG to BB, September 19, 1896; H/L, 66.
72. BB to ISG, January 14, 1900; H/L, 201.
73. BB to ISG, April 1, 1909, ISG to BB, October 21, 1896; BB to ISG, November 4, 1896; H/L, 440, 69.
74. MC, ISG&FC, 110.
75. Samuels, Connoisseur, 221.
76. BB to ISG, November 29, 1897; H/L, 104.
77. ISG to BB, December 3, 1897; H/L, 104.
78. ISG to BB, January 20 [1898]; H/L, 120.
79. ISG to BB, February 22, 1899; H/L, 168.
80. ISG to BB, January 28 [1897]; H/L, 74, 69.
81. BB to ISG, November 20, 1899; H/L, 195.
82. H/L, 195 n. 1; MC, "Gardner Museum," 142, 152–54.
83. ISG to BB, February 19 [1900]; H/L, 205.

84. MC, *ISG&FC*, 157. See also ISG to BB, February 11 [1900]; H/L, 204.

85. Ibid.

86. MC, *ISG&FC*, 158; see also MC, "Gardner Museum," 149.

87. BB to ISG, May 6, 1909; H/L, 445.

88. Samuels, *Connoisseur*, 225.

89. BB to ISG, January 23, 1897; H/L, 73.

90. ISG to BB, February 8 [1897]; H/L, 76.

91. Samuels, *Legend*, 70.

92. BB to ISG, January 9, 1898; H/L, 114.

93. For ISG's tax situation, see H/L, 251; Samuels, *Connoisseur*.

94. ISG to BB, November 4 [1901] July 29, 1902, June 30, [1902]; BB to ISG, March 21, 1898; H/L, 273, 295, 291, 130; De Wolfe, *After All*, 102.

95. ISG to BB, September 19 [1896]; H/L, 66.

96. BB to ISG, February 16, 1896; H/L, 50.

97. ISG to BB, April 25, 1896; H/L, 52. For the incense see BB to ISG, May 10, 1896; H/L, 54.

98. Trevor J. Fairbrother, "Painting in Boston," *The Bostonians* (Boston: Museum of Fine Arts, 1986), 76; hereinafter Fairbrother, "Painting in Boston."

99. Ibid., 72.

100. Kenyon Cox, "The Recent Work of Edmund C. Tarbell," *Burlington Magazine*, 14 (January 1909), 259.

101. Hirshler, "Artists' Biographies," 211.

102. MC, *ISG&FC*, 144; see also ISG to BB, April 25, 1896; H/L, 52.

103. ISG to BB, March 11 [1901], February 22, 1899, June 9 [1900], January 30, 1917, August 5 [1899], April 26, 1909; H/L, 25, 251, 168, 218, 222, 597, 185, 493–94.

104. ISG to BB, March 3 [1898]; H/L, 127.

105. ISG to BB, June 7, 1905; H/L, 365.

106. Samuels, *Legend*, 10, 20.

107. Samuels, *Connoisseur*, 219; Hadley calls ISG's commission modest, H/L, 36.

108. Richard Norton to ISG, September 14, 1898, GMA.

109. Ibid.

110. ISG to BB, September 25 [1898]; H/L, 154.

111. Samuels, *Connoisseur*, 301.

112. MB, diary entry, June 23, 1898, quoted H/L, 36.

113. Samuels, *Connoisseur*, 301.

114. Strachey, *Mary Berenson*, 82.

115. Meryle Secrest, *Being Bernard Berenson* (New York: Holt, Rinehart and Winston, 1979), 143, hereinafter Secrest, *Berenson*.

116. Samuels, *Connoisseur*, 302.

117. ISG to BB, January 22 [1899]; H/L, 167.

118. Locke, "Gardner," 31.

119. Samuel Eliot Morison, *One Boy's Boston* (Boston: Houghton, Mifflin, 1962), 8–10. See also Benstock, *Wharton*, 228.

120. Von Mehren, *Minerva*, 264.

121. Pilkington, *Crawford*, 127, 125.

122. Ibid., 120, 134.

123. FMC to ISG, December 1894, GMA; Elliott, *My Cousin*, 232.

124. Pilkington, *Crawford*, 134.

125. Seacrest, *Berenson*, 60.

126. Bates, *Puritans*, 200.

127. Edith Wharton, "The Fullness of Life," quoted Benstock, *Wharton*, 71. Crawford, a devout Roman Catholic with children, would have dis paraged divorce. Certainly Gardner did: see ISG to BB, June 11, 1924, quoted *H/L*, 667.

128. Sullivan, *Journal*, 5.

129. MC, *ISG&FC*, 156–57.

130. BB to ISG, January 19, 1896; *H/L*, 47; BB to Mary Costelloe, January 18, 1896, quoted in A. K. McComb, ed., *The Selected Letters of Bernard Berenson* (Boston: Houghton, Mifflin, 1964), 47.

131. ISG to BB, July 19, 1896; *H/L*, 59.

132. John P. Monks, *A History of Roque Island, Maine* (Boston: Colonial Society, 1964), 27, hereinafter Monks, *Roque Island.*

133. Smith, *Interesting People*, 154.

134. MB, diary entry, June 23, 1898; *H/L*, 36.

135. ISG to BB, August 13 [1909]; *H/L*, 453.

136. ISG to BB, September 4 [1909]; *H/L*, 455.

137. Paul Clemen, quoted MC, *ISG&FC*, 220.

138. BB to ISG, December 22, 1907; *H/L*, 416.

139. Unidentified newspaper clipping, GMA.

140. *H/L*, xvii.

141. Samuels, *Connoisseur*, 72.

142. BB to ISG, May Day, 1899; *H/L*, 173.

143. BB to ISG, March 19, 1900; *H/L*, 210.

144. BB to ISG, December 20, 1898; *H/L*, 210.

145. BB to ISG, January 28, 1900; *H/L*, 202.

146. BB to ISG, October 25, 1900; *H/L*, 231.

147. ISG to BB, November 7 [1900]; *H/L*, 233.

148. ISG to BB, May 25 [1900]; *H/L*, 217.

149. ISG to BB, August 25 [1899]; *H/L*, 188.

150. ISG to BB, June 8 [1899]; *H/L*, 179.

151. ISG to BB, May 23 [1899]; *H/L*, 176.

152. Ibid.

153. BB to ISG, October 16, 1901; *H/L*, 272.

154. ISG to Edmund Hill, June 21, 1917, GMA.

155. Edel, *James*, 243.

156. Ibid., 586.

157. Ibid., 242.

158. F. O. Matthiessen and Kenneth Murdock, *The Complete Notebooks of Henry James* (New York: Oxford University Press, 1961), 216.

159. Margaretta M. Lovell, *Venice, The American View* (San Francisco: The Fine Arts Museums, 1984), 11.
160. Ibid., 14.
161. Ibid., 16.
162. Arthur Symons, *Cities of Italy* (New York: Dutton, 1907), 77.
163. See Jack Basehart, "Palazzo Barbaro," *Italian Splendor* (New York: Universe, 1990), 44. James, Gardner, and Sargent all figure in this book.
164. William Vance, "Berenson and Mrs. Gardner," *New England Quarterly*, LXI (December 1988), 579; HJ, *The American Scene* in Richard Howard, ed., *Henry James: Collected Travel Writings–Great Britain and America* (New York: Library of America, 1993), 254.

CHAPTER ELEVEN: **The Age of Mrs. Jack**

1. Chiang Yee, *The Silent Traveller in Boston* (New York: Norton, 1959), 64–66.
2. W. G. Constable, *Art Collecting in the United States* (London: Thomas Nelson & Sons, 1964), 49.
3. Unidentified newspaper clippings, GMA. The "Whim of a Woman" clipping is from the *Boston Herald*, June 19, 1901.
4. MC, *ISG&FC*, 182–83.
5. Willard Sears, *Construction Diary*: entries of September 13, 1900; August 10, 1900; June 27, 1901; October 14, 1901, GMA, hereinafter Sears, *Diary*.
6. Bliss Perry, *The Saturday Club* (Boston: Houghton, Mifflin, 1958), 5–6, quoted Clara M. Kirk, *W. D. Howells and Art in His Time* (New Brunswick, N.J.: Rutgers University Press, 1965), Appendix IV, 314–15.
7. MC, *ISG&FC*, 183.
8. Ibid.
9. ISG to BB, March 19 [1900]; H/L, 210.
10. MC, *ISG&FC*, 184–85.
11. Susan Sinclair, Gardner Archivist, interview.
12. Smith, *Interesting People*, 160.
13. MC, *ISG&FC*, 190.
14. Ibid., 183–184.
15. Sears, *Diary*, October 23, 1900, GMA.
16. Ibid., September 16, 1901, GMA.
17. Smith, *Interesting People*, 168.
18. Ibid., 159.
19. Walter Muir Whitehill, "Boston Society of Architects," Marvin E. Goody and Robert P. Walsh, *Boston Society of Architects* (Boston: the Society, 1967), 33–34. The discussion makes plain that Cummings was the designing as well as the senior partner.
20. MC, *Reminiscences*, 24.
21. Henry-Russell Hitchcock, *A Guide to Boston Architecture* (New York: Reinhold Publishing Co., 1954), 22.
22. Doris Cole and Karen Cord Taylor, *The Lady Architects* (New York: Midmarch Arts Press, 1990), 4.

23. Lucy A. Paton, *Elizabeth Cary Agassiz* (Boston: Houghton, Mifflin, 1919), 377.

24. Dorothy M. Anderson, *Women, Design and the Cambridge School* (West Lafayette, Ind.: PDA Publishers, 1980), 13, 15; Doris Cole, *Eleanor Raymond, Architect* (Philadelphia: Art Alliance Press, 1981), 10.

25. For Edith Wharton as "designer" see Theresa Craig, *Edith Wharton, A House Full of Rooms* (New York: Monacelli Press, 1996).

26. MC, *ISG&FC*, 207.

27. Anscombe, *Woman's Touch*, 75.

28. Benstock, *Wharton*, 135. Beverly Russell, *Women of Design* (New York: Rizzoli, 1992).

29. Benstock, *Wharton*, 135; MC, *ISG&FC*, 199–201.

30. Saarinen, *Possessors*, 51.

31. Lesser, "T. S. Eliot," 31.

32. Carter, memorandum, July 19, 1930; MC, "Gardner Museum," 4.

33. This motto is carved in an escutcheon on the facade of the Gardner Museum.

34. HA to Elizabeth Cameron, August 22, 1906, Levenson, *Adams Letters* VI, 26; Edel, *James Notebooks*, 126; ISG to BB, September 19, 1896, July 19, 1896; H/L, 66, 59.

35. Saarinen, *Possessors*, 32.

36. Charles Eliot Norton to John Ruskin, July 1871, quoted J. Bradley and I. Ousby, eds., *The Correspondence of John Ruskin and Charles Eliot Norton* (Cambridge, MA: Cambridge University Press, 1987), 234.

37. Sears, *Diary*, September 13, 1900.

38. Cleota Read, *Henry Chapman Mercer and the Moravian Pottery and Tile Works* (Philadelphia: University of Pennsylvania Press, 1987), xxi.

39. Ibid., 99.

40. Ibid., 97.

41. Ibid. See also Ann O'Hagan, "The Treasures of Fenway Court," *Munseys* 34 (March 1906), 660.

42. ISG to H. Mercer, April 17, 1901.

43. ISG to BB, May 16, 1898; H/L, 137.

44. Edmund Hill dedicated the flowers to ISG. For ISG as horticulturalist see Benjamin Brooks, "A New England Garden Home," *Country Life in America* I–V (March 1902), 148–52.

45. The dahlia was named after her by Edmund Hill, GMA. MC, *ISG&FC*, 55.

46. Unidentified newspaper clipping, GMA.

47. Walter Cahn, "Romanesque Sculpture in American Collections," *Gesta* 8 (1969), 47.

48. Saarinen, *Possessors*, 51.

49. GMA. See also Samuels, *Legend*, 222; James F. O'Gorman, "Twentieth Century Gothic," *Essex Institute Historical Collections* 117 (April 1981), 95; Douglass Shand-Tucci, "First Impressions on the Rediscovery of Two New England Art Galleries by Ralph Adams Cram," *Currier Gallery Bulletin* (Fall 1979), 2–16.

50.   Constance G. Alexander, untitled biography of F. C. Powell, SSJE unpublished typescript ca 1950. SSJE Archives; MC, "Gardner Museum," 140. See also Douglass Shand-Tucci, *American Gothic*, vol. ii forthcoming of *Ralph Adams Cram: Life and Architecture* (Amherst, Mass.: University of Massachusetts Press, 1998).

51.   Smith, *Interesting People*, 158.

52.   Mary Cornille, "Isabella Stewart Gardner as a Landscape Gardener," unpublished paper, Boston University, Dept. of Art History, 1985, 1, 24, GMA. See also Hildegarde Hawthorne, "A Garden of the Imagination," *Century* LXXX (July 1910), 446–52.

53.   MC, *ISG&FC*, 191.

54.   MC, "Gardner Museum," 147.

55.   MC, memorandum, July 19, 1930, unpaged.

56.   Hilliard T. Goldfarb, *The Isabella Stewart Gardner Museum* (Boston: Gardner Museum, 1995), 119–20, hereinafter Goldfarb, *Gardner*.

57.   Paul Manship, quoted MC, *ISG&FC*, 248.

58.   A photograph in the GMA documents this.

59.   Pam M. Peterson, "Portraits in Black and White," *Fenway Court*, 1974: 38.

60.   For ISG's dogs see (for "Kitty Wink") H/L, 369; (for "Rolly"), MC, *ISG&FC*, 247.

61.   Interview with Susan Sinclair, Gardner archivist, June 12, 1995.

62.   Negative #D507, columns 13, 14. This is attached to *Inventory and Notebook of Collection*, GMA.

63.   John Coolidge, *Patrons and Architects* (Fort Worth, Tex.: Amon Carter Museum, 1989), 12, hereinafter Coolidge, *Patrons and Architects*.

64.   Goldfarb, *Gardner*, 30.

65.   Unidentified newspaper clipping, GMA.

66.   Goldfarb, *Gardner*, 109, 115.

67.   *ISG&FC*, 201.

68.   Walter Muir Whitehill, "A Fable for Historical Editors," *New England Quarterly*, 50 (1966), 513.

69.   ISG to Mary Berenson, October 22 [1906]; quoted H/L, 385.

70.   Nellie Melba, *Melodies and Memories* (London: Thornton Butterworth, 1925), 142–43; hereinafter Melba, *Melodies*.

71.   Ibid., 142.

72.   MC, *ISG&FC*, 206.

73.   ISG to BB, December 24, 1904; H/L, 355.

74.   MC, *Reminiscences*, 27.

75.   Unidentified newspaper clipping, GMA.

76.   Susan Sinclair, Gardner Archivist, interview September 1995.

77.   MC, "Gardner Museum," 155.

78.   Richard Klein, review of David Shaw's *The Pleasure Police*, *New York Times Book Review*, July 28, 1996, 25; William L. Vance, "Berenson and Mrs. Gardner," *New England Quarterly* LXI (December 1988), 578.

CHAPTER TWELVE: Stairway of Jade

1. Elsie De Wolfe to ISG. [1907], GMA.
2. Mrs. Frederick Winslow to ISG, February 28, 1910, GMA.
3. Ralph Curtis to BB, 1909, 1 Tatti, Harvard University Center for Renaissance Art.
4. Lady Gregory to ISG, January 18, 1914, quoted Susan Sinclair, "Lady Gregory and Mrs. Gardner," *Fenway Court* (1972), 61, hereinafter Sinclair, "Lady Gregory."
5. ISG to BB, January 25, 1906; H/L, 374.
6. BB to ISG, February 7, 1906; H/L, 375.
7. MB to her family, January 3, 1904, quoted Strachey, *Mary Berenson*.
8. ISG to BB, January 19 [1904]; H/L, 327.
9. ISG to BB, August 2 [1904]; II/L, 342.
10. ISG, *Commonplace Book*, 14.
11. Charles H. Garrett, "A Talk with Marion Crawford," *The Lamp* (October 1903), 216; quoted Pilkington, *Crawford*, 166.
12. Pilkington, *Crawford*, 174.
13. ISG to BB, April 9 [1909]; H/L, 440.
14. Pilkington, *Crawford*, 184.
15. Nathan Hale, quoted Strouse, *Alice James*, 106.
16. Gay, *Passion*, 337.
17. ISG to M. Lang, July 25 [1894], SSJE Archives. For reference to her facial neuralgia see ISG to BB, July 19 [1906] and December 3 [1897]; H/L, 380, 140. She went to Langen-Schwalbach, July 28–August 8, 1894.
18. ISG to BB, May 8, 1911; H/L, 487.
19. ISG to BB, August 22 [1910]; H/L, 497.
20. Kaplan, *James*, 532–36.
21. Ibid., 532, 533–34.
22. Nathan G. Hale, *James Jackson Putnam and Psychoanalysis* (Cambridge, Mass.: Harvard University Press, 1971), 11.
23. BB to ISG, January 19, 1907; H/L, 393–94.
24. MB to ISG, May 13, 1914; H/L, 522.
25. Stories abound of how anxious and nervous ISG was on "open days." See, for example, Smith, *Interesting People*, 166–67.
26. "Religion: Cowley Fathers," *Time* (August 14, 1936).
27. Mount, *Sargent*, 241.
28. MB to her family, December 24, 1920, quoted Strachey, *Mary Berenson*, 237.
29. MB to her family, November 17, 1903, quoted Strachey, *Mary Berenson*, 112.
30. HA to ISG, February 9, 1906, quoted MC, *ISG&FC*, 204.
31. Paul Goldberger, "Jane Jacobs," *New York Times Book Review* (May 1996), 39.
32. M. Prichard to S. D. Warren, November 1, 1904, quoted Whitehill, *MFA*, 201; Sox, *Bachelors*, 168, 171, 178.
33. Whitehill, *MFA*, 189; MC, "Gardner Museum," 6.
34. ISG to Loeffler, November 1910, GMA.

35. MC to A. Barr, March 13, 1951, GMA; Ernst Scheyer, *The Circle of Henry Adams* (Detroit: Wayne State University Press, 1970), 109. Scheyer is quoting Adams from his *Mont-Saint-Michel and Chartres* (Boston: Houghton, Mifflin, 1933), 60, 106.

36. ISG to BB., July 9 [1906]; H/L, 380.

37. M. Prichard to ISG, September 1, 1907, GMA.

38. MC, *Reminiscences*, 39.

39. ISG to BB, January 9 [1908]; quoted H/L, 417; MC, *ISG&FC*, 212; 209–10; 237; 211–12.

40. MC, *ISG&FC*, 206.

41. N. Melba to ISG, quoted MC, *ISG&FC*, 206.

42. Lawrence Gilman, "An Orchestral Master Work," *Harper's Weekly*, 51 (December 7, 1907), 1810, quoted Knight, *Loeffler*, 119.

43. ISG to BB, November 26 [1907]; H/L, 414.

44. Knight, *Loeffler*, 126.

45. Melba, *Melodies*, 143.

46. JSS to ISG, December 28, 1918, GMA.

47. Locke, "Gardner," 17.

48. Ibid., 22.

49. ISG to BB, December 7, 1916; H/L, 592.

50. Samuels, *Legend*, 70.

51. A. P. Andrew/Diary, December 18, 1912, GMA.

52. T. Whittemore to ISG, [Summer 1917], GMA.

53. Melba, *Melodies*, 144.

54. ISG to BB, December 17 [1917]; H/L, 605.

55. ISG to BB, May 2, 1904; H/L, 334.

56. ISG to BB, [March 1909]; H/L, 439.

57. Ibid.

58. Cleveland Amory, *The Proper Bostonians* (Orleans, Mass.: Parnassus Imprints, 1984), 134.

59. Coudenhove to ISG, September 4, 1918, GMA.

60. J. L. Smith to ISG, November 14, 1910, GMA.

61. ISG's Midnight Mass was much made of and is described as similar to the earlier Christmas Eve liturgy at the Advent in an unidentified newspaper clipping, GMA. Since her death the custom has been discontinued.

62. ISG to BB, December 19, 1904; H/L, 354.

63. When this gallery was or was not open is a vexing question. It never was included in published catalogs in ISG's lifetime and thereafter and must (like the Japanese Department of Boston's Museum of Fine Arts) have been closed during World War II. Yet many impressions and remembrances of it survive: see Elliott, *Generations*, 377, for an impression during ISG's lifetime and thereafter see Lincoln Kirstein, *Mosaic* (New York: Farrar, Straus & Giroux, 1994), 21, the most recent published reference. B. Hughes Morris recalls the room being open to the public prior to World War II (Interview, August 18, 1997). Its three great

Buddhas were purchased through William Sturgis Bigelow and Yamanaka, the famous export/import house in 1902: see Bigelow to ISG, March 22, 1902, GMA. The contents of the room were sold at auction, and the Buddha Room's upper part is now the Gardner Café! One other interior destroyed since ISG's death is the Vatichino, a small library off the Macknight Room. At some point ISG's private oratory on the fourth floor was also dismantled; some of its religious sculpture may have been given to the Cowley Fathers.

64. MC to H. J. Coolidge, January 5, 1931, GMA.
65. James Lees-Milne, *Harold Nicolson* (London: Archon, 1980), 5.
66. For Okakuro Kakuzo see "East Meets West," *Mrs. Gardner in Japan* (Boston: Gardner Museum, 1992).
67. Whitehill, *MFA*, 131.
68. J. La Farge to ISG, March 22, 1904, GMA.
69. MC, *ISG&FC*, 223.
70. Walter Denny, "Far Eastern and Islamic Art," *The Isabella Stewart Gardner Museum* (Boston: Gardner Museum, 1978), 73. Both the Rembrandt and the beaker have subsequently been stolen.
71. Okakura Kakuzo to ISG, November 22, 1910, quoted MC, *ISG&FC*, 235.
72. Ibid., n.d., quoted MC, *ISG&FC*, 235–36.
73. MB to her family, January 10, 1914, quoted Strachey, *Mary Berenson*, 194.
74. Martin L. Smith, MS of sermon ca 1995, SSJE Archives.
75. Okakura Kakuzo, "The Taoist"; see "East Meets West," 28, 29, 30.
76. ISG to BB, January 22, 1905; H/L, 360.
77. ISG to BB, May 28, 1908; H/L, 421.
78. ISG to BB, January 23, 1911; H/L, 482.
79. ISG to BB, July 27, 1914; H/L, 525.
80. ISG to BB, April 10, 1914; ISG to BB, April 22, 1914; H/L, 517, 520. For the three Buddhas see 63 above, this chapter. For *El Jaleo* see MC, *Reminiscences*, 53.
81. BB to ISG, January 1, 1897; H/L, 72; Smith, *Interesting People*, 154.
82. JSS to ISG, n.d., GMA.
83. R. H. Ives Gammell, "The Mural Decorations of John Singer Sargent," unpub. ms., iv, 4, 27–31, 49. Private collection.
84. Coolidge, *Patrons and Architects*, 10.
85. Goldfarb, *Gardner*, 92.
86. For Joseph Urban see John Dizikes, *Opera in America* (New Haven: Yale University Press, 1993).
87. Ibid., 366.
88. Ibid., 368.
89. MHE, *Generations*, 377.
90. Eaton, *Opera Company*, 139.
91. MHE, *Generations*, 377.
92. Okakura Kakuzo, "The Staircase of Jade," quoted MC, *ISG&FC*, 223–24.
93. Van Wyck Brooks, *New England: Indian Summer* (New York: Dutton, 1940), 438.

CHAPTER THIRTEEN: The New Woman

1. Ralph M. Eastman, "Boston Aviation," *Proceedings of the Bostonian Society* (1946), 39; material on ISG's attendance is in the GMA.
2. Linda V. Hewitt, "T. S. Eliot," *Fenway Court* (1972), 34.
3. Bernard Bergonzi, *T. S. Eliot* (New York: Macmillan, 1972), 29.
4. T. S. Eliot to ISG, April 4, 1915, and late June or early July 1915, GMA. For both see V. Eliot, ed., *The Letters of T. S. Eliot*, I (New York: Harcourt, Brace & Jovanovich, 1988).
5. MHE et al, *Julia Ward Howe*, 156, 157. See also MC, *ISG&FC*, 114–15.
6. Locke, *Gardner*, 13, 37. This early performance of the Schoenberg was by the Flonzaley Quartet.
7. Knight, *Loeffler*, 162.
8. Locke, "Gardner," 22.
9. Knight, *Loeffler*, 95, 100.
10. M. Loeffler to ISG, January 27, 1895, GMA.
11. Knight, *Loeffler*, 105; H/L, 105.
12. M. Loeffler to ISG, August 10, 1893, GMA.
13. Knight, *Loeffler*, 240–41.
14. Because of the absence of abstraction at Fenway Court it has always been assumed ISG had no use for Modernism.
15. Hirshler, *Bunker and His Circle*, 8; Charles Mount, *Monet* (New York: Simon & Schuster, 1966), 360.
16. Moore, *Blackbird*, 87.
17. Henry James, "New Moses," *New York Tribune* May 13, 1876.
18. Fairbrother, "Painting in Boston," 85. ISG did help Tarbell; see May 16, 1898; H/L, 137. The unidentified painter has since been identified from ISG's guestbook. GMA.
19. MB to ISG, February 3, 1921; H/L, 622. For an example of the sort of animosity the whole matter has engendered see (a perfectly appalling book) Patricia Jobe Pierce, *Edmund C. Tarbell and the Boston School of Painting* (Hingham, Mass.: Pierce Galleries, 1980), 53, 58, 60.
20. Leah Lipton, *George Hawley Hallowell's New England Vision* (Framingham, Mass.: Danforth Museum, 1996), 6; see also Hendy, *Gardner*, 117.
21. Karen Haas, "Dodge Macknight," *Fenway Court* (1982), 38, 42. See also JSS to ISG, 1919.
22. Hirschler, "Artists' Biographies," 218.
23. Brooks, *New England: Indian Summer*, 438. See also ISG to BB, December 2, 1895; H/L, 43.
24. BB to ISG, December 14, 1905; BB to ISG, December 14, 1905; both H/L, 372.
25. JSS to ISG, 1903, GMA.
26. Hirshler, *Bunker and His Circle*, 56.
27. For Thomas Whittemore see Charles Graves, "Whittemore, Thomas," DAB xx, 172–73.

28. T. Whittemore to ISG, August 25, 1911, GMA.

29. Hans Janson, *History of Art* (New York: Abrams, 1971), 521.

30. Goldfarb, *Gardner*, 28.

31. M. Prichard to ISG, November 4, 1913, GMA.

32. Virginia Woolf, *Roger Fry* (New York: Harcourt, Brace, 1940), 140; M. Prichard to ISG, June 6, 1922, quoted Sox, *Bachelors*, 193.

33. Karen E. Haas, "Henri Matisse," *Fenway Court* (1985), 42, hereinafter Haas, "Matisse."

34. See Patrick McMahon to J. Minor, March 21, 1995, GMA. ISG was also interested in the Steins. See the ISG/BB correspondence, September 4 and 27 [1909]; H/L, 454, 456; M. Prichard to ISG, June 26, 1914, GMA.

35. Haas, "Matisse," 37.

36. M. Prichard to ISG, June 6, 1922, quoted Haas, "Matisse," *Fenway Court*, 19, 47.

37. Walker Hancock, "Paul Manship," *Fenway Court* (October 1966), 1–2.

38. Jones, *Modern Art at Harvard*, 56.

39. Ibid., 44.

40. Guy Davenport, quoted Eric M. Selinger, "Lambs Amaze," *The Boston Phoenix* (July 1995), 8. T. S. Eliot to ISG, April 4 [1915], GMA.

41. For Walker and ISG's Matisse see Moore, *Blackbird*, 347; for the Harvard Society for Contemporary Art see Elizabeth Sussman, "Taking a Risk," *Dissent* (Boston: Institute of Contemporary Art, 1985), 10.

42. Robert A. M. Stern, *Pride of Place* (Boston: Houghton Mifflin, 1986), 94–95; Hugh Kenner, "A Change of Mind" (June 29, 1997), 24; William R. Everdell, *The First Moderns* (Chicago, 1997), 99; Lisa Zeidner, "The Way of Donald Barthelme" (July 27, 1997), 27; Morris Dickstein, "The Last Modernist" (August 3, 1997), 11; all *New York Times Book Review*. The Andrew diary is in GMA.

43. JSS to ISG, May 31, 1918, GMA.

44. ISG to BB, May 28, 1908; H/L, 421.

45. Richards/Elliott, *Howe*, II, 151.

46. Susan Sinclair, interview, September 1995. See also MC, *ISG&FC*, 141–42. For the Howe birthday lunch see Richards/Elliott, *Howe*, 151.

47. Boyer, "Howe," 228.

48. Ibid., 227.

49. Kaledin, *Mrs. Henry Adams*, 225.

50. William L. Vance, "Redefining Bostonian," *The Bostonians* (Boston: Museum of Fine Arts, 1986), 23.

51. Joan von Mehren, *Minerva and the Muse* (Amherst, Mass.: University of Massachusetts Press, 1994), 3.

52. Ibid.

53. Anne Higonnet, "Images," Georges Duby and Michelle Perrot, eds., *A History of Women in the West* (Cambridge, Mass.: Belknap Press, 1993), IV, 247.

54. Ibid., 260–61.

55. McCarthy, *Women's Culture*, 153.

56. Ibid., 161.

57. MC, *ISG&FC*, 142.

58. MC, *ISG&FC*, 112–14; Rogers, *Two Lives*; Nicholas Slonimsky, ed., "Lang, Margaret Ruthaven," *The Concise Edition of Baker's Biographical Dictionary of Musicians* (New York: Schirmer, 1994), 554.

59. Unidentified newspaper clipping, GMA.

60. Knight, *Loeffler*, 120.

61. Eaton, *Boston Opera*, 141.

62. Amy Lowell to ISG, June 19, 1916, GMA.

63. ISG to Amy Lowell, ca 1916, GMA.

64. Amy Lowell to John G. Fletcher, quoted S. Foster Damon, *Amy Lowell* (Boston: Houghton, Mifflin, 1935), 364.

65. Sinclair, "Lady Gregory," 60.

66. Doris Kearns Goodwin, *The Fitzgeralds and the Kennedys* (New York: St. Martin's Press, 1987), 241–42.

67. Sinclair, "Lady Gregory," 58–59.

68. Ibid., 59.

69. Ibid., 59.

70. A. P. Andrew, quoted MC, *ISG&FC*, 234.

71. Karl Keller, *The Only Kangaroo Among the Beauty* (Baltimore: Johns Hopkins University Press, 1979), hereinafter Keller, *Kangaroo*.

72. Ibid., 247.

73. Ibid., 228.

74. Ibid., 222–23.

75. Ibid., 243.

76. Ibid., 228.

77. Beauvoir, *Second Sex*, 112; Keller, *Kangaroo*, 296.

78. McCarthy, *Women's Culture*, 149–50 or 160.

79. Thomas H. Johnson, *The Poems of Emily Dickinson* (Cambridge, Mass.: Belknap, 1951).

CHAPTER FOURTEEN: End Game

1. Adeline R. Tinter, *The Cosmopolitan World of Henry James* (Baton Rouge, La.: Louisiana State University Press, 1991), 199.

2. Unidentified newspaper clipping, GMA.

3. MB to her family, October 19, 1903, quoted Strachey, *Mary Berenson*, 11.

4. Ibid., October 27, 1903, quoted H/L, 111.

5. De Wolfe, *After All*, 103. ISG's explanation, on another occasion, was the servant problem: "Labour here has got to the grotesque stage. Imagine how my stockings look! I wash and darn them!!!!!!!" she wrote BB, November 28, 1908; H/L, 610.

6. Clayton Johns, quoted in Samuels, *Connoisseur*, 413.

7. Benstock, *Wharton*, 135.

8. Louise Hall Tharp, *Saint-Gaudens and the Gilded Era* (Boston: Little, Brown, 1969), 353.

9. ISG to BB, April 22 [1898]; H/L, 133.

10. MC, *Reminiscences*, 53–54.

11. G. Muck to ISG, n.d., GMA.

12. ISG to BB, September 25 [1916]; H/L, 588.

13. M. Mower to ISG [1919], GMA.

14. Helen Howe, *The Gentle Americans* (New York: Harper & Row, 1965), 111.

15. MC, radio interview transcript, 21.

16. ISG to Joseph Lindon Smith, n.d., ca March 1919.

17. Joseph Lindon Smith to ISG, March 22, 1919.

18. "I was to have no ideas of my own," wrote MC in *Reminiscences*, 24.

19. ISG to BB, July 4, 1917; H/L, 603.

20. ISG to BB, May 18, 1917; H/L, 602.

21. Ibid.

22. S. Burton to ISG, April 10, 1919, SSJEA.

23. "Religion: Cowley Fathers," *Time*, August 14, 1936. See also "The Churchman Afield," *Boston Evening Transcript*, October 5, 1929, where it is stated that Gardner's "only stipulation was that on the anniversary of the day a Mass should be said by a member of the Society in the chapel of the Gardner Museum. . . . This condition has been complied with each year both before and since Mrs. Gardner's death and is a perpetual charge on the Society."

24. Henry Adams to Elizabeth Cameron, October 6, 1912, and February 1, 1918, Levenson, *Adams Letters*, vi, 563, 782.

25. Weeks, *Green Age*, 106–7.

26. MC, *ISG&FC*, 245.

27. S. Burton to ISG, April 13, 1920, SSJEA.

28. H/L, xxiii. No source is given. The phrase occurs in none of BB's published letters or books so far as I can tell, but like "precinema star" (see above) is assumed by Hadley as genuine. I do not quarrel with that assumption. For a seemingly related sobriquet, "Cleopatra of the Charles," see MB to ISG, December 30, 1920, H/L, 620.

29. Powell to ISG, February 9, 1922, and Palm Sunday 1919, SSJEA.

30. Powell to ISG, June 20, 1921, July 6, 1923, SSJEA.

31. See H/L, 421, where ISG writes "monk's garden," cf. Ibid. 429 where she writes "Monks Garden." It is widely assumed but so far as I know nowhere documented that ISG named this garden after her favorite niece, Olga Monks. My mother, Geraldine Groves Tucci, a student at Simmons College in the 1930s, noticed then a monk more than once reading there, the background for my own assumption the garden was named in honor of the Cowley Fathers.

32. Powell to ISG, April 13, 1920, SSJEA.

33. JSS to ISG, February 8, 1920, GMA.

34. JSS to ISG, November 16, 1923, GMA.

35. ISG to Loeffler, June 11, n.y., GMA.

36. For "Was-a-bella" see Samuels, *Legend*, 70.

37. ISG's letter to Coudenhove, November 15, 1922, GMA.

38. Weeks, *Green Age*, 106–7.

39. Alice De Lamar, "Some Little Known Facts," *Forum* 3 (Fall 1960), 30.

Samuels, *Legend*, 282–83, is somewhat fuller.

40. Smith, *Interesting People*, 157.

41. Alvin H. Rosenfield, ed., *The Collected Poems of John Wheelwright* (New York: New Directions, 1971), 226–228.

42. ISG, "Directions for my Funeral," GMA.

43. William Endicott to JSS, July 24, 1924, GMA.

44. Olga Monks to BB, September 14, 1924; H/L, 668.

45. Bruce Metzger, "*Breaking the Code* (Nashville, Tenn.: Abingdon, 1993), quoted in a review of same by Rodney L. Petersen, *Anglican Theological Review*, LXXVIII (Winter 1996), 166.

46. Chapman, "Gardner."

Index

About the Author

DOUGLASS SHAND-TUCCI is a historian of American art and architecture and New England studies. His most recent book, *Boston Bohemia,* was one of five 1996 PEN/Winship Award finalists for best book of the year by a New England author. He lives in Boston's Back Bay at the Hotel Vendôme, a place much frequented once by both Isabella Stewart Gardner and John Singer Sargent.